国際取引のための
イギリス法

Makoto Shimada
島田真琴

慶應義塾大学出版会

はしがき

　イギリス契約法の基礎知識は、国際取引に関する法務に従事する、いわゆる国際法律家にとって不可欠な素養といってよい。同法は、イングランド及びウェールズの国内法であると共に、アメリカ、カナダ、オーストラリア、ニュージーランド、インド、パキスタン、シンガポール、マレーシア、南アフリカその他多数の国の法制度のモデルであり、世界中の法律家が学んでいる。しかも、国際金融取引、国際合弁事業、国際物品売買、プラント輸出、海上・航空運送、海上保険その他の多国間に跨る重要な取引は、元々イギリス法に基づいて形成されており、現在でも、同法に準拠することが多い。これらの取引に関与する法律家として諸外国の弁護士と対等に渡り合い、これに係わる法務を適切に処理していくためには、自国法に精通するだけでなく、当該取引の基盤である制度を理解し、相手方と共通の認識を持った上で、取引やその交渉に臨むことが要請される。

　本書は、そのような要請に応えようとする方々のため、イギリス契約法の基本原則からこれに基づく法律実務までをわかりやすく紹介し、コモンロー（判例法）に関する予備知識が全くなくても、本書を読むだけで同法の全体像を掴めるようにすることを目指している。

　この目的のため、本書は、第1編（イギリスの法律制度と司法制度）、第2編（イギリス契約法）、第3編（国際取引法実務とイギリス法）の3部構成をとっている。

　第1編は、イギリス法入門というべき部分であり、コモンローとは何か（第1章）、イギリスの裁判制度（第2章）と法律専門職（第3章）、イギリス法の法源（第4章）、判例法の読み方、使い方（第5章）など、英米法律家には常識であっても日本人にはなじみの薄い事項を簡潔に説明している。本編を読め

ば、本書第2編以降を理解する上ではもちろん、今後、他の英米法の専門書を読むための助けともなる、コモン・ローの制度に関する基礎知識が得られるはずである。

　第2編は、本書の根幹をなす部分であり、全12章において、日本の企業人や実務家が国際取引法務に関与する前に知っておくと役に立つ、イギリス契約法の法理や法原則を体系的に説明している。各章の本文中においてイギリスの主要な法源である判例法の基礎理論を抽出して説明すると共に、別に【CASES】という項目を設け、特に重要と思われる判例を選択のうえ、その事案と判決要旨を紹介するようにした。読者は、本文の説明と【CASES】で紹介した関連判例とをあわせて読むことにより、それぞれの法原理や法原則が実務のどのような場面で適用されるのかについて、イメージをつかむことができるはずである。また、重要な制定法は、本文での解説に加え、【STATUTES】の項に関連条文を掲載した。

　第3編は、応用編として、国際契約交渉（第1章）、英文契約書のドラフト（第2章）、国際取引紛争（第3章）という、いわば国際取引法務の実践現場において、第2編で取りあげた法理論がどのような働きをするのかを紹介している。この第3編まで読み進んだ読者は、冒頭で述べたこと、すなわち、国際取引法務に従事する者にとってイギリス契約法の基礎知識が不可欠であることの理由について、実務的な観点から具体的に理解できるはずである。

　本書においては、イギリス法上の概念、用語、表現をすべて英文で表記し、また、判例要旨や制定法もあえて和訳せず英文だけで記述している。イギリス法を用いた国際取引のほとんどが英語にて行われる以上、その内容を日本語だけで学習・理解してもあまり意味がないからである。なお、本文中の語句・表現には、日本法との対比の便宜を考慮して、なるべく和訳を付するようにしたが、異なる法制度に基づく概念を一言の和文で表現するのは元来不可能に近い。文中の和訳には重きを置かず、一応の参考とするに留めていただきたい。

　本書は、法科大学院におけるイギリス法や国際取引法務に関する授業の教科書として利用することを本来の目的として執筆したものだが、コモン・ローの基礎理論を紹介するだけではなく、最新の判例法、制定法及びこれに基づく法律実務まで網羅し、実務家の参考書として利用できるように工夫している。

はしがき

　イギリス契約法の重要性は国際取引社会で広く認識されているにかかわらず、これを体系的に勉学・研究した経験のある日本人の実務家はあまり多いとはいえない。現に国際法務に携わっている企業人・法律実務家やこれからこの分野での活躍を目指している方々に、イギリス法を知るための契機として本書を手に取っていただければ幸いである。

　最後に、本書出版の労をおとりいただいた慶應義塾大学出版会編集部・堀井健司氏には、編集作業上、多大のご尽力をいただいた。心より感謝の意を表したい。

　　2006年8月

島田真琴

目　次

第Ⅰ編　イギリスの法律制度と司法制度

第1章　コモンローとは何か
  1．Common Law（コモンロー）の発生　2
  2．コモンロー（Common Law）とは何か　3
  3．Common Law（コモンロー）と Equity（衡平法）　4
  4．成文法の発展　6
  5．イギリス法の分類　7

第2章　イギリスの裁判所
  1．Civil law（民事法）と criminal law（刑事法）　13
  2．The Courts（裁判所）の種類　14
  3．Civil Court（民事裁判所）　15
  4．Criminal Courts（刑事裁判所）　22

第3章　法律専門職（Legal Profession）
  1．Solicitors（ソリシター）　26
  2．Barristers（バリスター）　27
  3．The Judiciary（裁判官）　29
  4．Magistrates（治安判事）　32
  5．その他の法律専門職　32

第4章　イギリス法の法源（Sources of English Law）
  1．国内法規（Domestic Legislation）　34

v

2．European Community Law（EU 法）　40
3．Common law（判例法）――Judicial precedents（先例法）　44
4．Subsidiary sources（副次的法源）　45

第5章　先例拘束性の原理（Stare Decisis）
1．判例調査（Finding Cases）　47
2．判例の分析（Finding Precedent）　48
3．判例法の適用・区別（Applying／Distinguishing Cases）　50

第II編　イギリス契約法

第1章　契約の成立（1）
　　　　――申込と承諾（Offer and Acceptance）
1．イギリス法における契約（Contract）　54
2．Invitation to treat（申込の誘引）　57
3．Acceptance（承諾）　59
4．Qualified acceptance（条件付承諾）　60
5．契約交渉と契約成立時期　60
6．Battle of forms（書式間の闘争）　61
7．Postal rule（郵便ルール）　62
8．Methods of acceptance prescribed by the offeror（申込人による承諾方法の指定）　63
9．Termination of offer（申込の失効）　63

第2章　契約の成立（2）
　　　　――Consideration（約因）と Promissory Estoppel（約束的禁反言）
1．約因（Consideration）の意義・目的　73
2．Executory consideration（未履行約因）と executed consideration（既履行約因）　74

3．Past consideration（過去の約因）　75
4．Consideration の価値　75
5．Performance of an existing obligation（既存の債務の履行）　75
6．Part-payment of debt（金銭債務の一部弁済）　77
7．Promissory estoppel（約束的禁反言）　79
8．金銭債務の一部弁済（Part payment of debt）と Promissory estoppel　81
9．Promissory estoppels の限界　81

第3章　契約の成立（3）
　　　　──Intention, Certainty, Completeness, Formality（契約意思、明確性、完全性、要式）
1．Intention to create legal relations（法的拘束力発生の意思）　93
2．Letter of Intent　94
3．Certainty（明確性）、Completeness（完全性）　97
4．Conditional agreement（条件付合意）　99
5．Formal requirement（要式性）　100
6．Deed（捺印証書）　101

第4章　契約の条項（Contractual Terms）
1．Term（契約条項）　109
2．Terms（条項）と Representations（表示）の区別　109
3．Classification of Terms（契約条項の分類）　110
4．Implied Terms（黙示条項）　114
5．The Sale of Goods Act 1979　115

第5章　契約の解釈（Interpretation of Contract）
1．契約解釈上の基本原則　127
2．The Parol Evidence Rule（口頭証拠排除の原則）　129
3．Entire Agreement Clause（完全合意条項）　131

第6章　Exclusion Clause（責任排除条項）の一般原則
　1．Exclusion Clause（責任排除条項）　134
　2．Incorporation into the contract（契約の内容となること）　135
　3．Exclusion clauseの適用に関する特別な解釈原則の適用　137
　4．The Unfair Contract Terms Act 1977　138
　5．The Unfair Terms in Consumer Contracts Regulations 1999　141

第7章　Misrepresentation（不実表示）
　1．Misrepresentationの定義と要件　153
　2．MisrepresentationのRemedies（不実表示の法的効果）　157

第8章　Mistake、Duress、etc.（錯誤、強迫等）
　1．Mistake（錯誤）　167
　2．Duress、Undue Influence and Unconscionability　172

第9章　Discharge of Contract（契約の終了）
　1．Discharge by Agreement（合意による契約終了）　183
　2．Discharge by Breach（契約違反による終了）　184
　3．Discharge by Frustration（契約目的不達成による履行義務の終了）　185
　4．The Law Reform (Frustrated Contracts) Act 1943　190

第10章　Remedies for Breach of Contract（契約違反の救済措置）
　1．Damages（損害賠償）の基本的性質　201
　2．損害の範囲　201
　3．損害の種類と損害額の算定　203
　4．損害額の限定　208
　5．Liquidated Damages（損害賠償額の予定）　210
　6．Restitution（原状回復）　212
　7．Specific Performance（特定履行）　212

8．Injunction（差止命令）　213

第11章　Privity of Contract（契約関係）
　1．Doctrine of Privity（契約関係の法理）　228
　2．Avoiding the Doctrine of Privity（契約関係の法理の回避）　228
　3．Exclusion clause and third party（責任排除条項と第三者）　232
　4．Contracts（Rights of Third Parties）Act 1999　233

第12章　Transfer of Contractual Rights and Obligation（契約上の権利義務の移転）
　1．Contractual rights の法的性質　242
　2．Assignment の一般原則（制定法によらない場合）　243
　3．Statutory Assignment（法令の規定による債権譲渡）　244
　4．Equitable Assignment（衡平法上の債権譲渡）　245
　5．Exclusion of Assignment（譲渡制限）　247
　6．債務者の抗弁権（Subject to equities）　248
　7．Novation（更改）　248

第Ⅲ編　国際取引法実務とイギリス法

第1章　国際契約交渉とイギリス法
　1．契約交渉の目的　254
　2．イギリス法に基づく契約交渉中における当事者の義務　256
　3．契約交渉中に交わす書面　259
　4．Subject to contract と Without prejudice　264
　5．契約交渉の一方的な破棄と当事者の責任　265
　6．契約交渉の準拠法　266

第2章　英文契約書のドラフト
　1．契約書作成の目的　270

2．契約書作成の方法　　270
　　3．契約書の構成　　271
　　4．契約書作成上の注意事項　　279
　　5．契約解釈の基本原理とドラフト　　283

第3章　国際取引に関する紛争の解決方法
　　1．裁判と仲裁　　287
　　2．裁判所の選択　　288
　　3．判決の執行　　296

参考文献　　303
索引　　307

第Ⅰ編
イギリスの法律制度と司法制度

第1章

コモンローとは何か

1．Common Law（コモンロー）の発生

　イギリス法は、1066年のノルマン候ウィリアムによるイングランド征服（the Norman Conquest）及びイングランド王国の成立をその起源としている。ウィリアム征服王（William I, the Conquer）は、イングランドの全ての土地を支配下においた上、これをノルマンディから連れてきた臣下に分配し、王への忠誠と引換に土地利用を許可した。王から土地使用権を賜った臣下は、その部下たちに更に使用権を分配し、部下たちは更に、それぞれの家来に土地利用を認めるという形で、国王を頂点とするピラミッド型の土地利用体系が出来上がった。いわゆる封建制度の成立である。イギリスの封建制度の際立った特徴は、土地利用権をめぐる全ての争いに関し、国王が紛争解決の権限（裁判権）を保持した点である。すなわち、ある地方貴族の領地内において土地利用を認められたその末端の家臣は、土地に関する自己の権利が侵害されたとき、土地利用権を付与してくれた直接の上司やその領主である地方貴族だけでなく、ロンドンにいる国王に対しても紛争解決のための裁判を求めることが許されていた。また、土地以外の財産に関する争いも、その価値が40シリング（2ポンド）を超えるときは国王に裁判を求めることができた。この上限金額はその後のインフレによりほとんど無意味に等しくなる。このように国王の下にある単一裁判所により統一的な司法判断を行う制度は、イングランド統一とほぼ同時に生まれていたわけである。ノルマン時代の王立裁判所はウエストミンスターに設置され、12人の裁判官により全事件を処理していた。この12人の裁判官は、年に2回、2人1組で全国を巡回して各地で裁判をし、法制度の均一化を図った。これは the system of assizes（巡回裁判所制度）と呼ばれ、1971年まで続けられてきた。この制度の下で全国を巡回した裁判官は、それぞれの地方の紛

争を合理的と思われる慣習に従って審理判断し、悪しき慣習は他の地方の慣習や新しい慣習に置き換えていった。こうして、ある地域における1つの事件での判断が他の地域における類似事件に適用されるようになり、先例拘束性の原理（the doctrine of precedence）が生まれた。裁判官たちは、巡回を終えてウエストミンスターの王立裁判所に戻った際、それぞれが扱った事件について報告・協議し、徐々に common law（共通法、ius communis）が形成されていった。

　こうして生まれたコモンローが全国的な制度として確立したのは、1189年以降のことである。この年は limit of legal memory と呼ばれ、それ以前は、time immemorial（誰もが記憶できる限界時期）と呼ばれている。

　なお、ウェールズは12世紀中、アイルランドは13世紀初頭にイングランドに征服され、それぞれイングランドと同じコモンローを採用している。他方、スコットランドは、1704年にイングランドに統合されてイギリスがグレート・ブリテンとなるまで独立を維持していた。スコットランドは、現在もイングランドとは異なる civil law の法律制度を採っている。

2．コモンロー（Common Law）とは何か

　上記のとおり、コモンローという名称は、その沿革上各地域の local law に対する共通法として形成された法律を意味していたが、現在では、これと異なる様々な意味に用いられている。

(1) 法制度上の定義——Common Law 対 Civil Law

　判例法に基づく法律制度は、国が制定し法典化（codify）されたいわゆるローマ法を起源とする civil law の法律制度（日本及びヨーロッパ大陸の多くの国が採用している法制度）に対する法制度として common law と総称されている。なお、後述するとおり civil law の語も多義的に使われている（本編第2章1）。

(2) 領域上の定義——アメリカ、commonwealth（英連合）諸国の法制度

　コモンローの法制度を採っている米国、カナダ、オーストラリア、ニュージーランド、シンガポール、インド、パキスタン、バングラディシュその他を総称して、common law countries と呼ぶことがある。なお、これらのうち、アメリカ以外の国々は、かつて大英帝国の下にあったことから独立後もイギリスとの親密な関係を維持して英連合（Commonwealth）を形成し、Commonwealth countries と呼ばれることがある。イギリスの EU 加盟以降、英連合の政治的な重要性は日を追って希薄化している。なお、旧英連邦構成国の内には、たとえばニュージーランドのように、今でも自国内の裁判手続上の最終審をイギリスの裁判所（the House of Lords の裁判官が構成する the Judicial Committee of the Privy Council）としている国もある。

(3) 法形式上の定義——Statute（制定法）と Case law（判例法）

　イギリスの全ての成文法に対する概念として、判例によって形成された全ての法源（case law）をコモンローと呼ぶこともある。この意味でのコモンローには、以下に述べる equity も含まれている。

(4) 法分野上の定義——Common law（普通法）と Equity（衡平法）

　エクイティ（equity）は、上記1の経緯で生まれてきたコモンローとは異なる沿革から生まれ、異なる種類の裁判所により形成されてきた1つの法体系である。イギリス法の中で、common law の語は、この equity に対比される法律という意味で用いられることが多い。

3．Common Law（コモンロー）と Equity（衡平法）

　王立裁判所の裁判手続は、原告が訴えた請求事項を記載した royal writ（勅令状）の発行により開始する制度（the writ system）が採られていたが、この writ は、伝統的に、特定の種類の請求を記載できる書式だけに限定されていた。このためこの書式に適合しない多くの訴訟申立ては裁判所に取り上げてもらえなかった。最大の問題は、他人に託した土地利用権の取り戻し請求を記

載できるwritが認められていなかったことである。イギリスの封建制度上、土地利用権者が死亡した場合、相続人は国王に1年分の賃料に相当する税金（primer seisin）を支払わなければならなかった。また、相続人が未成年（当時は21歳未満）の場合、当該土地は、相続人が成人に達するまでその直属の上司が管理することとされていたが、この間に上司が土地の全収穫を剥ぎ取ってしまう事態が横行した。そこで、国王の税金や領主の管理を避けるため、被相続人が友人1、2名に対し、息子が成人に達するまでの約束で土地利用権を託する方法が一般化していた。Common law上、この場合の土地利用権は、贈与（gift）されたものとして友人たちに移転し、友人たちが約束に違反して土地を息子に返さなかったとしても、これを取り戻すためのwritが存在しなかった。

　Common lawの制度の欠陥により生じたこの不公平を解消するため、14世紀以降、common lawによって取り上げてもらえない訴えは、国王に対して直接申立てられるようになった。国王は、その精神的な助言者であるthe Lord Chancellor（大法官）に指示し、そのような事件を衡平の原則（the principle of equity）に基づいて解決した。すなわち、trust（信託）に関する事件は、法律上の義務（obligations at law）ではなく衡平（エクイティ）に基づく義務（obligations in equity）が生じているとして処理されるようになった。こうして、trust事件に関するthe Lord Chancellorによる裁判所（the Court of Chancellor）の裁判管轄権が15世紀までに確立した。

　その後、the Court of Chancellor（大法官裁判所）は、trust以外の紛争に関してもcommon law上は解決困難な問題を取り扱うようになった。たとえば、金銭賠償（damages）及び土地返還請求というcommon law上の救済手段では充分な救済を受けられない者を、injunctions（差止命令）やspecific performance（特定履行）の方法で救済する等である。このようにして、イギリスの裁判上common law及びequityという2種類の異なる法体系が別個に発展していった。当初、両制度の解決が一致しない場合にどうすればよいかが問題となったが、1616年のthe Earl of Oxford判決により、equityがcommon lawに優先する旨が決定された。この原則は、the Judicature Acts 1873-1875において法文化された。

The Judicature Acts 以前においては、the Court of Chancellor のみが equity に基づく判断をすることを許されていたため、equity による判断を求める訴えが the Court of Chancellor に集中し訴訟遅延を招いていた。そこで、Common law courts と the Court of Chancellor は the Judicature Acts に基づいて the High Court（高等法院）に統合され、1876年以降は全ての裁判所に common law 及び equity の双方を適用する権限が与えられた。

　このようにして両制度が1つの裁判所に統合された後でも、equity に基づく trust の法概念は独自の発展を続け、また、injunctions（差止命令）や specific performance（特定履行）等の equity に基づく救済手段（equitable remedies）は、common law による救済（すなわち damages）が不十分な場合に裁判官の裁量により認められる例外的な制度として機能する等、equity は common law とは異なる実体法及び手続法上の法分野を形成している。

　Equity の役割は、20世紀半ば以降、Lord Denning（デニング卿、1899-1999）という1人の裁判官の出現により飛躍的に拡大した。彼は、1943年から1981年までの38年間裁判官を勤め、特に後半20年は the Master of the Rolls（記録長官）として the Court of Appeal の民事事件を統括した。そして、この間に関与した多くの事件において、硬直化して時代に合わなくなった common law の諸原則を equity によって修正する判断を示し続け、他の裁判官や lawmaker（立法者）に多大な影響を与えた。伝統的な法理や慣習を無視した彼の判断手法は未だによく批判されるが、彼の示した諸判決がイギリス法の発展に貢献した点は誰もが認めている。実際上、Lord Denning のような人物がいなかったとしたら、中世に生まれたイギリス判例法が、今日でも合理的な取引法として通用し得たかどうかかなり疑わしい。

　なお、equity は、裁判におけるフェアプレイの原則を補完する役割を担うものとされているので、誠実義務に違反する行為をした者がこれに基づく主張をすることは許されない（clean hands（クリーンハンド）の原則）。

4．成文法の発展

　1215年、イギリス国王ジョン（King John）は、その直接の臣下である貴族

たち (barons) との間で the Magna Carta (マグナカルタ、大憲章) を合意した。マグナカルタの条項の大半は、ジョン王の一方的な課税その他の圧政に反対していた barons との和解に関するものだが、商人の保護や裁判を受ける権利等、一般市民の権利にかかわる条項も一部加えられた。その内容以上に重要なのは、国王がその家臣との間の合意（法）に従うことを約束したこと、及び国王とその家臣の代表者との間で合意（法）を作ったことの2点である。前者は法の支配 (rule of law)、後者は議会主義の契機といわれている。この後国王の執政を監視し、専横を抑えるために、貴族の代表による Parliament と呼ばれる評議会が定期的に開催されるようになり、1265年には貴族以外の各地方の庶民の代表もこれに加わることが許された。こうして、14世紀半ば以降、国王 (King 又は Queen Regnant)、聖職貴族 (the Lord Spiritual)・世俗貴族 (the Lord Temporal) で構成される the House of Lords (貴族院)、地域別に選出された一般庶民 (commons) からなる the House of Commons (庶民院) という3つの機関により構成される立法府として、the King in Parliament (国王の議会) が生まれた。

イギリスの制定法は、日本を含む civil law の制度の国とは異なり、あくまでも裁判所が作った判例法 (common law) を補完又は修正するものと認識され、機能している。

5．イギリス法の分類

(1) Public Law（公法）

イギリス法を大別すると public law (公法) と private law (私法) の2種類に分けられる。Public law は、国家と個人の間を規律している法律の総称であり、これには、以下の constitutional and administrative law (憲法及び行政法)、criminal law (刑事法) の他、immigration law (移民法)、civil liberties and social welfare law (市民権法及び社会保障法) 等も含まれている。

(i) Constitutional Law（憲法）

主要な政府機関と市民との間を規律する法律の総称である。議会の最高機関

性（parliamentary sovereignty and supremacy）、三権分立（the separation of powers between the executive, the legislature and the judiciary）、地方自治体の構成（the structure of local government）、警察及び軍隊組織に関する事項、及び国家に対する個人の権利を定める法律がこれに含まれる。イギリスには、これらの事項を包括的に成文化した憲法典が存在せず、個別的な制定法（たとえば、マグナカルタ、人権に関する the Human Rights Act 1998等）、慣習及び判例法の集合体を constitutional law と呼んでいる。したがって、constitutional law の改正は、他の法律同様、通常の手続を経た the Act of Parliament によって行われる。

(ⅱ) **Administrative Law**（行政法）

Constitutional law と同様、政府の権限行使及びその制約に関する法律である。ただし、政府機関の組織よりも各機関の機能や役割の詳細に関する事項を中心に定めている。

政府や行政機関の constitutional law や administrative law 違反に関する事項は、司法審査（judicial review）請求の手続きにより、the High Court が取り扱う。

(ⅲ) **Criminal Law**（刑事法）

犯罪に該当する行為及び国家が公共のために犯罪人を訴追し、審理・判決するための手続きを定める法律である。犯罪には、殺人（murder）のように判例法（common law）に基づくもの及び個別的な制定法によるもの（たとえば、Theft Act 1968）の2種類がある。刑事裁判において、犯罪の証明は検察側（prosecutions）が行う。犯罪が成立するために、prosecutions は、被告人（the accused 又は the defendant）による犯罪行為（actus reus）、責任（men rea）及び被告人が主張している阻却事由（defense）の不存在について、合理的な疑いが生じない程度（beyond reasonable doubt）の立証をしなければならない。

(2) **Private Law**（私法）

Private law とは、個人間、法人間又は個人と法人の間の関係を規律する法律である。ただし、基本的には civil law の分野に属している法律であっても、

成文法の個々の規定の中には criminal law に該当するものが含まれている。たとえば、会社法は、詐欺的取引やインサイダー取引を犯罪として規定している。

(ⅰ) Contract Law（契約法）

この法律はあらゆる商事法の基礎となっている。契約がいつどのような内容で成立したかの問題に関する諸規則は、数百年前に遡る判例法に準拠している。ただし、特に21世紀以降は、議会が定める成文法により重要な修正がなされている。一般に、契約（contract）に基づく義務は、当事者間の合意（agreement）の効果であるとされているが、最近では、両当事者が意図的に合意していない義務や条件が契約に含まれる場合が増大している。特に、消費者契約（consumer contract）や電力その他生活必需品の供給契約等、契約条件を当事者間で交渉することがほぼ不可能な契約については、成文法の規定により多くの条項が黙示的に加えられている。また、契約当事者以外の者による当該契約上の権利の行使は、the doctrine of privity（契約関係の法理）により禁じられているが、この原則も、2000年から施行された the Contracts (Right of Third Parties) Act 1999によって、大幅な修正を受けている（第Ⅱ編第11章参照）。契約違反により損害（damages）を蒙った者は、契約が合意どおりに履行されていたとした場合におけるその者の状態を回復するために必要な賠償金の支払（damages）を受けることができる。

(ⅱ) Law of Torts（不法行為法）

Tort とは、当事者間の合意ではなく、法の運用に基づいて創設された義務に違反する民事上の違法行為である。裁判所又は議会が違法と認めた tort により損害を蒙った者は、当該 tort がなかったとした場合におけるその者の状態を回復するために必要な賠償金の支払（damages）を受けることができる。Tort には、negligence（過失）、nuisance（生活妨害）、trespass（侵害行為）、occupier's liability（占有者・所有者責任）、deceit（詐欺）、conversion（横領）、defamation（名誉毀損）、privacy（プライバシー）侵害等の種類がある。

(ⅲ) Law of Trusts（信託法）

既述のとおり、trust は、その沿革上は、封建制度下の国王や領主の干渉を排除する目的で他人の土地を預かった者の管理義務を基礎づける equity の制

度に基づいているが、今日では、土地に限らず物品、金員、債権を含むあらゆる財産に関して広く用いられている。Trust が成立するには、trust property（信託財産）、及び settler（設定者）、trustee（受託者）、beneficiary（受益者）の3当事者が存在する必要がある。Settler と trustee は同一人でも構わない。Trust の設定は、通常、settler が設定する意思を表明し、trust property を trustee に移転、又は（settler と trustee が同一人の場合）trust property を分離する方法で行われ、特別な要式を必要としない。また、trust 設定の意思表明がないままに財産を他人に移転してしまった場合でも、裁判所が信託の成立を擬制して不公平の是正を図ることもある。これを constructive trust（擬制信託）という。たとえば、売主が無償で使用を継続する旨の口頭の約束の下に土地を安価で処分した場合に、売主を beneficiary とし、買主を trustee とする constructive trust を認定してこの使用権を保護したり（Bannister v Bannister（1948）2 All ER 133、Binions v Evans（1972）Ch 359）、土地を購入してその名義人となる者との間で、当該土地に関する権利の2分の1を享受する旨の口頭合意の下に、購入代金の2分の1を支払った者を trustee と認定して、2分の1の持分について equity 上の財産権を認める等である（Lloyds Bank v Rosset [1991] 1 AC 107）。

(ⅳ) **Property Law**（財産権法）

Property には、real property（土地）、personal property（物、無体財産権、有価証券、債権等）及び chattels real（土地に関する利用権）の3種類があるが、property law の対象となっているのは、主として、land law（土地の所有権その他利用権に関する法律）及び law of landlord and tenant（不動産賃借権に関する法律）の2つである。

イギリスには、1066年の the Norman Conquest（ノルマン征服）以来の封建制度の下、国王の絶対的所有権を頂点として、重層構造の様々な複雑な土地利用権が生まれていたが、1925年以降、the Law of Property Act 1925及びその関連法規により、freehold（永久的な独占的土地利用権）と leasehold（5年、10年、99年、125年等の期間を定めた独占的土地利用権）の2種類だけに単純化された。さらに、the Land Registration Act 1925により土地の売買（conveyance）手続に land registry（土地登録所）への登録制度が導入され、

現在では、freehold、期間7年以上のleasehold及びその他の土地に対する第三者の権利（easement（通行地役権）、mortgage（抵当権）等）は、若干の例外を除き、land registryに登録され、確認可能となっている。このland registryは、the Land Registry Act 2002により順次にオンライン化されている。

Landlord and tenant lawは、leaseholdにおける貸主、借主（テナント）の関係を規律する法律であり、事業用地リースか居住用地リースか、居住用地の貸主が公的機関（public sector）か私人（private sector）か、リース期間の長短等の事情によって異なる規制がなされている。一般に、事業用土地のリースの場合や民間（private sector）による短期リース（1ヶ月、6ヶ月、12ヶ月等）の場合のテナント保護は限定的であり、貸主は、リース終了後に一定の期間が経過すれば、通知等の手続を踏んで立退きを求めることができる（事業用地につきthe Landlord and Tenant Act 1954 Part II、private sectorのリースにつきthe Housing Act 1996）。他方、政府その他公的機関（public sector）によるリースや21年以上の長期リースのテナントは、貸主に対し割引価格での強制的買取権が与えられる等、比較的厚く保護されている（public sectorによる居住地リースにつきthe Housing Act 1985、長期リースにつきthe Leasehold Reform Act 1967）。また、居住用集合住宅の一部のテナントは、the Landlord and Tenant Act 1985及びthe Service Charges (Consultation Requirements) (England) Regulations 2003により特別の保護が与えられている。テナントを違法に退去させた貸主の刑事罰等を定めるthe Protection from Eviction Act 1977も重要である。

(ⅴ) **Company Law（会社法）**

Company lawは、会社の設立、機能、組織、計算、倒産等を扱う法律であり、the Companies Act 2006及びthe Insolvency Act 1986等の制定法及びこれらに関する判例法が重要な法源である。イギリスの会社には、public company（公開会社）とprivate company（非公開会社）の2種類があり、株式や社債の公募ができるのは前者だけである。Public companyであるためには、定款（the memorandum of association）にその旨の記載があり、社名にPublic Limited Company又はplcの文字を含み、授権資本が5万ポンド以上

であり、かつ授権資本の4分の1以上の払い込みがなされていなければならない。これらを充たさない会社は、全て private company である。イギリスの会社の目的、本支店所在地、資本金、役員（通常、directors 及び secretary）、財務状況（BL 及び PS）、社債、担保等の情報は、London の the Registrar of Companies（会社登録所）において登録、公開され、オンラインにより誰でも入手することができる。もちろん、public company には、より詳細な財務情報開示義務が課されている。Companies Act は、長年に亘る判例法を条文化した規定と議会が政策的に設けた規定の集合体である。2007年に施行された現行会社法では、株主参加の促進、及び小規模な非公開会社に関する規制を簡素化し手続上の負担を軽減する制度などが新設されている。

（vi）その他の私法として、家族法（family law）、相続法（law of succession）、雇用法（employment law）その他多数がある。

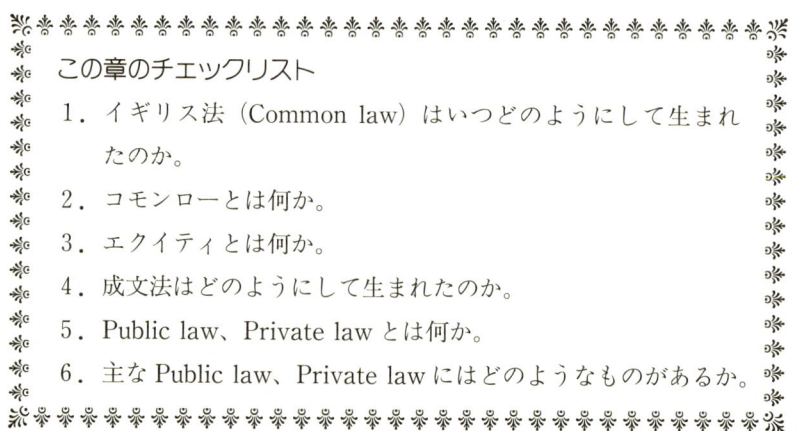

この章のチェックリスト
1．イギリス法（Common law）はいつどのようにして生まれたのか。
2．コモンローとは何か。
3．エクイティとは何か。
4．成文法はどのようにして生まれたのか。
5．Public law、Private law とは何か。
6．主な Public law、Private law にはどのようなものがあるか。

第2章

イギリスの裁判所

1. Civil law（民事法）と criminal law（刑事法）

　前章において、イギリス法を public law と private law に分類したが、これと異なる観点からの分類として、civil law（民事法）と criminal law（刑事法）の区別も重要である。ある事件がこのいずれに属する法律に関するものであるかによって、当該事件を取り扱う裁判所が決定されるからである。

　Civil law は private law の一部であるから、civil law に関する事件において判決を取得して権利を行使するのは専ら私人であり、国家その他の行政機関が直接にかかわることはない。他方、criminal law は国家と個人の間を規律している public law の一部であるから、criminal law に関する裁判手続は国の責任において開始し、かつその進行には国家が主体的に関与する。Criminal law が違法な（illegal）犯罪（crime）から社会を護るための法律であるのに対し、civil law は tort（不法行為）その他一切の不法な（unlawful）civil wrongs（民事上の権利侵害）による被害を蒙った私人を救済するための法律である。Crime（犯罪）とは、大まかに言えば、秩序ある文明社会において禁ずる必要がある、社会に害悪をもたらす行為一般（窃盗、殺人等）を意味している。他方、civil wrongs は、人身や財産を害する行為のうち、被害を蒙った者が求めたときに法律が個人的な救済措置を与えてくれるものをいう。ただし、刑事手続（criminal proceedings）の対象となる多くの行為は、その被害者にとっては民事訴訟（civil action）における請求の原因ともなる。

　この手続上の違いに加え、civil case（民事事件）と criminal case（刑事事件）とでは、裁判手続上の用語も異なっている。

　すなわち、criminal cases（刑事事件）は the Crown（女王）、the Crown Prosecution Service（公訴局）又は the Director of Public Prosecution（公

訴局長官）が訴訟を提起し（これを prosecutions（起訴、訴追）という。）、criminal court（刑事裁判所）において審理される（tried）。Criminal case の手続は、the Crown が the Attorney General（司法長官）を通じて止めることができるが、被害者（victim）には手続きを止める権限がない。

他方、civil cases（民事事件）は、被害者（wronged person 又は victim）である私人のみが suits（訴え）を提起し、civil court（民事裁判所）で審理され（tried）又は審尋される（heard）。訴訟を提起する私人は claimant（原告）と呼ばれる。Claimant はいつでも手続きを止めることができ、the Crown は民事手続きに介入できない。

Criminal case の判決言い渡しを受けた offender（犯罪者）には sanctions（制裁）が科せられる。Civil case の victim（被害者）は remedies（救済手段）により compensate（補償）を受ける。

Criminal case の判決において guilty（有罪）と判断された者には criminal record（前科）が残る。しかし、民事上 liable（有責）と判断されても何らの record も残らない。

なお、前述のとおり、civil law という用語は、法典化（codify）されたいわゆるローマ法に基づく法律制度（日本及びヨーロッパ大陸の多くの国が採用している法制度）を表す語としても用いられる。判例法に基づくイギリスの法律制度は、これに対して common law と総称されている。

イギリスの法制度上、civil law（市民法）は、ecclesiastical law（教会法）及び military law（軍事法）に対立する語としても用いられることがある。

2．The Courts（裁判所）の種類

イギリスの裁判所は、the Department for Constitutional Affairs（憲務省）の執行機関である Her Majesty's Courts Service（女王の下の裁判部）が運営している。

裁判所には、上位裁判所（superior courts）と下位裁判所（inferior courts）の2種類があり、前者としては、the House of Lords（貴族院）、the Court of Appeal (Civil Division & Criminal Division)（控訴院民事部及び同刑

事部)、the High Court（高等法院）及び the Crown Court（刑事法院）が、後者は、Small Claims Courts（少額裁判所）、County Courts（県裁判所）、Magistrates' Courts（治安判事裁判所）及び Youth Courts（少年裁判所）が設けられている。

　イギリスの裁判制度は、the Judicature Acts 1873-1875により確立された。これにより、それ以前に混在していた多数の様々な裁判所が廃止され、the Court of Appeal（Civil Division & Criminal Division）、the High Court 及び the Crown Court が設置された。これら（すなわち、the House of Lords 以外の上位裁判所）は、the Supreme Court of Judicature（最高法院）と呼ばれている。

3．Civil Court（民事裁判所）

　民事事件を取り扱う上位裁判所は、the House of Lords 及び the Supreme Court of Judicature のうちの the Court of Appeal 及び the High Court of Justice である。ただし、ほとんどの民事紛争は、上位裁判所の手続にはよらず、out-of-court settlements（裁判外の和解）又は County Courts において解決されている。County Courts は、the County Courts Act 1959により設けられた下位裁判所であり、the Supreme Court of Judicature には含まれない。

(1) Out-of-court Settlement（裁判外の和解）

　ほとんどの民事紛争は、裁判制度の直接的な助けを借りずに、当事者間の話し合いで解決されている。紛争解決のために両当事者が第三者に調停（conciliation）を頼むこともあるが、日本と異なり、裁判上の調停制度は存在しない。近年、紛争解決における conciliation その他裁判外の解決手段（ADR）の有効性が世界的に見直されており、イギリスでも、契約締結の際に調停前置の条項を合意しておくケースが増えている。裁判外の解決手段として、当事者間で仲裁（arbitration）合意をすることも少なくない。

(2) County Courts（県裁判所）

County Courts は全国約280箇所に設置され、民事事件全体の約90％を処理している。その事物管轄の範囲は、the Courts and Legal Services Act 1990以降飛躍的に拡大され、請求金額にかかわらず契約、土地返還請求、親族相続に関する紛争及び不法行為事件の大半の管轄（jurisdiction）を有している。ただし、不法行為のうちでも professional negligence（専門家の過失責任）、fatal accident（死亡事故）、defamation（名誉毀損）、civil actions against police（警察に対する民事訴訟）等の重大事件については管轄がない。County Courts の事物管轄の基準は、the High Court and County Court Jurisdiction Order 1991及び the Amendment Order 1999により、次のように定められている。

（ⅰ）契約又は不法行為に基づく請求事件：請求金額5万ポンド未満の人身損害に関する訴訟及び1万5000ポンド未満のその他の訴訟は、County Court に提起しなければならない。

（ⅱ）土地その他の財産権に関する返還請求事件は、目的物の価額が3万ポンド相当未満の場合は County Court に提起しなければならない。

（ⅲ）Mortgage（抵当）、trust（信託）等 equity（衡平法）に関する請求事件及び遺言（probate/will）に関する事件は、3万ポンド以下の場合は County Court の管轄とする。

County Courts にしか事物管轄がない事件を the High Court に提起した場合、裁判官は損害賠償額の25％までを減額することができる。

County Courts に配置される裁判官は、特定の複雑な事件だけを担当する circuit judge（巡回裁判官）、それ以外の事件をパートタイムで取り扱う recorder（レコーダー、非常勤裁判官）及びその他の少額事件のみを担当する district judge（地区裁判官、以前は the registrar（補助裁判官）と呼ばれた。）の3種類である。

County Court における訴訟は、事件の性質や規模に応じて、the small claims procedure（少額請求手続）、the fast-track（迅速手続）又は the multi-track（多面的手続）のいずれかの手続で審理される。Small claim procedure は、district judge（地区裁判官）による非公式の small claims arbitration（少額請求仲裁）であり、請求金額5000ポンド未満の事件の場合は、損害賠償請求金額（2次的損害分を除く。）が1000ポンドを超える人的損害賠償請求事件を除き、自動的にこの手続に回される。多くの場合、この small claims arbitration の審理は、chamber（裁判官室）において代理人なしで実施される。この手続は、事案の単純な消費者契約に関する少額請求事件等の解決に適しているが、複雑な法律上の争点がある事件では使えない。Small claim arbitration に適さない事件のうち、請求金額が1万5000ポンド未満であり、裁判所が1日以内に審理できると判断した事件は、fast-track により解決される。これは、比較的小規模な事件の審理を迅速かつ安価に進めるために設けられた手続であり、裁判官は、あらかじめ書類の提出時期、認否の時期等の手続進行スケジュールを厳格な期限を設けて定め、これに遅れた当事者には punishments（刑罰）を課す方法で強制する。Small claims track、fast-track のいずれにも適さない事件は、multi-track と呼ばれる手続に回され、裁判官がその事件毎の特色に応じて適宜に手続内容を決定・監督する方法で審理される。

County Court の判決に対する上訴（appeal）は、通常は the High Court に申し立てられるが、the Access to Justice Act 1990により the Court of Appeal に直接申し立てられる場合もある。

(3) The High Court（高等法院）

The High Court はロンドンに1つだけ存在するが、裁判官はイギリス内の各 County Court 所在地に出張し裁判を行うことができる。したがって、原告は、ロンドンの the Royal Courts of Justice 又は地元の County Court のいずれにも訴訟を提起できる。The High Court は、the Administration of Justice Act 1970により、Queen's Bench Division（女王座部）、Chancery Division（大法官部）及び Family Division（家事部）の3部門に分かれている。それぞれの部門の取扱事件は、次のとおりである。

（ⅰ） Queen's Bench Division：契約、不法行為等の common law に関するほとんどの民事事件を扱い、かつ海事裁判所（the Maritime Court）、商事裁判所（the Commercial Court）及び技術・建築裁判所（the Technology and Construction Court）を含んでいる。

（ⅱ） Chancery Division：土地法（land law）、信託（trusts）、抵当（mortgages）、会社法（company and partnership law）、破産（bankruptcy）、税法（tax）等を扱う。

（ⅲ） Family Division：離婚、婚姻及び親子関係事件を扱う。

この3つの部門は、それぞれのsenior judge（首席裁判官）が統括している。Queen's Bench Divisionのsenior judgeはthe President of the Queen's Bench Division（女王座部首席裁判官）Chancery Divisionはthe Chancellor of High Court（大法官部長官）、Family Divisionはthe President of the Family Division（家事部首席裁判官）である。なお、The Lord Chief Justice（裁判所長官）は、以前は高等法院のsenior judgeだったが、現在は、全裁判所を統轄する裁判官の役職名である。The High Courtの一般の裁判官は、puisne judge（ピューニ・ジャッジ、普通裁判官）と呼ばれている。Puisne judgeは10年以上の法廷実務経験のある弁護士でなければならない。弁論の権限はbarrister（バリスター、法廷弁護士）に与えられている。ただし、the Courts and Legal Services Act 1990により、solicitor（ソリシター、事務弁護士）も代理権証書を取ればthe High Courtで弁論ができる（本編第3章1）。

The High Courtの審判は、名誉毀損事件（defamation）、誣告事件（malicious prosecution）、不当監禁事件（false imprisonment）及び詐欺事件（fraud、deceit）を除き、陪審（jury）にはよらず1名のpuisne judgeにより行われる。

The High Courtの判決に対する上訴裁判所は、常にthe Court of Appealである。

(4) **The Divisional Court（Civil Division）（付属裁判所民事部）**

The High Courtの各部門には、Divisional Courts（付属裁判所）が設けられており、それぞれ一定の機能を果たしている。

（ⅰ） The Divisional Court of the Queen's Bench Division：Queen's Bench Divisionの裁判官2名以上によって構成されている。下位裁判所（inferior courts）、tribunal（審判機関）及び地方機関を監督し、その職務の

履行や管轄権の逸脱禁止を命ずる等の監督権限、及び the Administrative Court（行政裁判所）を通じて政府機関その他公的機関の決定、たとえば土地開発許可決定等を再検討し、取り消す権限（judicial review）を有している。また、Magistrates' Courts や Crown Courts の判決が case stated（当事者の合意により法律問題のみの判断を求める手続、特別上告）の方式で上訴された場合、その審理を行う権限も有している。

（ⅱ）The Divisional Court of the Chancery Division：County Courts の破産事件に関する決定に対する上訴事件等を取り扱う。

（ⅲ）The Divisional Court of the Family Division：The Family Proceedings Court（家事訴訟裁判所）からの上訴を受ける。

(5) The Court of Appeal (Civil Division)（控訴院民事部）

County Courts 及び the High Court の判決に対する上訴事件のほとんどは、the Court of Appeal において審判される。The Court of Appeal の長官は、the Master of the Rolls（記録長官、M.R.）と呼ばれ、全ての民事裁判所を統括している。The Court of Appeal における裁判は、通常、the Master of the Rolls を含む3名の裁判官により審判される。各裁判官は、記録を読み、バリスターの弁論を聞いて再審理し、原判決を維持、取消し又は変更する。The Court of Appeal の判決は、下級裁判所及び the Court of Appeal のその後の裁判所を拘束する。

(6) The House of Lords（貴族院）

正式には、the Appellate Committee of the House of Lords（貴族院上訴裁判所）と呼ばれ、イングランド、ウェールズのみならず、スコットランド及び北アイルランドの裁判に対しても最終の上訴裁判所として機能している。The House of Lords の裁判は、3名、5名又は7名の裁判官（Law Lords（法律貴族）又は Lords of Appeal in Ordinary（常任上訴貴族）という。）により審理される。各裁判官の判断は written speech（口述筆記）として言い渡され、裁判官の多数決で判決が決まる。判決は先例拘束力を有し、全ての下級裁判所を拘束する。第一審裁判所における裁判官は、当該事件に特定の法律問題が含

まれていると考えた場合、両当事者の同意に基づき、the Court of Appeal を leapfrogging（飛び級）して the House of Lords に事件を移管することができる。

なお、2005年3月24日に成立した the Constitutional Reform Act 2005により、2009年秋に the Judicial Committee of the House of Lords は廃止され、新たに the Supreme Court（最高裁判所）が設置されることになった。（現在、Supreme Courts の語は、the High Court、the Crown Court 及び Court of Appeal の3つを併せた裁判所の総称として用いられているが、新たに設けられる the Supreme Court はもちろんこれとは関係がない。）ただし、the Supreme Court の取扱事件及び機能は、これまでの the House of Lords と基本的に全く同じである。

(7) The Judicial Committee of the Privy Council（枢密院司法委員会）

The House of Lords と同一の裁判官で構成され、特定の Commonwealth 諸国における判決の上訴裁判所として機能している。形式上、the Judicial Committee of the Privy Council は、the Crown に advice（助言）をするに過ぎないが、この助言は必ず判決として採用される。未だに the Privy Council への上訴制度を残している国はわずかであるが、過去におけるいくつかの重要な判断がイギリス法に重要な影響を与えている。ただし、イギリスの法制度上、これらは persuasive precedent（本編第5章参照）としてしか機能しない。The Privy Council は、弁護士、裁判官の懲戒手続に関する管轄裁判所でもある。

(8) The European Court of Justice（欧州裁判所）

The European Court of Justice（ECJ）は、EC Treaty により、EU 加盟国の裁判所からの付託その他により European law に関する様々な事項を審理する管轄権が与えられている。イギリスの国内裁判所は、事件の付託を行うか否かの裁量権を有している。どのような場合に付託すべきかについて、明確な基準はないが、Lord Denning は、HP Bulmer v J Bollinger SA 判決（［1974］2 All ER 1226,［1974］Ch 401）において、以下の考慮事項に基づいて付託すべき旨を判示している。

（ⅰ） ECJ に付託できるのは European law に関する問題に限られる。
（ⅱ） ECJ に付託された問題に対する解答が当該事件の判断のために必要な場合に限られる。
（ⅲ） 実質的に同一の問題に対する解答が既に下されている場合、国内裁判所はこれに従わなければならない。
（ⅳ） 争われている問題に対する解答が明白である場合は付託の必要がない。
ECJ から付託事項に対する回答を受領したイギリスの裁判所は、これに従わなければならない。
ECJ は15名の裁判官により構成され、8名の Advocates General（法務官）がこれを補佐している。通常、1つの事件は7名の裁判官によって審理される。
なお、フランスの Strasbourg に the European Court of Human Rights（欧州人権裁判所、ECHR）という司法機関があるが、これは EU 法の裁判所として Luxembourg に設置されている ECJ とは、設置根拠、目的及び機能が異なる全く別個の裁判所であり、EU の機関ではない。ECHR は、欧州市民の人権保護のために the Council of Europe が起草し、1953年に発効した The European Convention of Human Rights and Fundamental Freedoms（欧州人権条約）に関する事件を処理するために設置された特別な裁判所であり、欧州内の個々人や団体は、人権侵害を受けたときにはいつでもこの裁判所に救済を求めることができる。イギリスは、当初からこの人権規約に批准していたが、約50年後の the Human Rights Act 1998によって、同規約はようやく国内法として採択された。しかし、それ以前から、イギリスの個人や団体は、政府や行政機関等の人権侵害（人権規約違反）について頻繁に ECHR に訴えを提起している。

⑼ Magistrates' Courts（治安判事裁判所）
Magistrates' Court は、主として刑事事件を扱うが、民事に関する一定の事項についても管轄を有している。特に、the Domestic Proceedings and Magistrates' Courts Act 1978及び the Children Act 1989により、Family Proceedings Court（家事訴訟裁判所）として家事手続に関する広範な管轄権を有している。Adoption（養子縁組）、public houses（パブ）、betting house（賭博

場)、casino 等の営業免許及び off-licences（酒類販売免許）も Magistrates' Courts が取り扱う。

4．Criminal Courts（刑事裁判所）

(1) Magistrates' Courts（治安判事裁判所）

　イングランド及びウェールズに435の Magistrates' Courts が存在し、イギリスの刑事事件の約98％を処理している。全ての刑事事件は、まず Magistrates' Court に持ち込まれ、このうち、駐車違反、自動車保険未加入等の軽犯罪（summary offences）については、Magistrates' Court が第一審裁判所として審理する。他方、殺人、強姦等の重大犯罪（indictable offences）の場合は、事件を陪審（jury）にかけるため the Crown Court（刑事法院）に付託する。この両者の中間程度の犯罪（triable either way offences）に関しては、被告人の同意があったときのみ magistrates が自ら審理し、そうでない場合は、the Crown Court に付託する。

　Magistrates（治安判事）は全国に約3万人おり、全て Lord Chancellor により選任された素人の男女である。Magistrates は2、3人で裁判所を構成し、法曹資格のある書記官（clerk）の助言を受けて判断する。いくつかの裁判所には district judge（地区裁判官）というプロの裁判官も配属されている。District judge は約85名おり、単独で審判する。

　Magistrates は、原則として、6ヶ月以下の懲役又は5000ポンド以下の罰金刑しか言い渡すことができない。Magistrates がこれより重い刑が相当であると判断した場合は有罪の決定のみを行い、刑の言い渡しのために被告人を the Crown Court へ移送しなければならない。

　被告人が18歳未満である場合、Magistrates' Court の一部として設けられた Youth Court（少年裁判所）において審理する。この審理は、特別なトレーニングを受けた、男女混合の3名の magistrates により行われる。この裁判は、通常の法廷とは異なる部屋において非公開で行われる。18歳未満の被告人は、殺人その他の重大犯罪で起訴された場合を除き、Youth Court により処理される。

Magistrates' Court の判決に対する上訴裁判所は、通常の場合 the Crown Court（刑事法院）である。上訴権は被告人にのみ与えられている。ただし、the Crown Court は Magistrates' Court が言い渡した刑を加重することもできる。被告人が純然たる法律事項に関してのみ争いたい場合は、cases stated（合意事実記載書）を提出する方法により the Divisional Court of the Queen's Bench Division（女王座部付属裁判所）に上訴することができる。上訴があったとき、the Divisional Court は、magistrates の法律判断を否認、是認又は変更する。この case stated の方法による上訴は、the prosecution（検察官）の側も行うことができる。この場合、the Divisional Court は、事件を Magistrates' Court に差し戻して有罪判決又は量刑変更の指示をしてもよいし、自ら判断することもできる。

(2) The Crown Court（刑事法院）

The Crown Court は、殺人その他の全ての重大犯罪（trial on indictment）を第一審裁判所として処理し、かつ Magistrates' Court の判決に対する上訴事件も取り扱う裁判所である。全ての裁判は、12人の素人からなる陪審（jury）の評決により審判する。ただし、jury は事実問題のみを判断し、法律判断は judge が行う。

理論上、the Crown Court は1個の裁判所とされているが、実際上は、100箇所前後の大都市における地方裁判所により構成されている。各裁判所は、judge の経験年数に応じて、重大事件を扱う法廷とそれ以外の事件を扱う法廷とに分かれている。

The Crown Court の判決に対する上訴裁判所は the Court of Appeal（Criminal Division）（控訴院刑事部）である。ただし、the Access to Justice Act 1999により、法律問題に関しては、case stated の方式で the Divisional Court of the Queen's Bench に上訴することもできる。

(3) The Court of Appeal（Criminal Division）（控訴院刑事部）

The Crown Court で陪審により審理された事件の有罪判決又は量刑に対する上訴事件は、the Court of Appeal において審理される。The Court of

Appealの裁判所は、通常、the Lord Chief Justice及びその他のthe Lords Justices of Appeal又はthe High Court裁判官の3名によって構成される。被告人は、法律問題、事実問題、量刑の当否のいずれに関しても上訴することができるが、事実問題のみについて上訴しようとする場合、原審の裁判官又はthe Court of Appealの許可を受けなければならない。検察側は原則として量刑以外に関しては上訴することはできない。ただし、the Criminal Justice Act 2003により、検察官は、the Court of Appealに対して、殺人、強姦等重大犯罪事件の再審査や法律問題の検討を要求することができる。

(4) The House of Lords（貴族院）

The Judicial Committee of the House of Lords（貴族院司法委員会）は、the Court of Appealの判決における法律判断について、（ⅰ）the Court of Appeal又はthe House of Lordsが当該法律問題についてthe House of Lordsの判断を受けるべきであると判断し、かつ（ⅱ）the Court of Appealが当該法律事項は公共のために重要であることを証明した場合に限り、上訴審として審理する。この上訴は、検察側、被告人の双方が行うことができる。

The House of Lordsは、the Divisional Court of the Queen's Bench Divisionの判決に対する上訴事件も審理する。

―――――――――――――――――――――――
この章のチェックリスト
1. ある者が他人の行為によって被害を蒙ったとする。当該他人の行為が民事上の違法行為（civil wrong）か刑事上の犯罪（crime）であるかを区別することは、被害者にとってなぜ必要か。
2. 以下の各用語は、criminal proceedingsとcivil proceedingsの内、どちらの手続きにおいて用いられるか。Defendant, Prosecuted, Guilty, Damages, Illegal, Liable, Fined, Sentenced, Awarded, Sued, Accused, Unlawful
3. Civil lawの反対語は何か。

4．An appellate court と a court of first instance との違いを述べなさい。

第3章

法律専門職（Legal Profession）

　イングランド及びウェールズにおける弁護士には、solicitors（ソリシター、事務弁護士）と barristers（バリスター、法廷弁護士）の２種類がある。現在、ソリシターの人数は約９万人、バリスターは１万人である。現行制度上のそれぞれの役割、資格を概説すると以下のとおりである。

1．Solicitors（ソリシター）

(1) 役割

　ソリシターは、通常の場合は下位裁判所（County Courts 及び Magistrates' Courts）においてのみ代理人として弁論でき、一定の事件に限って、the Crown Court でも活動できる。ただし、自分で事務所を経営しているソリシターは、the Courts and Legal Services Act 1990 に基づき、上位裁判所における弁論資格を申請することができる。この許可は、the Lord Chancellor の Advisory Committee on Legal Education and Conduct（司法教育・指導諮問委員会）が行う。ソリシターがこの資格を取得するためには、一定の研修を受けなければならない。

　ソリシターの仕事のほとんどは、事務所内における不動産譲渡手続、遺言書作成、会社設立手続その他の非争訟業務、及び訴訟におけるバリスターのための下準備作業である。

　従来、一般人がバリスターに事件を依頼したい場合、まずソリシターに依頼し、ソリシターを通じてバリスターに接触しなければならなかったが、2004年７月以降、ソリシターを通さずに直接バリスターに事件処理を頼むことが可能になった。これは、公正取引庁（the Office of Fair Trading）の批判を受けて、バリスター団体総評議会（Bar）が一般人の弁護士費用負担の軽減を図る

ために行った改革の一部である。しかし、実際上、素人がソリシターのサービスを受けずに直接に事件を管理し、バリスターに適切な指示を与えるのは困難なので、今でも、ほとんどの事件はソリシターを通じて依頼されている。ソリシターは、the brief と呼ばれる事件の報告書を作成して、これをバリスターに提示し、依頼事項の説明をする。訴訟以外の一般的な法律問題に関する助言は、特に専門的な法律知識が必要な場合を除き、ソリシターが直接処理している。

　ソリシターの自治団体は、the Law Society（ロー・ソサイエティ、ソリシター協会）である。The Law Society はソリシターの能力維持と誠実性の確保のため、厳格な行動準則（code of conduct）を設けている。ただし、ソリシターの不正行為を処罰する権限を有しているのは、the Law Society とは独立した the Solicitors' Disciplinary Tribunal（ソリシター懲戒審判委員会）と呼ばれる行政機関である。この機関は、ソリシターに対し、資格剥奪又は5000ポンド以下の罰金を科する権限を有している。

(2) **資格**
　ソリシターの資格を取得するための最も一般的な方法は、大学の法学部において、所定の基本法7科目（contract、tort、public law、trusts、real property、criminal law 及び the law of the European Union）を履修し、law degree を採った上、Legal Practice Course と呼ばれる1年間の研修コースを受講することである。このコース終了後、ソリシターの法律事務所において2年間の実習（apprenticeship）を受けなければならない。この実習を training contract と呼ぶ。大学で法律以外の degree を修取した者は、law degree に代えて Graduate Diploma Course という1年間の速習コースを受け、Common Professional Examination という試験に通ってから Legal Practice Course に進む方法を採ることができる。

2．Barristers（バリスター）

　バリスターとは、伝統的には、裁判所において代理人として活動する gentlemen（ジェントルマン、紳士）を意味していた。昔は、バリスターになるためには Inns of Court（インズ・オブ・コート）と呼ばれるロンドンの排他的クラブに加入し、このクラブにおいて所定の回数食事をするだけでよかった。

(1) 役割

　ほとんどのバリスターは、法廷における代理活動を主要な業務としている。ただし、その業務時間の大半は、事務所（chamber と呼ばれている。）における準備書面（the pre-trial documents）の作成に費やされている。バリスターは、あらゆる裁判所において訴訟活動をすることができる。The General Council of the Bar（バリスター団体総評議会）というバリスターの統治団体が、ソリシターにおける the Law Society と同等の機能を果たしている。

　バリスターが上位裁判所（superior courts）に出頭する場合は、wig と呼ばれる白髪のかつら、bib と呼ばれる前垂れのような物（ネクタイではない）、黒いガウンの着用等の厳格なドレスコードを護らなければならない。時代劇染みてはいるが、現在でもバリスターの大半は、このドレスコードの継続を望んでいる。ソリシターが裁判所に出頭し弁論する場合もガウンの着用は必要であるが、wig は不要とされている。

　バリスターは、依頼を受けたあらゆる事件を差別なく引き受けるべき義務を負っている。これを the "cab rank" principle（タクシー乗車の原則）と呼ぶ。実績を上げたバリスターは、女王の勅選弁護士（Queen's Counsel）になることがある。これを "take silk"（シルクを纏う）という。バリスターはパートナーシップを組むことができないが、通常、Queen's Counsel を所長とする chambers（事務所）の１つに所属して執務する。バリスターは数多くの伝統的な慣習による制約を受けているが、the Courts and Legal Services Act 1990 により、そのいくつかが廃止された。たとえば、新たに chamber を設けることが自由化され、business manager（事務所経営者）としての clerk を設けるべき義務も廃止された。また、pupilages（実習）を無給とする原則も廃止された。

　最近まで、バリスターは、その過失により敗訴しても責任を問われないものとされていた。この特権は、Arthur J S Hall v Simons（[2000] 3 WLR 543）

判決によって廃止された。

(2) 資格

　バリスターとなるための法曹教育上の資格要件は、ソリシターと似通っている。大学での law degree 又はこれに代わる Graduate Diploma Course（ただし、ソリシターの必須7科目とは若干異なり、real property の代わりに civil procedure、criminal procedure を加えた8科目の degree が必要である。）を取った上で、Bar Vocational Course と呼ばれる1年間の特別研修を受け、その後、バリスターの chamber で1年間の実習をすることが必要である。バリスターの実習又は見習いは pupilage、実習生は pupil と呼ばれている。最近までこの実習期間中は無給とされていたため、バリスターになることができるのは、経済的に余裕のある者に限られていた。現在は実習を受けている chamber から最低給与額以上の支払を受けることができるが、training contract 中のソリシターが事務所から受ける給与に比べれば薄給である。

　以上の教育上の要件に加えて、Bar Vocational Course を受けようとする者は、ロンドンにある4つの Inns of Court（インズ・オブ・コート、法曹院）のうちの1つに加入し、研修期間に所定の回数（原則24回）の晩餐（dinners）を当該 Inn 内の dinning room（ダイニング・ルーム）でとらなければならない。これは dinning（ダイニング）と呼ばれる制度で、バリスターが gentlemen（ジェントルマン）だった頃から続いている。現在は地方で実習を受ける者が多いので、一度に2度ずつ dinner をとった扱い（double-dining という。）にして12回に減らすことが許されている。

3．The Judiciary（裁判官）

(1) 選任

　イギリスは職業裁判官の制度を採っていない。The Lords of Appeal in Ordinary（常任上訴貴族）から stipendiary magistrates（有給治安判事）に至るまでのイギリスの全裁判官は、弁護士（主としてバリスター）の中から選ばれる。

The High Court の裁判官（puisne judges of the High Court）及び County Courts の裁判官の内、circuit judges（巡回裁判官）、recorders（レコーダー、非常勤裁判官）、the district judge（地区裁判官）は、the Lord Chancellor（大法官）の推薦により女王が任命し、裁判官補以下については the Lord Chancellor が任命する。裁判官の選任基準には不明瞭な部分が多かったが、2006年4月3日から、裁判官を選任するための独立機関として the Judicial Appointments Commission（司法任命委員会、JAC）が新たに設置され、実質的な選任は、この委員会の協議に基づいて行うことになった。現在、the Lord Chancellor は、JAC が推挙した候補者しか推薦、任命できない。

　イギリスで最高位の裁判所である the House of Lords の長官、the Lord Chancellor（大法官）は、専ら政治的な観点から首相の助言の下に女王が選任する。最初の Chancellor が選ばれたのは605年である。2003年6月12日、当時の Lord Chancellor であった Lord Irving of Lairg は、65万ポンドの国費を費やして彼が居住していた公邸を改装したこと等で社会的非難を浴び、ブレア首相により解任された。ブレアは、この機に乗じて裁判所改革を議会に諮り、2005年、the Constitutional Reform Act（裁判所組織改革法）が成立した。2006年4月3日以降、Lord Chancellor の権限は大幅に縮減され、全裁判官の統括権限は the Lord Chief Justice（裁判所長官）に移管されている。

　The Lord Chief Justice、High Court の各 division を統括する senior judge、the Court of Appeal（控訴院）の裁判官である the Lords Justice of Appeal（控訴院裁判官）やその長である the Master of the Rolls（記録長官）、及び The House of Lords の裁判官である the Lords of Appeal in Ordinary（常任上訴貴族）は、JAC が推挙した候補者を the Lord Chancellor が首相に進言し、首相の助言に基づいて女王が任命する。

(2) **資格**

　裁判官の選任資格は、the Courts and Legal Services Act 1990に以下のとおり規定されている。

　（i）　Lord of Appeal in Ordinary（the Judicial Committee of the House of Lords の裁判官）：上位裁判所（the High Court 又は the Court of Appeal）

の裁判官の職に2年以上の期間就いていた者、又はSupreme Courtsでの弁論資格を15年以上有していた者（2009年秋以降に任命されるSupreme Court Judgeの選任資格も同様である。）

（ⅱ） Lords Justice of Appeal（the Court of Appealの裁判官）：The High Courtでの弁論資格を10年以上有していた者、又はthe High Courtの裁判官であった者

（ⅲ） High Court Judges（puisne judges）：The High Courtでの弁論資格を10年以上有していた者、又は2年以上circuit judgeをしていた者

（ⅳ） Circuit Judges及びRecorders：10年以上the Crown Court又はCounty Courtsでの弁論資格を有していた者

(3) 訓練

The Judicial Studies Board（司法研修委員会）がtrainee assistance recorder（補助レコーダー研修生）及び新任のcircuit judges（巡回裁判官）のための入門セミナーや経験のある裁判官のための強化セミナー（refresher seminar）を実施している。

(4) 解任

The High Court以上の裁判所の裁判官は、議会の申立てにより女王が解任する場合を除き、定年退職まで職務に就いている。

それ以下の裁判所の裁判官は、the Lord Chancellorが弾劾裁判所（tribinal）の報告に基づき解任することができる。裁判官が弾劾を受けて退任に至ることは滅多にない。先例としては、密輸入で有罪となったcircuit judgeが1名解任されたことがあるだけである。

原則として、裁判官は、70歳に達したとき引退しなければならない。ただし、the Lord Chief Justice他の役付裁判官の定年は75歳である。

4．Magistrates（治安判事）

イギリスには、約700の治安判事裁判所（magistrates' court）があり、約3

万人の無給かつ非常勤の素人治安判事（part-time lay magistrates）及び約85人のプロの常勤地区裁判官（district judges、正式には、stipendiary magistratesすなわち有給治安判事という。）が勤務している。

District judgesは、7年以上の実務経験があるソリシター又はバリスターである。Magistratesは法律上の資格は何も持っていない。彼らは、仕事に就く前に1年間の準備コースを受けているが、裁判所における法的な問題は、ソリシター又はバリスターの資格のある the justice' clerk（裁判所書記官）が処理している。

Magistratesは、the Lord of Chancellorが local advisory committee（地域諮問委員会）と相談の上選任する。Local advisory committeeは、地方における利益団体（政党、労働組合等）が提案する者を magistrates候補として推薦するので、結局、それらの団体の利益を代表する者が選任されることになる。実際上、ほとんどの magistratesは、中産階級の中年の白人である。このような状況を是正するため、最近、地方政府は、ラジオの地方局やバスの車体広告等で magistratesの募集広告を始めている。

被告人が無罪判決を受ける確率は、Crown Courtの陪審評決を受けた場合の方が magistratesの判決より2対1位の割合で高い。

5．その他の法律専門職

職業法律家に準じる職業としては以下のものがある。

(1) Licensed Conveyancers（不動産譲渡士）：Conveyanceすなわち土地売買の手続を処理する業務は、1985年までソリシターが独占していたが、the Administration of Justice Act 1985によりこの独占状態は崩され、現在は、不動産売買手続の処理業のみを扱う conveyancerという資格を取ることができるようになった。この結果、不動産売買手続費用は、以前よりもいくらか下がってきている。

(2) Legal Executives（法律専務職員）：ほとんどのソリシターは、高度の法律業務を処理するソリシター以外のスタッフを雇っている。これらのスタッフは、一定の実務経験と一連の試験に受かることを条件として、legal execu-

tives という資格を得て、the Institute of Legal Executives（法律専務協会）に登録することができる。現在、legal executives は2万人を超えており、その中にはソリシターを目指している者も少なくない。

(3) Assistant Lawyers（補助弁護士）：国際的な事件を扱う大規模のソリシター事務所には、イギリス国外の弁護士も多数勤務している。この中には、ソリシターの資格を取らないまま、外国弁護士という資格だけで執務する者も多い。イギリスでの work permit（就業許可）上の就労条件としては、通常、かつてソリシターの独占業務だった conveyance（不動産譲渡事務）及びかつてバリスターの独占業務だった litigation（訴訟）以外の一切の法律業務の遂行が許可される。なお、EU 加盟国の弁護士は、イギリスでも自由に就業できる。

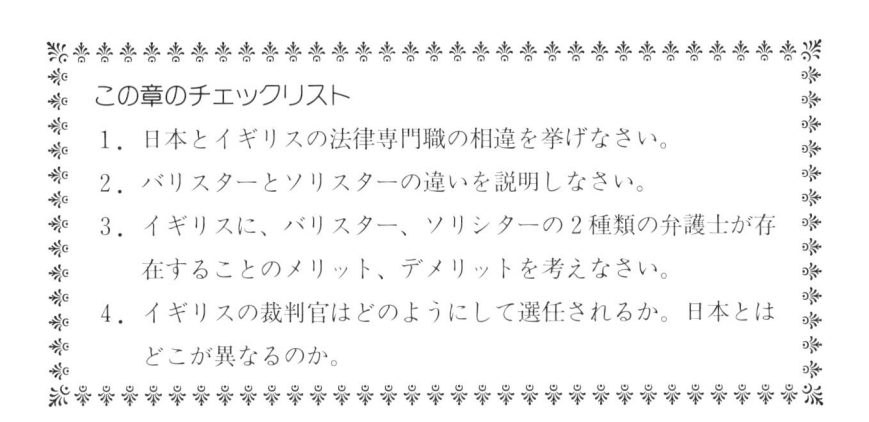

この章のチェックリスト

1．日本とイギリスの法律専門職の相違を挙げなさい。
2．バリスターとソリシターの違いを説明しなさい。
3．イギリスに、バリスター、ソリシターの2種類の弁護士が存在することのメリット、デメリットを考えなさい。
4．イギリスの裁判官はどのようにして選任されるか。日本とはどこが異なるのか。

第4章

イギリス法の法源
(Sources of English Law)

イギリスには、次の4つの種類の法源が存在する。
（ⅰ） Domestic legislation（国内法規）としての statutes（制定法）及び statutory instruments（命令、規則）
（ⅱ） European Community Law（EU法）、すなわち、EUの treaties（条約）、regulations（規則）、directives（指令）及び decisions（決定）
（ⅲ） Case law（common law）（判例法）
（ⅳ） Custom（慣習）

1．国内法規（Domestic Legislation）

(1) Statute（制定法）とは

　Statutes は、the Queen In Parliament（女王の議会）が制定する Acts of Parliament（議会制定法）のことである。Acts of Parliament はイギリスにおける第一義的な法律（primary legislation）であり、判例法その他のあらゆる国内法令に優先し、所定の手続きに従わない限り、原則として覆すことができない。これを議会（Parliament）の主権及び優位性（sovereignty and supremacy）という。ただし、法律の制定における Parliament の権限には、以下のような限界がある。
　第1に、statute により将来の議会による立法行為を制限することはできない。
　第2に、the European Communities Act 1972に基づき、EU法は、イギリス国内法に優先する。よって、EU法施行と同時にこれに反する国内法の規定は効力を失うことになる。ただし、議会は、この1972法自体を廃止する権限を

有している。

　第3に、the Human Rights Act 1998により、議会は the European Convention on Human Rights（欧州人権条約）に基づいて保障されているイギリス国民の権利と自由を尊重しなければならない。同法19条に基づき、各大臣は、立法に当り、法案が同条約に抵触しないことを明確に示さなければならない。ただし、理論上は、この1998法もまた、議会が廃止を議決することが可能であり、その結果人権条約上の義務を免れることができる。

(2) 制定法の立法過程

　Statute を制定するには、法案（a Bill）が the House of Commons（庶民院）及び the House of Lords（貴族院）の双方を通過し、the Royal Assent（女王の裁可）を受けなければならない。

　The House of Commons とは、総選挙（general election）又は補欠選挙（任期中に議員が死亡した場合）で国民に選ばれた議員（Members of Parliament）によって構成される議会である。英国は、各選挙区から1名ずつを選出する小選挙区制を採っている。選出された議員が最も多い政党が政府を組織し、その政党の代表が the Prime Minister（首相）となる。1999年以降スコットランドは独自の議会を持ち、教育、社会保障等に関し、スコットランド地方だけに適用される法律を制定する特定の権限の委譲（devolution）を受けている。このスコットランド議会の議員は比例代表制で選出されている。ただし、スコットランド議会に委譲された権限は限定的であり、スコットランドの利害に影響する一般的な法律のほとんどは、ウエストミンスターの中央議会で制定されている。ウェールズにも、Welsh National Assembly（ウェールズ議会）と呼ばれるミニ議会があるが、その権限はスコットランド議会よりも更に限定的である。

　The House of Lords は、伝統的に、家柄に基づく世襲貴族（hereditary peers）とその者の善行や政治的な嗜好により選任される終身貴族（life peers）によって構成されてきたが、the House of Lords Act 1999により、世襲貴族は、90の例外を残して廃止され、2003年7月、労働党政府は、この90議席分についても世襲貴族の特権を全廃した。The House of Lords は、法案の

成立を最長1年まで（予算案の承認は1ヶ月まで）遅らせることができるだけである。

　女王による裁可（the Royal Assent）は、現在では、女王が両院において法律の略名を読み上げるだけの形式的な行為である。1707年以降、女王又は国王が法律の承認を拒んだことは一度もない。

　ほとんどの法律は政府が議会に提出した法案に基づいて制定されているが、各議員も Private Member's Bill（議員提出法案）の方式で法案を提出することができる。議員提出法案は、複雑な審議、採決手続を経なければならないため、滅多に可決されない。

　法案が議会に提出されてから可決に至るまでの通常の手続きは次のとおりである。

（ⅰ）　政府の the Legislation Committee（立法委員会）が当会期中の立法計画を決定し、通常11月中である会期の開始日に女王が the Queen's Speech（女王の施政方針演説）において発表する。

（ⅱ）　政府は、法案の内容を記載した Green Paper（グリーン・ペーパー）と呼ばれる諮問書（最初の草案）を作成の上発行し、関係者の意見を求める。

（ⅲ）　Green Paper に対する回答を検討の上、政府は White Paper（白書）と呼ばれる最終の公式提案書を発表する。この提案書は、最終的な法律の形で発表され、法案（Bill）となる。

（ⅳ）　Bill は、以下の5つの手続きを経た後に、他の House に送られる。両院で可決された場合、the Royal Assent に回される。

（a）　First Reading：法案名及び提案者名の正式発表及び法案の印刷。

（b）　Second Reading：法案の趣旨・目的について幅広く議論する。過半数が賛成した場合、法案は、審議のために委員会に送られる。

（c）　Committee Stage：法案が綿密に審査され、議論の上修正される。常設委員会は、主要な政党の代表を含む20名前後の議員により構成される。重要な法案の場合は、議員全員で議論される。

（d）　Report Stage：常設委員会より、修正後の法案が議会に上程され、さらに討議、修正される。

（e）　Third Reading：最終討議の上、採決がなされる。法案が可決した場合、

他の院に回され、両院で可決した後は女王に上程される。

（ⅴ） 2番目に審議するHouseがbillを修正した場合は、最初のHouseに戻されて再度審議採決される。この過程は、法案の修正がなされる度に繰り返される。1つの会期中に最終的に可決されなかった法案は廃案となる。

(3) 委任立法（Delegated Legislation）

　Delegated legislationとは、the Parliament（議会）から授権を受けたthe Parliament以外の機関によって制定された法規（legislation）のことであり、subordinate legislation又はsecondary legislationとも呼ばれる。これには、statutory instruments（命令、規則）、orders in council（枢密院令）及びbye-law（条例）が含まれる。Statutory instrumentsの制定権は、statuteにおいて、特定の大臣その他の役人やthe Lord Chancellorに対して付与される。毎年約40乃至50の法律が制定されるのに対し、statutory instrumentsの数は年間4000以上である。これらの規則は、Houseによる異議申し立ての機会を保障するため、原則として40日間、施行が据え置かれる。Order in councilは、the Emergency Powers Act 1920に基づき、特に緊急を要する事態が生じたときに限り、大臣が宣告して遅滞なく実施することができる命令である。Bye-laws（条例）は、議会が各地方自治体に対し、当該地方に影響がある事項に関してのみ制定権を付与する法規である。法律による委任の範囲を超える立法行為は、ultra-vires（権限ゆ越）行為となり、当該法規は無効とされる。

(4) 法規解釈（Statutory Interpretation）

　裁判所による法規解釈とは、ある特定の法律における1つの語句について複数の意味内容が考えられる場合、その内の1つの意味を選択する作業のことである。歴史的に、イギリスの裁判所は、法規解釈に当ってその法規の文言の客観的な意味だけを探求し、議会が立法に当って何を意図していたか等の事情を法文以外の資料から検討するような行為は試みない方法（literal approach、文理解釈手法）を採っていた。この手法は、比較的最近までは支配的かつ絶対的な法規解釈方法とされ、現在でも多数の裁判官がこれに従っている。ただし、今日では、少なくともEU法の解釈に限っては、purposive approach（目的

論的解釈方法)の方が主流となりつつある。目的論的解釈の方法を採った場合、裁判所は、法規の文言を離れて、the Law Commission Reports(法律の制定過程を記録した報告書)やHansard(英国国会議事録、議会手続の公式報告書)のような信頼の置ける資料から立法意図を探求することができる。日本ではごく一般的なこの解釈手法がイギリスでも採られるようになったのは、EU法の法規解釈にこの手法が不可欠であることがわかったためである。ただし、EU法規及びその実施のために制定された国内法規以外の法律の解釈にも目的論的手法を用いることができるかどうかについては、裁判官の間でまだ意見が分かれている。Lord Denningは、伝統的な文理解釈の手法に反対し、一般の法規においても目的論的解釈を採るべき旨を主張したが(Northman v London Borough of Barnet [1988] 1 AER 1243)、彼の見解はthe House of Lordsにより否定された。ただし、全法規の解釈に目的論的手法を採用しようとする裁判官の人数が徐々に増えていることは確かである。

　裁判官は、上記の文理解釈手法(literal approach)によって法規を解釈する際、以下のような解釈準則(the rules of interpretation)を用いている。

　(ⅰ)　まず、最も基本的な決まりごととして、法律は、特に明記されている場合を除き、既に存在する他の法律を変更せず、また遡及的な効力を生じないものとされている。

　(ⅱ)　The Literal Rule(文理準則):法文中の語句は、当該法律が特に定義している場合を除き、辞書に記載されたとおりの一般的な意味を有していることを前提とすべしとする解釈準則である。ただし、実際には、裁判官は、辞書など使用せず、文脈上適当と思われる通常の法律用語の技術的な意味を採用しているのが通常である。この準則は、ある語句について、文脈上適当な意味が2つ以上ある場合や、文字どおりの意味に解釈すると明らかに不合理な結果を招くときには適用できない。

　(ⅲ)　The Mischief Rule(弊害準則):ある法規が特定の弊害の除去を目的としていることが明らかな場合は、その法規における語句は、その目的に合わせて解釈すべしとする準則である。これは、1584年の判例(Heydon's Case 1584)により確立された解釈準則であるが、16世紀当時の制定法には、その目的や趣旨について長文の導入文が記されていたので、literal approachと矛盾

することはなかった。しかし、今日では、この準則を利用するためには、法規の文言だけでなく Law Commission Report や Hansard その他の立法資料まで参考にして法律の目的を探求しなければならないため、法規の文理（literal meaning）に反する場合が生じている。したがって、現在では、むしろ目的論的な解釈手法（purposive approach）のための準則ということができ、これがどの範囲の法規まで（すなわち EU 法以外にまで）適用できるかについては見解が分かれている。

（ⅳ）　The Golden Rule（黄金律）：この準則は、ある語句が 2 つ以上の異なる意味に用いられていて、上記の the literal rule の適用だけでは、確定困難な場合にのみ使用できる。第 1 に、語句の意味が文理上あいまいな場合、裁判所は最も合理的と思われる意味を採用して解釈すべきものとされている。第 2 に、literal rule を適用すると明らかに不合理と思われる場合、裁判所は golden rule により合理的な意味に解釈することができる。この第 2 の golden rule を用いる場合、裁判官は政策的な判断に基づいて法規解釈を行うことになる。

（ⅴ）　Human Rights（人権準則）：The Human Rights Act 1998 に基づき、裁判官は、あらゆる法律について、the European Convention on Human Rights（欧州人権条約）に基づく基本的人権とできる限り矛盾しないように解釈しなければならない。

（ⅵ）　補充的な解釈準則：Literal rule を補充するその他の解釈準則として、次のような原則がよく使用されている。

（a）　The noscitur a sociis principle（近辺用語類推原則）：The contextual rule（文脈準則）とも呼ばれる。ある特定の文中における 1 つの語句の意味を決める上で、法律全体及びその語句の他の文での使用方法を考慮することができるとする原則である。

（b）　The ejusdem generis principle（同類解釈原則）：列記事項の末尾が「and other items」のような一般的な言い回しで終わった場合、この「other items」にはその前に列記した事項と同じ種類の事項だけが含まれるとする解釈原則である。

（c）　The expressio unius est exclusio alterius principle（規定外排除原

則）：条文中に特定の事項が列記されている場合、特定されていない事項は除外する趣旨であるとする解釈原則である。

2．European Community Law（EU法）

(1) 意義

　EU法とは、欧州共同体に加盟する諸国間で批准された条約（treaties）及びこの条約に基づき、これを補足するためにEU共同体の関連機関が制定した2次的法規、すなわちregulations（規則）、directives（指令）及びdecisions（決定）のことである。イギリスは、1972年にローマ条約に批准することによってthe European Economic Community（欧州経済共同体）に加盟し、議会はこれを受けてthe European Communities Act 1972を制定した。イギリスの法原則上、一般に、treatyは国家間の約束に過ぎず、これによって国内の各個人、法人、機関等に対する権利義務が直ちに創設されるものではないが、このthe European Communities Act 1972により、the European Communityに関するtreaty（条約）は当然に国内法の一部となり、また、the European community lawと他の国内法との間に不一致があるときはthe European Community lawが優先することとなった。この点に関し、the European Communities Act 1972のSection 2(1)は以下のとおり規定している。

> All such rights, power, liabilities, obligations and restitutions from time to time created or arising by or under the Treaties, and all remedies and procedures from time to time provided for, by or under the Treaties, as in accordance with the Treaties are without further enactment to be given legal effect or used in the United Kingdom shall be recognized and available in law, and be enforced, allowed and followed accordingly, and the expression 'enforceable Community right' … shall be read as referring to one which this subjection applies.

　この規定に基づき、EU加盟国間のtreaties及びこれに基づいてEUの機関が決定したregulationsは、個別的な議会の承認を得なくても自動的にイギリスの法源となる。イギリス議会はこれによって自らの立法権限に制限を付した

わけだが、少なくとも理論上、議会はいつでもこの法律を廃止して the European Community から脱退することができるという意味において、parliamentary sovereignty and supremacy（議会の最高機関性）が維持されている。

(2) European Institutions（EU 機関）

EU には、the European Commission（欧州委員会）、the European Council of Ministers（欧州首脳協議会）、the European Parliament（欧州議会）及び the European Court of Justice（欧州裁判所）が設けられている。

European Commission は EU の政策を実施・遂行する執行機関である。欧州委員会の本部はブラッセルにあるが、各国の主要都市にオフィスを設け、その機能を分散している。The European Council of Ministers（ECM）は、加盟各国政府の首脳（president, prime minister 等）の集まりであり、基本的な政策やその実施方法を決定する機関である。現在の ECM の議長はイギリスのブレア首相である。The European Parliament は、各国が選出した代表による会議体であり、フランスのストラスブルグ（Strasbourg）に所在している。この代表として選出された委員の総数は626名であり、イギリスからは77名が送り込まれている（2005年）。この機関は、欧州委員会に対する助言、勧告が主要な役割であるが、予算の承認に関しては実質的な権限を持っている。EU の司法機関としては、ルクセンブルグ（Luxembourg）に the European Court of Justice が設けられ、加盟国の条約上の義務違反の判断や条約解釈の決定等を行っている。この裁判所には、加盟各国から1名ずつの裁判官が派遣されている。

(3) The Treaties（条約）

EC 法の主要な法源は、1951年のパリ条約（the Treaty of Paris 1951）、及び1957年の2つのローマ条約（the first and second Treaties of Rome 1957）の3条約である。パリ条約により the European Coal and Steel Community（ECSC、欧州石炭鉄鋼共同体）が、また2つのローマ条約により、the European Atomic Energy Community（Euratom、欧州原子力共同体）及び the

European Economic Community（EEC、欧州経済共同体）がそれぞれ形成された。The European Economic Community は、その後は単に the European Community（EC、欧州共同体）と呼ばれるようになり、the Single European Act 1986及び the Maastricht Treaty 1992ではこれが正式名称となった。これら条約の全条項は、the Treaty of Amsterdam 1997により全て単一の条約に統合され、条項番号が付け替えられた。

　これらを含む主要な EC 条約は以下のとおりである。

　（ⅰ）　The European Coal and Steel Community Treaty（ECSC）1951

　（ⅱ）　The European Community Treaty 1957（the EC Treaty, the Treaty of Rome）

　（ⅲ）　The European Atomic Energy Community Treaty（Euratom）1957

　（ⅳ）　The Merger Treaty 1965（ECSC、Euratom 及び EC の統合）

　（ⅴ）　The Single European Act 1986（単一市場形成）

　（ⅵ）　The Treaty of European Union 1992（TEU）（the Maastricht Treaty）

　（ⅶ）　The Treaty of Amsterdam 1997（全条約の統合）

　（ⅷ）　Treaty of Nice 2000（EU 憲法の検討）

　以下の各 Treaty は、EU が拡大してきた過程を示している。

　（ⅰ）　Treaty of Accession 1972（UK、Ireland 及び Denmark 加盟）

　（ⅱ）　Second Treaty of Accession 1979（Greece 加盟）

　（ⅲ）　Third Treaty of Accession 1986（Spain 及び Portugal 加盟）

　（ⅳ）　Fourth Treaty of Accession 1993（Austria、Finland 及び Spain 加盟）

　（ⅴ）　Fifth Treaty of Accession 2003（Cyprus、the Czech Republic、Estonia、Hungary、Latovia、Lituania、Malta、Poland、the Slovak Revablic 及び Slovania 加盟）

　なお、EC 条約を引用する場合、たとえば、article 249 [ex. 189] EC のように、2種類の条文が示されることが多いが、この括弧内（189）は当該条約のオリジナルの条番号であり、その前に示されたもの（249）は、the Treaty of Amsterdam 1997により付け替えられた条番号である。

(4) 2次的 EU 法規 (Secondary EU Legislation)

EU の各機関には一般的な立法権は与えられていない。ただし、条約の個別的な規定に基づいて特定の機関 (European Commission 又は European Council of Ministers) に権限が付与された場合に限り、当該機関は、関連する2次的法規を制定することができる。このような2次的法規に関して、the EC Treaty (ローマ条約) の249条 (article 249 [ex. 189] EC) は以下のとおり規定している。

> In order to carry out their task and in accordance with the provisions of this Treaty, that European Parliament acting jointly with the Council and the Commission shall make regulations, issue directives, take decisions, make recommendations or deliver opinions.
>
> A regulation shall have general application. It shall be binding in its entirety and deliver applicable in all Member States.
>
> A directive shall be binding as to the result to be achieved, upon each Member State to which it is addressed, but shall leave to the national authorities the choice of the form and methods.
>
> A decision shall be binding in its entirety upon those to whom it is addressed.
>
> Recommendations and opinions shall have no binding force.

Regulations (EU 規則) は、the Council of Ministers 又は the European Commission が策定する法規であり、各加盟国の議会による採択を待たず、制定と同時に全加盟国を拘束し、各国の裁判所において国内法に優先して適用される (In Re: Tachographs: EC Commission v The United Kingdom (1979))。農業政策、競争政策等、EC が直接的に管轄を持つべき重要事項に関しては、regulations が利用される。

The Council of Ministers 及び the European Commission は、それぞれの役割に応じて、directives (指令) を発行する権限を与えられる。Directives は、直ちに加盟国を拘束するものではなく、各加盟国に対し、一定の期間内

（2年くらい）に国内法をEU法に適合させるように要求して発せられる指令である。たとえば、イギリスは、消費者保護のためのEuropean Commissionが発行したEC Directive on Unfair Terms in Consumer Contracts（93/13/EC）の指令に基づいて、the Unfair Terms in Consumer Contracts Regulations 1999を制定している。Directivesは、会社法、銀行法、取引法等、EUが定めた法規だけで各国の法制を直接的に変更するのは実務的に困難な分野において用いられる。

　Decisionsは、加盟国内の個人、法人、機関、国家等から持ち込まれた特定の事項に関してEC Commissionが行う決定である。当該決定はその名宛人を直ちに拘束する。たとえば、ある加盟国の農業政策に関して当該加盟国を名宛人とする決定、企業の競争制限行為を調査の上当該企業に対して出される決定等である。

　Recommendations及びopinionsは、単なる助言、勧告に過ぎず、法的拘束力はない。

3．Common law（判例法）——Judicial precedents（先例法）

　Common lawには前述のとおり様々な意味があるが、法源（sources of law）としてのcommon lawはcase law（判例法）の意味で用いられる。Common law（判例法）とは、過去の事件の裁判において裁判所が示した一定の規範的な判断のうち、その後の事件を拘束する効力を有している部分のことである。Common lawは、その効力においてActs of Parliamentであるstatutesに劣後するが、statuteの適用がない分野には広く適用されると共に、statuteの解釈法としても重要な機能を有している。また、contract（契約）、tort（不法行為）、homicide（殺人）等、最も基本的かつ重要な法分野の根幹部分はcommon lawによって規律されている。

4．Subsidiary sources（副次的法源）

(1) Custom（慣習）

全ての common law は元々各地方の慣習を基礎に形成されてきたものなので、これまで裁判所で採用されたことのない慣習があれば、今後の裁判における法源となり得る。

(2) 参考書

裁判所は、適切な先例が見つからない場合、著名な法律学者の書物における意見を参考にすることがある。

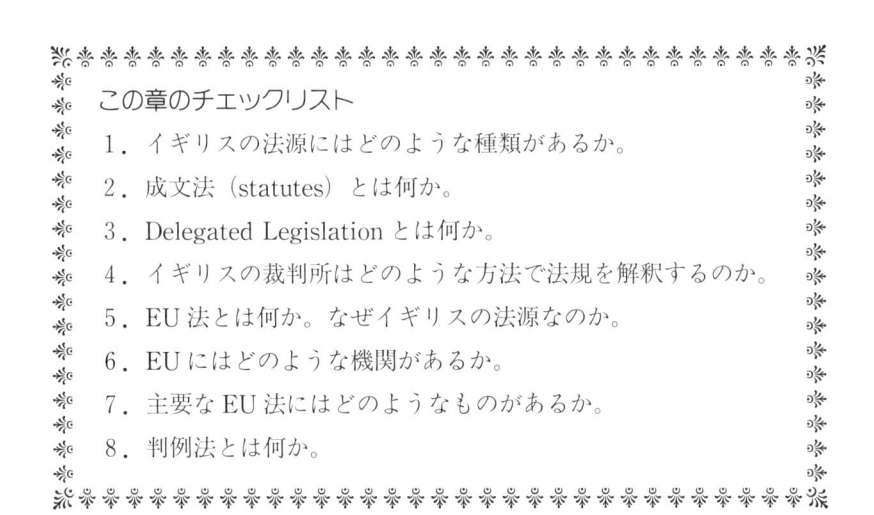

この章のチェックリスト
1．イギリスの法源にはどのような種類があるか。
2．成文法（statutes）とは何か。
3．Delegated Legislation とは何か。
4．イギリスの裁判所はどのような方法で法規を解釈するのか。
5．EU 法とは何か。なぜイギリスの法源なのか。
6．EU にはどのような機関があるか。
7．主要な EU 法にはどのようなものがあるか。
8．判例法とは何か。

第5章

先例拘束性の原理（Stare Decisis）

　Stare decisis（the doctrine of precedence、先例拘束性の原理）とは、（ⅰ）裁判所が、過去の先例（すなわち、過去の裁判における裁判官の決定）に従わなければならないこと、（ⅱ）上位の裁判所の判断は下位裁判所の判断を拘束すること、及び（ⅲ）事実関係の重要な部分が同一の事件は同様の取扱いを受けるべきことを内容とする、判例法の適用に関する基本原理である。イギリスの裁判官は、裁判において、この基本原理の存在を前提とし、過去の判決を分析して判例法に当る規範的判断を見つけ出し、それが現事件の事実関係に適用できるか否かを決定することにより、事件を解決している。

　The doctrine of precedence の下では、たとえ過去の裁判所の判断が不適当であってもその後の裁判官はこれに従わなければならないので、時代の状況に応じた柔軟な事件解決や裁判を通じての法の発展を妨げているとの批判がある。しかし他方において、裁判官個々人の信条や世界観にかかわらず同一の事実関係において常に同一の判断が期待できる点で、この法原理が裁判の公平及び安定性を高める働きをしていることも確かである。特に、取引社会では、紛争が生じた場合はできる限り裁判手続を経ずに解決することが望まれるところ、この法原理を採れば、類似する先例さえあれば裁判所が示すであろう判断を確実に予見できるので、これに基づいて当事者間で紛争を効率的に解決することが可能となる。このことから、先例拘束性の原理の存在は、イギリス法が国際取引の準拠法として好まれる理由の1つであるといわれている。

　裁判官は、the doctrine of precedence に基づいて common law を適用する場合、（ⅰ）先ず現に取り扱っている事件の争点と類似、関連する問題を扱った判例を探し（finding cases）、（ⅱ）次にその判例の中で裁判官が示している規範的な判断が先例拘束性のある binding precedent（判例法）であるのか、それとも法に関する裁判官の意見、すなわち persuasive precedent（説得的先

例）又は non-binding precedent（拘束力のない先例）に過ぎないのかを選別し（finding precedent）、(iii)最後にこれを当該事件に適用できるか否かを分析（applying cases 又は distinguishing cases）する必要がある。以下に、この３つの作業の具体的な内容を説明する。

１．判例調査（Finding Cases）

Common law を適用する大前提として、まず先例を報告した判例集（case report）を入手して調査しなければならない。

判例集には様々な種類のものが存在し、その質も玉石混合である。1272年から1535年までの間は Year Books（年書）と呼ばれる裁判速記録のようなものが編纂されていたが、1535年から1865年までの間は廃止され、代わりに報告者の名前の入った様々な非公式の判例集が民間企業により出版された。これらの中には全く信頼に値しないものも少なからず含まれていた。1865年、ロンドン市内の４つの Inns of Court（インズ・オブ・コート）及び Law Society（ロー・ソサイエティ）は、法律家が監修した上級裁判所判決集を出版するための協議会（the Incorporated Council of Law Reporting 又は ICLR）を発足し、毎週発行する the Weekly Law Reports 及び年次の the Law Reports の編纂を開始した。これ以外にも、民間企業が、特に特定の専門分野の判決を中心に集めた判例集（たとえば、the Industrial Law Reports、Lloyd's List Law Reports 等）を出版している。現在50種類以上の判例集が存在するが、重要なものは以下の４つである。

① The Law Reports：上記の ICLR が1865年以降発行しているもので、Appeal Cases（AC）、Queen's Bench Division（QBD）& King's Bench Division（KBD）、Chancery Division（Ch.）及び Family Division（Fam.）の４つに分かれている。
② Weekly Law Report（WLR）
③ All England Law Reports（All ER）
④ English Reports：1865年以前から発行され、ICLR のリポート以降に適宜廃止された様々な判例集をまとめて再発行したもの。

なお、the Court of Appeal の実務指導により、裁判手続で判例を引用する場合、原則として ICLR 発行の公式判例集によることとし、その他の判例集は、これに載っていない事件を引用するときにだけ使用すべきものとされている。

今日では、リーガルデータベースの出現により、判例調査作業は飛躍的に単純化し、容易化した。LEXIS 及び WESTLAW のデータベースには、最近のほとんどの判例が含まれている。

2．判例の分析（Finding Precedent）

(1) Ratio Decidendi と Obiter Dicta の区別

関連する判例が見つかった場合、次に当該判例を分析し、当該判例が示している判例法が何かを確定しなければならない。判決文には、通常、当該事件の事実が記載され、更に裁判官による先例の分析と当該事件における争点の判断が説示されているが、その全てが binding precedent となってその後の裁判所を拘束するわけではない。先例として拘束力を持つのは、当該事件の争点を決定する上で本当の理由となった部分だけである。この部分は、ratio decidendi、すなわち判決理由事項（the reason for deciding）と呼ばれている。

判決文中においては、裁判官が、当該事件の解決とは実際上関係がない事項についてまで意見を述べていることが少なくない。たとえば、被告がもっと若かったらどうか、身体障害者だったらどうなっていたか、原告にも非があったらどうなったか等々である。このような仮説の提示は、そのとおりの事態が起こったときに裁判官がどのように判断するかを推測する上で有益であるが、その意見自体が binding precedent となるわけではない。判決のこの部分は、obiter dicta、すなわちその他の判示事項（other thing said）と呼ばれている。また、そのような意見部分は、判例法ではないにしても、裁判官を説得する上で役に立つという意味で、persuasive precedent（説得的先例）とも呼ばれる。

判決文中の裁判官の説示に関して、descriptive ratio（記述的判決理由）と prescriptive ratio（規範的判決理由）という区別が用いられることがある。Descriptive ratio とは、当該事件に関して裁判所に提示された事実関係に基

づく裁判官の具体的な判断を意味し、prescriptive ratio は、当該事件から導き出される法規範を意味している。一般に、拘束力ある法と言えるのは、抽象的な法規範として抽出される prescriptive ratio の方である。ただし、descriptive ratio も、当該判例における ratio が類似の他の事件においてどのように適用されるかを判断する上で有益なので、軽視することはできない。

　裁判官や弁護士は、binding precedent を見つけるに際し、判例法に関するいくつかの神話（myths）を前提としている。これには、以下のものが含まれている。

（ⅰ）　Ratio は判決文を読めば誰にでも容易に発見できること
（ⅱ）　１つの判決には ratio が１つ存在すること
（ⅲ）　Ratio はいつまでも変わらないこと
（ⅳ）　あらゆる問題に関して、適用されるべき precedent が存在すること

　ただし、実際にはこれらの神話が当てはまらない判決や事件は数多く存在し、裁判上、ある事件の判決における ratio はどのような内容か、判決に示された複数の理由のうちのどれが ratio か、過去の判例が ratio として示した判断は今も同一内容か、当該事件に適用ある precedent が本当に存在するのか等の問題が頻繁に争われている。

(2)　Hierarchy of the Courts（裁判所間のヒエラルキー）

　裁判所が他のどの裁判所の判断に拘束され、どの裁判所の判断には拘束を受けないかについては、裁判所間のヒエラルキーに従って決められている。その基本的なルールは以下のとおりである。

（ⅰ）　The House of Lords：イギリス国内の法律問題について、他の全ての裁判所の判断に拘束されない。ただし、European Law（EU法）に関する事項については、European Court（欧州裁判所）の判断に従わなければならない。1966年以降、the House of Lords は、the House of Lords 自身の先例についても適当と考えるときは従わなくてもよいとされている。

（ⅱ）　The Court of Appeal：The Civil Division については、the House of Lords 及び the Court of Appeal 自身の先例の拘束を受ける。The Criminal Division については、the House of Lords の判断のみに拘束される。

(iii) The High Court：The Court of Appeal 及び the House of Lords の判例に拘束されるが、自らの先例には拘束を受けない。

(iv) The Divisional Court：The Court of Appeal 及び the House of Lords の判例に拘束される。また、2名以上の裁判官による判決の場合、the Divisional Court 自身のその後の裁判及び下位裁判所を拘束する。

(v) The Crown Court、Magistrates Courts 及び County Courts：上位裁判所の判例に拘束されるが、自らの判断は先例拘束力を有しない。

(vi) The Privy Council：英連合に属する国の事件（Commonwealth cases）について the House of Lords の裁判官によって構成される the Privy Council が上訴審として下した判決は、イギリスでは先例拘束力を有しないが、persuasive precedent として重要である。

3．判例法の適用・区別（Applying／Distinguishing Cases）

裁判所が示す ratio には、当該判例法が適用されるための要件とそれが充たされた場合の効果（たとえば、損害賠償）が含まれているが、この要件の中には、たとえば reasonableness 等、一定の評価が必要なものもある。また、裁判官は、ratio の適用範囲が限定的であることを明らかにするため、in the absence of special circumstances 等の限定文言を入れて ratio を示す場合も少なくない。ある事件に ratio の適用があることを争おうとする者は、このような qualification（限定文言）を手掛かりとし、ratio を示している判決における事実関係と本件の事実関係とが重要な部分において相違することを示して、両事件を区別しなければならない。この作業を distinguishing cases（判例の区別）という。判決において、ratio を適用するために示した具体的な事実関係、すなわち、上記の descriptive ratio の分析は、この作業を行う上で不可欠である。

この章のチェックリスト

1. The doctrine of precedence とは何か。
2. 判例集（case reports）にはどのような種類のものがあるのか。
3. 判例集に掲載されている判決はその全文が判例法（case law）となるのか。
4. 全ての裁判所の判決が判例法を形成するのか。
5. Descriptive precedent とは何か。

第II編
イギリス契約法

第1章

契約の成立(1)
―― 申込と承諾（Offer and Acceptance）

1．イギリス法における契約（Contract）

(1) Contractとは何か

　イギリス法における契約（contract）とは、人又は団体（会社、パートナーシップ、国家等）と他の人又は団体との間における一定の内容の行為や給付を行うこと、又は行わないことの約束（promise）、すなわち、当事者間における義務負担の合意（an agreement between the parties to undertake obligations）であって、かつ法的拘束力（enforceability）を有するものを意味している。「法的拘束力を有する」とは、裁判所が、（ⅰ）当事者の一方がその約束を破ったとき、すなわち、当該合意に違反（breach）したときに、その結果不利益を被った相手方当事者に対して一定の救済手段（remedy）を与え、かつ（ⅱ）違反の有無にかかわらず、そのような効果を伴う義務の存在を認めるということである。

　現代におけるイギリスの代表的な契約法学者、トライテル教授（G. H. Treitel）は、その著書 The Law of Contract (11th edition, Sweet & Maxwell, 2003) の冒頭において、contractを次のように定義している。

> A contract is an agreement giving rise to obligations which are enforced or recognized by law. The factor which distinguishes contractual obligations from the other obligations is that they are based on the agreement of the contracting parties.

　Contractは、原則として、（ⅰ）当事者間における合意（agreement）、（ⅱ）価値のある約因（valuable consideration）及び（ⅲ）法的拘束力を生じさせる当事者の意思（intention to create legal relations）という3つの要素が備わ

った場合に成立する。土地の権利に関する契約、一定の金額を超える消費者金融契約その他の例外を除き、契約成立のためには、書面の作成その他の特別な要式を必要としない（本編第3章5参照）。

　上記3要素の1つである agreement は、当事者の一方の申込（offer）とこれに対応する承諾（acceptance）によって成り立っている。

　Offer（申込）とは、申込人（offeror）が、相手方（offeree）が承諾（accept）することによりそのとおりの法的拘束を受けること（法的拘束力のある義務を負担すること）を意図して行った契約条件の申し入れ（a statement of terms upon which the offeror is prepared to be bound upon their acceptance by the offeree）のことであり、acceptance（承諾）とは、申込を受けた条件に対する無条件の合意（an unconditional agreement to the terms of the offer）のことである。

(2)　Bilateral Offer（双方的申込）と Unilateral Offer（一方的申込）

　Offer には、bilateral offer（双方的申込）と unilateral offer（一方的申込）の2種類があり、前者によって成立する契約を、bilateral contract（双方的契約）、後者による契約を unilateral contract（一方的契約）という。これらは日本法上の双務契約、片務契約とは全く異なる法概念である。

　Bilateral contract とは、当事者の一方（X）が相手方（Y）に対し、Yが一定の行為（AAA）をする旨（又はしない旨）を約束することの見返りとして、XがYのために一定の行為（BBB）をすること（又は一定の行為をしないこと）の申込（bilateral offer）をし、Yがこれに承諾することによって成立する合意（agreement）のうち法的拘束力を有するものであり、この結果、XはYに対し、YはXに対し、それぞれ自己の約束した行為を行う（又は行わない）義務を負うことになる。

　他方、契約の一方当事者（X）が、「YがAAAをしたら自分（X）はBBBをしてあげよう」との申し入れをすることがある。この場合、YはXの申し入れた AAA の行為を行う義務を負うわけではないが、これを行った場合、Xは約束どおり BBB の行為を行うべき義務を負うことになる。このような申入れが unilateral offer（一方的申込）であり、これにより成立する契約が unilateral contract（一方的契約）である。たとえば、X が「Y が家の庭の芝生を刈ってくれたら 5 ポンドあげよう」と約束する場合や、X が「誰かが家の犬を見つけてくれたら、その人に 5 ポンドあげよう」と約束する場合等がその例である。Unilateral contract の場合、X の申込（unilateral offer）に対し、その申込を受けた相手方 Y（特定人の場合もあれば、特定又は不特定多数の内の誰かに対する申込の場合もある）が申入れどおりの行為を行うことが承諾（acceptance）に当る。

　ある offer が unilateral offer、bilateral offer のどちらであるかの区別は、以下に述べる承諾（すなわち、合意成立）の有無（本章 3）や申込の撤回（revocation of offer）の可否（本章 9 (1)）などを判断する上で重要な意味を持っている。

(3) 契約成立の判断基準――Objective Test（客観基準）

　契約が成立したか否かを決定するには、一方当事者の他方に対する通知や表明が offer に当るか否か、及び相手方がこれに対応する acceptance をしているか否かを判断、評価しなければならない。この判断は、いわゆる objective test（客観基準）を用い、各当事者の言動に基づいて、一般人の立場から見て契約が成立したと合理的に判断することができるか否か（whether or not a reasonable person would believe so）を客観的に決定すべきものとされている。この際、当事者の内心の意思がどうであったかは問題としない。判例（Smith v Hughes (1871) LR 6 QB 597）は、この基準について以下のとおり述べている。

> If, whatever a man's real intention may be, he so conducts himself that a reasonable man would believe that he was assenting to the terms proposed by the other party, and that the other party upon that belief enters into a contract with him, the man thus conducting himself would be equally bound as if he had intended to agree to the other party's terms. (per Blackburn J.)

　Offer は、この objective test に従って、契約の申込みであることが明らかにわかるような表現で行われなければならない。たとえば、Harvey v Facey

判決（［1893］AC 552（Privy Council：Jamaica））では、商品購入希望者（X）が売主（Y）に対し、「Will you sell us Bumper Hall Pen? Telegraph lowest cash price.」との電報を出し、Y が、「Lowest price for Bumper Hall Pen £900.」との回答を返電したので、X が「We agree to buy Bumper Hall Pen for £900 asked by you.」と返した場合について、裁判所（the Judicial Committee of the Privy Council）は、客観基準に基づき、Y の返信は単なる最低価格の通知（mere price indication）であるから申込の誘引（invitation to treat）に過ぎず、契約は成立していないとの認定を示している。

2．Invitation to treat（申込の誘引）

申込は、相手方の承諾によって法的義務を負担する旨の確定的な約束の表明でなければならず、単なる契約交渉の申し入れでは足りない。後者のことは講学上 invitation to treat 又は invitation to make an offer と呼ばれる。Invitation to treat と unilateral offer とは一見区別がつきにくいので、契約が成立したか否かについて問題が生ずることがある。判例法は以下のような場合に関して offer の有無の判断基準を示している。

(1) Shop display（店舗の商品展示・陳列）

小売店舗のショーウィンドーに展示された商品や店内に陳列された商品は、たとえ値札が付いていたとしても、原則として、invitation to treat に過ぎない（Pharmaceutical Society of Great Britain v Boots Cash Chemists［1953］1 QB 401(CA)①、Fisher v Bell［1961］1 QB 394(CA)②）。小売店が展示品の購入希望者全員の需要に応ずるのは通常不可能なので、客観基準に照らし、展示しただけで売却義務を負う旨の意思があるとは考えられないからである（上記 Fisher v Bell 判決の obiter）。

(2) Advertisement（広告）

商品の宣伝広告文は、客観的に見て、当該商品の購入を希望する全ての者と契約する意図とは解されないので、原則として申込の誘引（invitation to treat）に過ぎない（Partridge v Crittenden［1968］2 All ER 421③）。

　ただし、広告主が、特定の者から申込があったときは必ず法的義務を負担する意思があることを明確に示す表現を用いた場合、広告文であっても申込（offer）と解されることがある（Carlill v Carbolic Smoke Ball Co［1893］1 QB 256(CA)④、Lefkowitz v Great Minneapolis Surplus Store（1957）86 NW 2d 689⑤）。

(3) Auction sale（競売）

　Auction sale は、競売人がハンマーを叩く等の慣習上の方法で手続終了を宣言し、かついずれかの入札者が当該宣言までに入札を申し入れていた場合に成立する（the Sale of Goods Act 1979 s 57(2)）。Auction が 'without reserve（価格無制限、権利保留なし）' として行われる場合は、取引慣習上、競売人がハンマーを打った時に最高値の bidder（入札者）との間で成立する（Warlow v Harrison（1859）1 E&E 309；120 ER 925(Exchequer Chamber)、Harris v Nickerson(1873)LR 8 QB 286(QB)、Barry v Davies［2000］1 WLR 1962 (CA)⑥）。

(4) Tender（入札）

　通常の場合、tender の申し入れは申込の誘引（invitation to treat）に過ぎない（Spencer v Harding（1870）LR 5 CP 561(CP)、Harvela Investments Ltd. v Royal Trust Co. of Canada［1985］2 All ER 966(HL)、Blackpool and Fylde Aero Club v Blackpool BC［1990］3 All ER 25(CA)）。よって、最も高額の回答をした者との間で直ちに契約が成立するわけではない。

　なお、期間を定めて商品の継続的購入を申し入れた tender に対する承諾は、tender に従った商品販売の申込にあたるので、申込の撤回をする前に商品供給の請求を受けたときに契約が成立し、これに従って供給すべき義務が発生する（Great Northern Railway v Witham(1873)LR 9 CP 16⑦）。

3．Acceptance（承諾）

Offer に対する acceptance がなされたか否かを決定する上で、先ず当該 offer が bilateral offer、unilateral offer のどちらであるかを確定しておく必要がある。

(1) Bilateral offer の場合

申込を受けた者に承諾の意思があったとしても、その意思が申込人に通知されない限り契約は成立しない（Felthouse v Bindley(1862)11 CB(NS)869⑧）。すなわち、申込に対する沈黙が承諾となったり、承諾とみなされたりすること（acceptance by silence）はない。

ただし、申込に対して沈黙しながら承諾したことを前提とする行為を行ったとき、これによって契約を承諾したこと（acceptance in silence）になる場合がある（Brogden v Metropolitan Railway(1877)2 App Cas 666(HL)⑨）。

なお、商品を一方的に送りつける方法による購入申込がなされた場合に関しては、消費者保護のため、the Unsolicited Goods and Services Act 1971 s. 1(2)が以下のとおり定めている。

> When goods are sent unsolicited other than for the purposes of a trade or business, and either; a) They are not collected within 6 months; or b) The sender does not collect the goods within 30 days of being sent notice; then the recipient may treat the goods as a gift.

(2) Unilateral Offer の場合

Unilateral offer に対する承諾は、offer があることを知りながら、offer されたとおりの行為を行うことであり（R. v Clarke(1927)40 CLR 227-Australian case）、当該行為を行った理由や動機までは関係がない（Williams v Cawardine(1833)5 C&P 566⑩）。

4．Qualified acceptance（条件付承諾）

契約が成立するには、申込に対する無条件の承諾（unqualified acceptance）がなければならない。条件付の承諾（qualified acceptance）は、相手方の申込の拒絶（rejection）プラス新たな申込（counter-offer）である（Hyde v Wrench(1840) 3 Beav 334⑪）。

ただし、申込人に対する単なる問い合わせは、counter-offer とはいえない。この場合は、最初の申込が存続し、これに対する承諾があれば契約は成立する（Stevenson, Jacques v Mclean(1880) 5 QBD 346⑫、Gibson v Manchester C. C.［1979］1 WLR 294(HL)⑬の obiter、Norfolk C.C. v Dencora Properties［1995］9 Nov. 1995(CA)）。

5．契約交渉と契約成立時期

契約は、その内容、対価その他の多くの契約条件に関する長期間の交渉を経て合意に至ることが多い。たとえば、建物工事請負契約の場合は、請負った作業の範囲、内容、請負代金、完成時期、仕様及び品質基準等の条件などが交渉の対象となる。このような場合、契約交渉中のどの時点において契約が成立したといえるかが問題となる。

裁判所は、Trollope & Colls Limited and Holland, Hannen & Cubitts Ltd. v The Atomic Power Construction Ltd.判決（［1962］3 All ER 1936）及び Pagnan S.p.A. v Feed Products Ltd.判決（［1987］2 Lloyd's LR 601）において、この問題に関するガイドラインを示している。これらを要約すれば、以下のとおりとなる。

（ⅰ）契約が契約交渉中に成立したか否かを決定するためには、交渉全体を斟酌しなければならない。

（ⅱ）両当事者は、契約が成立に至るまで継続して契約を締結する意思を有していなければならない。

（ⅲ）契約成立日において、両当事者は、契約が存在するために必要とみなされる全ての契約条件について合意していなければならない。

（ⅳ）両当事者間で合意している契約条件は、意図的であるか無意識であるかにかかわらず、契約が商業的に実施可能であるならば実際上合意しておくことが必要不可欠な契約条件の1つでも欠いていてはならない。

（ⅴ）両当事者間で必須条件以外の契約条件についてまだ交渉が継続している場合は、両当事者が未だ合意に達していないその他の契約条件について合意に至らない限り契約に拘束されない意思を有しているのか、あるいは、両当事者が未だ交渉中のその他の条件があるにかかわらず直ちに契約に拘束される意思を有しているのかにより、契約が成立したか否かを決定する。

（ⅵ）契約の申込をした者が、申込を受けた者に対して、承諾の方法に関して十分に明確な指定をしている場合には、当該申込に対する承諾は、申込に際して指定された方式に従って行われなければならない。

6．Battle of forms（書式間の闘争）

契約交渉において、申込（offer）に対し、条件の変更を申し入れた再度の申込（counter-offer）が交互に繰り返される状態を battle of forms という。企業間の取引交渉で、互いの契約条件について、それぞれが自己の用いている印刷された標準契約書式（standard form of contract）の条件による契約を交互に繰り返して申し入れる場合が典型例である。特に建物建築工事請負契約（building and engineering contracts）やその下請契約（subcontracts）等に関して、このような状況になったときの契約成立時期について争われることが多い。

契約成立の一般原則に従えば、この battle の勝者は、最後の申込を行った側の当事者（the party who fires the last shot）となるはずである。これを受け取った側の当事者が特に異議を述べずに契約の履行に着手したとき、conduct（行為）によって、最後の契約条件に承諾したものと解されるからである（Butler Machine Tool Co., Ltd. v Excell-o Corporation (England) Ltd. [1979] 1 All ER 965⑭、Sauter Automation v Goodman (HC)(Manchester Services)[1987] CLY⑮）。上記 Butler Machine Tool v Excell-o Corporation 判決では、申込人の標準書式による申込に対し、承諾者が自社の標準書

式によることを条件として合意する旨を回答しても、その時点では契約が成立していないと判示した。契約は、最後の無条件承諾があったときに、その直前に受けた申込の書式により成立することになる。

　Lord Denning M.R.は、このように契約成立時期を画一的、形式的に決定する考え方に反対し、契約の成立は、両当事者が互いに相手方に提示した契約条件を総合的に考慮の上、両者間で重要な契約条件について合意があったと認定できるときに成立すると解すべきである旨を主張した。上記の Butler Machine Tool 事件において、Lord Denning M.R.は以下のとおり述べて多数意見を批判している。しかし、彼の見解は、未だ the House of Lords には受け入れられていない。

> In many of these cases our traditional analysis of offer, counter-offer, rejection, acceptance and so forth is out-of date ... The better way is to look at all the documents passing between the parties and glean from them, or from the conduct of the parties, whether they have reached agreement on all material points.

7．Postal rule（郵便ルール）

　上記のとおり、契約は原則として申込に対する承諾が申込人に到達したときに成立するが、イギリスの判例法上、承諾の通知方法が郵送である場合には、その例外として、承諾通知書を投函したときに承諾の効力が発生し、契約が成立したものと見なされる。これを postal rule といい、その具体的な内容は以下のとおりである。

　(1)　申込に対する承諾の方法として、郵便の方法による承諾が合理的な場合、契約は承諾通知を投函したときに成立する（Adams v Lindsell (1818) 106 ER 250)。

　(2)　郵便による承諾は、投函しさえすれば到達の有無を問わない（Household Fire and Carriage Accident Insurance Co., Ltd. v Grant (1879) 4 Ex D 216(CA)）。

　(3)　申込人が当該申込に対する承諾に関して postal rule を排除した場合は、

その適用がない (Holwell Securities v Hughes [1974] 1 All ER 161(CA))。

(4) Postal rule は、承諾 (acceptance) の通知だけに適用される rule であり、申込の撤回 (revocation) 通知には適用がない (Byrne & Co. v Van Tienhoven & Co.(1880)5 CPD 344)。

(5) Postal rule は、ファックスやテレックス等、通知の発信と同時に到達する伝達手段 (instantaneous communications) には適用がない。この場合、acceptance は相手方に到達しなければならない (Entores v Miles Far East Corporation [1955] 2 QB 327(CA)⑯、Brinkibon Ltd. v Stahag Stahl [1983] 2 AC 34(HL)⑰)。

8．Methods of acceptance prescribed by the offeror（申込人による承諾方法の指定）

申込人 (offeror) は、申込に際して承諾の通知の方法等を指定することがあるが、一般的には、承諾は必ず申込人が指定した方法によって通知しなければならないわけではない (Tinn v Hoffman & Co(1873)29 LT 271⑱)。申込人が特定の方法によらない限り承諾を受けない意思であるなら、そのことを明確に示しておかなければならない (Manchester Diocesan Council for Education v Commercial and General Investments [1969] 3 All ER 1593(Ch D)⑲、Yates Building Co. v R J Pulleyn & Sons (York)(1975)119 SJ 370)。

9．Termination of offer（申込の失効）

Offer は、申込人による撤回 (revocation)、申込に際して指定した有効期限又は合理的な期間の経過 (express time limits or lapse of reasonable time)、及び条件付申込における解除条件の成就 (condition satisfied in case of conditional offer) によって失効する。

(1) Revocation（撤回）

申込の revocation（撤回）の時期は、bilateral offer の場合と unilateral

offer の場合とで若干異なる。Bilateral offer は、原則として、承諾があるまではいつでも撤回できる。Bilateral offer の申込人が承諾期間を設けた場合であってもこれに拘束されず、申込人は、承諾期間中でも自由に撤回できる（Dickinson v Dodds(1876) 2 ChD 463(CA)⑳）。ただし、撤回の通知をすることが必要である（Byrne & Co v Van Tienhoven & Co.(1880) 5 CPD 344㉑）。この撤回の通知は、申込人本人ではなくても、信頼できる第三者（reliable third party）が行えば十分である（上記 Dickinson v Dodds 判決）。

　Unilateral offer の場合の撤回は、相手方が履行に着手した後はできない（Errington v Errington and Woods [1952] 1 All ER 149、Daulia Ltd. v Four Millbank Nominees [1978] 2 WLR 621(CA)㉒）。なお、不特定多数人に対する unilateral offer の場合、その撤回通知を申込と同一又は同等の方法で行なえば、相手方が撤回通知を知らなくても構わない、すなわち相手方に現実に到達しなくても撤回の効力が生ずると解されている（Shuey v United States (1875) 23 L ed 697, 92 US 73㉓、ただし、アメリカの判決）。

(2) Time limits（承諾期間）

　申込に有効期限（express time limits）を設けた場合、その期間が経過した後に承諾しても契約は成立しない。

　期限を設けていない申込は、その性質に応じた合理的期間の経過（lapse of reasonable time）により失効する（Ramsgate Victoria Hotel Co., Ltd. v Montefiore (1866) LR 1 Ex 109㉔）。

(3) Conditional offers（条件付申込）

　解除条件付申込は条件成就（occurrence of condition）後には accept（承諾）できない。この条件は、implied condition（黙示的条件）の場合もあり得る（Financial Ltd. v Stimson [1962] 3 All ER 386㉕）。

【CASES】

① *Pharmaceutical Society of Great Britain v Boots* [1953] 1 QB 401 (CA)
　　Under the Pharmacy and Poisons Act 1933, certain drugs containing poisons

may only be sold 'under the supervision of a pharmacist.' Boots was charged to have broken this rule by putting supplies of its drugs on open shelves in a self-service shop. Boots, however, contended that there was no sale until a customer brought the goods, which he had selected, to the cash desk at the exit and offered to buy them. A qualified pharmacist was stationed at this point. It was held that goods displayed in shops are merely invitations to treat, and that it is the customer who makes the offer to buy, so the shop may decide whether to accept or reject.

② *Fisher v Bell* [1961] 1 QB 394 (CA)

Mr. Bell ran a shop called 'Bell's Music Shop'. He displayed in his shop window a flick-knife behind which was a ticket reading 'Ejector knife −4 shillings'. He was charged with offering a flick-knife for sale, contrary to the Restriction of Offensive Weapons Act 1959. He argued that it was not an 'offer' in the contractual sense, but merely an invitation to passers-by to come in and make a bargain, which he could then refuse. It was held that the display of the flick-knife was not an offer, but merely an invitation to treat. The court referred to obiter of another case that if a supplier is also a manufacturer his display may be an offer to sell as he could theoretically make any number of offered goods to order.

③ *Partridge v Crittenden* [1968] 2 All ER 421

Mr. Partridge inserted the advertisement 'Bramblefinch cocks, bramblefinch hens, 25s each' in the column of 'Classified Advertisement' in a publication called 'Cage and Aviary Birds'. A man answered the advertisement sending cheque for 25 shillings, and asking that a 'bramblefinch hen' be sent to him. Partridge sent one in a box, which was opened in the presence of inspector, Mr. Crittenden. Crittenden brought a prosecution against Partridge, alleging that he had offered for sale a wild brambling contrary to the Protection of Birds Act 1954. The Divisional Court of the QBD accepted that the bird was a wild brambling, which sale was prohibited under the Act, however, since Partridge had been charged with 'offering for sale' the conviction could not stand.

"I think when one is dealing with advertisements and circulars, unless they come from manufacturers, there is business sense in their being construed as invitations to treat and not offers for sale." (per Lord Parker C.J.)

④ *Carlill v Carbolic Smoke Ball Co* [1893] 1 QB 256 (CA)

Carbolic Smoke Ball Co ("CSB") is a proprietor of a medical preparation called 'The Carbolic Smoke Ball'. CSB published the following advertisement in various newspapers: "£100 reward will be paid by the Carbolic Smoke Ball Co to any person who contracts the increasing epidemic influenza, colds or any disease caused by taking cold, after having used the ball three times a daily for two weeks according to the printed directions supplied with each ball. £1,000 is deposited with the Alliance Bank, Regent Street, showing our sincerity in the matter." Mrs. Carlill bought a smoke ball, used it as indicated and duly caught flu. CSB refused to pay, saying it was not an offer, but a mere advertising 'puff'. The court, admitting Carilill's claim, held that CSB made a unilateral offer by the advertisement.

"... it intended that the £100 should, if the conditions were fulfilled, be paid? The advertisement, and that it would be an insensate thing to promise £100 to a person who used the smoke ball unless you could check or superintend his manner of using it. The answer to that argument seems to me to be that if a person chooses to make extravagant promises of this kind he probably does so because it pays him to make them, and, if he has made them, the extravagance of the promises is no reason in law why he should not be bound by them...It was also said that the contract is made with all the world- that is, with everybody; and that you cannot with everybody. It is not a contact made with all the world. There is the fallacy of the argument. It is an offer made to all the world; and why should not an offer be made to all the world that is to ripen into a contract with anybody who comes forward and performs the condition? It is an offer to become liable to anyone who, before it is retracted, performs the condition, and, although the offer is made to the world, the contract is made with the limited portion of the public who come forward and perform the condition on the faith of the advertisement." (per Bowen L.J.)

⑤　*Lefkowitz v Great Minneapolis Surplus Store* 86 NW 2d 689 (1957)

The store published an advertisement in a newspaper, stating: 'Saturday 9 am sharp; 3 Brand new fur coats, worth $100. First come first served, $1 each' Lefkowitz was one of the first three customers at the shop, but the store refused to sell him a coat, claiming that the offer was only open to woman. It was held that this was an offer open to both men and women.

⑥　*Barry v Davies* [2000] 1 WLR 1962 (CA)

At an action without reserve Barry had made the only bid for two engine analysers. The auctioneer considered his price was too low, withdrew them from the sale and sold them privately a few days later. It was held that the auctioneer was liable. Applying Warlow v Harrison, the court said that at an action without reserve there was a collateral contract between the auctioneer and the highest bidder, whereby the auctioneer agreed to sell to the highest bidder.

⑦　*Great Northern Railway v Witham* (1873) LR 9 CP 16

Railway company advertised for tenders for the continuous supply for one year of certain types of goods as it might think fit to order. Mr. Witham submitted a tender, stating 'I undertake to supply the company for twelve months with such quantities of the goods as the company may order from time to time'. The company accepted his tender, and ordered goods under this continuous supply contract. Eventually, Witham refused to supply goods ordered by the company. It was held that Witham was in breach of the contract.

⑧　*Felthouse v Bindley* (1862) 11 CB (NS) 869, 142 ER 1037, 31 LJCP 204

Felthouse offered to buy a horse belonging to his nephew John. Eventually the uncle wrote: '*If I hear no more about him, I consider the horse is mine at £30 15s.*' The nephew did not reply, and the uncle claimed that they had a contract of sale. It was held that there was no contract. The uncle could not stipulate inaction as a means of acceptance.

⑨　*Brogden v Metropolitan Railway* (1877) 2 App Cas 666 (HL)

Brogden had supplied coal to the railway company for 4 years without a formal agreement. The company sent Brogden a draft form of agreement, wishing to formalize the arrangement. Brogden inserted a term and returned it marked 'approved.' The company's agent did not acknowledge it, but put it in a drawer. For two years Brogden and the company dealt in accordance with the terms of the written agreement. A dispute arose, and Brogden claimed that as the company had never acknowledged this altered draft, there was no contract. It was held that the contract had been accepted by the actions of the parties in performing the terms without actually notifying acceptance.

⑩　*Williams v Carwardines* (1833) 5 C&P 566

Carwardiness published a handbill stating that he would pay £20 to any person who should give information concerning the murderer called Williams. A girl friend of Williams, the murderer, was seriously beaten by him. She gave information leading to the conviction of Williams for the murder. Carwardines in refusing to pay the reward, insisted that she was not induced to give the information by the reward of £20, but by motives of revenge. It was held that she was nevertheless entitled to the reward for she had seen the handbill and had given the information. Her motive in accepting it was immaterial.

⑪　*Hyde v Wrench* (1840) 3 Beav 334

Wrench offered to sell his farm for £1,000. Hyde replied that he would pay £950. Wrench turned down the £950 offer, whereupon Hyde wrote saying that he accepted the original £1,000 offer. Wrench did not accept it. It was held that there was no contract because Hyde's counter-offer of £950 was an implied rejection of the original offer to sell at £1,000.

⑫　*Stevenson, Jacque & Co. v Mclean* (1880) 5 QBD 346

Mclean offered to sell to Stevenson, Jacque & Co. ("SJC") a quantity of iron at 40 shillings net cash per ton open till Monday (close of business). On Monday morning, SJC telegraphed asking whether Mclean would accept 40 shillings for delivery over two months, or if not what was the longest limit Mclean could give. Since no reply came, SJC accepted Mclean's original offer in the afternoon. However, Mclean had already sold the iron elsewhere. SJC claimed breach of contract, and Mclean alleged that SJC's first telegram had been a counter-offer. It was held that SJC's first telegram was a mere inquiry for different terms which did not amount to a rejection of Mclean's original offer, so that the offer was still open when SJC accepted it.

⑬　*Gibson v Manchester C.C.* [1979] 1 WLR 294 (HL)

The county council sent a letter to its tenants, stating that they could buy their rented houses. The letter to Gibson stated: 'The corporation may be prepared to sell the house to you at the purchase price of £2,725 less 20 per cent.' During the negotiations for the sale of a house, Gibson asked the council whether the price could be reduced as there were repairs to be done to the property. The council replied that such factor had been taken into account when fixing the price. Gibson replied that in that case he wished to proceed with the purchase at the original price. It was stated obiter that Gibson's letter was merely a request for information, but on the facts the council had not actually made an offer, there was nothing for Gibson to accept.

⑭　*Butler Machine Tool Co., Ltd. v Excell-o Corporation (England) Ltd.* [1979] 1 All ER 965

The seller of a machine offered to supply it for a specified sum, but their written conditions of sale included a price escalation clause by which the price might rise by the date of delivery. The buyer ordered the machine on its own written terms which did not include a price- escalation clause. These conditions also contained a tear-off slip which the seller was to sign, which stated that the order was accepted 'on the terms and conditions stated therein'. The seller signed the slip, but then tried to rely on the price-escalation clause in its original offer. It was held that the seller was not entitled to do so since the buyer had made a counter-offer, which the seller had accepted.

⑮ *Sauter Automation v Goodman (HC) (Manchester Services)* [1987] CLY

Sauter tendered to supply the control panel of a boiler. The tender contained a title retention clause. Goodman accepted on the basis of its standard terms of contract which did not contain retention clause. Sauter did not formally accept Goodman's counter-offer, however, it delivered the panel. When Goodman went into liquidation, the court held that Sauter could not recover the panel or the proceeds of the sale on the ground of the title retention clause since the contract was formed on Goodman's terms, which did not contain a retention arrangement, by Sauter's deemed acceptance.

⑯ *Entores v Miles Far East Corporation* [1955] 2 QB 327 (CA)

Entores in London made an offer by telex to the agents in Holland of Miles Far East Corporation ("MFE") in New York. The offer was accepted by a communication received on Entores' telex machine in London. Later, MFE was in breach of contract and Entores wished to sue them in London. For this, Entores had to serve notice of writ on MFE in New York and the rules of Supreme Court allow service out of jurisdiction when the contract was made in England. MFE argued that the contract was made in Holland. The Court of Appeal held that the rule about instantaneous communications was different form the postal rule, and that the contract in such cases is made where the acceptance is received, i.e. England.

⑰ *Brinkibon Ltd. v Stahag Stahl* [1983] 2 AC 34 (HL)

Where a telex of acceptance was sent from London to Vienna, it was held that the contract was concluded in Vienna, where the telex arrived, and accordingly, the writ could not be served out of the jurisdiction. By this, Entreos' rule was confirmed by the House of Lords.

⑱ *Tinn v Hoffman & Co* (1873) 29 LT 271

Acceptance was requested 'by return of post'. It was held that this did not exclusively require a reply by letter by return of post. Any equally expeditious method would suffice.

⑲　*Manchester Diocesan Council for Education v Commercial and General Investments* [1969] 3 All ER 1593 (Ch D)

A request for tender stated that acceptance of the winning tender would be sent by letter to the address given on the tender. Acceptance was actually sent via the winner's surveyor. It was held that although an offeror is entitled to insist on acceptance in a particular way, when a method of acceptance is merely prescribed, any equally efficient method of acceptance will suffice.

"Where the offeror has prescribed a particular method of acceptance, but not in terms insisting that only acceptance in that method shall be binding, I am of the opinion that acceptance communicated to the offeror by any other mode which is no less advantageous to him will conclude the contract...If an offeror intends that he shall be bound only if his offer is accepted in some particular manner, it must be for him to make it clear." (per Buckley J.)

⑳　*Dickinson v Dodds* (1876) 2 ChD 463, 34 LT 607 (CA)

On Wednesday June 10, Mr. Dodds delivered a signed letter to Mr. Dickinson offering to sell his house for £800, '*this offer to be left over until Friday, 9 o'clock am, June 12*'. The next afternoon, Mr. Berry, a friend of Dodds, told Dickinson that Dodds had offered to sell the house to somebody else. Dickinson rushed over to Dodds to accept the offer, but the house had been sold. Dickinson purported to accept the offer made to him, and sued for breach of contract. It was held that there was no contract between Dickinson and Dodds as Dickson was communicated Dodds' revocation from Berry

㉑　*Byrne & Co v Van Tienhoven & Co* (1880) 5 CPD 344

On October 1, van Tienhoven posted a letter to Byrne, offering to sell them 1000 boxes of tinplates, but on October 8, it posted a letter revoking its offer. On October 11, Byrne telegraphed acceptance, and on 15, he confirmed his acceptance by letter. On October 20 Tienhoven's letter of revocation reached Byrne. It was held that there was a contract. The letter of revocation was not valid until it was actually communicated, which was after the acceptance had arrived. The postal rule does not apply to revocations, only to acceptances.

㉒　*Daulia Ltd v Four Millbank Nominees* [1978] 2 WLR 621 (CA)

Four Millbank Nominees ("FMN") promised Daulia that if Daulia produced a signed contract and a banker's draft of the purchase price by 10 a.m. the next day, FMN would sell certain properties to it. Daulia did all this but FMN refused to counter-sign the contract. It was held that FMN was not entitled to withdraw their unilateral offer once Daulia had embarked upon performance.

"Whilst I think the true view of a unilateral contract must in general be that the offeror is entitled to require full performance of the condition which he has imposed and short of that he is not bound, that must be subject to one important qualification, which stems from the fact that there must be an implied obligation on the part of the offeror not to prevent the condition being satisfied, which obligation it seems to me must arise as soon as the offeree starts to perform. Until then the offeror can revoke the whole thing, but once the offeree has embarked on performance it is too late for the offeror to revoke his offer." (per Goff LJ)

㉓ *Shuey v United States* (1875) 23 L ed 697, 92 US 73

On April 20 1865, the Secretary of War published an announcement in the public newspapers offering a reward for information leading to the arrest of certain criminals. On November 24 1865, the President issued an order revoking the offer which was published in a similar way. Shuey discovered and identified one of the criminals in 1866, unaware of the notice of revocation. It was held that there was no contract. The offer had been revoked with the same 'notoriety' as the original offer, and this was sufficient to cancel it, even for those who had not read it.

㉔ *Ramsgate Victoria Hotel Co., Ltd. v Montefiore* (1866) LR 1 Ex 109

An offer to buy shares was held to have lapsed when an acceptance was attempted five months later.

㉕ *Financial Ltd. v Stimson* [1962] 3 All ER 386

Stimson signed a hire-purchase form and took possession of a motor car from the dealer. The hire-purchase form had not yet countersigned by Financial Ltd., a finance company who owned the car. Subsequently, Stimson dissatisfied the car and returned it to the dealer. The car was stolen from the car dealer's premises and was badly damaged. Financial Ltd., without knowing these facts, then countersigned the hire-purchase form and demanded payment of instalment under the contract. It was held that hire-purchase agreement was not binding on Stimson since there was an implied condition in the offer that the car was in substantially the same condition when the offer was accepted as when it was given.

> ## この章のチェックリスト
> 1. イギリス法における契約とは何か。契約成立の要素は何か。
> 2. Unilateral offer と bilateral offer とはどこが違うのか。
> 3. Offer があるか否かはどのような基準で判断するのか。
> 4. Invitation to treat とは何か。以下の場合、どちらのどの行為が offer に当るのか。
>   (1) Shop display
>   (2) Advertisement
>   (3) Auction sale
>   (4) Tender
> 5. Acceptance の通知なしに契約が成立する場合があるか。Bilateral offer の場合と unilateral offer の場合とで異なるか。
> 6. Qualified acceptance とは何か。どのような法的意味があるのか。
> 7. Battle of forms とは何か。いつ契約が成立するのか。
> 8. Postal rule とは何か。
> 9. Offer が失効するのはどのような場合か。
> 10. Offer の撤回はいつまでできるか。Unilateral offer の場合と bilateral offer の場合とで異なるか。

第2章

契約の成立(2)
——Consideration(約因)と Promissory Estoppel(約束的禁反言)

1. 約因(Consideration)の意義・目的

　Consideration(約因)とは、ある者(promisor)が他の者(promisee)に対して財産の交付、役務の提供その他の一定の行為をすること(act)やしないこと(forbearance)の約束(promise)をしたことに対する見返りとして、そのようなpromiseを受けた者、すなわち被約束者(promisee)が約束者(promisor)のために行う一定の作為(act)もしくは不作為(forbearance)又は一定のactもしくはforbearanceをする旨の約束(promise)のことである。そのような作為、不作為又はその約束の存在によって、約束者(promisor)が被約束者(promisee)に対して行った約束(promise)は、法的拘束力(enforceability)のある合意(agreement)、すなわち契約(contract)となる。Sir Frederick Pollock は、Dunlop v Selfridge 判決([1915] AC 847 (HL))においてこのことを以下のとおり述べている。

　　An act or forbearance of one party, or the promise thereof, is the price for which the promise of the other is bought, and the promise thus given for value is enforceable.

　イギリス法上、considerationのない合意は、捺印証書(deed)による契約その他後述する一定の例外を除き、法的拘束力を生じない。これを the doctrine of consideration(約因の法理)という。この法原則は、何らの見かえりのない無償の約束にまで裁判所の保護を与える必要がないとする、相互主義の理念(idea of reciprocity)に基づき、裁判所が訴訟数を限定するために形成してきた伝統的法理の1つであるが、現代ではその合理性に疑問が持たれてい

る。実際上、義務負担を約束した者が当該義務を不当に免れようとする際、合意したときに偶々considerationを失念していたことを利用し、この法理を方便として主張することが少なくない。よって、裁判所はconsiderationの要件を形式的、画一的に解することはせず、様々な政策的な目的を考慮しながら、比較的柔軟にその適否を判断している。

Considerationという語の通常の和訳は「対価」であるが、契約成立の要素としてのconsiderationは、日常用語として使用されている対価（たとえば、不動産売買の対価としての売買代金、賃貸借の対価としての賃料等）とは異なるものも含まれるので、これと区別するために「約因」という日本語が用いられる。

Considerationの提供は、必ずpromiseにより利益を受ける者（promisee）が行わなければならない（Dunlop v Selfridge [1915] AC847 (HL)）。ただし、considerationの提供を受ける者やその利益を受ける者は、promisor、すなわち義務の負担を約束した者以外の第三者でも構わない（Shadwell v Shadwell (1860) 9 CB NS 159）。

2．Executory consideration（未履行約因）と executed consideration（既履行約因）

Considerationには、「当事者の一方による作為もしくは不作為（an act or service provided as consideration of promise)」と「当事者の一方による作為もしくは不作為の約束（promise as consideration of promise)」の2種類がある。前者の例は、たとえば、飼い犬を探した人に50ポンド支払うとの広告を見て、犬を見つけてくる行為等であり、他方、1000ポンドでパソコンを購入するとの申込を承諾してパソコンの搬入を約束すること等が後者である。前者はexecuted consideration、後者はexecutory considerationという。通常の場合、unilateral contract（一方的契約）における約束に対するconsiderationはexecuted considerationであり、bilateral contract（双方的契約）の場合はexecutory considerationである。

3．Past consideration（過去の約因）

　Past considerationとは、相手方が約束をする前に相手方の要求を受けることなく提供（実行）した作為又は不作為のことである。原則として、past considerationは、その後の約束の約因とはなり得ない（Roscorla v Thomas (1842) 3 QB 234①、Re McArdle (1951) Ch 669 (CA)②）。

　ただし、過去の行為が当事者間の合意（一方当事者が相手方に対して当該行為を依頼し、相手方がこれを承諾すること）に基づいて行われ、かつ当該行為に対して対価を支払うことが当初から意図されていた場合には、たとえ対価の金額が未定であっても、past　considerationにはならない（Lampleigh v Braithwait (1615) Hob 105③、Pao On v Lau Yiu Long (1980) AC 614 (Privy Council: Hong Kong)④）。

4．Considerationの価値

　Considerationは、経済的価値（value）のあるものでなければならないが、約束や義務の価値に見合った経済的価値（たとえば、売買の目的物の時価に見合った代金）を有するものである必要はなく、何らかの経済的価値のあるものでさえあれば、nominal value（名目的価値）でもよい（Currie v Misa (1875) LR 10 Ex 153 (HL)、Chappell v Nestle (1959) 2 All ER 701⑤、Edmonds v Lawson [2000] QB 501 1091 (CA)⑥）。Considerationという要件は、私人間の取引上のミス（bad bargain）を是正するために存在するわけではないからである。もちろん、gift of onerous property（負担付贈与）もvaluable consideration（経済的価値ある約因）である。

5．Performance of an existing obligation（既存の債務の履行）

　Considerationに経済的な価値（value）があるか否かの問題に関連し、約因を提供すべき者が既に負担している義務を履行することやその履行を約束することが有効な約因（good consideration）といえるか否かがしばしば問題と

なる。判例法上、約因として履行する義務が法律上の義務（obligation imposed by law）である場合と契約上の義務（contractual duties）である場合とでは、若干取り扱いが異なっている。

(1) Legal duties（法律上の義務）

法律上の義務（obligation imposed by law）の履行は原則として consideration とはならない（Collins v Godefroy（1831）1 B & Ad 950⑦）。ただし、法律上の通常の義務履行を尽くしたと認められる限度を超えて履行することやその履行を約束することは、public policy（公序則）に反しない限り consideration となり得る（Glasbrook Bros. Ltd. v Glamorgan C.C.（1925）A.C. 270 (HL)⑧、Harris v Sheffield United Football Club Ltd.（1987）2 All ER 838 (CA)⑨、Ward v Byham（1956）2 All ER 318 (CA)、White v Bluett（1853）23 LJ Ex 36）。

(2) Contractual duties（契約上の義務）

相手方との間で既に締結している契約上の義務の履行（obligation imposed by contract with promisor）は、原則として、当該相手方による新たな約束の約因にならない（Stilk v Myrick（1809）2 Camp 317⑩）。

ただし、この例外として、当初の契約上予定されていた義務の範囲を超えた行為を行う場合は、約因となり得る（Hartley v Ponsonby（1857）7 E&B 872⑪）。

Williams v Roffey Bros and Nicholls (Contractors) Ltd. 判決（(1991) 1 QB 1 (CA)⑫）は、役務提供や物品供給に関する義務履行に関し、上記 Hartley v Ponsonby 判決が示した例外の適用場面を拡大し、(ⅰ)債権者が、債務者による約定どおりの義務履行は困難である旨を合理的に判断し、かつ(ⅱ)債務者に対して約束した期限内に義務を履行したら追加の報酬を支払う旨を約束した場合、当該義務の履行は新たな約束の consideration となると判示した。同判決の裁判官は上記 Stilk v Myrick 判決の原則を変更するわけではないと述べているが、実質的には、obligation imposed by contract with promisor が consideration にはならない旨の上記 Stilk 判決が示した原則の適用範囲は、

Williams v Roffey 判決により大幅に制約を受けることになった。

(3) Contractual duties with third parties（第三者との契約に基づく義務）

　約束者（promisor）による約束の対価として、約束を受けた者（promisee）が第三者との間の契約に基づいて負担した義務（obligation imposed by contract with a third party）を履行した場合、当該義務履行は約束者（promisor）の約束の約因（consideration）となる（Scotson v Pegg（1861）6 H & N 295、New Zealand Shipping Co., Ltd. v A.M. Satterhwaite, The Eurymedon（1975）AC 154 (PC)⑬）。

　また、約束者（promisor）による約束の対価として、promisee が第三者との間の契約上の義務を履行することを promisor に対して約束した場合、当該約束は、強迫、威嚇によるものでない限り、promisor の約束の約因となる（Shadwell v Shadwell（1860）9 CB NS 159 (Court of Common Bench)⑭）。

6．Part-payment of debt（金銭債務の一部弁済）

(1) 原則

　金銭債務に関する契約において、借金等の返済に窮した借主と貸主との間で、借主がその一部だけ支払えば残金の返済を免除する旨を約束することがある。借主がいわれたとおりの金額を支払った後に貸主が残債務免除の約束を反故にして残金を請求してきた場合、貸主による約束は法的拘束力があるのか、すなわち、金銭債務の一部履行は、残債務免除の consideration となり得るのかが問題となる。金銭債務の一部履行も契約上の義務の履行ではあるが、イギリスの裁判所は、古くからこの問題に関して上記5(2)とは異なる法原則を採ってきた。すなわち、原則として、金銭債務の全部弁済の代わりにその一部を弁済しても残債務を免除する約束に対する consideration とはならず、債権者は、残債務免除の約束を無視して残額を請求することができる（Pinnel's case（1602）5 Co. Rep 117、Foakes v Beer（1884）9 App Cas 605 (HL)⑮、Re Selectmove（1995）2 All ER (CA)⑯）。Pinnel's case は、この原則について以下のとおり述べている。

> Payment of a lesser sum on the day in satisfaction of a greater cannot be any satisfaction for the whole, because it appears to the judges, that by no possibility can a lesser sum be a satisfaction to the plaintiff for a greater sum.

(2) 例外

裁判所は、上記6(1)の原則によって生ずる不合理な結果から債務者を救済するため、以下のような様々な例外を設けて、Pinnel's case 及びその後にこれを確認した Foakes v Beer 判決の適用場面を限定している。

(ⅰ) **Claims disputed in good faith**（正当に争われている債務）

争いのある債務の一部弁済は、それ以上の債務が存在しない旨の約束の約因となり得る。ただし、一部弁済金額の受領により残債務を免除する意思がある場合でなければならない（Ferguson v Davies（1997）1 All ER (CA)⑰）。

(ⅱ) **Variations in debtor's performance**（債務者の履行条件の変更）

債務弁済に関する履行条件の変更を伴う場合であれば、当該変更の合意が残債務免除の consideration となり得る（Sibree v Tripp（1846）15 M. & W. 23⑱）。これについて Sibree v Tripp 判決の裁判官は、「5ポンド支払って100ポンドの債務免除を受けることはできないが、5ポンド相当の馬を提供すれば免除を受けられる」と述べている。この例外によれば、債務の一部の繰上げ弁済を条件に残債務の免除を受ける方法等も可能となる。ただし、現金に換えて小切手により支払うことにする程度では履行条件の変更に当らない（D&C Builders Ltd. v Rees [1965] 3 All ER 837）。

(ⅲ) **Part-payment by a third party**（第三者による一部弁済）

債権者が、第三者による債務の一部弁済がなされたときに残債務を免除する旨を合意した場合、第三者による弁済は consideration となり、当該残債務免除の合意は法的拘束力を生ずる（Hirachand Punamchand v Temple（1911）2 KB 330 (CA)⑲）。

(ⅳ) その他の例外として、composition agreement（任意整理契約、Good v Cheeseman（1831）2 B&Ad 328）、forbearance to enforce claim（反対債権の放棄）、promissory estoppel（約束的禁反言、下記7）等が挙げられ

る。

7．Promissory estoppel（約束的禁反言）

　Estoppel（禁反言）は、相手方に信頼を生じさせる行為をした者に対して、その後に自己の行為に反する主張をすることを裁判所が禁ずるために生まれた、裁判上の証拠法則である。すなわち、ある者が、他人に一定の事実の存在を信じさせる行為をしたとき、これを信頼して自己の利害関係を変更した者の利益を保護するため、この事実を覆す主張をすることを禁止する旨の法原則である。この原則に基づき、契約どおりの権利（strict legal rights）を実行しない、又は権利行使を停止すると信じさせた契約当事者は、その後に当該権利の行使をすることができないことになる。

　Common law 上の estoppel は当事者の行為（conduct）及び事実の表示を基礎とし、これに反する将来の行為や事実の主張を禁じていたが、19世紀後半になって、事実の表示だけではなく、将来の意思の表示、すなわち約束についても、equity に基づいて estoppel を認める判例が現れた（Hughes v Metropolitan Railway (1877) 2 App Cas 439 (HL)[20]）。Hughes v Metropolitan Railway 判決では、契約の一方当事者が consideration を新たに提供せずに契約上の権利行使をしないことを約束（promise）した場合において、その約束に反して権利行使をすることが衡平に反すること（inequitable）を根拠として、promisor による権利行使を制限した。この判決は、その後の Central London Property Trust v High Trees House Ltd.判決（[1947] KB 130）において、Denning J.が obiter の中で取り上げたことにより脚光を浴び、以降、約束的禁反言（promissory estoppel）の法理は、consideration を欠いた合意（agreement）に関する不公平な結果を是正する上で重要な役割を果たすようになった。

　Promissory estoppel の主張は consideration の法理の例外に過ぎないので、無限定に認められるわけではない。どのような場合に認められるのかについて、上記 Hughes v Metropolitan Railway 判決や Central London Property v High Trees 判決では、equity に反するか否かという基準しか示されていなか

ったが、それ以降の裁判において、以下の3つの要件が作り出されている。

(1) 契約当事者の一方が相手方に対して、契約どおりの権利（strict legal rights）を行使しない旨の明白かつ明瞭な約束（a clear and unequivocal promise）をしていること（Woodhouse A.C. Israel Cocoa Ltd. S.A. v Nigerian Produce Marketing Co., Ltd.［1972］AC 741（HL）㉑）。この点に関し、Lord Hailsham は、Woodhouse v Nigerian Produce Marketing Co 判決において、以下のとおり述べている。

To give rise to an estoppel, representations should be clear and unequivocal. If a representation is not made in such a form as to comply with this requirement, it normally matters not that the representee should have misconducted it and relied upon it.

(2) そのような約束を受けた相手方当事者（promisee）がこの約束を信頼して何らかの重要な行動（conduct on reliance）をとったこと。相手方が信頼に基づく行動によって何らかの不利益（detriment）を被ったことまでを立証する必要はない（W.J. Alan v El Nasr Export & Import Co［1972］2 QB 189（CA）㉒）が、約束者（promisor）が直ぐに撤回した場合等には信頼に基づく重要な行動があるとは認められないことがある（Brikom Investments Ltd. v Carr［1979］QB 467、The Post Chaser［1982］1 All ER 19）。

(3) Equity に基づく制度における本質的な要件として、約束者（promisor）が約束を反故にすることが衡平に反する（inequitable）こと。相手方（promisee）が威嚇や強迫的な手段を用いて約束者（promisor）に権利の放棄や不行使の約束を強要した場合（D&C Builders Ltd. v Rees［1966］2 QB 617（CA）㉓）や約束した後にその前提を覆すような重大な事情の変更があった場合（William v Stern（1879）5 QBD 40㉔）には、この要件が充たされないことになる。ただし、この要件の適否の判断に当たっては、個々の裁判官による裁量の余地が大きい。

8．金銭債務の一部弁済（Part payment of debt）と Promissory estoppel

　上記6のとおり、イギリス法には古くから、債務の全部弁済の代わりにその一部を弁済しても、残債務を免除する約束に対する consideration とはならない旨の法原則がある（Pinnel's case (1602) 5 Co. Rep 117）。Promissory estoppel を最初に認めた上記 Hughes v Metropolitan Railway 判決（1877）は、当初は、金銭債務の一部弁済の場合には適用されないものと解されていた（Foakes v Beer (1884) 9 App Cas 605 (HL)）。ところが、上記 Central London Property Trust Ltd. v High Trees House Ltd.判決（[1947] KB 130㉕）の obiter において、Denning J.は、残債務免除を約束して一部弁済を受け入れた場合であっても promissory estoppel の適用があるとの判断を示した。彼の判断と既に判例法として確立している Foake's v Beer 判決との整合性が不明であるし、そもそも obiter（傍論）は判例法としての先例拘束性を有しないはずであるが、その後の裁判において、彼の obiter は ratio（判例法）であるかのように取り扱われ、promissory estoppel の要件が充足されたときは Foakes v Beer 判決を適用しない旨の判決が次々と下されてきた。結局、Foakes v Beer 判決の法理は Central London Property v High Trees 判決によって修正されたに等しい状態となっている。

9．Promissory estoppels の限界

　上記7の3要件に加え、promissory estoppel の主張は、以下のような制限を受けることがある。ただし、これらの制限がどのような場合に及ぶかは、未だ流動的である。

(1)　Effect normally suspensory（一時停止効を原則とする）

　債権者からの義務履行請求に対する promissory estoppel の主張は、原則として、義務の履行を停止する働きをするだけであり、義務を完全に消滅させるものではないと解されている（上記 Hughes v Metropolitan Railway (1877)

判決)。したがって、義務の免除や猶予を約束した当事者 (promisor) は、相手方 (promisee) に権利行使の通知をした後に合理的な期間を経過したとき、原則として、元の契約上の地位を回復し、それ以降に発生する債権に関しては権利を行使することができる (Tool Metal Manufacturing v Tungsten Electric [1955] 2 All ER (HL)㉖)。

ただし、相手方当事者が約束をしたとき以前の状態に戻ることができない場合や権利の復活を認めては衡平に反する場合は、通知をしても元の契約上の地位を回復することができない (W.J. Alan v El Nasr Export & Import Co. [1972] 2 QB 189 (CA)㉗)。

(2) A shield, not sword (抗弁とはなるが、請求の根拠にはならない)

Promissory estoppel は、原則として、相手方による権利行使から防御するため、すなわち請求に対する抗弁 (defense) としてのみ主張でき、これを根拠として consideration を伴わない約束の履行を請求することはできない (Combe v Combe [1951] 2 KB 215 (CA)㉘)。なお、コモンローの法制度を有する国の中でも、オーストラリア (Waltons Stores (Interstate) Ltd v Maher (1988) CLR 387 (High Court of Australia)) やアメリカ (the American Restatement (2d) Contracts (1979) s90(1)) においては、一定の制約の下で promissory estoppel を請求原因 (cause of action) とする請求が認められている。イギリスの the Court of Appeal は、上記 Waltons Stores 判決(オーストラリア)後も Combe v Combe を変更していないが (Baird Textile Holdings Ltd v Marks & Spencer plc [2001] EWCA Civ 274, [2002] 1 All ER (Comm)737)、最近、一切の例外が認められないのかについて論争がなされており、将来裁判所がこの制限を修正する可能性もある。

【CASES】

① *Roscorla v Thomas* (1842) 3 QB 234

Thomas sold a horse to Roscorla for £30. After the sale Thomas promised that the horse was free from vice, which was not true. It was held that Roscorla could not sue on this promise as he had already agreed to pay for the horse when the promise was made.

② *Re McArdle* (1951) Ch 669 (CA)

Majorie McArdle was the wife of one of the children of McArdle family, and carried out certain improvements to the property of the family. The children signed a document addressed to her stating: 'In consideration of your carrying out certain alterations and improvements to the property ... at present occupied by you, the beneficiaries under the Will of William Edward McArdle hereby agree that the executor .... shall repay to you from the said estate when so distributed the sum of £488 in settlement of the amount spent on such improvements...' However, the children refused to authorise payment. It was held that the work done by her was past consideration and so invalid.

"As the work had in fact all been done and nothing remained to be done by Mrs. Majorie McArdle at all, the consideration was wholly past consideration, and, therefore, the beneficiaries' agreement for the repayment to her of the £488 out of the estate was nudum pactum, a promise with no consideration to support it. That being so, it is impossible for her to rely upon this document as consisting an equitable assignment for valuable consideration." (per Jenkins L.J.)

③ *Lampleigh v Braithwait* (1615) Hob 105

Braithwait had killed a man, and asked Lampleigh to do all he could to get him a pardon from the King. After Lampleigh had done this at great trouble and expense Braithwait promised him £100, but then refused to hand it over, claiming that Lampleigh's actions were past consideration. It was held that Lampleigh was entitled to his money, as he had done the act on Braithwait's request and it was clear at the time Braithwait asked him for help that he would be paid for his trouble.

④ *Pao On v Lau Yiu Long* (1980) AC 614 (Privy Council: Hong Kong)

The minority shareholders in a private company agreed to sell their shares to the majority shareholders in return for shares in a public company. They also agreed not to sell 60% of shares in such public company for a year, in order not to depress the market. Before they completed the agreement, the minority shareholders insisted on an indemnity against the loss which might occur if the market were to rise and they were unable to sell the shares. The majority agreed to this and bought the shares, however, and then they refused to honour the indemnity on the ground that such indemnity was past consideration. The Privy Council held that it was not past consideration and clarified the three conditions which must be satisfied to decide that the past act was not a past consideration:

1. The act must have been done at the request of the promisor;

2. The parties must have understood that a payment was to be made for the service when it was requested; and

3. The contract (had it been made in the normal way) must have been a legally enforceable one.

⑤ *Chappell & Co., Ltd. v Nestle Co., Ltd.* (1959) 2 All ER 701

Chappell owned the copyright in a dance tune called 'Rockin' Shoes', and Nestle was using records of this tune as a part of an advertisement scheme. A record company made records of such tune and sold to Nestle for 4 pence each. Nestle then sold them to the public for 1 shillings 6 dime, plus the wrappers from 3 chocolate bars. The wrappers were immediately thrown away when received. Chappell sued Nestle for infringement of the copyright. Under the Copyright Act 1956, a person recording musical works for retail sale need not get permission but had merely to serve the copyright holder with notice and pay 6 and 1/4 per cent of the selling prices as royalty. Chappell asserted that Nestle was not retailing the goods as it was selling for money plus valueless wrappers, which could not be a part of consideration, and accordingly Nestle needed Chappell's consent. It was held that even the most worthless items can be good consideration.

"A contracting party can stipulate for what consideration he chooses. A peppercorn does not cease to be good consideration if it is established that the promisee does not like pepper and will throw away the corn." (per Lord Somervell)

⑥ *Edmonds v Lawson* (2000) QB 501 1091 (CA)

Ms. Edmonds, a pupil barrister, claimed for minimum wage under the National Minimum Wage Act 1998, claiming that her 12 months pupillage was a contract of employment. Chambers argue that the offer of pupillage was not enforceable as a contract since she had not provided any consideration. It was held that although there was no contract between the pupil and the pupil-master, there was a contract between the pupil and the chambers as it is to the benefit of the chambers to attract talented pupils who may compete for tenancies at that chambers.

"On balance, we take the view that pupils such as the claimant provide consideration for the offer made by chambers ... by agreeing to enter into the close, important and potentially very productive relationship which pupillage involves." (per Lord Bingham)

⑦　*Collins v Godefroy* (1831) 1 B & Ad 950

Godefroy was involved in a lawsuit, and caused Collins to be subpoenaed to attend. Godefroy offered to pay Collins six guineas as an attendance fee. It was held that as Godefroy was legally bound to attend anyway it was not good consideration to do so.

⑧　*Glasbrook Bros. Ltd. v Glamorgan C.C.* (1925) A.C. 270 (HL)

During a miners' strike, the colliery manager ("James") requested the local police superintendent ("Smith") to provide extra forces to protect the working men against the strikers. Smith thought that the workers were adequately protected by the policemen already available, but on Jame's insistent request provided an extra 70 policemen, who remained on the premises until the end of the strike. The colliery owners were then sent a bill for the extra policemen, which they refused to pay on the ground that the police was only performing its legal duty to protect the public. It was held that although the police cannot accept extra money for doing their normal statutory duty, when special services are required beyond the normal call of their duty, they are entitled to be recompensed.

⑨　*Harris v Sheffield United Football Club Ltd.* (1987) 2 All ER 838 (CA)

As a result of the violent behaviour of spectators at Sheffield United's grounds, it became necessary to have a substantial police presence to maintain law and order. The South Yorkshire Police Authority (represented by John Harris) claimed £51,699.54 from Sheffield United in consideration for these "special services". The club denied liability on the basis that in attending the matches the police was merely fulfilling its duty to enforce the law. It was held that police who was on duty during the football match was providing services beyond those of its normal public duties of maintaining law and order, and therefore entitled to claim extra monies.

⑩　*Stilk v Myrick* (1809) 2 Camp 317

A ship crew were promised extra pay by the captain if they would continue on a voyage despite the desertion of two of the seamen. It was held that they were not entitled to extra pay as it was part of their contract to continue on the voyage.

⑪　*Hartley v Ponsonby* (1857) 7 E&B 872

A ship left England for Bombay with crew of 36. By the time it arrived en route to Port Philip, only 19 remained of whom only 5 were able seamen. The captain offered the remaining able seamen an extra £40 for completing the voyage. It was held that the seamen had provided good consideration as what they were asked to do was deferent from what they had agreed to do when there was a full crew.

⑫ *Williams v Roffey Bros and Nicholls (Contractors) Ltd.* (1991) 1 QB 1 (CA)

Roffey Bros ("RB"), who held a building contract, hired Williams, who was a carpenter, as a subcontractor to perform a contract between RB and a third party for £20,000. Williams got into financial difficulty because the agreed price was too low for him to operate. RB was concerned that it may incur a penalty under the main contract for late performance if Williams did not finish on time and so offered him an extra £10,300 to complete on time. RB later refused to make full payment, insisting that Williams had given no consideration as he was merely fulfilling the original contract. It was held that as there was no suggestion of duress by Williams, he was entitled to the extra money. The court said that he had provided consideration in return for the promise to pay him extra in that RB received various benefits of (i) ensuring that Williams would continue to work and not stop in breach of the sub-contract; (ii) avoiding the penalty for delay; and (iii) avoiding the trouble and expense of engaging other people to complete the work.

"The present state of the law on this subject can be expressed in the following proposition:-

(i) If A has entered into a contract with B to do work for, or to supply goods or services to, B in return for payment by B; and

(ii) at some stage before A has completely performed his obligations under the contact B has reason to doubt whether A will, or will be able to, complete his side of the bargain; and

(iii) B thereupon promises A an additional payment in return for A's promise to perform his contractual obligations on time; and

(iv) as a result of giving his promise, B obtains in practice a benefit, or obviates a disbenefit; and

(v) B's promise is not given as a result of economic duress or fraud on the part of A; then

(vi) the benefit to B is capable of being consideration for B's promise, so that the promise will be legally binding...

If it be objected that the propositions above contravene the principle in Stilk v Myrick, I answer that in my view they do not; they refine, and limit the application of that principle, but they leave the principle unscathed e.g. where B secures no benefit by his promise." (per Glidewell L.J., p.15)

⑬ *New Zealand Shipping Co., Ltd. v A.M. Satterhwaite, The Eurymedon* (1975) AC 154 (PC)

The maker of a drilling machine entered into a contract for the carriage of the machine by sea to New Zealand. Under the contract of carriage (the bill of lading), the maker promised not to sue the carrier and its servant or agent, including independent contractors. The machine was damaged by the stevedore employed by the carrier in the course of unloading, and the maker sued the stevedore. The issues were (ⅰ) whether the stevedore was a party to the contract, containing exemption clause, and if so, (ⅱ) whether they provided consideration. It was held that (ⅰ) the stevedore was a party to the bill of loading since it accepted the maker's offer when it unloaded the machine (Carlill v Carbolic Smoke Ball Co (1893) applied) and (ⅱ) the performance of services by the stevedore in discharging cargo was sufficient consideration.

⑭ *Shadwell v Shadwell* (1860) 9 CB NS 159 (Court of Common Bench)

Lancey Shadwell was engaged to marry Ellen Nicholl. In 1983 his uncle wrote a letter to him, stating: 'I am glad to hear of your intended marriage with Ellen Nicholl and, as I promised to assist you at starting, I am happy to tell you that I will pay one hundred and fifty pounds yearly during my life and until your income derived from your profession of Chancery barrister shall amount to six hundred guineas....'. Lancey married with her and his income never exceeded six hundred. The uncle died 18 years after the marriage. He paid 12 annual sums and stopped payment. On his death, Lancey sued the executor for the balance. The executor argued that as Lancey was contractually bound to marry Ellen anyway, he provided no consideration to the uncle. It was held that his marriage was a sufficient consideration to support his uncle's promise, for by marrying, he had incurred responsibilities and changed his position in life. The uncle probably derived some benefit in that his desire to see his nephew settled had been satisfied.

⑮ *Foakes v Beer* (1884) 9 App Cas 605 (HL)

Mrs Beer was owed £2,090 19 shillings by Dr Foakes, and agreed with him that he should pay it in instalments, after which time she promised she would take no further action. The sum was paid over five years, and Mrs Beer then sued for £360 interest. It was held that she was entitled to it. Her promise not to take further action was not binding as Dr Foakes had given her no consideration for it. The House of Lords confirmed the decision in Pinnel's Case.

⑯   *Re Selectmove Ltd* [1955] 1 WLR 474 (CA)

In July 1997, a company which owed the Inland Revenue considerable sums in income tax and national insurance contributions had made a proposal at a meeting with the collector of taxes that in future it should pay the tax as it fell due and repay the arrears in instalments. The Revenue later demanded payment in full and eventually presented a petition to have the company wound up. The company argued that the petition should be dismissed since there was a contract by which the Revenue had agreed to accept smaller payments. The judge ordered compulsory winding up on the basis that there was no such agreement. He also stated obiter that there was no consideration to support it.

⑰   *Ferguson v Davies* (1997) 1 All ER (CA)

In February 1992, Ferguson sold some specialist records to Davies, who was a dealer. The contract provided that Davies would either 'pay' Ferguson with £600 worth of records by a certain date, or would pay him £1,700 in cash. Davies delivered only £143.50 worth of records and £5 in cash to Ferguson. Ferguson sued for a further £486.50. Davies denied the claim, but sent Ferguson a cheque for £150. which Ferguson cashed. Ferguson then increased his claim to balance of the £1,700 (plus interest), but Davies claimed that in cashing the cheque, Ferguson had accepted a settlement of a lesser amount and could not sue for any more. It was held that Ferguson had not compromised his position by accepting the cheque. In sending the cheque Davies was not necessarily representing this as the whole sum owed. He could simply have been admitting to owing at least £150. Ferguson was entitled to understand Davies' offer in that sense, and so his acceptance of the cheque did not give rise to a settlement which would deny him the possibility of claiming the balance of the debt.

⑱   *Sibree v Tripp* (1846) 15 M. & W. 23

"It is undoubtedly true that payment of a portion of a liquidated demand, in the same manner as the whole liquidated demand ought to be paid, is payment only in part; because it is not one bargain, but two; namely payment of part and an agreement, without consideration, to give up the residue...But if you substitute a piece of paper or a stick of sealing wax, it is different, and the bargain may be carried out in its full integrity. A man may give, in satisfaction of a debt of £100, a horse of the value of £5, but not £5. Again, if the time or place of payment be different, the one sum may be in satisfaction of the other." (per Baron Alderson)

⑲ *Hirachand Punamchand v Temple* (1911) 2 KB 330 (CA)
   Lieutenant Temple had borrowed 3,600 rupees from the money lenders, and had given them a promissory note. His father, Sir Richard Temple, offered them 1,500 rupees in full settlement and sent a draft. The lenders cashed the drafts but then brought an action against the son for the balance. It was held that the lenders had no further claim against the son.

⑳ *Hughes v Metropolitan Railway* (1877) 2 App Cas 439 (HL)
   A tenant was required by his landlord to do certain repairs within six months. During that time, the landlord started to negotiate with the tenant for the purchase of the lease, so the tenant did not do the repairs. The negotiations broke down after the six months had elapsed, and the landlord immediately sued the tenant (for forfeiture) on the grounds that the repairs had not been done. The House of Lords held that it would be inequitable to allow the landlord to enforce this part of the contract when he had led the tenant to suppose he would not do so. He should have given the tenant a reasonable time to do the repairs from the date the negotiations broke down.

㉑ *Woodhouse A.C. Israel Cocoa Ltd SA v Nigerian Produce Marketing Co. Ltd* [1972] AC 741 (HL)
   A sale contract provided for payment in Nigerian pounds. Woodhouse, the buyer, had asked if the seller would be prepared to accept pound sterling, and the seller had relied that 'payment can be made in sterling.' Later, the pound sterling was devalued to worth 85% of the Nigerian pound, and the seller claimed the deference in value. The buyer argued that the seller was estopped from going back, however, it was held that the seller's representation was not sufficiently precise to found an estoppel.

㉒ *W.J. Alan v El Nasr Export & Import Co* [1972] 2 QB 189 (CA)
   In a contract for sale of coffee, the price was expressed in Kenyan shillings. The buyer made part payment in pound sterling and the seller accepted. While the shipment was in progress sterling was devalued and the seller claimed the deference in price between the value of Kenyan shillings and sterling shillings. It was held that the seller by accepting payment in sterling had irrevocably waived their right to be paid in Kenyan currency or had accepted variation of

the sale contract, and that a party who has waived his rights cannot afterwards insist on them if the other party has acted on that belief, even though he could not have been shown to have acted to his detriment in reliance on the promise.

"The principle of waiver is simply this: If one party, by his conduct, leads another to believe that the strict rights arising under the contract will not be insisted on, intending that the other should act on that belief, and he does act on it, then the first party will not afterwards be allowed to insist on the strict legal rights when it would be inequitable for him to do so .... There may be no consideration moving from him who benefits by the waiver. There may be no detriment to him acting on it. There may be nothing in writing. Nevertheless, the one who waives his strict rights cannot afterwards insist on them." (per Lord Denning M.R.)

㉓ *D&C Builders Ltd. v Rees* [1966] 2 QB 617 (CA)

D&C Builders, a small company, did work for Rees for £480. Rees did not pay despite repeated request. Six months later, the wife of Rees offered on his behalf £300 in full settlement, knowing that the builder was in financial difficulty. The builder accepted, but later sued for the balance. In defense Rees claimed estoppel. It was held that since D&C Builders had been forced by Rees into giving the promise, it was not fair of them to be bound by it.

"In the present case, on the facts as found by judge, it seems to me that there was not true accord. The debtor's wife held the creditor to ransom. The creditor was in need of money to meet his own commitments, and she knew it. When the creditor asked for payment of the £480 due to him, she said in effect: 'We cannot pay you the £480. But we will pay you £300 if you will accept in settlement. If you do not accept it on those terms you will get nothing. £300 is better than nothing ...' She was making a threat to break the contract (by paying nothing) and she was doing it so as to compel the creditor to do what he was unwilling to do (to accept £300 in settlement): and she succeeded. He complied with her demand...No one can insist on a settlement procured by intimidation." (per Lord Denning M.R.)

㉔ *William v Stern* (1879) 5 QBD 40

A creditor promised not to seize the debtor's furniture which had been put up as security for a loan. However, he went back on this promise when he discovered that the debtor's landlord was about to seize the furniture himself to cover unpaid rent. It was held that going back on the promise was reasonable in the circumstances.

㉕ *Central London Property Trust Ltd. v High Trees House Ltd.* [1947] KB 130

In 1937 Central London Property Trust as landlord leased to High Trees House a block of flats for a term of 99 years at a rent of £2,500 a year. In 1940, many of the flats were empty, on account of the war, and the landlord agreed to reduce the rent to £1,250. By 1945 the flats were again full. The landlord claimed the full original rent both the future and also for the last two quarters of 1945. Denning J upheld the claim since the agreement to reduce the rent was only meant to last during the war, and had ceased early in 1945. The importance of the judgment lies in his obiter, stating that, had the plaintiffs sued for the full rent between 1940 and 1945, it would have been estopped by its promise from asserting its legal right to demand in full on the basis of Hughes v Metropolitan Railway.

"A promise to accept a smaller sum in discharge of a larger sum, if acted upon, is binding notwithstanding the absence of consideration: and if the fusion of law and equity leads to this result, so much the better. That aspect was not considered in Foakes and Beer. At this time of the day, however, when law and equity have been joined together for over seventy years, principles must be reconsidered in the light of their combined effect" (per Denning J.)

㉖ *Tool Metal Manufacturing v Tungsten Electric* [1955] 2 All ER (HL)

In 1938 Tool Metal Manufacturing ("the licensor") granted to Tungsten Electric ("the licensee") a licence to import, make, use and sell certain hard metal alloys it had patented. The licensee was to pay royalties and, if the licensee sold more than certain amount, an extra sum of 'compensation'. During the war, the licensor agreed to suspend its right to compensation. In 1945, the licensor claimed to have revoked its suspension and to be entitled compensation from 1 January 1945, but the claim failed since the revocation was premature as no adequate notice had been given to the licensee. In 1950, the licensor brought an action again, claiming compensation from 1 January 1947. It was held that the licensor had effectively revoked its promise to suspend its legal rights and that it was entitled to the compensation claimed.

㉗ *W.J. Alan v El Nasr Export & Import Co.* [1972] 2 QB 189 (CA)

"[The creditor] may on occasion be able to revert to his strict legal rights for the future by giving notice in that behalf, or otherwise making it plain by his conduct that he will insist upon them. But there are cases where no withdrawal is possible. It may be too late to withdraw: or it cannot be done without injustice to the other party. In that event he is bound by his waiver. He will not be allowed to revert to his strict legal rights. He can only enforce them subject to the waiver he has made." (per Lord Denning M.R.)

㉘　*Combe v Combe* [1951] 2 KB 215 (CA)
　A husband during divorce proceedings promised to pay £100 per annum to his wife who, in reliance on this promise, did not apply to the court for maintenance. When he stopped paying her, she sued him on the promise, but it was held that she could not claim estoppel when she was the plaintiff since the doctrine should not 'create new causes of action'.

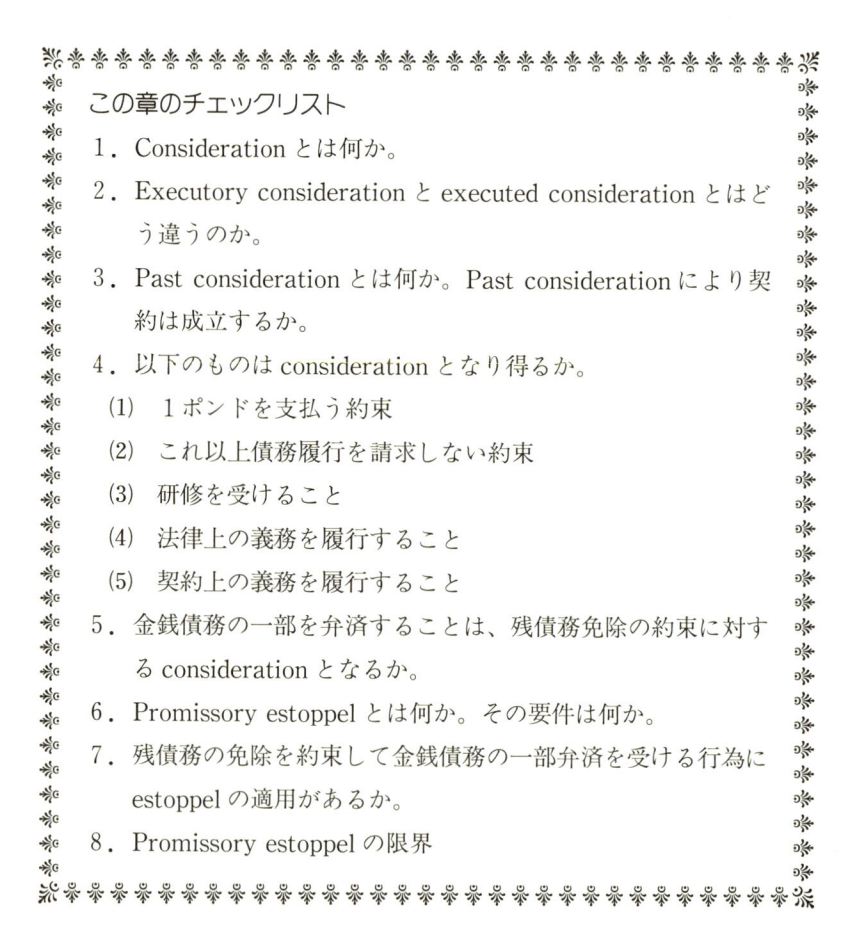

この章のチェックリスト

1．Consideration とは何か。
2．Executory consideration と executed consideration とはどう違うのか。
3．Past consideration とは何か。Past consideration により契約は成立するか。
4．以下のものは consideration となり得るか。
　(1)　1 ポンドを支払う約束
　(2)　これ以上債務履行を請求しない約束
　(3)　研修を受けること
　(4)　法律上の義務を履行すること
　(5)　契約上の義務を履行すること
5．金銭債務の一部を弁済することは、残債務免除の約束に対する consideration となるか。
6．Promissory estoppel とは何か。その要件は何か。
7．残債務の免除を約束して金銭債務の一部弁済を受ける行為に estoppel の適用があるか。
8．Promissory estoppel の限界

第3章

契約の成立(3)
——Intention, Certainty, Completeness, Formality
（契約意思、明確性、完全性、要式）

1．Intention to create legal relations（法的拘束力発生の意思）

　当事者が一定の義務を負担する旨の合意（agreement）をした場合であっても、その者に合意どおりの法的拘束を受ける意思（intention to create legal relations）がない場合、当該合意は法的に有効（enforceabe）な契約とはならない。そのような意思の有無を判断する上では、まず当該合意がどのような状況で行われたかを確定する必要がある。特に、家族間の合意であるか、それとも取引上の合意であるかによって判断基準が異なっている。

(1)　Domestic Agreement（家族間の契約）
　家庭内の契約は原則として法的拘束力がないとされている。ただし、別居夫婦間の離婚条件の合意等はその例外である（Merritt v Merritt [1970] 2 All ER 760 (CA)）。

(2)　Commercial Agreement
　取引に関する合意は、通常法的拘束力を受ける意思があるものと解される。ただし、合意に関する書面の中に、「binding in honour only」、「subject to contract」、「in principle only」等の文言が入っている場合は、原則として法的拘束力を生じさせない意思があるものと解釈される（Rose and Frank Co v Crompton (JR) & Brothers Ltd [1925] AC 445①、Jones v Vernon's Pools [1938] 2 All ER 626②）。

2．Letter of Intent

　重要な取引に関する契約交渉（negotiation）中の当事者間で、交渉開始時又は交渉がある一定の段階に達したとき、正式な契約とは異なる何らかの書面を交わすことがある。これは、一定の取引分野においては、契約交渉段階において一応の合意に達した契約条件や取引条件を書面化して確認しておくことが実務上必要とされているからである。また、契約書作成手続に入る前に、契約の履行の一部とも言うべき一定の準備作業や調査作業を行う必要がある場合にも、そのような作業の根拠やこの段階における当事者の関係を示すために、何らかの書面の締結が要請される。実務上、このように契約締結前における当事者間の合意や確認事項を記載した書面（pre-contractual document）には、letter of intent（レター・オブ・インテント）、letter of commitment（レター・オブ・コミットメント）、heads of agreement（ヘッド・オブ・アグリーメント）、memorandum of understanding（メモランダム・オブ・アンダースタンディング）等の表題が付けられている（第Ⅲ編第1章参照）。

　イギリスでは、特に建築請負取引の分野において、契約交渉中の請負人が、契約上の義務の一部となるべき作業を契約締結に至る前に行う際、注文者から何らかの保証を得ておくための手段としてこれらの書面がよく利用されている。よって、関連する判例法は、建築請負契約に関連するものが最も多い。

　Letter of intent 等の内容は、当事者間の合意により自由に定められるものであり、実際上も状況に応じて様々であるが、建築請負取引の場合における標準的な letter of intent には、一方当事者（注文者側）が将来の一定の時期に相手方当事者（請負人側）と契約を締結する意思を有していることの表明と相手方当事者が報酬受領を対価として契約締結前に一定の作業に着手する意思があることの表明とが記載される。

　Letter of intent その他契約締結前書面の法的効果に関する問題には、当該書面がこれを締結した状況下においてどのように解釈されるかという問題と当該書面自体の法的性質の分析に関する問題の両面がある。前者は、正式に契約を締結していないにかかわらず、契約締結前書面を交わしたことによって当事者間で交渉している取引に関する最終的な契約（正式契約）が成立したものと

解される場合があるか否かの問題として、後者は、当該書面によって正式契約とは異なる内容の付随的な契約が成立したか否かの問題として、それぞれ議論される。以下、それぞれの問題を分けて説明する。

(1) 正式契約（final contract）の成否

　Letter of intent というタイトルの通常の意味には、当該レターが契約としての法的拘束力を有する約束を形成しないものであるという意味が含まれている。実際上、そのような拘束力を生じさせないことが、agreement ではなく letter of intent という形式の書面を締結することの主要な目的であることが少なくない（British Steel v Cleveland Bridge［1984］1 All ER 504③、Kleinwort Benson Ltd. v Malaysia Mining Corporation, Berhad［1989］1 All ER 785－第Ⅲ編第1章①）。たとえば、British Steel v Cleveland Bridge 判決において、裁判官（Robert Goff J.）は、以下のとおり判示し、契約の成立を前提とする Cleveland Bridge の請求を斥けた。

　　In these circumstances, if the buyer asks the seller to commence work pending the parties entering into a formal contract, it is difficult to infer from the buyer acting on that request that he is assuming any responsibility for his performance, except such responsibility as will rest on him under the terms of the contract which both parties confidently anticipate they will shortly enter into …

　ただし、letter of intent に記載された文言の解釈及び当該書面作成に至った状況によっては、その作成、交換の結果、両当事者間における拘束力ある合意が形成されることもある。たとえば、Wilson Smithett v Bangladesh Sugar 判決（［1986］Lloyd's LR 1986 Vol.1 378④）において、裁判所は、security deposit（担保預託金）又は performance bond（履行保証状）の交付を求めること等を内容とする letter of intent の作成・交付は相手方の契約申込（offer）に対する承諾（acceptance）の意思表示であると認定し、法的拘束力ある正式契約の成立を認めている。

　裁判所は、letter of intent その他の pre-contractual documents（契約締結前書面）を作成したときに正式契約（formal contract）が成立したか否かの

判断を、当該書面の記載だけではなく、(ⅰ)当該 pre-contractual document の目的、(ⅱ)契約交渉の内容及び経過、(ⅲ)当該 pre-contractual document において確定していなかった契約条件があったか否か、(ⅳ)当事者が pre-contractual document に基づく義務や引受行為の一部を履行したか否か、(ⅴ)関連する業界における取引慣行その他の事項を考慮して認定している。これは、後記の the parol evidence rule（口頭証拠排除の原則）に基づいて契約書以外の外部要素を排除することを原則とする、契約解釈の一般法則（本編第5章参照）とは異なった解釈方法なので、注意を要する。

(2) 付随的契約（Ancillary Contract）の成否

　Letter of intent 等に関しては、各事件における具体的な事実関係の下で、これを交わしたことにより、正式契約とは異なる内容の付随的な契約（ancillary contract）が成立したものとし、当該付随的契約に基づく法的責任が認められる場合もある。たとえば、Turiff v Regalia（[1971]（QBD）9 BLR 20⑤）では、裁判所は、letter of intent に当事者の義務は「受け入れ可能な契約の締結を条件とする（subject to agreement on an acceptable contract）」旨の記載があったとしても、この条件は、正式な契約（the full contract）に基づく義務だけに関わるものであり、予備的契約（the preliminary contract）には関係していないと判示し、被告に対し、当該予備的契約に基づき、正式契約締結に先立って原告が実施した作業に関する合理的な費用を支払うように命じた。裁判所は、当該予備的契約は、letter of intent の交換によって締結されたものであり、そこには、被告は原告に対しその作業に対する合理的な金額を支払わなければならない旨の黙示の契約条項（implied term）が含まれていると判断したものである。ただし、付随的な契約も契約である以上、客観基準に基づいてそのような内容の合意（agreement）に達していることが認められ、かつ約因（consideration）及び契約意思（intention to create legal relations）が備わっていなければ、法的拘束力を生ずることはない。

　なお、仮に付随的契約の成立が認められなかったとしても、一方当事者が相手方の依頼に基づいて相手方のために作業を行った場合は、restitution（不当利得）を根拠として、依頼に基づいて行った作業の費用の支払を請求できるこ

とがある（本編第10章6参照）。たとえば、上記 British Steel v Cleveland Bridge 判決において、裁判所は、letter of intent による正式契約の成立は否定し、原告は、被告が当該 letter において要求した作業に関して、履行遅滞による契約違反の責任を負うものではないとしながら、原告に作業の依頼をした被告は、当該依頼に従って行われた作業に対し、合理的な費用を支払うべき法律上の義務があるとして、British Steel の賠償請求を認めている。

3．Certainty（明確性）、Completeness（完全性）

(1) 契約の必須条項が不明確又は不完全な場合（Uncertainty or incompleteness of essential terms）

　契約は、取引上の常識（commercial common sense）に照らして契約を実行するために必要不可欠な条項（essential terms）を全て含んでいなければならない。たとえば、典型的な建築請負契約において、契約が実行可能となるためには、作業の範囲、完成時期、請負代金のような事項が確定していることが必要である。ただし、契約の必須条件が何であるかについて、あらゆる場合に共通する決まりがあるわけではない。実務上、建築請負契約における請負代金の金額が契約成立の必須条件であるか否かがしばしば争われる。この問題は、個々の事件における両当事者の言動及び意図を総合的に斟酌して、何が当該契約にとって必須の条件であったかを判断して決めなければならない。たとえば、前記 British Steel Corp. v Cleveland Bridge 判決では、請負代金額は実際上必須の契約条件であり、それが決定されない限り最終合意に達していないので契約は成立していないと判断されている。

　契約の条項、条件は、両当事者間の合意により決定される。契約の重要な要素に関する合意の内容が不明確である場合は、原則として法的拘束力を生じない（Scammell & Nephew v Ouston［1941］AC 251 (HL)⑥）。ただし、不明確な合意であっても、取引慣行（trade practices）その他に基づき、契約内容を明確化できる場合もある。また、当事者の一方が不明確な事項を明確化する義務（duty on one party to resolve uncertainty）を負うことが合意されている場合や不明確な事項について第三者に対して判定、決定の委託（reference to third party）をするための手続きが合意されている場合は、契約締結後に契約内容を明確化する手続が確保されているので、不明確な条項を含む契約であっても有効である（Foley v Classique Coaches Ltd［1934］2 KB 1⑦）。ある契約条項について複数の可能な解釈があって、その内のどれであるかが不明であるような場合、裁判所は、最も合理的と思われる解釈を客観的見地から選択した上で、契約を有効と解している（Martinez v Ellessee International SPA［1999］CLY 861（CA）⑧）。

イギリス法上、将来契約するために交渉することの合意（agreement to negotiate、agreement to agree）は、原則として法的拘束力を有しない（Courtney & Fairbairn Ltd v Tolaini Brothers (Hotels) Ltd［1975］1 WLR 297 (CA)）。したがって、agreement to negotiateであることを根拠として契約不成立と判断されることを避けるためには、将来合意するための仕組みを契約に明記（criteria or machinery specified）しておく必要がある（Foley v Classique Coaches Ltd.［1934］2 KB 1）。

契約交渉中の当事者の一方が、相手方に対し交渉中の取引と競合又は矛盾する事項について第三者とは契約交渉しない旨（agreement not to negotiate with third parties）を約束することがある。たとえば、不動産や株式の売主が第三者とは対象物の売買契約交渉に入らないことを合意する場合等である。そのような合意のことをlock-out agreement（ロックアウト契約）という（第Ⅲ編第1章3(4)参照）。裁判所は、交渉禁止期間について合意があるlock-out agreementは法的拘束力を有するが、期間の定めがない場合は無効であると判示している（Walford v Miles［1992］2 WLR 174⑨）。

なお、イギリス法上契約は口頭の合意だけでも成立するので、裁判所は、契約書を作成していないこと（non-execution of formal documents）だけを根拠にして契約上の責任を負わないとの主張は認めない傾向がある（DMA Financial Solutions Ltd v BaaN U.K. Ltd.［2000］WL 1629568⑩）（第Ⅲ編第1章3参照）。

(2) 必須条項以外の条項

契約に無意味な条項や意味不明の条項があったとしても、その他の条項によ

り拘束力ある契約が完成している場合、裁判所は、無意味な条項だけを除外 (meaningless term ignored) し、契約のその他の条項の法的拘束力には影響しないものとしている (Nicolene Ltd. v Simmonds [1953] 1 All ER 822 (CA)⑪)。

いわゆる努力義務条項 (obligation to use reasonable endeavours) は、無意味又は不明確であるとして争われることがあるが、それ自体としては執行不能な程に不明確な合意とはいえない。当該努力義務の目的となっている事項を達成するために何らの行為をも行わない等、明白な努力義務の不履行がある場合は義務違反 (breach of contract) となる (Lambert v HTV Cymru (Wales) [1998] FSR 874⑫)。

4. Conditional agreement（条件付合意）

イギリス法上、condition という語には、(ⅰ)全ての契約条件 (terms and conditions)、(ⅱ)契約解除の原因となる重要な契約条件 (conditions instead of warranties)、(ⅲ)契約の効力発生又は契約上の当事者の義務の発生や消滅の前提となっている事象の発生や行為等、複数の意味がある（本編第4章3）。この(ⅲ)の意味でのconditionには、当事者の支配を離れた偶発的事実が条件となっている contingent condition（偶発的条件）と当事者による義務の履行自体を条件とする promissory condition（約束的条件）の2種類があり得る。たとえば、「明日雨が降ったら仕事をする」という場合の「明日雨が降ること」は前者で、「明日中に仕事が終わったら報酬を支払う」という場合の「明日中に仕事を終えること」は後者である。Conditional agreement における condition は、この contingent condition という意味である。

Contingent condition には、(ⅰ)当該事実や行為が生じない限り契約が成立せず、又は契約上の義務が生じないという効果が生ずる condition precedent（停止条件）及び(ⅱ)condition となっている事実や行為の発生によって契約上の義務が消滅することになる condition subsequent（解除条件）の2種類がある。Conditional agreement は、一定の contingent condition（偶発的条件）が発生することが契約成立の条件となっている契約のことである。

一般に、contingent condition 自体は契約上の義務ではないが、condition 付きで義務負担の合意をした場合、これによって、以下のような付随的な義務が発生することがある。

(1) Duty not to prevent occurrence（条件成就妨害の禁止）：Condition precedent to performance（義務履行の停止条件）を付して義務の負担を約束した者は、原則として、条件成就の意図的な妨害をしてはならない（Blake & Co v Sohn [1969] 1 WLR 1412、Thompson v ASDA-MFI Group plc [1988] Ch 241)。

(2) Duty to make reasonable efforts（合理的努力義務）：Condition precedent の内容によっては、当事者は、黙示の合意による義務（implied term）として、条件成就のために合理的な努力を払うべき義務（duty to make reasonable efforts）を負う場合がある（Hargreaves Transport Ltd. v Lynch [1969] 1 WLR 215⑬)。

(3) Prevention of withdrawal before occurrence（条件成就前の撤回禁止）：Condition precedent の達成が相手方の行為にかかる場合は、当該条件付の契約は unilateral contract（一方的契約）となるので、condition precedent to performance（義務履行の停止条件）を付して負担を約束した義務を条件成就前に撤回・取消すること（withdrawal before occurrence）は許されない（Smith v Butler [1900] 1 QB 694⑭)。

5．Formal requirement（要式性）

Contract は、原則として口頭（orally 又は by parol）の合意だけで成立するが、以下の契約に限っては、書面によることが必要とされている。

(1) **捺印証書（deed）によるべき契約（contract to be made by deed）**
期間３年超の不動産賃貸借契約（lease of more than 3 years term）（the Law of Property Act 1925 ss52、54)

(2) **書面によるべき契約（contract to be made in writing）**

(ⅰ) 有価証券（negotiable instruments）（the Bills of Exchange Act 1882 ss3(1)、17(2)、the Bills of Sale Act (1878) Amendment Act 1882）
(ⅱ) 25,000ポンド以下の消費者金融契約（consumer credit agreement）（the Consumer Credit Act 1974 s61）
(ⅲ) 土地に関する権利の処分に関する契約（contract for disposition of interest in land）（the Law of Property (Miscellaneous Provisions) Act 1989 s2(1)）
(ⅳ) 海事保険契約（contract of marine insurance）（the Marine Insurance Act 1906 s22）

(3) **書面によって証明することを要する契約（contract to be evidenced in writing）**

　保証（guarantee）（The Statute of Frauds 1677 s4）：保証契約（contract of guarantee）とは、他人の債務不履行に対して責任を負うことを約束する契約のことである。主たる債務者の義務の存在を前提として、その不履行の場合の責任を約束する点において、他人に生じた損害を単純に塡補する旨の合意である indemnity contract（損害塡補契約、損害補償契約）と区別される。Indemnity contract に関しては書面による証明の要件は存在しないので、この両者の区別は重要である（Actionstrength Ltd. v International Glass Engineering [2002] 1 WLR 566⑮）。

6．Deed（捺印証書）

　イギリス法上、合意が契約としての法的拘束力が有するためには、原則として consideration（約因）がなければならない。ただし、当該合意が deed（捺印証書）により作成された場合は、consideration がなくても法的拘束力を生ずる。
　Deed とは、第三者を証人として書面により行った約束（an attested promise in writing）であり、作成した者が署名、押印、引渡（signed, sealed and delivered）することによって成立する。Deed により作成されたあらゆる約束

（promises）は法的拘束力を有している。

Deed は以下の要件を全て充たす書面でなければならない（the Law of Property (Miscellaneous Provisions) Act 198 s1(2)、(3)）。

(1) Deed であることが当該書面上に明記されていること（express statement as 'deed'）。

(2) 作成者が第三者の面前で署名し、かつ当該第三者にその証人となってもらうこと（attested 又は witnessed by third party）。なお、作成者以外の者が作成者の代理人として署名する場合は、2名以上の証人の面前で署名しなければならない。

(3) Sealing（押印）すること。

ただし、作成者が individual（自然人）である場合は押印不要である。

作成者が法人の場合は、原則として、登録された common seal（会社印）の押印が必要となる。ただし、作成者がイギリスの1985年又は2006年会社法（the Companies Act 1985 or 2006）に基づいて設立された company である場合は押印不要となり、その代わりに会社法上の契約作成要件を充たしていなければならない。すなわち、取締役（directors）2名以上もしくは取締役1名と会社書記官（secretary、会社法上の会社役員）が署名し、かつ会社のために作成した書面であることを契約書面上に明記することが必要である。

作成者が外国法人の場合、当該外国法人の設立準拠法に基づいて有効とされている方法で作成された書面は、common seal の押印が不要である。日本の会社の場合は、日本法上 common seal の制度がないので、登録された代表者印による記名押印、又は登録された代表者のサインによる署名が、押印に代わる deed の成立要件である。

(4) 作成者による引渡しがなされること（delivered）。作成者は、引渡のために、契約の相手方や第三者に契約書を手渡すことまでは要しないが、当該契約書が法的拘束力のあるものとして完成したことを明らかにするための何らかの言動をしなければならない（Xenos v Wickham (1867) LR 2 HL 296）。

(5) なお、conditional deed（条件付捺印証書）の場合は、当該条件の成就（conditions satisfied）が要件となる。たとえば、不動産の売買契約において、売主は、代金が支払われるまでは契約を発効させない意図で契約証書を条件付

で第三者に預け入れる（escrows）のが通常であるが、この場合は、代金支払がdeedの要件となる（Alan Estates Ltd v W.G. Stores Ltd［1982］Ch 511）。

【CASES】

① *Rose and Frank Co v Crompton (JR) & Brothers Ltd* ［1925］AC 445 (HL)

Rose and Frank ("R&F"), an American distributor, entered into a distributorship agreement with Crompton & Bros. ("CB"), a British manufacturer, whereby CB appointed R&F as sole agent for sale in the USA of CB's products. The agreement included the following clause: 'This agreement is not entered into.... as a formal or legal agreement and shall not be subject to legal jurisdiction in the Law Courts either of the United States or England, but it is only a definite expression and record of the purpose and intention of the three parties concerned, to which they honourably pledge themselves.' CB terminated the agreement without giving notice, and refused to deliver the goods ordered by R&F although CB had accepted such orders. It was held that the agreement was not binding for the future, however, the orders actually given and accepted were binding contract of sale.

"The overriding clause in the document is that which provides that it is to be a contract in honour only and unenforceable at law." (per Lord Phillimore)

② *Jones v Vernon's Pools* ［1938］2 All ER 626 (Liverpool Assizes)

Jones said that he sent in a winning football coupon to Vernon, who denied that they have received it and relied on a clause printed on every coupon, stating that the transaction should not 'be legally enforceable … but … binding in honour only.' It was held that the clause meant that this was not a contract.

③ *British Steel v Cleveland Bridge* ［1984］1 All ER 504

Cleveland Bridge ("CB") entered into negotiations with British Steel ("BS") for BS to manufacture steel nodes. CB sent BS a letter of intent stating their intention to place an order for the steel nodes, and requested BS to commence work immediately pending the issue of the formal contract. BS went ahead with the manufacture of the nodes as requested, however, the parties did not reach agreement on the contractual terms and no formal written contract was executed. BS had delivered most of nodes but the last one was delayed. CB refused payment and sought damages on the basis that BS's delay in delivery of the last node constituted a breach of a binding contract. It was held that there was no formal contract, and accordingly, the work performed under the letter of intent was not referable to any contractual terms as to payment and performance. However, since CB received a benefit at the expense of BS, the count said that it would be unjust for CB to retain the benefit without recompensing BS for the reasonable value of the nodes delivered.

④　*Wilson Smithett v Bangladesh Sugar* [1986] Lloyd's LR 1986 Vol.1 378

Wilson was a sugar merchant and responded by a tender to an invitation by the defendant (Bangladesh Sugar). Negotiations were conducted between the parties and Wilson presented to the defendant his letter of offer which was to remain valid for the defendant's confirmed and irrevocable acceptance. The defendant issued its letter of intent stating 'We are pleased to issue this letter of intent to you for supply of the following materials ... All other terms and acceptance will be as per your ... offer ... You are advised to submit security deposit/performance bond ...' Later the defendant decided not to go ahead with the deal with Wilson. It was held that the letter of intent was intended to have contractual significance and effect; the reference to a performance bond could not be regarded as constituting a condition.

⑤　*Turriff Construction Ltd. and Turriff Ltd v Regalia Knitting Mills Ltd.* [1971] (QBD) 9 BLR 20

Regalia negotiated with Turriff, a building contractor, for the design and construction of a new factory. On 2 June 1969, Regalia told Turriff that it wanted Turriff to carry out a part of the project based on completion in 1972. Turriff asked an early Letter of Intent in order to meet Regalia's requirement. On 17 June, Regalia sent a letter to Turriff stating: '... it is the intention of Regalia to award a contract to Turriff to build a factory ... The whole to be subject to agreement on an acceptable contract.' After Turriff spent an interim payment of £3,500 in respect of design cost, Regalia decided to appoint another group for the work. It was held that Regalia were liable to the cost done by Turriff under an 'ancillary' contract, which came into existence since Turriff offered to carry out work with the urgency required by Regalia, and Regalia apparently accepted such offer by sending a Letter of Intent.

⑥　*Scammell and Nephew Ltd v Ouston* [1941] AC 251 (HL)

Ouston wished to acquire a motor-van and negotiated with Scammell based on the understanding that part of the purchase price should be paid on 'hire-purchase terms'. Arrangements were made with a finance company, but the actual terms were not agreed. The seller also agreed to take Ouston's present van in part exchange, but later refused to take it. Ouston sued for damages, alleging breach of contract. It was held that a purchase made 'on hire-purchase terms' was not valid, as the terms were not specified, and hire-purchase terms may vary considerably.

⑦ *Foley v Classique Coaches Ltd* [1934] 2 KB 1

Foley sold part of his land to a coach company for use as a coach station, on condition that the company would buy all their petrol from him 'at a price to be agreed between the parties'. It was also agreed that any dispute arising from the contract should be submitted 'to arbitration in the usual way'. Three years later, the company felt that it could get petrol at a better price, and refused to buy petrol from Foley. It was held that the agreement was binding since there was a way of ascertaining the price under the terms of the contract.

⑧ *Martinez v Ellessee International SPA* [1999] CLY 861 (CA)

By a contract with Ellessee International, Conchita Martinez was entitled to US$550,000 bonus if she was ranked the world's number two tennis player in any contract year. There are two possible ways of calculating ranking: one is to take the player's rank for the best week in each month, and then to average that out over the year; the other is to compare the player's ranking with those of other players. In 1996, Martinez's average ranking based on the first method was 2.5 and she claimed her bonus. It was refused on the basis that by the second method her ranking was 4.00 as there were three players above her (S. Graff, M. Seles and A. Vicario). The Court of Appeal held that the terms of her bonus required that the first method should be used, but as she was still only 2.5 (as opposed to 2.0) by such calculations she was not entitled to the bonus anyway.

⑨ *Walford v Miles* [1992] 2 WLR 174

In the course of negotiation concerning sale of the Miles' business for £2 million to Walford, Miles agreed that they would break any negotiations with any third party and would not consider any other alternative and would not accept a better offer but would deal exclusively with Walford. However, Miles continued to keep in touch with another party and sold the business to such party. Walford sued for breach of contract. The Court of Appeal held that it was only an agreement to negotiate and was unenforceable. On appeal, the House of Lords held that a lock-out agreement could be enforceable if it was covered fixed period of time, however, this agreement was unenforceable as it did not specify for how long it was to last.

⑩　*DMA Financial Solutions Ltd v BaaN U.K. Ltd.* [2000] WL 1629568

　　BaaN owned the rights in a computer programme called Coda, which was designed for use in financial accounting systems. BaaN decided to outsource the provision of training, and in 1998 entered into negotiations with DMA for DMA to become the authorised provider of training. At the end of 1998 there were no outstanding issues between the parties and the matter was referred to BaaN's legal department for a formal agreement to be drafted. The legal department raised objections to some of the terms and attempted to substitute the BaaN standard form agreement. DMA claimed that the contact was made in 1998 and that therefore the terms were no longer negotiable. BaaN claimed that the 1998 agreement was not a contract either because negotiations remained subject to the execution of a written contract or because there were still some matters of detail which required negotiation. It was held that the contract was concluded in 1998. There was no understanding that the contract was subject to a written agreement and a complete agreement was reached orally in 1998. The agreement did not omit any crucial element without which there would be no contract at all on grounds of uncertainty. Since the essential terms were agreed it did not assist BaaN to argue that there was no agreement on matters which had not been raised in the original negotiations. The parties were bound notwithstanding that there was a formal written agreement.

⑪　*Nicolene Ltd. v Simmonds* [1953] 1 All ER 822 (CA)

　　Nicolene claimed Simmonds' breach of contract of sale for steel bars. The contract provided that 'We are in agreement that the usual conditions of acceptance apply'. Simmonds insisted that there was no contract at all since there were no usual conditions of acceptance so that the words were meaningless. It was held that the contract was enforceable.

　　"In my opinion a distinction must be drawn between a clause which is meaningless and a clause which is yet to be agreed. A clause which is meaningless can often be ignored, whilst still leaving the contract good; whereas a clause which has yet to be agreed may mean that there is no contract at all, because the parties have not agreed on all the essential terms." (per Denning LJ)

⑫　*Lambert v HTV Cymru (Wales) Ltd and Another* [1998] FSR 874; [1998] 15 LS Gaz R 30

　　Lambert owned the copyright for certain cartoon characters and had granted HTV an exclusive licence to exploit the work and assigned all existing and future copyright to them. Under the terms of the assignment HTV promised to 'use all reasonable endeavours' to obtain for Lambert a first right of negotiation for book publishing from any future assignee. HTV assigned copyrights to a film maker and assigned other publishing rights to another company without obtaining for Lambert the first right of negotiation in respect of the publishing rights. Lambert claimed that HTV was in breach of the assignment terms. It was held that there was sufficient certainty in respect of the obligation of HTV. Although the right to first negotiation might itself not be enforceable, as HTV had no endeavours at all this was clearly not 'all reasonable endeavours'.

⑬ *Hargreaves Transport Ltd. v Lynch* [1969] 1 WLR 215

Land was sold by Hargreaves to Lynch subject to the condition that Lynch, the purchaser, should obtain planning permission to use the land as a transport depot. It was held that the purchaser was bound to make reasonable efforts to obtain the permission, but he was free from liability when those efforts failed.

⑭ *Smith v Butler* [1900] 1 QB 694

Butler bought a land from Smith on condition that a loan to Smith, which was secured by a mortgage on the premises, would be transferred to Butler. It was held that Butler could not withdraw before the time fixed for completion, and was bound to wait until then to see whether Smith could arrange the transfer.

⑮ *Actionstrength Ltd. v International Glass Engineering* [2002] 1 WLR 566

The first defendant (the "contractor") sub-contracted with the claimant (the "subcontractor") to provide workforce for building glass factory owned by the second defendant (the "factory owner"), however, the contractor delayed payment to the subcontractor under the subcontract. The factory owner promised orally with the subcontractor to pay the amounts due from the contractor if the subcontractor would keep the workforce. Later, the factory owner did not pay to the subcontractor, and was sued by it under the oral contract. The claim was dismissed since the oral contract was held to be a guarantee, not an indemnity.

この章のチェックリスト

1. 当事者間における合意に法的拘束力を生じさせないためには、通常どのような方法がとられるか。

(1) Domestic agreement の場合
　　(2) Commercial agreement の場合
 2．Letter of intent とは何か。どのような場合にどのような目的で作成されるのか。
 3．Letter of commitment、heads of terms、memorandum of understanding とは何か。
 4．Letter of intent はどのような法的効力を有しているのか。
 5．契約交渉において、未だ合意に達していない条項があるにかかわらず契約が成立することはあるか。
 6．Agreement to agree はどのような効力があるか。
 7．努力義務条項（best effort clause）はどのような効力があるか。
 8．Conditional agreement とは何か。
 9．Conditional agreement の condition が達成されないにかかわらず当事者が何らかの責任を負うべき場合はあるか。
10．書面によるべき契約にはどのようなものがあるか。
11．Deed とは何か。
12．Deed はどのようにして作成するのか。

第4章

契約の条項（Contractual Terms）

1．Term（契約条項）

　一般に、term という語は用語とか専門用語（technical term）の意味で用いられることが多いが、契約法上、この語はこの通常の用法と異なるいくつかの意味を有している。第1は契約期間という意味、第2は property law 上の定期土地利用権（term of years）という意味、第3は、契約や合意において当事者の義務や負担の内容を定めている条項や条件という意味である。ここでは、この第3の意味で用いる。

　契約は、口頭の契約であれ書面による契約であれ、法的拘束力を有する以上必ず terms を規定している。Terms の内には、express terms（明示条項）と implied term（黙示条項）の2種類があり、通常の契約にはこの双方が含まれている。Express term は、契約上明記又は明示的に言及されており、当事者間で合意されていることが明らかにわかる term のことである。Implied term とは、契約上明らかに示されてはいないが、当事者の黙示の意思、取引慣行又は法律により、契約の一部に含まれているとみなされる term のことである。

2．Terms（条項）と Representations（表示）の区別

　契約交渉中に当事者の一方が他方に対して、ある特定の事実や事項（statement）を告げた場合、そのことが契約の express term として契約の一部となっているのか、それとも単なる事実の表示（mere representation）に過ぎないのかが争われることがある。この区別に関する判例法上の原則は以下のとおりである。

(1)　売主が、買主による契約品購入の決定に重大な影響を及ぼす事実を告げ

た場合、その事実は mere representation ではなく express term となる（Bannerman v White (1861) 10 CB NS 844①、Couchman v Hill [1947] KB 554 (CA)②）。ただし、買主が、当該事実の真否にかかわらず購入したであろう場合は、term にはならない（Oscar Chess v Williams [1957] 1 WLR 370③）。

(2) 契約の目的物に関して、専門知識や特殊技能（special knowledge or skill）を有している当事者が相手方に告げた事実は、原則として express term と解される（上記 Oscar Chess v Williams 判決、Dick Bentley Productions Ltd v Harold Smith (Motors) Ltd [1965] 2 All ER 65 (CA)④）。

(3) 契約の対象事項に関して専門知識を有し、相手方が告げた事実の真偽を容易に確認できる立場にいる当事者に対して告げられた事実や事項は、原則として express term にはならない（Drake v Thos. Agnew & Sons Ltd. [2002] EWHC 294⑤）。

3．Classification of Terms（契約条項の分類）

イギリス法上、terms（契約条項）には以下の3種類がある。

（ⅰ） Conditions（契約条件条項）：契約の根幹を成している重要な条項

（ⅱ） Warranties（付随的条項）：Conditions ほど重要ではない、付随的な条項。事実に関する保証や約束の場合も多い。

（ⅲ） Innominate terms（無名条項）又は intermediate terms（中間条項）：契約が成立した時点では、conditions、warranties のどちらにも分類できない、両者の混合というべき条項。

個々の term が condition、warranty、innominate term のいずれであるかは、契約締結の時から決定している場合もあるが、実務上は、breach of term（契約条項違反）等に関する紛争が生じた後に、裁判所がその term が重要かつ本質的であるか否かを判断して決定することが多い。

(1) Conditions（契約条件条項）

Conditions は、契約の根幹にかかわる重要な条項である。Condition 違反の

結果損害を蒙った契約当事者は、違反した当事者に対し、当該損害の賠償を請求することができ、更に契約を解消してこれに基づく全ての義務を終了させること（rescission）ができる。Rescission（契約解消）により、当事者双方の契約上の義務が消滅するが、損害を受けた当事者は、契約が履行されていたとしたら得られたであろう遺失利益の賠償を受けることができる。契約を解消せずに追認（affirmation）し、損害賠償（damages）のみを請求してもかまわない。

　Conditionの語には、他にも複数の意味がある。第1に、conditions、warranties、innominate termsを含む全ての契約条項という意味で使われることがある。この意味では、terms and conditionsという表現がよく用いられる。第2に、契約の成立や契約上の権利義務の発生や消滅を偶発的な出来事や行為に拠らしめている場合の当該事実や行為もconditionsと呼ばれる。前述のとおり（本編第3章4）、このconditionsには、当事者とは関係のない事象の発生が契約の成立や義務の発生、消滅の条件となっているcontingent condition（偶発的条件）と当事者の行為や約束の履行が条件となっているpromissory condition（約束的条件）の2種類がある。後者はそれ自体、本章で扱うtermとしてのconditionでもある。

(2) Warranties（付随的条項）

　一般に、warrantiesとは、契約の条項（terms）の内、その不履行が契約の根幹に影響を与えない程度の付随的な条項のことである。

　Warranty違反があったとしても契約当事者の契約上の義務が消滅することはないが、その結果損害を蒙った当事者は、違反当事者に対して損害賠償を求めることができる。いずれの当事者も、契約上のその他の義務を免れることはできない。

　なお、warrantyの語も、termsの1種類という意味以外の意味で用いられることがある。第1に、製品のメーカーなどが最終消費者にwarrantyする場合は、商品の瑕疵について修理や取替えを約束することを意味している。これは、イギリス法上のいわゆるguarantee（保証）とほぼ同じ意味（ただし、guaranteeにも複数の意味がある。）であり、この意味でのwarrantyは「保

証」と和訳されている。保証としてのwarrantyも契約条項の1つではあるが、付随的条項という意味のwarrantyと常に一致するわけではない。第2に、保険契約（insurance contract）において、被保険者が一定の事実の存否や条件充足の事実を表明、表示することもwarrantyと呼ばれるが、一般的なwarrantyとは効果が異なる。保険者は、被保険者による保険契約上のwarranty違反を根拠に、保険事故発生時における保険金支払義務の免除を受けることができる（The Good Luck（1991）2 Lloyd's ep. 410）。

(3) Condition と warranty の区別

売買契約の買主が、対象となる商品が一定の品質を有さない場合にはその商品は購入しないことを明示していた場合、その品質が備わっていることを保証する旨の売主の合意（term）はconditionと解されることが多い。買主がそのような意思を明示していない場合は、一般的に言われている基準として、当該termが契約の重要な要素といえる場合はconditionとされ、比較的重要度の低い場合はwarrantyと解される（Behn v Burness（1863）3 B&S 751⑥、Couchman v Hill [1947] KB 554 (CA)）。このように、conditionとwarrantyの区別は、個々の契約条項の性質に応じて客観的に判断できるかのように説明されている。しかし、実際上、裁判所は従前から、契約条項そのものがconditionかwarrantyかを決定するというよりも、当該条項違反の程度や結果を考慮した上で契約解消という救済手段を与えるべきかどうかを先に判断し、契約解消が適当な場合にはcondition、そうでない場合はwarrantyと認定しているのではないかと思われる場合が少なくなかった（Poussard v Speirs（1876）1 QBD 410⑦、Bettini v Gye（1876）1 QBD 183⑧、Aerial Advertising Co. v Batchelor's Peas Ltd. (Manchester) [1938] 2 All ER 788⑨）。たとえば、Poussard v Spiers判決とBettini v Gye判決は、いずれもオペラ出演契約におけるオペラ歌手のリハーサル参加及びオペラ出演義務の不履行を理由に、主宰者が契約を解消しようとした事件である。裁判所は、リハーサルのみならず開演初日にも間に合わなかった前者の事件ではcondition違反による契約解消を認めたのに対し、リハーサルに数日遅れた程度の違反に過ぎなかった後者の事件ではwarranty違反と認定し、主宰者による契約解消を認めなかっ

た。同じ年に言渡されたこの2つの判決は、ほぼ同内容の条項でも、違反の程度により condition と解されたり warranty と解されたりすることを示している。

(4) Innominate terms（無名条項）

　上記(3)のとおり、契約条項の文言だけからでは、それが condition か warranty かを区別することができない場合があることは古くから認識されていた。その典型例は、charterparty（傭船契約）における seaworthiness clause（耐航性条項）である。この条項は、船の運航を不可能とするエンジンの欠陥から、数日出航を遅らせる程度の備品不足に至るまでのあらゆる耐航性に関する義務違反に適用があるので、当該条項の性質上 condition、warranty の両方を含んでいると言うほかない。そこで、20世紀後半に入ると、契約条項には、上記の seaworthiness clause のように、その性質上 warranty、condition のいずれかに分別することが不可能なもの、すなわち当該条項に定める義務違反があった後でなければ、それが契約解消に値するほど重要な義務なのか、それとも損害賠償だけを認めれば足りる程度の些細な義務なのかの判断ができない条項が存在することを正面から認める判決が現れた（Hong Kong Fir Shipping Co., Ltd. v Kawasaki Kisen Kaisha Ltd.［1962］2 QB 26 (CA)⑩）。このような条項は、warranties と conditions の中間という意味で intermediate terms（中間条項）、又はどちらとも決められないという意味で innominate terms（無名条項）と呼ばれるようになった。ある条項が innominate term である場合、裁判所は、その条項違反の程度や結果の重大性に基づき、condition 違反と同様に契約解消（rescission）まで認めるか、それとも warranty 違反と同じ効果（すなわち、damages のみ）しか認めないかを判断することになる（Cehave N.V. v Bremer Handelsgesellschaft mbH, The Hansa Nord［1976］QB 44 (CA)⑪）。

(5) Classification by the Parties（当事者による区別）

　契約当事者間で特定の条項を condition とするか warranty とするかについて合意した場合、裁判所は、原則としてこの合意どおりに判断する（上記

The Hansa Nord ［1976］QB 44 (CA)、Lambard North Central plc v Butterworth ［1987］QB 527 (CA)⑫。ただし、違反の程度及び結果が軽微な場合、裁判所はある条項を condition とする旨の合意や条項違反を解除事由と定める合意があるにかかわらず、当該条項違反による契約の解消を認めないこともある（L. Schuler AG v Wickman Machine Tool Sales ［1974］AC 235 (HL)⑬、Rice (T/A The Garden Guardian) v Great Yarmouth Borough Council ［2003］TCR 1,（2001）3 LGLR 4 (CA)⑭）。

4．Implied Terms（黙示条項）

Terms は、当事者間に明示的な合意がない場合でも、取引慣行（custom）、当事者間の意思（intention of the parties）、法律（court、statute）等により発生し、契約の一部となることがある。これを implied terms（黙示条項）といい、その発生原因に基づいて以下のような種類に分けられている。

(1) Terms implied by custom（商慣習による黙示条項）：特定の産業団体が設定した標準契約条項（standard terms）が当該業界内の取引において普及している場合等である。取引慣行に基づく implied term は、当事者間の別段の合意により排除できる。

(2) Terms implied by the courts in fact（裁判所の認定による黙示条項）：以下のような基準に基づいて裁判所が定める term であり、当事者間にそのような term を排除する旨の明示的な合意がないときのみ適用される。

（ⅰ） The Business Efficacy Test：当事者間で意図された取引を実行する上で不可欠であると客観的に判断される事項を implied term とする（The Moorcock（1889）14 PD 64⑮）。

（ⅱ） The Officious Bystander Test of common but unstated understanding：当事者間の契約交渉に officious bystander（お節介な見物人）が立ち会っていたとしたら、当然に指摘していたであろう事項、すなわち中立的な第三者の目から見て、当事者間で明示の合意がなかったとしても当然に契約の terms に含まれているはずであると判断される事項は terms に含まれる（Shirlaw v Southern Foundries (1926) Ltd. ［1939］2 KB 206 (CA)⑯、

Malik v BCCI［1997］3 WLR 95 (HL)⑰）。

 (3) Terms implied by the courts in law（判例法による黙示条項）：特定の種類の契約において、当事者間の合理的な意思に合致するか否かにかかわらず、裁判所が公共政策的な見地から implied term を設定することがある。この implied terms は、当事者間の明示的な合意によって排除することができない（Liverpool City Council v Irvin［1977］AC 239 (HL)⑱）。

 (4) Statutory implied terms（制定法に基づく黙示条項）：物品売買（sale of goods）その他特定の種類の契約に関しては、特別の制定法（the Sale of Goods Act 1979等）によって一定の implied terms が定められている。この implied terms は、当事者間の合意によって排除することができる場合とできない場合とがある（the Unfair Contract Terms Act 1977 s6）。

5．The Sale of Goods Act 1979

 Statute（制定法）に基づく implied terms として最も重要なものは the Sale of Goods Act 1979が売買契約に関して規定する terms である。

 (1) 同法には、以下の implied conditions が定められている。

（ⅰ） 売主が対象商品を販売する権限（the right to sell）を有していること（s12）；

（ⅱ） 対象商品が売主による商品表示に一致（comform to their description）していること（s13(1)）；

（ⅲ） 対象商品が完全な品質（satisfactory quality）を有していること（s14(2)）；

（ⅳ） 対象商品が、買主が売主に知らせた使用目的に合理的に適合（reasonably fit for the purpose make known to the seller）していること（s14(3)）.

 (2) 同法は、更に以下の implied warranties を定めている。

（ⅰ） 対象商品に、買主が告知したもの以外の第三者の権利が設定され、又は付着していないこと（ss12(2)(a)、12(4)）

（ⅱ） 購入した対象商品の買主による占有が妨害されない（quiet possession) こと (ss12(2)(b)、12(5))。

ただし、当事者間で上記(ⅰ)、(ⅱ)の条項を condition とする旨の明示の合意をすれば、原則としてその合意が優先する。

(3) 同法は、コモンロー上の諸原則に一定限度で修正を加えている。たとえば、事業者間の売買取引における売主による condition 違反に関しては、当該違反が、これを根拠とする買主の契約解消権を認めては不合理な程度に小さい場合 (where the breach of condition is slight such that it would be unreasonable for the purchaser to rescind)、当該 breach of condition は、a breach of warranty として取り扱うべきものとしている (s15A(1))。すなわち、condition 違反があるにかかわらず、損害賠償請求だけしかできないことになる。また、消費者契約 (consumer agreement) に関して、消費者である買主は、damages、rescission に加えて、商品の修理や取替えを要求する権利 (option to repair or replace the goods) も与えられている (s48A(1))。

【CASES】

① *Bannerman v White* (1861) 10 CB NS 844

A buyer of hops asked the seller if sulphur had been used in the cultivation, adding that, if it had, he would not even bother to ask the price. The seller assured that sulphur had not been used. This was held to be a term.

② *Couchman v Hill* [1947] KB 554 (CA)

Couchman bought Hill's heifer at auction. The catalog described that the heifer was unserved. It also stated that no warranty was given as to description. Couchman required unserved heifer and verified this with both Hill and the auctioneer before sale. Later, the heifer suffered miscarriage and died, and Couchman successfully sued Hill for breach of warranty.

"... there was clearly an oral offer of a warranty which over-rode the stultifying condition in the printed terms..." (per SCOTT LJ)

③ *Oscar Chess v Williams* [1957] 1 WLR 370

A motor dealer sold a car described as a 1948 Morris 10. In fact it was a 1939 model. It was held that this was not a term. The buyer might still have entered into the contract if he had known the truth, though he would have paid less price. The court also considered it to be significant that the seller was relying in good faith on the forged log-book and that he was dealing with a motor dealer who could have got the information checked themselves.

 "The seller did not intend to bind himself so as to warrant the car was a 1948 model. If the seller was asked to pledge himself to it, he would at once have said 'I cannot do that. I have only the log-book to go by, the same as you'." (per Denning LJ)

④ *Dick Bentley Productions Ltd. v Harold Smith (Motors) Ltd* [1965] 1 All ER (CA)

A dealer sold a Bentley car, claiming that it had done only 20,000 miles since a replacement engine was fitted. In fact it has done nearly 100,000. His statement was held to be a warranty since he was in a better position to know the truth than the buyer.

⑤ *Drake v Thos. Agnew & Sons Ltd* [2002] EWHC 294

Callan, an art dealer, bought from Agnew a painting described as 'by Sir Anthony van Dyck' as being agent of Richard Drake, a Texan millionaire, who requested him to acquire an Old Master to add his art collection. The painting had been bought by Agnew from Sotheby's, who had described it in the catalogue as being 'after Sir Anthony van Dyck' which indicated that it was a copy. In fact, there had been expert debate about its provenance. Agnew did not mention it, but it volunteered to answer any questions Callan may have about the painting before purchase, and he could easily have found it. It was held that Agnew's statement that it was 'by van Dyck' ought to have known that the statement was merely an opinion which Callan should verify himself.

⑥ *Behn v Burness* (1863) 3 B&S 751

A ship was stated in the contract of charterparty to be 'now in the port of Amsterdam', however, she was not in that port at the date of the contract. The statement was held to be a condition, since this is the common understanding of charterers.

⑦ *Poussard v Speirs* (1876) 1 QBD 410

Mme Poussard was engaged by Spiers to play the leading part of Friquette in a new opera which was to open at the Criterion Theatre on November 28, 1874, and which was to run for up to three months. On November 23 she fell ill and was unable to attend rehearsals. On November 25 Spiers entered into a contract with Miss Lewis, by which she was to play the part from November 28 to

December 25 if Mme Poussard had not recovered by the opening night. Mme Poussard continued ill until December 4, when she asked for her part back, but was refused. Mme Poussard claimed that her contract had been wrongfully repudiated. It was held that Spiers was entitled to cancel Mme Poussard's contract. The requirement for her to be available for rehearsals and on the opening night was a condition of the contract which she had breached.

⑧　*Bettini v Gye* (1876) 1 QBD 183

Gye, the director of the Royal Italian Opera at Covent Garden, engaged Bettini to sing in concerts and operas 'to fill the role of primo tenor assoluto in the theatres, halls, and drawing rooms in Great Britain and Ireland' from March 30 to July 13 1875. He was required 'to be in London without fail at least six days before the commencement of his engagement for the purpose of rehearsals.' Bettini was prevented by temporary illness from being in London until March 28. He gave no advance notice of this delay to Gye, and when he arrived in London, Gye refused to accept his services. It was held that this refusal was unjustified. Bettini was only in breach of a warranty, not a condition as missing a few rehearsals was not significant to a 15-week season.

⑨　*Aerial Advertising Co. v Batchelor's Peas Ltd. (Manchester)* [1938] 2 All ER 788

Aerial Advertising ("AA") conducted an advertising campaign for Batchelar's Peas ("BP") by flying over various towns trailing behind the aeroplane a banner saying 'Eat Batchelor's Peas'. It was agreed that the proposed schedule of flight be confirmed every day, however, on 11 November 1937, AA's pilot failed to contact BP and flew over Manchester and Salford on his own decision. This was Armistice Day, and people gathered in the main square of Salford observing two minute silence while the aeroplane towing the banner appeared. Letters poured into BP's threatening to boycott its products. BP refused further performance of the contract since the effect of this breach of contract was too serious. It was held that the term was a condition, and the breach led to the repudiation of contract.

⑩　*Hong Kong Fir Shipping Co., Ltd. v Kawasaki Kisen Kaisha Ltd.* [1962] 2 QB 26 (CA)

Hong Kong Fir Shipping chartered a ship to Kawasaki Kisen for 24 months, 'being in every way fitted for ordinary cargo service.' The chief engineer was incompetent and the ship was ancient, and as a result, 20 weeks out of 24 months were lost. It was held that Kawasaki Kisen was not entitled to rescind the contract as the breach was not sufficiently substantial.

"There are many contractual undertakings...which cannot be categorized as being 'conditions' or 'warranties' ... Of such undertakings, all that can be predicted is that some breaches will and others will not give rise to an event which will deprive the party not in default of substantially the whole benefit which was intended that he should obtain from the contract; and the legal consequences of a breach of such an undertaking, unless provided for expressly in the contract, depend on the nature of the event to which the breach gives rise and do not follow automatically from a prior classification of the undertaking as a 'condition' or a 'warranty'." (per Diplock LJ)

⑪ *Cehave N.V. v Bremer Handelsgesellschaft mbH, The Hansa Nord* [1976] QB 44 (CA)

Bremer sold citrus pulp pellets to Cehave under the term that 'shipment to be made in good condition'. When a particular consignment of goods arrived at Rotterdam, the market price had fallen and 1,260 tons out of total 3,293 tons was found to be damaged. Cehave rejected the whole cargo on the ground of the breach of the term. It was held that the contractual term 'shipment to be made in good condition' was not a condition, but an innominate term.

"If a small portion of the whole cargo was not in good condition and arrived a little unsound, it should be met by a price allowance. The buyer should not have the right to reject the whole cargo unless it was serious or substantial" (per Lord Denning MR)

⑫ *Lambard North Central plc v Butterworth* [1987] QB 527 (CA)

Lambard leased a computer to Butterworth. The agreement provided that punctual payment of each instalment of hire was the essence of the agreement, and failure entitled the lessor to terminate the agreement. The lessee was late in paying the third, fourth and fifth instalments, and when the sixth was overdue, Lambard terminated the agreement. It was held that prompt payment was a condition of the contract, and the lessor may terminate the contract if any payment was not made, even though such breach was not regarded as giving rise to serious consequence.

⑬ *L. Schuler AG v Wickman Machine Tool Sales* [1974] AC 235 (HL)

Wickman, an English company, was given sole selling rights for German company's panel presses. The distribution contract provided that it was a 'condition of agreement' that the distributor should visit six named customers a week to solicit orders. It was held that such clause was not a condition in the sense that a single trivial breach would entitle the innocent party to terminate the contract.

⑭　*Rice T/A The Garden Guardian v Great Yarmouth Borough Council* [2001] 3 LGLR 4 (CA)

A standard form contract prepared by the Great Yarmouth Borough Council for providing Rice (the contractor) of leisure management and grounds maintenance services contained the following provisions:

Clause 6: During the contract period the contractor shall provide the service in a proper and skilful and workmanship manner, to the contract standard and to the entire satisfaction of the authorized officer.

Clause 23: If the contractor commits a breach of any of its obligations under the contract, the council may, without prejudice to any accrued rights or remedies under the contract, terminate the contractor's employment under the contract by notice in writing with immediate effect.

The Council invoked the termination clause and cancelled the contract since it was not satisfied with the contractor's work (the summer bedding was not completed in time and the football pitches were not ready for the start of the season. It was held that this was a classic example of an innominate term, and that as the cumulative effect of the breaches did not justify a termination, the Council was liable to the contractor for wrongful termination. A clause in the contract, providing for a right to terminate for breach of any obligations, could not have been intended that there should be a right to terminate for any breach of any term.

⑮　*The Moorcock* (1889) 14 PD 64

The appellants who were wharfingers and jetty owners claimed that they were not liable for the damage sustained by the respondent's vessel whilst lying at their jetty as they had never said that the berth would be safe for the ship when the tide went out. The court held that the jetty owners were liable, as there was an implied term that the mooring would be safe.

"I think if they let out their jetty for use they imply that they have taken reasonable care to see whether the berth, which is the essential part of the use of the jetty, is safe, and if it is not safe, and if they have not taken such reasonable care, it is their duty to warn persons with whom they have dealings that they have not done so." (per Bowen LJ)

⑯ *Shirlaw v Southern Foundries (1926) Ltd.* [1939] 2 KB 206 (CA)

Shirlaw was appointed to be management director of the Southern Foundries (the "Company") for 10 years. The company was then taken over by another company, whose articles allowed the removal of a director by two other directors and the company secretary. Shirlaw was removed as a director, resulting his losing the job as managing director under the contract. It was held that the Company was in breach of two implied terms that (ⅰ) the Company should not remove Shirlaw from his position of director during the term, and (ⅱ) the Company would not alter its articles of association to enable someone else to remove him from his office.

"Prima facie that which in any contract is left to be implied and need not be expressed is something so obvious that it goes without saying; so that, if while the parties were making their bargain an officious bystandarder were to suggest some express provisions for it in their agreement, they would testily suppress him with a common, 'Oh, of course'." (per MacKinnon LJ)

⑰ *Malik v BCCI* [1997] 3 WLR 95 (HL)

Malik, a former employee of BCCI, claimed damages for the adverse effect on his future employment prospects as a result of dishonesty and corruption of BCCI. It was held that there was an implied term in all employment contracts that the employer will not, without reasonable and proper cause, conduct himself in such a manner as to destroy or seriously damages the relationship of confidence and trust between the employer and the employee, unless such term has been expressly amended by the parties.

⑱ *Liverpool City Council v Irvin* [1977] AC 239 (HL)

The tenants of a block of flats withheld the rent on the basis that the landlord (the Council) was in breach of contract for not keeping the lifts and communal stairwells in a reasonable state of repair. There was no formal agreement that the landlord was responsible for this, but the House of Lords held that, as a matter of policy, there were implied terms to this effect.

【*STATUTE*】
SALE OF GOODS ACT 1979
12. Implied terms about title, etc.

(1) In a contract of sale, other than one to which subsection (3) below applies, there is an implied term on the part of the seller that in the case of a sale he has a right to sell the goods, and in the case of an agreement to sell he will have such

a right at the time when the property is to pass.

(2) In a contract of sale, other than one to which subsection (3) below applies, there is also an implied term that—

  (a) the goods are free, and will remain free until the time when the property is to pass, from any charge or encumbrance not disclosed or known to the buyer before the contract is made, and

  (b) the buyer will enjoy quiet possession of the goods except so far as it may be disturbed by the owner or other person entitled to the benefit of any charge or encumbrance so disclosed or known.

(3) This subsection applies to a contract of sale in the case of which there appears from the contract or is to be inferred from its circumstances an intention that the seller should transfer only such title as he or a third person may have.

(4) In a contract to which subsection (3) above applies there is an implied term that all charges or encumbrances known to the seller and not known to the buyer have been disclosed to the buyer before the contract is made.

(5) In a contract to which subsection (3) above applies there is also an implied term that none of the following will disturb the buyer's quiet possession of the goods, namely—

  (a) the seller;

  (b) in a case where the parties to the contract intend that the seller should transfer only such title as a third person may have, that person;

  (c) anyone claiming through or under the seller or that third person otherwise than under a charge or encumbrance disclosed or known to the buyer before the contract is made.

(5A) As regards England and Wales and Northern Ireland, the term implied by subsection (1) above is a condition and the terms implied by subsections (2), (4) and (5) above are warranties.

(6) Paragraph 3 of Schedule 1 below applies in relation to a contract made before 18 May 1973.

13. Sale by description

(1) Where there is a contract for the sale of goods by description, there is an implied term that the goods will correspond with the description.

(1A) As regards England and Wales and Northern Ireland, the term implied by subsection (1) above is a condition.

(2) If the sale is by sample as well as by description it is not sufficient that the bulk of the goods corresponds with the sample if the goods do not also correspond with the description.

(3) A sale of goods is not prevented from being a sale by description by reason only that, being exposed for sale or hire, they are selected by the buyer.

(4) Paragraph 4 of Schedule 1 below applies in relation to a contract made before 18 May 1973.

14. Implied terms about quality or fitness

(1) Except as provided by this section and section 15 below and subject to any other enactment, there is no implied term about the quality or fitness for any particular purpose of goods supplied under a contract of sale.

(2) Where the seller sells goods in the course of a business, there is an implied term that the goods supplied under the contract are of satisfactory quality.

(2A) For the purposes of this Act, goods are of satisfactory quality if they meet the standard that a reasonable person would regard as satisfactory, taking account of any description of the goods, the price (if relevant) and all the other relevant circumstances.

(2B) For the purposes of this Act, the quality of goods includes their state and condition and the following (among others) are in appropriate cases aspects of the quality of goods—

(a) fitness for all the purposes for which goods of the kind in question are commonly supplied,

(b) appearance and finish,

(c) freedom from minor defects,

(d) safety, and

(e) durability.

(2C) The term implied by subsection (2) above does not extend to any matter making the quality of goods unsatisfactory—

(a) which is specifically drawn to the buyer's attention before the contract is made,

(b) where the buyer examines the goods before the contract is made, which that examination ought to reveal, or

(c) in the case of a contract for sale by sample, which would have been apparent on a reasonable examination of the sample.

(2D) If the buyer deals as consumer or, in Scotland, if a contract of sale is a consumer contract, the relevant circumstances mentioned in subsection (2A) above include any public statements on the specific characteristics of the goods made about them by the seller, the producer or his representative, particularly in advertising or on labelling.

(2E) A public statement is not by virtue of subsection (2D) above a relevant circumstance for the purposes of subsection (2A) above in the case of a contract of sale, if the seller shows that—

　(a)　at the time the contract was made, he was not, and could not reasonably have been, aware of the statement,

　(b)　before the contract was made, the statement had been withdrawn in public or, to the extent that it contained anything which was incorrect or misleading, it had been corrected in public, or

　(c)　the decision to buy the goods could not have been influenced by the statement.

　(2F)　Subsections (2D) and (2E) above do not prevent any public statement from being a relevant circumstance for the purposes of subsection (2A) above (whether or not the buyer deals as consumer or, in Scotland, whether or not the contract of sale is a consumer contract) if the statement would have been such a circumstance apart from those subsections.

　(3)　Where the seller sells goods in the course of a business and the buyer, expressly or by implication, makes known—

　(a)　to the seller, or

　(b)　where the purchase price of part of it is payable by instalments and the goods were previously sold by a credit-broker to the seller, to that credit-broker, any particular purpose for which the goods are being bought, there is an implied term that the goods supplied under the contract are reasonably fit for that purpose, whether or not that is a purpose for which such goods are commonly supplied, except where the circumstances show that the buyer does not rely, or that it is unreasonable for him to rely, on the skill or judgment of the seller or credit-broker.

　(4)　An implied term about quality or fitness for a particular purpose may be annexed to a contract of sale by usage.

　(5)　The preceding provisions of this section apply to a sale by a person who in the course of a business is acting as agent for another as they apply to a sale by a principal in the course of a business, except where that other is not selling in the course of a business and either the buyer knows that fact or reasonable steps are taken to bring it to the notice of the buyer before the contract is made.

　(6)　As regards England and Wales and Northern Ireland, the terms implied by subsections (2) and (3) above are conditions.

　(7)　Paragraph 5 of Schedule 1 below applies in relation to a contract made on or after 18 May 1973 and before the appointed day, and paragraph 6 in relation to one made before 18 May 1973.

　(8)　In subsection (7) above and paragraph 5 of Schedule 1 below references to the appointed day are to the day appointed for the purposes of those provisions

by an order of the Secretary of State made by statutory instrument.
15A. Modification of remedies for breach of condition in non-consumer cases
　(1)　Where in the case of a contract of sale—
　　(a)　the buyer would, apart from this subsection, have the right to reject goods by reason of a breach on the part of the seller of a term implied by section 13, 14 or 15 above, but
　　(b)　the breach is so slight that it would be unreasonable for him to reject them,
then, if the buyer does not deal as consumer, the breach is not to be treated as a breach of condition but may be treated as a breach of warranty.
　(2)　This section applies unless a contrary intention appears in, or is to be implied from, the contract.
　(3)　It is for the seller to show that a breach fell within subsection (1)(b) above.
　(4)　This section does not apply to Scotland.

この章のチェックリスト

1．Terms とは何か。
2．契約交渉中における特定の事実や事項の告知が term であるか representation であるかをどのように区別するか。
3．Conditions と warranties とはどこが違うのか。
4．裁判所は conditions と warranties をどのようにして区別しているか。
5．Innominate terms とは何か。
6．Implied terms はどのような場合に発生するか。
　(1)　Terms implied by custom
　(2)　Terms implied by the courts in fact
　(3)　Terms implied by the courts in law
　(4)　Statutory implied terms
7．裁判所はどのような判断基準で implied terms を認定するか。
　(1)　The Business Efficacy Test
　(2)　The Officious Bystander Test

8. The Sale of Goods Act に基づく implied terms にはどのようなものがあるか。

 (1) Implied conditions

 (2) Implied warranties

第5章

契約の解釈
（Interpretation of Contract）

1．契約解釈上の基本原則

　契約当事者の一方が裁判所に対して相手方の契約違反による救済を求めてきたとき、裁判所はまず、違反があると主張している契約条項がどのような義務を定めているのかを判断するために契約解釈を行わなければならない。契約解釈とは、契約条項に用いられているある1つの語句や表現が複数の意味を有する場合に、その内の1つを選択して契約条項の意味内容を確定する作業のことである。伝統的に、イギリスの裁判所は、契約条項の意味内容を確定するに当たって、そのような合意をする際に両当事者が用いた言動のみに基づいて、合理的な通常人（reasonable person）ならばどのような意図でそのような言動をするであろうかを客観的に判断し、当事者が実際にどんな意図を持っていたか等の当事者の内心にかかわる事情は考慮の対象にしない手法を採っている。これを objective approach（客観的手法）という。本編第1章1で述べたとおり、Smith v Hughes 判決（(1871) LR 6 QB 597）は、契約成立の判断基準としてこの客観的手法を用い、以下のとおり判示している。

　　If, whatever a man's real intention may be, he so conducts himself that a reasonable man would believe that he was assenting to the terms proposed by the other party, and that the other party upon that belief enters into a contract with him, the man thus conducting himself would be equally bound as if he had intended to agree to the other party's terms.（per Blackburn J.）

　裁判所は、この手法を用いて書面による契約（written agreement）を解釈する際、以下の解釈準則（rules of interpretation）を適用している。

まず、契約書を交わした両当事者の意思（parties' intention）は、原則として、契約書の文言そのものから解釈しなければならない（Intention must be normally ascertained from documents itself）（British Movietonews, Ltd. v London and District Cinemas, Ltd.［1952］AC 166 (HL)①）。そして、契約書の文言は、平易かつ単純に字義どおりの意味（plain and literal meaning）に理解されなければならない（Robertson v French (1803) 4 East 130）。これは契約の解釈に関する最も基本的な原則であり、literal rule（文理準則）と呼ばれている。この解釈方法を採るに当っては、個々の条項の字句だけには拘泥せず、契約書全体から（from the whole of the agreement）両当事者の合理的な意思を推定すべきものとされている（Ford v Beech (1848) 11 QB 852）。これを the noscitur a sociis principle（近辺用語類推原則）という。

　上記の literal rule の帰結として、契約書の文言が明確な場合、契約交渉中における当事者の言動その他契約締結前の事情によって契約文言の通常の意味と異なる解釈をすることは、原則として許されない（Negotiations prior to contract inadmissible）。また、契約締結後における当事者の言動（subsequent conduct of the parties）も、原則として契約文言と異なる解釈をする根拠や契約における合意内容を変更する証拠になり得ない（L. Schuler AG v Wickman Machine Tool Sales［1974］AC 235 (HL)）。

　他方、契約書の文言が不明確な場合には、契約交渉（negotiations）中の事実関係（Prenn v Simmonds［1971］1 WLR 1381）、取引実務（market practice）、業界の取引慣行（custom in the industry）その他の外部的証拠（external evidence）を用いて当事者意思を解釈し、合意の内容を確定することができる（Ambiguities may be resolved by external evidence）。

　なお、2つ以上の意味に解される余地がある条項は、できる限り当該契約を有効とする意味に解釈しなければならないとされている（Words susceptive of two meanings receive that which will make the instrument valid）。

　上記に加え、裁判所は、literal rule に従った契約解釈のため、以下のような解釈原則をしばしば用いている。これらは、両当事者の意思が上記準則だけでは明確にできない場合のみに適用すべき2次的な解釈準則である。

　（ⅰ）The expressio unius est exclusio alterius principle（規定外排除原

則）：契約文中の語句や条項が一定の事項についてのみ言及しているときは、その他の類似する事項を排除する意図と解される。たとえば、工場と家屋の売買において、契約書が「家屋内の家具も売買の対象とする」旨を記載していた場合、工場内の設備は売買の対象から除く意図と解される（Hare v Horton (1883) 5 B & Ad 715）。

（ⅱ） The ejusdem generis principle（同類解釈原則）：いくつかの事項に言及した後に「and others」と記載されているとき、この「others」に含まれる事項は、既に言及されている事項により限定を受ける。たとえば、傭船契約（charterparty）において「war, disturbance, or any other cause」による事故の場合は責任を負わない旨の条項があった場合、「any other cause」は「war, disturbance」と同種の原因による事故に限られるので、流氷（ice）による事故の場合は免責されない（Tillmanns v S.S. Knutsford [1908] 2 KB 385）。

（ⅲ） The contra proferentem rule（「起草者の不利に」の原則）：あいまいな規定は、当該条項により利益を受けることとなる者の不利益（against the party putting forward）に解釈すべしという原則である。本編第6章の責任排除条項（exclusion clause）の解釈に関してよく用いられるが、それ以外の条項の解釈にも適用されることがある。

2．The Parol Evidence Rule（口頭証拠排除の原則）

The parol evidence rule は、不明確な主張を排斥して裁判手続の長期化を避けることを目的とする証拠法上の原則の1つであるが、事実上、上記1の書面による契約に適用される文理準則を補完する働きをしている。この parol evidence rule に基づき、書面による契約の当事者は、契約書に記載されていない事項が契約に含まれること、契約書に記載された事項が変更されていること、契約書が間違っていること等を立証するために契約書以外の証拠（extrinsic evidence）を提出することが禁じられる。

判例（Jacobs v Batavia and General Plantations (1924) 1 Ch 287）はこの原則を以下のとおり定義している。

Parol evidence will not be admitted to provide that some particular term, which had been verbally agreed upon, has been omitted (by design or otherwise) from a written instrument constituting a valid and operative contract between the parties.

　この法原則に基づき、書面による契約があるときは、契約の全てのtermsが書面化されているとの推定が働く。ただし、契約の意味を明らかにする証拠、契約が見せかけに過ぎないこと（a mere sham）の証拠、契約の変更の証拠、estoppelの根拠事実の証拠等を示してこの推定を争うことは許されている。すなわち、以下に列挙するような事情を主張立証するために、契約書以外の事項を用いることは可能である。

　(1) 書面による契約が不完全であること：書面契約の完全性の推定に対する反証のためであれば、外部証拠を提出することができる。契約の一部が口頭で成立しているとして争う場合等である。（J. Evans & Son (Portsmouth) Ltd v Andrea Merzario Ltd ［1976］1 WLR 1078 (CA)②）。

　(2) Implied terms（黙示条項）の存在：契約中に明記されていない事項について、implied termsの存否、内容は、外部証拠により証明できる（Gillespie Bros. & Co v Cheney Eggar & Co ［1896］2 QB 59）。書面化された契約と矛盾しない追加的合意を証するために慣習や取引慣行（custom or trade usage）の存在を立証することも許される。

　(3) 契約の履行を停止するための証拠、契約の有効性を争う証拠：条件付契約におけるconditions precedent、conditions subsequent（停止条件、解除条件）が成就した事実、consideration（約因）の有無、contractual intentionの存否、misrepresentation（本編第7章参照）、mistake（本編第8章1）等の立証は、外部証拠により行うことができる。

　(4) Rectification（契約書の誤記）：当事者間の口頭合意を書面化した場合等において、契約書に不正確な記述がある場合、これを訂正（rectify）するための証拠として、口頭合意の内容を証明できる（本編第8章1(4)）。

　(5) Identification of subject matter（目的物の特定）：当事者間の契約書が契約の目的物を明確に示していない場合は、契約書以外の事項は、目的物を特定するための証拠となり得る。土地売買における土地の所在地を証明する場合

等である。

(6) Collateral contract（付随的な契約）：書面化された契約の変更、追加ではなく、独立した別個の口頭契約が存在することの証明は許される。たとえば、被告がその所有する建物の修繕を約束し、原告が修繕後に建物をリースする約束を口頭でしていたが、後日リース契約だけが書面化された場合、原告は口頭契約を根拠に被告に修繕を請求できる（Mann v Nunn（1874）30 L.T. 526）。Collateral contract の内容が書面化された契約の条項と抵触する場合であっても構わない（City and Westminster Properties（1934）Ltd v Mudd [1959] Ch 129③）。

3．Entire Agreement Clause（完全合意条項）

　国際取引に関する標準的契約書には、たいていの場合、当該書面には当事者間の合意の全てが記載されていることを確認する旨の条項が含まれている。これは entire agreement clause（完全合意条項）又は sole agreement clause（唯一の合意条項）と呼ばれ、当該契約の解釈に関する問題に the parol evidence rule が適用されることを明確にすること、及び上記2に示した the parol evidence rule の例外の一部（2の(2)、(4)、(6)等）を排除することを主たる目的とするものである（Inntrepreneur Pub Co. v East Crown Ltd [2000] 2 Lloyd's Rep 611④）。国際取引に関する契約は必ずイギリス法に準拠するとは限らないので、契約文言に反する解釈をされないようにする上で重要な規定である。

　典型的な entire agreement clause の例は、以下のとおりである。

　　This Agreement constitutes the entire agreement and understanding between the parties hereto with respect to the subject matter hereof and merges and supersedes all prior discussions, agreements, contracts or understandings, expressed or implied, between the parties hereto, and neither party shall be bound by any condition, definition, warranty or representation other than as expressly provided for herein.

【CASES】

① *British Movietonews, Ltd. v London and District Cinemas, Ltd.* [1952] AC 166 (HL)

A film distributors ("BM") contracted with the owner of a chain of cinemas ("LDC") to supply films. The contract permitted either party to terminate the contract by giving four weeks notice. In 1943, because of World War II, the film supply was restricted by the governmental order, and the parties entered into a supplementary agreement providing that 'the principal agreement shall remain in full force and effect until such time as the order is cancelled.' At the time of this agreement, the parties expected that the order would have been abrogated immediately after the war was over. However, the order was continued in force even after the war. In 1948, LDC gave BM a four weeks prior notice for termination of the contract pursuant to the termination clause of the original contract. BM refused and sued for breach of contract. In the Court of Appeal, it was decided that in light of the parties' presumed intention the supplementary agreement was to endure only as long as war-time conditions persisted, and that since the continuance of the order beyond that period was quite uncontemplated by the parties, LDC should be relieved from liability under the termination clause of the original contract. However, the House of Lords decided that the intention of the parties must be ascertained by the document itself, and the court should not rewrite it in the light of what the parties might have had in mind at the time of the contract. According to the clear and unequivocal wordings of the supplementary agreement, LDC was bound by the contract.

② *J. Evans & Son (Portsmouth) Ltd v Andrea Merzario Ltd* [1976] 1 WLR 1078 (CA)

An importer of machines ("Evans") contracted with the carrier for carriage of machines to England. Under the written contract, the carrier was given complete freedom as to method of transportation. After execution of the written contract, the carrier proposed to transport machines in containers and gave Evans an oral assurance that the containers would be shipped below deck. Evans agreed. Later, a container was shipped on deck and fell overboard. Evans sued the carrier in breach of the oral promise. It was held that the oral assurance was an express term of the contract, and as the contract was partly oral and partly written, evidence of the oral term was admissible.

③ *City and Westminster Properties (1934) Ltd v Mudd* [1959] Ch 129

Mudd was a tenant of a shop and had lived in the office at the back of the shop. The landlord proposed a draft renewal contract, containing a covenant by the lessee 'not to permit or suffer the demised premises to be used as a place for lodging or sleeping'. The tenant executed the contract since the landlord's agent told him that the landlord would not object to his continuing to live in a shop if he signed the lease. Later, the landlord sought forfeiture of the lease on the ground of breach of that covenant. It was held that the tenant was entitled to rely on the promise by the landlord's agent since he had signed the lease only because of that promise.

④ *Inntrepreneur Pub Co. v East Crown Ltd* [2000] 2 Lloyd's Rep 611

Inntrepreneur Pub Co. leased a public house to East Crown with a covenant that the tenant had agreed to purchase its supply of beer from the landlord. The tenant later alleged that a collateral warranty, made orally, whereby the covenant was released. It was held that even if a collateral warranty was established (which had not been established), it would be deprived of legal effect by the entire agreement clause in the lease contract, making it clear that the only agreed terms were those in the written contract.

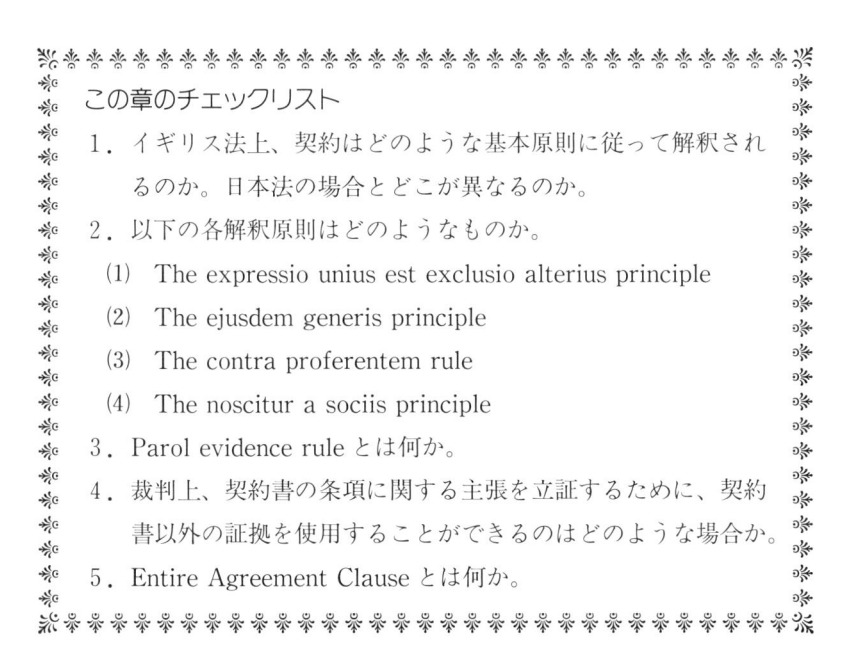

この章のチェックリスト

1. イギリス法上、契約はどのような基本原則に従って解釈されるのか。日本法の場合とどこが異なるのか。
2. 以下の各解釈原則はどのようなものか。
   (1) The expressio unius est exclusio alterius principle
   (2) The ejusdem generis principle
   (3) The contra proferentem rule
   (4) The noscitur a sociis principle
3. Parol evidence rule とは何か。
4. 裁判上、契約書の条項に関する主張を立証するために、契約書以外の証拠を使用することができるのはどのような場合か。
5. Entire Agreement Clause とは何か。

第 6 章

Exclusion Clause（責任排除条項）の一般原則

1．Exclusion Clause（責任排除条項）

　商取引に関する契約（business contract）には、通常、当事者の義務や責任を何らかの方法で排除又は制限することを内容とする明示条項（express terms）が規定される。これらは、exclusion clause、exemption clause、limitation clause 等と呼ばれている。ここでは、総括して exclusion clause（責任排除条項）と呼ぶ。Exclusion clause による責任制限の方法には、損害賠償額の限定（limiting compensation payable）、救済措置の限定（limiting remedies available）、請求期限（time limits）、証拠制限（conclusive evidence）、黙示条項の排除（excluding implied terms）、契約上の義務の限定（limiting contractual obligations）等の種類がある。

　イギリスの裁判所は、契約成立要件を充足した契約の条項には当事者間で合意したとおりの法律効果を認めることを原則としている。しかし、exclusion clause に関しては、一方当事者が取引上優越した立場を利用して強要したり、相手方の無知に乗じて契約書に盛り込んだりすることが少なくないので、不合理な条項の適用範囲を政策的に限定するため、様々な手段が講じられている。現在のイギリス法上、契約当事者が exclusion clause に依拠して契約違反の責任を免れるためには、（ⅰ）当該条項が契約の内容になっていること（incorporated into contract）、（ⅱ）当該条項の解釈上、適用される場合であることが明確なこと、（ⅲ）the Unfair Contract Terms Act 1977 の適用がないこと、又は適用がある場合はその要件を充たしていること、（ⅳ）the Unfair Terms in Consumer Contracts Regulations 1999 の適用がないこと、又は適用がある場合はその要件を充たしていることという 4 つのハードルを越えなければなら

ない。以下、それぞれについて説明する。

２．Incorporation into the contract（契約の内容となること）

　イギリス契約法上、express term（明示条項）は、両当事者が契約締結時にその term の存在に関する通知（notice）を受けていない限り契約の一部とはならない。この法原則は全ての明示条項に適用があるが、実際上、notice の存否は、exclusion clause に関して争われることが最も多い。ただし、ここでいう notice は、契約の相手方にその存在を現実に知らせていること（actual knowledge）という意味ではなく、合理的に知り得る状態にすることで足りる。
　ある条項について notice がなされたか否かの判断基準は、相手方が当該条項を記載した書面に署名した場合とそうでない場合とで異なっている。

(1)　Signing a document（署名）

　Terms を記載した書面に署名をした者は、原則として、当該書面に記載された全ての条項の拘束を受ける（L'Etrange v F. Graucob Ltd.［1934］2 KB394(CA)①）。ただし、exclusion clause の効果について相手方に事実と異なる説明（misrepresentation）をして、これを記載した書面に署名させた者は、当該条項に依拠することができない（Curtis v Chemical Cleaning and Dyeing Co.［1951］1 All ER 631②）。

(2)　Constructive notice（擬制通知）

　通常人の日常生活においては、小売店での商品売買、公共交通機関の利用、ホテル宿泊その他書面によらない契約を締結することがほとんどであるし、商取引においても契約書を用いないことがある。そのような契約の条項（terms）は、契約締結時において、合理的な人間であれば誰でもその存在を知るであろう方法で相手方に通知されていた場合に、当該 terms の通知があったものと擬制され、契約の内容となる（Parker v South Eastern Railway Co.(1877)2 CPD 416③）。この場合、相手方が当該 terms を現実に知らなかったことや相手方固有の事情（文盲等）で知り得なかったことは一切考慮されな

い（Thompson v London, Midland & Scottish Railway ［1930］1 KB 41④, Midland & Scottish Railway ［1930］1 KB 41）。このような通知を constructive notice（擬制通知）という。

ただし、通知の方法が不適当な場合（inadequate notice）、すなわち合理的な人間ならば知るであろう方法で通知されていない場合は、当該 terms を実際に読まない限り、その拘束を受けない（Chapelton v Barry UDC ［1940］1 KB 532 (CA)⑤）。

また、terms の通知は、契約締結時又はそれ以前になされている必要があり、契約締結後に通知しても（late notice）相手方はその拘束を受けない（Olley v Marborough Court Ltd. ［1949］1 KB 532⑥、Thornton v Shoe Lane Parking Ltd. ［1971］2 QB 163 (CA)⑦）。

(3) Notice by course of dealing（継続取引による通知）

当事者間で同種の取引が継続している場合は、その内のある１つの取引に関して偶々契約書を交わしていなかったとしても、当該取引に関する契約には、それまでの取引で交わしてきた契約に含まれていたものと同一の terms が含まれているものと解される（Spurling (J.) Ltd. v Bradshaw ［1956］1 WLR 461 (CA)、Hardwick Game Farm v Suffolk Agricultural etc., Association ［1969］2 AC 31⑧、British Crane Hire Corp. Ltd. v Ipswich Plant Hire Ltd. ［1975］QB 303 (CA)⑨）。

(4) 上記の例外として、exclusion clause が相手方当事者にとって特別に不利（particularly severe）な場合は、SPECIAL NOTICE が必要となる（Spurling (J.) Ltd. v Bradshaw ［1956］1WLR461(CA)⑩、Interfoto Picture Library v Stiletto Visual Programmes ［1989］QB 433 (CA)⑪）。SPECIAL NOTICE とは、赤字、太字、大文字などを用いて、当該条項の存在を特に際立たせて相手方の注意を引くように配慮して示した通知という意味である。この考え方は、1956年の Spurling (J.) Ltd. v Bradshaw 判決において、Denning 判事が obiter として最初に示し、その後の取引実務に影響を与えたが、イギリスの判例法となったのは、1989年の上記 Interfoto Picture Library v Sti-

letto Visual Programmes 判決以降である。

3．Exclusion clause の適用に関する特別な解釈原則の適用

　以下の解釈原則は、イギリスの契約解釈全体に関するものではあるが、裁判所は exclusion clause に関して適用することが多い。

　(1)　The contra proferentem rule（「起草者の不利に」の原則）：既に紹介したとおり（本編第5章1）、契約条項の意味があいまいな場合は、当該条項の作成者又はその条項に基づく主張をする者の不利に解釈すべしとする原則である（Houghton v Trafalgar Insurance Co., Ltd.［1954］1 QB 247 (CA)⑫、Andrews Bros. (Bournemouth) Ltd. v Singer & Co. Ltd.［1934］1 KB17(CA)⑬、Hollier v Rambler Motors (AMC) Ltd.［1972］2 QB 71 (CA)⑭）。以下の諸原則は、exclusion の解釈のために、この contra proferendem rule から派生して生まれた解釈原則といえる。

　(2)　Clear words to exclude negligence（過失免責の明記）：Liability for negligence（過失による責任）を免責するためには、契約書において、過失の有無にかかわらず免責する旨を明記しなければならないとする原則である（上記 Hollier v Rambler Motors (AMC) Ltd.判決⑭）。

　(3)　The repugnancy rule（矛盾原則）：Exclusion clause が契約の主たる目的と直接的に矛盾（repugnat）する場合、当該 clause は排除される（Pollock v Marcrae［1922］SC (HL) 192⑮）。

　(4)　The deviation (4 corners) rule（離路原則）：Exclusion clause は、契約の範囲内の行為による責任にしか適用されない（Thomas National Transport (Melborne) Pty Ltd. and Pay v May and Baker (Australia) Pty Ltd.［1966］2 Lloyd's Rep 347⑯）。

　(5)　The doctrine of fundamental beach（根幹義務違反の法理）：契約の一方当事者が契約の根幹に拘わる義務違反を行った場合（fundamental breach of the contract）、exclusion clause による免責を受けることは原則として許されないとする解釈原理である。1950年代から60年代頃の裁判所は、不公平な exclusion clause がもたらす不合理な結果を是正するためにしばしばこの解釈

方法を用いた。しかし、契約解釈の問題とする以上は、fundamental breach をも免責する旨を明記した条項に対しては適用できないという限界があった。そこで、Lord Denning は、fundamental breach があるときは合理的な理由がない限り exclusion clause の適用を認めないとする原則は、単なる契約の解釈準則（a rule of construction）ではなく、当事者の合意にかかわらずに適用されるべき法理（a rule of law）であると主張したが、数年間の論争の後、the House of Lords はそのような法理は存在しないことを確認した（Suisse Atlantique Societe d'Armement Martime SA v NV Rotterdamsche Kolen Centrale ［1967］1 AC 361 (HL)、Photo Production Ltd. v Securicor Transport Ltd. ［1980］AC 827 (HL)）。ただし、Lord Denning が主張した考え方は、その後、下記 4 の the Unfair Contract Terms Act 1977 により制定法として採り入れられている。

4．The Unfair Contract Terms Act 1977

The Unfair Contract Terms Act 1977（UCTA 1977）の制定は、契約の厳格解釈によって exclusion clause の適用を制限してきた裁判所とそのような解釈の余地のない条項を作成・締結しようとする企業（及びその弁護士）との間の闘争に重大な変革をもたらした。この法律の適用がある契約における exclusion clause の効力は、当該条項について当事者間の合意があった場合でも大幅に制限される。なお、UCTA 1977は、契約責任のみならず不法行為責任（liability in tort）にも適用される。

(1) 適用範囲

UCTA 1977は、business liability（商取引上の責任）のみに適用される。Business liability には、事業者間の契約に基づくものと事業者と消費者間の契約に基づくものの双方が含まれ、事業とは関係ない私人間の契約（private contract）だけが除外される。UCTA 1977の第 1 条(3)は、business liability を次のとおり定義している。

  liability arising from breach of obligations or duties arising from (i) things done or to be done in course of a business, or (ii) occupation of premises used for business purposes of occupier

(2) Clauses automatically void（当然無効条項）

　UCTA 1977の適用を受けるexclusion clauseには、理由や事情のいかんにかかわらず当然に無効となる条項とそのような条項を設けることに合理性が認められる場合は無効とならない条項の2種類が含まれている。もちろん、business liabilityに関するexclusion clauseであっても、同法のいずれの規定の適用をも受けない場合は、合理性の有無を問題とするまでもなく、その契約文言どおり有効である。

　当然に無効な条項（automatically void）とされるのは、以下の内容のexclusion clauseである。

　（ⅰ）　生命又は身体の侵害に対する責任を免除又は制限する条項（s2(1)）
　（ⅱ）　消費者（consumer）との契約において、the Sale of Goods Act 1979又はthe Supply of Goods (Implied Terms) Act 1973における一定の黙示条項（商品表示との合致、商品の品質、目的への適合性の保証に関する条項）違反に基づく消費者に対する責任を免責する条項（ss6(2)、7(2)）
　（ⅲ）　製造者によるguarantee（製造者保証）の規定において、製造又は販売上の消費者に対するliability for negligence（過失責任）を免責又は制限する条項（s5）

(3) Clauses required to be reasonable（合理性を必要とする条項）

　以下の内容のexclusion clauseは、合理性が認められれば有効である。
　（ⅰ）　Negligence（過失）による生命、身体の侵害以外の損害又は損失に対する責任を制限する条項（s2(2)）
　（ⅱ）　消費者契約以外の物品売買契約等（the Sale of Goods Act 1979又はthe Supply of Goods (Implied Terms) Act 1973の適用がある契約）であって、商品表示との合致、商品の品質及び目的適合性の保証に関する黙示条項（implied term）に基づく責任を制限する条項（ss6(3)、7(2)）
　（ⅲ）　契約当事者の一方が消費者である場合、又は当事者の一方が相手方当

事者の作成した standard terms of business(標準取引条項)を何らの修正なく受け入れた場合における以下の条項(ss3(1)、3(2))
　(a)　契約違反の責任を免除又は制限する条項
　(b)　契約上の義務の大幅な修正を一方的にすることができる条項
　(c)　契約上の義務の全部又は一部の終了に関する条項

　(4)　上記(3)の reasonableness(責任制限条項の合理性)は、以下のような要素を斟酌して決定する(s11(2)、(3)、Schedule 2：Guidelines For Application of Reasonableness Test 及び case law)。なお、UCTA 1977の s11(2)は、Schedule 2のガイドラインを物品に関する売買等の取引に適用すべき旨を規定しているが、裁判所は、それ以外の取引に関する契約における exclusion clause の合理性の認定の際も同様な基準を利用すべきものとしている (Stewart Gill v Horatio Meyer & Co [1992] 1 QB 600)。
　(ⅰ)　一方当事者の交渉力(bargaining power)の優越性
　(ⅱ)　不利な exclusion clause に合意した当事者が、そのような合意をした誘引は何か(代金、供給の困難性など)
　(ⅲ)　不利な exclusion clause に合意した当事者は、そのような合意をしなくても他の方法(他の者と同種の契約を締結する方法)で同じ目的を実現することが可能だったか否か
　(ⅳ)　不利な exclusion clause に合意した当事者は、当該条項の存在と効果を認識していたか否か(特に、取引慣行や過去における取引上、同様の条項が存在したか)
　(ⅴ)　一定の条件が充たされないことを責任免除又は責任制限の要件とする exclusion clause の場合、当該条件は、実務上、実現可能なものであったか否か
　(ⅵ)　物品取引に関する契約において、当該商品は顧客の特別注文により製造、加工又は適合されたものだったか
　(ⅶ)　責任制限の対象となっている契約違反のリスクについて、いずれの当事者が保険を付することができたか
　(ⅷ)　契約違反の程度、結果、当該免責規定が、実際にどのような結果をも

たらしたか

UCTA1977が最初に適用されたのは、George Mitchell (Chesterhall) Ltd. v Finney Lock Seeds Ltd.判決（[1983] 2 All ER 803 (HL)⑰）である。この事件では、商人が農家に表示と異なる品種のキャベツのタネ（cabbage seed）を販売した責任にexclusion clause（免責条項）の適用があるか否かが争われた。Lord Denningは、原審であるCourt of Appealの判決（[1983] 1All ER108）において、（ⅰ）売買代金に比べて損害額（収穫期までの労力等）が甚大であること、（ⅱ）契約当事者間の交渉力（bargaining power）が対等でなかったこと、（ⅲ）タネの同一性の瑕疵は売主（商人）でなければ予測困難だったこと、（ⅳ）売主は契約違反のリスクを保険によって回避可能だったこと、（ⅴ）契約違反は売主の重大な過失（serious negligence）を原因としていること等を理由にexclusion clauseの合理性を否定した。そして、上訴審であるthe House of Lordsは、合理性の認定基準は裁判官によって異なるが、原審が明らかな過ちを犯していない限りは原判決を尊重すべきである旨を述べてDenningの認定を支持し、UCTA 1977に基づいてexclusion clauseを無効とする判断を初めて示した。しかし、その後の裁判所は、契約条項の合理性を否定することには比較的慎重である。コンピュータソフトの開発契約におけるexclusion clauseの有効性が争われたWatford Electronic Limited v Sanderson CFL Limited判決（[2001] 1 All ER (Comm) 696 (CA)⑱）は、契約当事者の交渉上の地位が対等（equal bargaining power）の場合、原則として、両当事者は当該契約が取引上公平であること（the commercial fairness of the agreement）について最善の判断をしたはずであると述べ、UCTA 1977, s11の適用を否定している。

5．The Unfair Terms in Consumer Contracts Regulations 1999

商品売買や役務提供に関する契約におけるexclusion clauseは、UCTA 1977に加えて、the Unfair Terms in Consumer Contracts Regulations 1999（"UTCCR 1999"）の基準に照らしても適法と判断されなければ、これを適用することができない。UTCCR 1999は、the European Commission

（欧州委員会）がEC域内の消費者保護のために1993年に発したEC Directive on Unfair Terms in Consumer Contracts 1993（消費者契約における不公正条項に関する1993年欧州委員会指令）に応じて1994年に制定された法律の改正法である。

　この法律に基づき（ⅰ）事業者と消費者との間の物品売買や役務提供に関する契約（消費者契約）における条項であって（ⅱ）当事者間の個別的な交渉を経ていないもの（事業者の標準契約書式の条項等）は、unfair term（不公正条項）とみなされ（regs.4(1)、5(1)）、consumer（消費者）を拘束することができない（reg.8）。「Unfair term」とは、契約から生ずる両当事者の権利義務が、著しく不均衡（significant imbalance）に消費者に不利益をもたらす（to the detriment of the consumer）条項であり、かつ信義則に反するもの（contrary to the requirement of good faith）を意味する（reg.5(1)）。なお、契約の中に、当事者間で交渉した条項とそうでない条項とが混在する場合、交渉していない条項についてこの法律の適用がある（reg.5(3)）。

　この法律によって、信義則（good faith）という大陸法（civil law）上の概念が初めてイギリスに導入されたことになるが、good faithの定義規定が設けられていないし、これに関する判例法もないので、イギリス法上、この語句が何を意味するのか、未だに不明である。法律のSchedule 2は、「Unfair term」の指針としていくつかの条項を例示列挙している（reg.5(5)）。これらによれば、unfairな条項であるか否かは、（ⅰ）両当事者の契約交渉上の地位、（ⅱ）消費者はどのような誘引、動機により当該条項に同意したか、（ⅲ）契約の対象である物品やサービスは、消費者による特別な注文（special order）によって提供されたか、（ⅳ）売主又は供給者は、消費者を公正かつ対等に取り扱ったか否か等の要素を考慮して判断される（Schedule 2）。したがって、実際上の適用要件は、UCTA 1977と概ね重複することになる。なお、UTCCR 1999の適否が争われた最初の事件は、銀行の消費者金融契約書（consumer credit agreement）における遅延利息条項の有効性に関するthe House of Lordsの裁判である（Director General of Fair Trading v First National Bank plc [2001] 1 AC 481 (HL)）。この判決では、同法の適用を否定している。

第6章　Exclusion Clause（責任排除条項）の一般原則

【CASES】
① *L'Etrange v F. Graucob Ltd.* [1934] 2 KB 394 (CA)
　Mrs L'Etrange bought a vending machine and sued the supplier when it did not work. The supplier insisted that there was an exclusion clause in the contract she had signed. She contented that it was in small print and she had not read it. It was held that she was bound by the term contained in a signed document, even though she had not read the document and did not know its contents.
　"When a document containing contractual terms is signed, in the absence of fraud, or, I will add, misrepresentation, the party signing it is bound, and it is wholly immaterial whether he has read the document or not." (per Scrutton L. J.)

② *Curtis v Chemical Cleaning and Dyeing Co.* [1951] 1 All ER 631
　Miss Curtis took to the cleaning shop a white satin wedding dress to have it cleaned. The dress was trimmed with beads and sequins. The shop assistant gave her a form to sign and Curtis asked what it was all about. The assistant replied that it exempted the company from the risk of damage to the beads and sequins only, so Curtis signed. In fact, the form said the company was not liable for any damage at all. When the dress was returned, it was stained, and the shop tried to rely on the exclusion clause. It was held that the shop could not do so as it had misrepresented its effect.

③ *Parker v South Eastern Railway Co.* (1877) 2 CPD 416
　Parker's bag, deposited with the railway company's cloakroom, was stolen. A ticket of deposit was printed on the back that company would not be responsible for any package worth more than £10. A similar notice was displayed in the cloakroom. It was held that the sufficient notice of exclusion clause was given.
　"The railway company, as it seems to me, must be entitled to make some assumption respecting the person who deposits luggage with them: I think that they are entitled to assume that he can read, and that he understands the English language, and that he pays such attention to what he is about as may be reasonably expected from a person in such a transaction … I think that a particular plaintiff ought not to be in a better position than other persons on account of his exceptional ignorance or stupidity or carelessness." (per Mellish LJ)

④ *Thompson v London, Midland & Scottish Railway* [1930] 1 KB 41
　Thompson asked her niece to buy a railway ticket for her. The ticket, which

cost 2 shillings 7 dime had written on it that it was subject to the conditions set out in the company's timetable. This timetable cost nearly a fifth of the price of the fare, and on page 552 was an exclusion clause. It was held that even though Thompson was illiterate and was unlikely to have read the exclusion clause, she was still bound by it.

⑤　*Chapelton v Barry UDC* [1940] 1 KB 532 (CA)
Chapelton hired a deck chair for 2 dime from Barry UDC. He was given a ticket which he did not read, and was injured when the deck chair collapsed. Barry tried to rely on an exclusion clause on the back of the ticket, but it was held that the ticket was merely a receipt and it was not reasonable to expect it to contain any contractual terms.

⑥　*Olley v Marborough Court Ltd.* [1949] 1 KB 532
Mrs Olley, a guest, booked in at the reception desk of a hotel. She then went to the bedroom, where there was a notice on the wall saying that the hotel accepted no responsibility for lost or stolen items. Her furs were stolen. It was held that the hotel could not rely on the exclusion clause, as the guest had already made her contract before she had the chance to see the notice.

⑦　*Thornton v Shoe Lane Parking Ltd.* [1971] 2 QB 163 (CA)
Thornton had got a ticket from an automatic machine as he entered a car-park. On the ticket it said that the contract was subject to conditions displayed on the premises. A notice in a car-park purported to exclude liability for personal injury. He was injured. It was held that the contract was made when Thornton entered the car-park, so the notice on the ticket came too late.

⑧　*Hardwick Game Farm v Suffolk Agricultural etc., Association* [1969] 2 AC 31
It was held that where there has been a consistent course of dealing between the parties on certain terms, such terms may be incorporated even though notice has not been given in the particular case. In this case three contracts a month for three years was held to be sufficient 'course of dealing'.

⑨　*British Crane Hire Corp. Ltd. v Ipswich Plant Hire Ltd.* [1975] QB 303 (CA)
Ipswich Plant Hire Ltd. ("IPH") hired a crane from British Crane Hire Corp ("BCH"). Both were in the business of hiring out such machinery, and it was a usual condition of such hire contracts that the party taking the machinery would

indemnify the party hiring it out against expenses incurred in the use of it. Before IPH could sign the hire form containing this term, the crane sank. It was held that IPH was liable even though they had not signed the form. As IPH itself was in the trade, it should have known what the usual conditions of hire would be.

"It is clear that both parties knew quite well that conditions were habitually imposed by the supplier of these machines, and both parties knew the substance of those conditions ... In these circumstances, I think the conditions on the form should be regarded as incorporated into the contract. I would not put it so much on the course of dealing, but rather on the common understanding which is to be derived from the conduct of the parties, namely, that the hiring was to be on the terms of the plaintiff's usual conditions." (per Lord Denning MR)

⑩ *Spurling (J.) Ltd. v Bradshaw* [1956] 1 WLR 461 (CA)
"Some clauses I have seen would need to be printed in red ink on the face of the document with a red hand pointing to it before the notice could be held to be sufficient." (per Denning L.J.)

⑪ *Interfoto Picture Library v Stiletto Visual Programmes* [1989] QB 433 (CA)
Stiletto Visual Programmes ordered some transparencies from Interfoto Picture Library who sent them packed in a bag with a delivery note, which stated that if the transparencies were not returned on the due date, there would be a fee of £5 per transparency per day for each day they were late. They were returned two weeks late and Stiletto was charged £3,783.50. It was held that it had not been sufficiently notified of the term and so were not liable.

"'If one condition in a set of printed conditions is particularly onerous or unusual, the party seeking to enforce it must show that that particular condition was fully brought to the attention of the other party." (per Dillon LJ)

⑫ *Houghton v Trafalgar Insurance Co., Ltd.* [1954] 1 QB 247 (CA)
A car insurance policy included liability for damages 'caused or arising whilst the car is conveying any load in excess of that for which it was constructed'. A five-seater car was involved in an accident whilst carrying 6 people. It was held that the word 'load' only covered cases where there was a specified weight, and passenger was not a 'load'.

⑬ *Andrews Bros. (Bournemouth) Ltd. v Singer & Co. Ltd.* [1934] 1KB 17 (CA)

An exclusion clause in a dealership agreement covered all conditions, warranties and liabilities implied by statute, common law or otherwise. It was held that the car dealer could not rely on the clause as exempting it from liability for breach of express obligation that the car be new.

⑭ *Hollier v Rambler Motors (AMC) Ltd.* [1972] 2 QB 71 (CA)

A car left for repair was damaged in a fire caused by the garage owner's negligence. There was a clause that the garage owner was 'not responsible for damage caused by fire to customers' cars on the premises.' It was held that the term was not incorporated in the contract anyway, but even had it been, it would not have been effective, as it could be read as a simple warning that the garage owner was not generally liable (except for negligence) rather than as an actual exclusion clause.

⑮ *Pollock v Marcrae* [1922] SC (HL) 192

The marine engines built and supplied by the defendant had so many defects that they could not be used. The contract contained exclusion clause, protecting the defendant from liability for defective materials and workmanship. It was held that the exclusion clause did not apply as it was repugnant to the main purpose of the contract, which was to build and supply workable engines.

⑯ *Thomas National Transport (Melborne) Pty Ltd. and Pay v May and Baker (Australia) Pty Ltd.* [1966] 2 Lloyd's Rep 347

Thomas National Transport made a contract with May and Baker, the carrier, under which packages containing drugs and chemicals were to be carried from Melbourne. The carrier employed a subcontractor to collect the parcels and take them to the carrier's depot in Melbourne. When the subcontractor arrived late at Melbourne depot it was locked and so he kept them in a garage of his house. There was a fire and some of the parcels were destroyed. The High Court of Australia held that the carrier could not rely on the exclusion clause in the contract since there had been a fundamental breach. The intention of the parties was that the goods would be taken to the carrier's depot and not to the subcontractor's house.

⑰ *George Mitchell (Chesterhall) Ltd. v Finney Lock Seeds Ltd.* [1983] 2 All ER 803 (HL)

The seeds merchant agreed to sell 30 pounds of 'winter white cabbage seed' to the farmer, but delivered another type (i.e. autumn cabbage seeds of inferior variety) and as a result the crop failed. The question arose as to whether an exemption clause could cover this breach. The majority of the Court of Appeal held that the clause could not operate on the ground of fundamental breach (what was delivered was wholly different form what was agreed), however, the House of Lords held that it could since the obligation under the contract was to deliver seeds, and although this was a defective performance, it was not a non-performance. However, the House agreed with Lord Denning's decision of the Court of Appeal that it was not 'fair and reasonable' to allow reliance on the exemption clause, and accordingly the clause was not enforceable under s. 55 of the Sale of Goods Act 1979 (which is equivalent to s6(3) of the Unfair Contract Terms Act 1979).

"There will sometimes be room for a legitimate difference of judicial opinion as to what the answer should be, where it will be impossible to say that one view is demonstrably wrong and the other demonstrably right ... when asked to review such a decision on appeal, the appellate court should treat the original decision with the utmost respect and refrain from interference with it unless satisfied that it proceeded on some erroneous principle or was obviously wrong." (per Lord Bridge)

⑱ *Watford Electronic Limited v Sanderson CFL Limited* [2001] 1 All ER (Comm) 696 (CA)

Watford had purchased computer software on Sanderson's terms for the supply of software, which included an entire agreement clause (incorporating an acknowledgement of non-reliance on the part of Watford), an exclusion of liability for all indirect and consequential losses and a limitation of liability to the contract price. The systems supplied by Sanderson failed catastrophically for Watford; there were millions of pounds lost in profit, turnover, etc. An issue was raised regarding the reasonableness under s. 11 of the Unfair Contract Terms Act 1977 of clauses in Sanderson's written standard terms. The Court of Appeal held it did not fall foul of s.11. In so doing, the court considered that it was necessary to examine all the clauses, including the entire agreement and acknowledgement of non-reliance clauses, together. Watford and Sanderson were, as the court saw it, of equal bargaining power and Watford signed the contract with its eyes open.

"Unless satisfied that one party had effectively taken unfair advantage of the other, or that a term was so unreasonable as plainly not to have been understood or considered, the court should not interfere ..." (per Chadwick LJ)

⑲ *Director General of Fair Trading v First National Bank plc* [2001] 1 AC 481 (HL)

The bank's standard form of consumer credit agreement contained a provision that if a consumer was sued and ordered to pay in installments, he would not only pay the amount ordered by the court, but would also have to pay extra interest accruing until the payment in full. A consumer complained that the provision was unfair under the UTCCR. The Court of Appeal held it created unfair surprise for the consumer. On appeal, the House of Lords overturned such decision. It was held that the term about interest was clear and unambiguous and that the consumer could reasonably be suppose to understand its implication when he entered into the loan.

【STATUTES】
Unfair Contract Terms Act 1977
2. Negligence liability
⑴ A person cannot by reference to any contract term or to a notice given to persons generally or to particular persons exclude or restrict his liability for death or personal injury resulting from negligence.
⑵ In the case of other loss or damage, a person cannot so exclude or restrict his liability for negligence except in so far as the term or notice satisfies the requirement of reasonableness.
⑶ Where a contract term or notice purports to exclude or restrict liability for negligence a person's agreement to or awareness of it is not of itself to be taken as indicating his voluntary acceptance of any risk.
3. Liability arising in contract
⑴ This section applies as between contracting parties where one of them deals as consumer or on the other's written standard terms of business.
⑵ As against that party, the other cannot by reference to any contract term?
　(a) when himself in breach of contract, exclude or restrict any liability of his in respect of the breach; or
　(b) claim to be entitled―
　　(i) to render a contractual performance substantially different from that which was reasonably expected of him, or
　　(ii) in respect of the whole or any part of his contractual obligation, to render no performance at all,
except in so far as (in any of the cases mentioned above in this subsection) the contract term satisfies the requirement of reasonableness.
5. "Guarantee" of consumer goods

(1) In the case of goods of a type ordinarily supplied for private use or consumption, where
loss or damage—
  (a) arises from the goods proving defective while in consumer use; and
  (b) results from the negligence of a person concerned in the manufacture or distribution of the goods,
liability for the loss or damage cannot be excluded or restricted by reference to any contract term or notice contained in or operating by reference to a guarantee of the goods.

(2) For these purposes—
  (a) goods are to be regarded as "in consumer use" when a person is using them, or has them in his possession for use, otherwise than exclusively for the purposes of a business; and
  (b) anything in writing is a guarantee if it contains or purports to contain some promise or assurance (however worded or presented) that defects will be made good by complete or partial replacement, or by repair, monetary compensation or otherwise.

(3) This section does not apply as between the parties to a contract under or in pursuance of which possession or ownership of the goods passed.

6. Sale and hire-purchase

(1) Liability for breach of the obligations arising from—
  (a) section 12 of the Sale of Goods Act 1979 (seller's implied undertakings as to title, etc);
  (b) section 8 of the Supply of Goods (Implied Terms) Act 1973 (the corresponding thing in relation to hire-purchase),
cannot be excluded or restricted by reference to any contract term.

(2) As against a person dealing as consumer, liability for breach of the obligations arising from—
  (a) section 13,14 or 15 of the 1979 Act (seller's implied undertakings as to conformity of goods with description or sample, or as to their quality or fitness for a particular purpose);
  (b) section 9,10 or 11 of the 1973 Act (the corresponding things in relation to hire-purchase),
cannot be excluded or restricted by reference to any contract term.

(3) As against a person dealing otherwise than as consumer, the liability specified in subsection (2) above can be excluded or restricted by reference to a contract term, but only in so far as the term satisfies the requirement of reasonableness.

11. The "reasonableness" test

(1) In relation to a contract term, the requirement of reasonableness for the purposes of this Part of this Act, section 3 of the Misrepresentation Act 1967 and section 3 of the Misrepresentation Act (Northern Ireland) 1967 is that the term shall have been a fair and reasonable one to be included having regard to the circumstances which were, or ought reasonably to have been, known to or in the contemplation of the parties when the contract was made.

(2) In determining for the purposes of section 6 or 7 above whether a contract term satisfies the requirement of reasonableness, regard shall be had in particular to the matters specified in Schedule 2 to this Act; but this subsection does not prevent the court or arbitrator from holding, in accordance with any rule of law, that a term which purports to exclude or restrict any relevant liability is not a term of the contract.

(3) In relation to a notice (not being a notice having contractual effect), the requirement of reasonableness under this Act is that it should be fair and reasonable to allow reliance on it, having regard to all the circumstances obtaining when the liability arose or (but for the notice) would have arisen.

(4) Where by reference to a contract term or notice a person seeks to restrict liability to a specified sum of money, and the question arises (under this or any other Act) whether the term or notice satisfies the requirement of reasonableness, regard shall be had in particular (but without prejudice to subsection (2) above in the case of contract terms) to—

(a) the resources which he could expect to be available to him for the purpose of meeting the liability should it arise; and

(b) how far it was open to him to cover himself by insurance.

(5) It is for those claiming that a contract term or notice satisfies the requirement of reasonableness to show that it does.

SCHEDULE 2
"GUIDELINES" FOR APPLICATION OF REASONABLENESS TEST
Sections 11(2), 24(2)

The matters to which regard is to be had in particular for the purposes of sections 6(3), 7(3) and (4), 20 and 21 are any of the following which appear to be relevant—

(a) the strength of the bargaining positions of the parties relative to each other, taking into account (among other things) alternative means by which the customer's requirements could have been met;

(b) whether the customer received an inducement to agree to the term, or in accepting it had an opportunity of entering into a similar contract with other persons, but without having to accept a similar term;

(c) whether the customer knew or ought reasonably to have known of the existence and extent of the term (having regard, among other things, to any custom of the trade and any previous course of dealing between the parties);

(d) where the term excludes or restricts any relevant liability if some condition is not complied with, whether it was reasonable at the time of the contract to expect that compliance with that condition would be practicable;

(e) whether the goods were manufactured, processed or adapted to the special order of the customer.

The Unfair Terms in Consumer Contracts Regulations 1999
4. Terms to which these Regulations apply

(1) These Regulations apply in relation to unfair terms in contracts concluded between a seller or a supplier and a consumer.

(2) These Regulations do not apply to contractual terms which reflect-

(a) mandatory statutory or regulatory provisions (including such provisions under the law of any Member State or in Community legislation having effect in the United Kingdom without further enactment);

(b) the provisions or principles of international conventions to which the Member States or the Community are party.

5. Unfair Terms

(1) A contractual term which has not been individually negotiated shall be regarded as unfair if, contrary to the requirement of good faith, it causes a significant imbalance in the parties' rights and obligations arising under the contract, to the detriment of the consumer.

(2) A term shall always be regarded as not having been individually negotiated where it has been drafted in advance and the consumer has therefore not been able to influence the substance of the term.

(3) Notwithstanding that a specific term or certain aspects of it in a contract has been individually negotiated, these Regulations shall apply to the rest of a contract if an overall assessment of it indicates that it is a pre-formulated standard contract.

(4) It shall be for any seller or supplier who claims that a term was individually negotiated to show that it was.

(5) Schedule 2 to these Regulations contains an indicative and non-exhaustive list of the terms which may be regarded as unfair.

8. Effect of unfair term

(1) An unfair term in a contract concluded with a consumer by a seller or

supplier shall not be binding on the consumer.

(2) The contract shall continue to bind the parties if it is capable of continuing in existence without the unfair term.

この章のチェックリスト

1．Exclusion Clause とは何か。
2．Exclusion clause が契約に含まれるのはどのような場合か。
　(1) signing a document
　(2) constructive notice
　(3) notice by course of conduct
　(4) special notice
3．Exclusion clause の解釈のための特別な解釈原理として、以下のものを説明しなさい。
　(1) The contra proferentem rule
　(2) Clear words to exclude negligence
　(3) The repugnancy rule
　(4) The deviation (4 corners) rule
4．The Unfair Contract Terms Act 1977により無効とされる exclusion clause とは。
5．The Unfair Contract Terms Act 1977により reasonableness test の対象となる exclusion clause にはどのようなものがあるか。
6．Reasonableness test とは何か。
7．The Unfair Terms in Consumer Contracts Regulations 1999はどのような契約条項に適用があるか。

第7章

Misrepresentation（不実表示）

　イギリス法上の misrepresentation（不実表示）は、日本の民法における詐欺よりもはるかに適用範囲が広い法制度であり、契約を解消するための事由としても最も重要である。ただし、misrepresentation に基づく法律効果は、原則として契約の直接の相手方に対してしか主張できない。

1．Misrepresentation の定義と要件

　Misrepresentation とは、他人に契約締結を決断させるための勧誘手段として行う、十分に具体的で明確な真実ではない現在の事実の告知（a sufficiently concrete and unambiguous false statement of existing fact, which made to induce someone to enter into a contract）であり、これによって契約締結に至った者は、契約の相手方に対し、損害賠償（damages）の請求、及び場合によっては契約解消（rescission）を求めることができる。

　この定義から明らかなとおり、misrepresentation に基づく法的請求をするには、（ⅰ）a sufficiently concrete and unambiguous（十分に具体的で明確な）statement であること、（ⅱ）existing fact（現在の事実）に関する statement であること（ⅲ）false（虚偽の事実の）statement であること、（ⅳ）事実を statement（告知）すること、及び（ⅴ）inducement of the conclusion of the contract（契約締結の誘因）であることという、5つの要件が備わっていなければならない。以下、それぞれについて説明する。

(1) A SUFFICIENTLY CONCRETE and UNAMBIGUOUS（十分に具体的で明確な）statement of fact であること

　第1に、当該 representation は、十分に具体的（sufficiently concrete）な

表示でなければならず、宣伝文句のための単なる吹聴（a mere puff）は misrepresentation の対象とはならない。たとえば、中古住宅の販売（for sale of a second-rate house）のための広告文に「a desirable residence for a family of distinction（特別な家族のために理想的な邸宅）」と表示した程度では、単なる宣伝文句（a mere puff）に過ぎない（Magennis v Fallon (1828)）。また、abandoned and useless land（放棄された無価値の土地）の競売の際に競売人が「fertile and improvable（肥沃で改良可能)」な土地との誇張表示（flourishing' description）をしても、当該表示は訴求不能なセールストーク（merely sales talk and not actionable）に過ぎない（Dimmock v Hallett (1866) LR 2 Ch App 21 (CA)）。ただし、広告における宣伝文が具体的で明白な場合は、a mere puff とは解されないことがある（Carlill v Carbolic Smoke Ball Co [1893] 1 QB 256 (CA)）。

また、表示された言葉の意味を相手方が誤解して契約を締結しただけでは、misrepresentation による責任が生じることはない（Mclnery v Llyods Bank Ltd [1974] 1 Lloyd's Rep 246 (CA)①）。

(2) statement of EXISTING FACT（現在の事実）

第2に、当該 representation は、現在の事実（existing fact）の表示でなければならない。この要件に関してよく争われるは、当該表示は（ⅰ）事実（fact）の表示か意見（opinion）の表明か、（ⅱ）現在（existing）の事実か将来（future）の事実か、及び（ⅲ）事実（fact）の表示か法律（law）の表示かという点である。

（ⅰ） 意見（opinion）の表明は、原則として misrepresentation に当らない（Bisset v Wilkinson [1927] AC 177 (Privy Council: New Zealand)②）。ただし、意見を表明している者が当該意見に関する専門的知識を有し、かつ相手方が当該意見に依拠して契約を締結しようとしていることを知っている場合、当該意見表明は事実の表示（representation of fact）として扱われる（Smith v Land & House Property Corporation (1884) 28 ChD 7 (CA)③、Esso Petroleum v Marden [1976] QB 801 (CA)④）。

（ⅱ） 原則として、将来一定の行為をする旨の意思表明は misrepresentation に当らず、それが約束 (promise) に当って、契約の内容に condition 又は warranty として含まれる場合にのみ法的効果が生ずる（本編第4章参照）。ただし、当該行為を行う意思がないのにその意思があることを表明した場合は、意図的な虚偽事実の表示（fraudulent misrepresentation）と解されることがある（Edgington v Fitzmaurice（1885）29 ChD 459 (CA)⑤)。

(iii) 法律の表示（statement of law）は、原則として事実の表示に当らない。ただし、当該表示が間違っていることを知っている者が、相手方がこれに依拠していることを知りながら契約を締結した場合は、misrepresentation of fact として扱われる（West London Commercial Bank v Kitson（1884）13 QBD 360 (CA)⑥)。

(3) FALSE statement（虚偽事実）

Misrepresentation の主張を行うための第3の要件として、当該 representation の内容が虚偽でなければならない。なお、表示した事実の一部が真実であっても、虚偽が含まれていれば misrepresentation に当る場合がある（Dimmock v Hallett（1866）LR 2 Ch App 21(CA)⑦、Inntrepreneur Estates Ltd. v Hollard [2000] WL 1084502 (CA)⑧)。そのような事実は、half-truths（Suppresio veri, suggestio falsi）と呼ばれている。

(4) STATEMENT of fact（事実の告知）

第4に、representation は事実の告知でなければならず、単なる沈黙（mere silence）では足らない。イギリス法上、契約締結段階における信義誠実の原則に相当する法原理が存在せず、原則として、契約の交渉相手に対してその意思決定に影響を及ぼすべき事実を告げる義務は存在しないからである。ただし、以下の3つ場合はその例外として、事実を告げないことが misrepresentation となる。

なお、言葉（word）ではなく行動による事実の告知（misrepresentation by conduct）もあり得る（Spice Girls Ltd. v Aprilia World Service BV [2002] EWCA Civ 15)。

(ⅰ) Deliberate concealment（意図的な隠蔽）：相手方の意思決定に影響

する不利な事実を意図的、計画的に隠した場合、行為による事実表示（statement by conduct）があると解されることがある（Gordon v Sellico [1986] EGLR 71 (CA)⑨）。ただし、どのような場合がこれに当るか、若干不明確である。

（ⅱ）Change of circumstances（事情の変更）：契約交渉中に告げた事実が、契約締結前に状況が変更して真実でなくなった場合（subsequent untruth）には、当該事実の変更について相手方に開示すべき義務が発生し、これを怠った場合は、misrepresentation に当る（With v O'Flanagan [1936] 1All ER 727 (CA)⑩、Spice Girls Ltd. v Aprilia World Service BV [2002] WL 45121 (CA)⑪）。

（ⅲ）Contract Utmost Good Faith (Uberrimae fidei)（最高信義契約）：特定の種類の契約（家族間の財産分与契約、保険契約等）に関しては、その性質上当事者の一方がほとんど全ての重要な情報を有していることを前提に契約交渉に入るため、法律（制定法及び判例法）によって、重要事実の開示義務が課せられている。この義務違反があった場合は契約を解消（rescind）することができるが、損害賠償請求（damages）はできないので、通常の misrepresentation に関する法律（制定法及び判例法）が適用される場合とは区別される（Gordon v Gordon (1816) 3 Swan 400、Banque Keyser Ullman S.A. v Skandia (U.K.) Insurance Co., Ltd. [1991] 2 AC 249 (HL)）。

(5) INDUCE the contract（契約の誘引）

最後に、misrepresentation に基づく主張をするためには、表示された虚偽の事実に基づいて契約締結の意思決定をした場合でなければならない。よって、相手方が虚偽事実を表明していることを知りながら契約した者や当該表明には影響を受けずに自らの技能と判断で契約締結を決定した者は、原則として、misrepresentation に基づく法的主張をすることができない（Attwood v Small (1838) 6 Cl & F 232 (HL)⑫）。

他方、相手方の表明が虚偽であることを見破る機会があったというだけでは、misrepresentation の主張が許されなくなるわけではない（Redgrave v Hurd (1881) 20 ChD 1 (CA)⑬、Smith v Eric S. Bush [1990] 1 AC 831 (HL)⑭）。

ただし、容易に虚偽か否かを調べられる者があえて調査しない場合、その者は当該事実が真実か否かには関心がなかったとして、因果関係が認められない可能性がある（Drake v Thos. Agnew & Sons Ltd.［2002］EWCH294⑮、Smith v Eric S. Bush［1990］1 AC 831（HL）⑭の obiter）。

Misrepresentation によって契約したか否かの判断は、契約解釈の一般原則とは異なり、客観的な一般人基準（objective test）ではなく契約者本人を基準に行う（Smith v Chadwick（1884）9 App Cas 187）。

2．Misrepresentation の Remedies（不実表示の法的効果）

Misrepresentation には、fraudulent misrepresentation（詐欺による不実表示）、negligent misrepresentation（過失による不実表示）、innocent misrepresentation（善意の不実表示）の3種類がある。Misrepresentation があったときの救済手段は、この内のどの misrepresentation に当るのかによって異なっている。

(1) Fraudulent Misrepresentation（詐欺による不実表示）

Fraudulent misrepresentation は、misrepresentation を行う者が、当該事実が虚偽であることを知っているか、真実であるとは信じていない場合、又は真実か否かについて無関心（reckless）であった場合である。Fraudulent misrepresentation を主張する者は、misrepresentation をした者の fraud（詐欺）を立証しなければならない（Derry v Peek（1889）14 App Cas 337⑯）。この立証に成功した場合は、common law 上の権利として、rescission（契約解消）と damages（損害賠償請求）の2つの救済手段が与えられる。Damages は、tort（不法行為）の1つである tort of deceit として認められる。したがって、損害の対象は、misrepresentation によって発生することが契約締結時に合理的に予期、予見された範囲内のものに留まらず、misrepresentation の結果として発生した全損害に及ぶ。

(2) Negligent Misrepresentation（過失による不実表示）

　Negligent misrepresentation となるのは、不注意に、又は合理的な理由なしに真実であると信じて表示した場合である。The Misrepresentation Act 1967により、この場合の救済手段も rescission と damages の 2 つがあるが、rescission が認められるか否かは、裁判所の裁量に委ねられている。Misrepresentation の内容が軽微であり、その結果として被った損失に比べて、契約が解消されたとしたら misrepresentation を行った者が被る可能性がある損失の方が大きい場合、通常 rescission は認められず、damages のみが与えられる（the Misrepresentation Act 1967 ss2(1)、2(2)）。

　Damages の算定は、fraudulent misrepresentation（詐欺による不実表示）の場合と同様の基準で行われる。したがって、契約違反の場合の damages とは異なり、misrepresentation により生ずることが合理的に予期されたか否かにかかわらず、misrepresentation から直接発生した全損害の賠償が認められる（Royscott Trust Ltd. v Rogerson [1992] 2 All ER 294 (CA)⑰）。

　なお、the Misrepresentation Act 1967による remedy（救済手段）が与えられるのは、契約交渉中の当事者による misrepresentation があった場合だけである。したがって、契約当事者以外の者による misrepresentation を信じて契約を締結した結果として損害を被った者は、この法律に基づく rescission や damages を請求することができない。判例法は、そのような場合の救済手段として、tort（不法行為）の 1 つである negligent　misstatement に基づく damages（損害賠償）を認めている。ただし、misrepresentation を行った者とこれを信じた者との間に特別な関係（special relationship）が存在することを要件としている（Hedley Byre & Co Ltd. v Heller and Partners Ltd. [1964] AC 465 (HL)⑱）。

(3) Innocent Misrepresentation（善意の不実表示）

　Innocent misrepresentation は、事実の告知を行った者が、誠実かつ合理的に（honestly and reasonably）真実と信じていた場合のことである。

　The Misrepresentation Act 1967に基づき、innocent misrepresentation により契約を締結した者は、裁判所の裁量による契約の rescission を求めること

第7章　Misrepresentation

ができるが（s2(2)）、damagesを請求することはできない（s2(1)）。裁判所は、その裁量によりrescissionに代えてdamagesを認めることができる（s2(3)）。ただし、rescissionの権利が認められない場合にはdamagesも与えられない。

(4) Rescission（契約解消）の制限

Misrepresentationによるrescissionとは、契約を解消して、契約を締結する前と同じ状態に戻す権利である。この権利は、以下の場合に喪失する。

（ⅰ）　Affirmation（追認）：Rescissionできることを知りながら、契約をaffirm（追認）した場合（Long v Lloyd［1958］1 WLR 753 (CA)⑲）。

（ⅱ）　Status quo ante（原状の復元）が不可能な状態になった場合（Clarke v Dickson（1858）EB & E 148⑳）。

（ⅲ）　Lapse of time（期間の経過）：Innocent misrepresentation（善意の不実表示）及びnegligent misrepresentation（過失による不実表示）の場合において、契約締結後、合理的な期間が経過した場合（Leaf v International Galleries［1950］2 KB 86 (CA)㉑）。

（ⅳ）　以上に加え、善意の第三者（innocent third party）が誠実な取引により契約目的物に関する権利を取得した場合は、当該第三者から目的物を取り戻すことができない。これに関して、The Sale of Goods Act 1979のs23は、以下のとおり定めている。

> 23. Sale under voidable title
>
> When the seller of goods has a voidable title to them, but his title has not been avoided at the time of the sale, the buyer acquires a good title to the goods, provided he buys them in good faith and without notice of the seller's defect of title.

（ⅴ）　当事者間の合意によってmisrepresentationによる責任の減免やrescissionの禁止等の方法でremedy（救済手段）を制限する条項（exemption clause）を設けた場合、当該条項は、the Unfair Contract Terms Actの定めるreasonableness test（s11(1)）を充たしていることを立証しない限り適用されない（the Misrepresentation Act 1967 s3 - the Unfair Contract Terms

Act 1977に基づく追加条項)。

【CASES】

① *McInery v Llyods Bank Ltd* [1974] 1 Lloyd's Rep 246 (CA)
McInery wished to sell some companies and wanted the bank to guarantee the buyer's payment. The bank wrote a letter, stating that it was not possible to issue guarantee under banking regulations, but it could give an 'irrevocable credit'. McInery signed a contract with the buyer, thinking that 'irrevocable credit' amounted to be the same thing as a guarantee. When the buyer defaulted payment, McInery claimed negligent misrepresentation by the bank. It was held that the bank was not responsible for the misinterpretation of the letter as on a reasonable construction it had not given the assurance.

② *Bisset v Wilkinson* [1927] AC 177 (Privy Council: New Zealand)
The owner of a farm told a prospective buyer that he believed his farm would support 2,000 sheep if it were properly managed, though, as both parties knew, the land had never been used for sheep-farming. The buyer discovered that the farm could not support near that number of sheep and sought rescission on the grounds of misrepresentation. It was held that he was not entitled to rescission on the basis as the statement was merely an honest opinion, not a misrepresentation.

③ *Smith v Land & House Property Corporation* (1884) 28 ChD 7 (CA)
The vendor of a hotel (Land & House Property Corp.) described it as 'let to Mr. Frederick Fleck a most desirable tenant'. In fact the tenant had for some time been in arrears with his rent. It was held that the vendor had misrepresented a fact for he implied that he had information which could justify his opinion.
"In my opinion a tenant who had paid his last quarter's rent by driblets under pressure must be regarded as an undesirable tenant." (per Bowen LJ)

④ *Esso Petroleum v Marden* [1976] QB 801 (CA)
Esso assured the prospective tenant of one of their petrol stations that 200,000 gallons of their petrol could be sold there each year. In fact sales never came to anything like that figure. It was held that unlike the Bisset case Esso were much better placed than Marden to make a forecast of sales, given their special knowledge of the likely markets. Marden was awarded damages for breach of warranty and for negligent misrepresentation.

第 7 章　Misrepresentation

⑤　*Edgington v Fitzmaurice* (1885) 29 ChD 459 (CA)
　Directors of a company invited a loan, stating their intention to spend the money on improvements to the buildings. They actually intended to use the money to pay off existing debts. It was held that this was a misrepresentation.
　'There must be a misstatement of an existing fact, but the state of a man's mind is as much a fact as the state of his digestion." (per Bowen LJ)

⑥　*West London Commercial Bank v Kitson* (1884) 13 QBD 360 (CA)
　A tramway company was incorporated by an Act of Parliament, which gave it no power to accept bills of exchange. Directors accepted a bill on behalf of the company. It was held that the directors were liable for the implied misrepresentation as to the power of a company to accept bills. It was a representation of a matter of fact rather than a matter of law.

⑦　*Dimmock v Hallett* (1866) LR 2 Ch App 21 (CA)
　The land which was for sale was described as 'let to Hickson at £130p.a.' and 'let to Wigglesworth at £160p.a.'. Although this was true, the vendor omitted to mention that both tenants had given notice to quit. This was held to be a misrepresentation.

⑧　*Inntrepreneur Estates Ltd. v Hollard* [2000] WL 1084502 (CA)
　Inntrepreneur Estate leased its public house to Hollard on a twenty-year lease. In order to induce Hollard to take the lease, the lessor stated that the record showed the annual barrelage was about 480, which was accurate on the record they referred to. However, more recent record showed a barrelage of only 400. It was held that the statement of the lessor was a misrepresentation.

⑨　*Gordon v Sellico* [1986] EG 53 (CA)
　Sellico was an estate agent of a flat, who deliberately concealed patches of dry rot to make it more saleable. It was held that his concealment amounted to a misrepresentation.
　"In my judgment the concealment of dry rot by Mr Azzam was a knowingly false representation that Flat C did not suffer from dry rot, which was intended to deceive purchaser, and did deceive the plaintiffs to their detriment. I am satisfied that the plaintiffs would not have entered into a contract or accepted the lease had they known there was dry rot inside Flat C." (per Goulding J)

⑩　*With v O'Flanagan* [1936] 1 All ER 727 (CA)

Dr O'Flanagan told With that his medical practice was worth £2000 p.a., which was then quite true. For the next four months O'Flanagan was seriously ill and during his absence his practice became virtually non-existent. With bought the practice relying on the earlier statement, and then claimed rescission. It was held that rescission was granted as the seller had a duty to disclose the changed circumstances to the buyer.

"If A with a view to inducing B to enter into a contract makes a representation as to a material fact, then if at a later date and before the contract is actually entered into, owing to a change of circumstances, the representation then made would to the knowledge of A be untrue and B subsequently enters into the contract in ignorance of that change of circumstances and relying upon that representation, A cannot hold B to the bargain." (per Romer LJ)

⑪ *Spice Girls Ltd. v Aprilia World Service BV* [2002] EWCA Civ 15

Spice Girls entered into a sponsorship agreement for their European tour with AWS, a motor scooter manufacturer. They took part in a photo shoot and promotions for AWS scooter under the brand name "Spice Sonic". Before signing of the agreement, Geri Halliwell (Ginger Spice) told the other members that she wanted to leave the group, but AWS was not informed. It was held that their cooperation and negotiation in silence before execution of the contract amounted to a misrepresentation by conduct in respect of the fact that none of the members had intention to leave before the sponsorship ended. It was also held that AWS should have been told of the changed circumstances before the contract was concluded.

⑫ *Attwood v Small* (1838) 6 Cl & F 232 (HL)

Attwood negotiated with Small to sell some mines and iron works. Small asked about the earning capacity of the property, but had the answers checked by their own experienced agent. The agent reported that Attwood's representations were accurate, and on the strength of this Small bought the property. In fact they were grossly inaccurate, and Small sued Attwood for misrepresentation. It was held that Small had not relied upon Attwood's statements but on its own independent advisor's, so the action for rescission failed.

⑬ *Redgrave v Hurd* (1881) 20 ChD 1 (CA)

Hurd was induced to buy a solicitor's house and practice by an innocent misrepresentation as to the value of the practice. He was held to be allowed to rescind the contract even though he had been given the opportunity of examining the accounts and so discovering the truth. A vendor is under no obligation to check the facts, even if given the opportunity to do so.

⑭ *Smith v Eric S. Bush* [1990] 1 AC 831 (HL)
Smith bought a house with the aid of a mortgage, relying on a valuation which had been negligently conducted by the surveyor engaged by the lender. His claim in negligence succeeded despite the fact that he could have discovered the truth by employing his own surveyor, for it was not reasonable to expect him to do this since the house in question was of modest value. However, the House of Lords stated obiter that failure to make use of an opportunity to discover the truth could defeat a claim for negligent misrepresentation, but only where it is reasonable to expect the representee to make use of the opportunity.

⑮ *Drake v Thos Agnew & Sons Ltd.* [2002] EWCH 294
An art dealer did not check the provenance of a supposed van Dyck painting, even though he could easily have done so, because his only interest was to earn a large commission from Drake, an art collector who wanted an Old Master. It was held that the dealer had not relied on the statement by the seller about the provenance.

⑯ *Derry v Peek* (1889) 14 App Cas 337
The company advertised shares for sale, stating that it had permission to run steam trains. In fact, it did not, but the directors honestly believed that the permission would be granted by the Board of Trade. Derry, who had bought shares relying on such advertisement, brought an action against the directors in deceit based upon false statement. It was held that the directors were not liable since their dishonesty was not successfully proved.
"I think the authorities establish the following propositions: First, in order to sustain an action of deceit, there must be proof of fraud, and nothing short of that will suffice. Secondly, fraud is proved when it is shewn that a false representation has been made (1) knowingly, or (2) without belief in its truth, or (3) recklessly, carelessly whether it be true or false." (per Lord Herschell)

⑰ *Royscott Trust Ltd. v Rogerson* [1991] 2 All ER 294 (CA)
A customer agreed to buy a Honda Prelude on hire purchase from the dealer for £7,600, paying a deposit of £1,200. In order to meet the finance company's condition that at least 20% of the purchase price was paid by way of deposit, the dealer told Royscott Trust (the finance company) that the purchase price

was £8,000 of which £1,600 had been paid as deposit. The customer dishonestly sold the car to an innocent third party, who took good title to it. Royscott sued for compensation, and the issue arose as to whether damages should be assessed in tort or in contract. The court held that the correct measure of damages under s.2 (1) was that for the tort of deceit even though actual fraud was not proved. Thus, Royscott is entitled to any loss which has flowed from the defendant's misrepresentation, even if the loss could not have been foreseen.

⑱　*Hedley Byre & Co Ltd. v Heller and Partners Ltd.* [1964] AC 465 (HL)

Hedley Byre, a firm of advertising agent, wanted to know whether one of its clients was creditworthy, and asked its own bank, the National Provincial, to make enquiries. The bank then inquired of Heller, the clients' bank, and was told 'in confidence and without responsibility on our part' that the client was good for £100,000 a year. Hedley Byre relied on this statement and lost more than £17,000 when the client went into liquidation, and sued Heller for negligence. It was held that the words used by Heller meant that it accepted no liability for their statements and so was not liable. However, the court said obiter that where A in the ordinary course of business asks B for information, when it is clear that A is relying on B to exercise a reasonable degree of care in answering, and B knew or ought to have know that A was relying on him, then B will be under a duty to take reasonable care.

⑲　*Long v Lloyd* [1958] 1 WLR 753 (CA)

Long was induced to buy a lorry from Lloyd after hearing representations as to its condition and a statement that it would do eleven miles to the gallon. Long drove the lorry from Hampton Court to Sevenoaks. The next Wednesday he drove to Rochester, whereupon the dynamo ceased to function, an oil leak developed, a crack appeared in one of the wheels and the petrol consumption was 5 miles per gallon. He complained to Lloyd who offered to pay half the cost of new dynamo, and this offer was accepted. The next day the lorry broke down en route to Middlesborough and Long asked for his money back. It was held that rescission could not be granted since the representations were innocent, and, although the journey to Rochester was not affirmation as Long had to have an opportunity to test the vehicle, the acceptance of the money and the subsequent journey to Middlesborough amounted to affirmation.

⑳　*Clarke v Dickson* (1858) EB & E 148

Clarke bought shares in a mining company, which was wound up three years later, as a result of false misrepresentations. It was held that he was unable to give up the shares and recover the purchase price because the shares could not be restored in the same state as they were when he had purchased them three years earlier.

㉑ *Leaf v International Galleries* [1950] 2 KB 86 (CA)

Leaf was induced to buy a painting by an innocent misrepresentation that it was by Constable. Five years later he discovered the truth and claimed rescission. It was held that his remedy had been lost since it had not been exercised within a reasonable time.

[STATUTES]
MISREPRESENTATION ACT 1967

2. -(1) Where a person has entered into a contract after a misrepresentation has been made to him by another party thereto and as a result thereof he has suffered loss, then, if the person making the misrepresentation would be liable to damages in respect thereof had the misrepresentation been made fraudulently, that person shall be so liable notwithstanding that the misrepresentation was not made fraudulently, unless he proves that he had reasonable ground to believe and did believe up to the time the contract was made that the facts represented were true.

(2) Where a person has entered into a contract after a misrepresentation has been made to him otherwise than fraudulently, and he would be entitled, by reason of the misrepresentation, to rescind the contract, then, if it is claimed, in any proceedings arising out of the contract, that the contract ought to be, or has been, rescinded, the court or arbitrator may declare the contract subsisting and award damages in lieu of rescission, if of opinion that it would be equitable to do so, having regard to the nature of the misrepresentation and the loss that would be caused by it if the contract were upheld, as well as to the loss that rescission would cause to the other party.

(3) Damages may be awarded under subsection (2) of this section whether or not he is liable to damages under subsection (1) thereof, but where he is so liable any award under sub-section (2) shall be taken into account in assessing his liability under the said sub-section (1).

3. -If a contract contains a term which would exclude or restrict
  (a) any liability to which a party to a contract may be subject by reason of any misrepresentation made by him before the contract was made; or
  (b) any remedy available to another party to the contract by reason of such

a misrepresentation,
that term shall be of no effect except in so far as it satisfies the requirement of reasonableness as stated in section 11 (1) of the Unfair Contract Terms Act 1977 ; and it is for those claiming the term satisfies that requirement to show that it does.

この章のチェックリスト

1．Misrepresentation とは何か。

2．Misrepresentation の以下の要件を説明せよ。

   (1) Sufficiently concrete representation

   (2) Existing FACT

   (3) False statement

   (4) Statement of fact

   (5) Induce the contract

3．以下のそれぞれの Misrepresentation があったとき、どのような救済手段があるか。

   (1) Fraudulent misrepresentation

   (2) Negligent misrepresentation

   (3) Innocent misrepresentation

4．Rescission とは何か。

5．Rescission の権利はどのような場合に喪失するか。

第8章

Mistake、Duress、etc.（錯誤、強迫等）

1．Mistake（錯誤）

日本法において錯誤は重要な契約無効原因であるが、イギリス法上、契約がmistakeによって無効となるのは例外的な場合だけである。

Mistakeには、次の3つの種類があり、それぞれ法的効果が異なる。

（i）　Common Mistake（共通錯誤）：契約の両当事者が共通の認識の上で合意しているが、当該共通の認識が間違っていた場合である。これには売買契約の目的物が元々存在しなかった場合（a mistake res extincta）、契約前から目的物を買主が所有していた場合（a mistake res sua）、及び目的物が合意したとおりの品質を備えていなかった場合（quality mistake）がある。判決には、この共通錯誤のことをmutual mistakeと呼んでいるものもあり、以下の（ii）と混同しやすい。

（ii）　Mutual Mistake（相互的錯誤）：両当事者が合意したと思っている契約の目的物や内容が一致しておらず、実は合意に達していない場合のことである。

（iii）　Unilateral Mistake（一方的錯誤）：一方当事者が契約に関連する重要な事実を誤解しており、かつ他方当事者はそのことを知っていたか、又は知るべきであった場合をいう。

なお、契約書面上の記載に関するmistakeがあった場合についてはmistakeの法理の適用はない。後述のとおり、裁判上、このような場合の救済手段としては、rectification（修正命令）の方法による契約書面の訂正がなされている。

(1) Common (Bilateral) Mistake（共通錯誤又は双方的錯誤）

Common mistake とは、契約の目的物や品質に関して、当事者双方が同じ内容の誤解をしていた場合である。判例法上、誤解の対象に応じて、以下のとおり法律効果が異なっている。

（ⅰ） A mistake res extincta（目的物の存在の錯誤）：両当事者が存在すると思っていた契約の目的物が存在しなかったため契約を履行できない場合 (res extincta)、契約は無効（void）である（Coutrier v Hastie (1856) 5 HLC 673①）。The Sale of Goods Act 1979は、特定物売買に関して以下のとおりこの原則を確認している（s6）。

Where there is a contract for the sale of specific goods and the goods without the knowledge of the seller have perished at the time when the contract is made, the contract is void.

（ⅱ） A mistake res sua（目的物の権利の錯誤）：相手方から購入又は賃貸する契約の目的物が元々自分の物だった場合（res sua）、契約は無効である（Cooper v Phibbs（1867）LR 2 HL 149 (HL)②）。

（ⅲ） A mistake as to quality（品質の錯誤）：契約の目的物の品質に関して当事者間で認識していたとおりではなかったとしても、misrepresentation（不実表示）の適用がある場合を除き、契約の効力に影響を及ぼさないのが原則である（Bell v Lever Brothers Ltd.［1932］AC 161 (HL)③、Leaf v International Galleries［1950］1 All ER 693 (CA)④）。ただし、the House of Lords は、Bell v Lever Brothers 判決の obiter において、quality に関する mistake によって契約の目的物が本質的に異なるものになると考えられるときは目的物の同一性に錯誤があり、上記（ⅰ）の適用により契約が無効となる場合があることを認めている。

以上の判例法上の原則に対し、Lord Denning は、Solle v Butcher 判決（［1950］1 KB 671 (CA)⑤）において、目的物の品質に関する共通錯誤（common mistake as to quality）がある契約は equity（衡平法）に基づき voidable（取消可能）である、すなわち、衡平の原則に反するとき、当事者は契約を解消（rescind）することができる旨の判断を示した。この判決後の約半世紀の間、イギリスの法学界及び実務界は、この判決（the Court of Appeal 判

決)と上記(iii)の Bell v Lever Brothers 判決(the House of Lords の判決)とは両立し得るのか、すなわち、common mistake as to quality(品質の共通錯誤)のある契約を equity に基づいて解消できる(voidable)場合があるのか否かについて大論争となった。しかし、この問題は、2002年の Great Pearce Shipping v Tsavliris Salvage 判決([2003] QB 679 (CA)⑥)において、the Court of Appeal が Bell v Lever Brothers 判決を正しい法として認めたこと(すなわち、Solle v Butcher 判決における Lord Denning の見解を否定したこと)によって一応解決した。

(2) Mutual Mistake(相互的錯誤)

Mutual mistake とは、契約締結の際に、一方当事者が実際に認識していた契約の目的物その他の条件と他方当事者の実際の認識とが異なっていることである。そのような場合であっても、objective test(客観基準)に従って契約内容が確定できる場合、すなわち、当事者本人ではなく合理的な一般人(reasonable person)を基準として合意したであろう事項が確定できる場合は、両当事者は、そのようにして確定された契約内容に従って法的拘束を受ける(Smith v Hughes(1871)LR 6 QB 597 (CA)⑦)。他方、客観基準によって合意内容が確定できない場合は、契約は成立していないと判断される(Raffles v Wichelhaus(1864)2 HC 906⑧)。

(3) Unilateral Mistake(一方的錯誤)

Unilateral mistake は、契約の一方当事者が契約に関連する重要な事実や契約条項について重大な誤解をし、かつ相手方がそのことを知りながら、又は知るべきであったにかかわらず契約を締結した場合における前者の錯誤のことである。判例法上、一方的錯誤の対象が契約の本質にかかわる重要事項(fundamental mistake)である場合、そのような錯誤に陥った当事者は契約の無効(void)を主張することができる。Fundamental mistake(本質的な錯誤)に当たる可能性がある錯誤は、mistake as to terms(契約条件の錯誤)の場合と mistake as to identity(当事者の同一性の錯誤)の場合の2つである。これに対し、契約の目的物の性質や当事者の属性に関する錯誤(mistake as to quality or attribute) は、misrepresentation による契約解消 (rescission) ができる場合 (voidable) を除き、契約の効力に影響しない。

　契約を無効とするほどの unilateral mistake がある場合は、相手方の詐欺行為 (fraud) が介在しているのが通常であり、misrepresentation (不当表示) を根拠とする rescission (契約解消) や damages (損害賠償) の請求も可能なことが多い (本編第7章)。しかし、rescission は契約の相手方に対してのみ主張できる救済手段なので、たとえば、相手方が契約の目的物を第三者に転売してしまった場合、目的物を善意 (a bona fide) で取得した第三者に対して rescission を主張して目的物を取り戻すことはできない。したがって、錯誤によって処分した目的物を第三者に転売されてしまった後にこれを転得者から取り戻したい場合は、mistake による void の主張ができるか否かが決め手となる。

　（ⅰ）　Mistake as to terms（契約条件の錯誤）：契約の一方当事者が契約条件について重大な (fundamental) 誤解をしていて、相手方がそのことを合理的に知り得た場合は、前者は契約の無効を主張することができる (Hartog v Colin and Shields [1939] 3 All ER 566⑨)。

　（ⅱ）　Mistake as to identity（当事者の同一性の錯誤）：契約当事者の同一性に錯誤があるとき、すなわち、契約の相手方が A であると信じて契約を締結したところ、実際には B であった場合は、B との間では契約が成立しない。また、A との間でも B に代理権がない以上契約は成立しない。ただし、特に商取引に関する契約の場合、当事者にとって重要なのは、相手方の支払能力 (creditworthiness) その他当事者の属性 (attributes) だけであり、当事者が A なのか B なのかという問題はその関心の対象外であることが多い。上述のとおり、その程度の錯誤は fundamental mistake とはいえず、契約の成否に影響しない。判例法上、当事者の同一性の錯誤と属性の錯誤とを区別する基準は、相対取引 (face to face transaction) によって成立した契約の場合と書面交換のみによる契約の場合とで異なっている。

　まず、契約当事者が一度も相対することなく、書面だけで契約が成立した場合は、原則として、契約当事者はその書面に当事者として記載されている者である。したがって、たとえば、詐欺師 (rogue) が他人の名を使って商品注文

書を送付した場合、注文書の名義人を注文者と信じて商品を送付した売主と当該詐欺師との間では契約が成立しない（Cundy v Lindsay（1878）3 App Cas 459 (HL)⑩）。ただし、詐欺師が実在しない会社の名義で注文した場合は、架空名義人の存在を信じて注文に応じた売主は、注文者の creditworthiness（信用力）の mistake をしたに過ぎないと解される場合がある（King's Norton Metal v Edridge, Merrett & Co.（1897）14 TLR 98 (CA)⑪）。

これに対し、直接相対しての取引（face to face transaction）の場合、詐欺師が自分の名前を偽ったとしても、契約当事者は対面している詐欺師本人であり、その名前に関する錯誤は、原則として、契約相手の creditworthiness（信用力）その他の属性（attributes）に関する mistake に過ぎないと推定される（Phillips v Brooks Ltd.［1919］2 KB 243⑫、Lewis v Averay［1971］3 All ER 907⑭）。この推定を覆して詐欺師との契約が mistake as to identity（契約当事者の同一性に関する錯誤）により void（無効）であることを主張するためには、当該契約を締結する上で当事者が誰であるかが本質的な要素であったことを証明しなければならないが、そのような主張が認められる場合は、当事者の才能や個性に基づく役務や成果の提供を内容とする特殊な契約（作曲契約、演奏契約、出演契約等）を除き、あまり考えられない。Phillips v Brooks Ltd.判決（［1919］2 KB 243⑫）と Ingram v Little 判決（［1961］1 QB 31 (CA)⑬）は、いずれも、売買代金支払のために他人名義で cheque（小切手）を作成した詐欺師を、売主が小切手名義人本人と信じて物品（前者は指輪、後者は中古車）を売却した事件である。前者は、売主の mistake は当事者の信用力（creditworthiness）に過ぎないと判示したが、後者では、小切手による代金受領を拒んでいた売主が小切手名義人の実在を確認した上で小切手での支払に応じたとき、買主が誰であるかが契約の本質的な要素となった旨を認定し、売買の錯誤無効（void）を理由に転買人に対する自動車返還請求を認めた。しかし、後者でも、売主の錯誤の実質的な内容は、前者同様小切手の有効性、すなわち買主の支払能力（creditworthiness）に過ぎなかったはずであり、区別の基準が不明確である。よって、後者（Ingram v Little 判決）に対しては、批判的な意見の裁判官が少なくない（Lewis v Averay［1971］3 All ER 907⑭、Shogun Finance Ltd. v Hudson［2003］3 WLR 1371 (HL)⑮）。

(4) Rectification（修正命令）

　当事者間で明確な口頭の合意をした上でこれを書面化して契約書を作成する際、何らかの書き違いや書き落とし等の書類上の錯誤（mistake in documents）があった場合、裁判所は equity に基づいて、当該書き違い、書き落としの訂正を命ずることができる。これは、両当事者が書き違いに気づかずに契約を交わした場合（common mistake）、又は一方が気づいていながら黙っていた場合（unilateral mistake）に適用がある救済手段である。ただし、修正が命じられるのは以下の要件が備わっている場合に限られる（Frederick E Rose (London) Ltd. v William Pim & Co., Ltd.［1953］2 QB 450 (CA)⑯）。

　（ⅰ）　書面化する前に、両当事者間で契約の内容に関して明確な意思の合致があること

　（ⅱ）　両当事者が意図していた内容と書面化された内容が異なることについて、明らかな証拠があること

　（ⅲ）　書面作成上の mistake であり、取引そのものに関する mistake ではないこと

2．Duress、Undue Influence and Unconscionability

(1) Duress（強迫）

　Duress には、以下のとおり、（ⅰ）duress to the person（人に対する強迫）、（ⅱ）duress to goods（財物に対する強迫）、（ⅲ）economic duress（経済的強迫）の3種類がある。Duress により締結された契約や gift（贈与）は、原則として取消すことができる（avoidable）。

（ⅰ）　Duress to the persons（人に対する強迫）

　他人の身体、自由、生命に対して暴力を加えること、又は加える恐れを与えることをいう。Duress により契約したことの立証を要するが、duress が唯一の原因である必要も主要な原因である必要もない。

（ⅱ）　Duress to goods（財物に対する強迫）

　他人の財物に危害を加えること、又はその危険にさらすことによる強迫である。ただし、法律上の権利の行使等をする旨の通知はこれに当らない。

Duress to the persons と異なり、この場合は、duress が契約締結の主たる原因であることの立証を要する。また、他により有効かつ実際的な解決手段（an effective and practical alternative）がある場合は契約の解消の請求は認められない。

（iii） Economic duress（経済的強迫）

不正な手段（in an illegitimate way）で優越的な経済的地位を利用して契約を強要する場合がこれに当る（Universe Tankships Inc. of Monrovia v International Transport Workers' Federation ［1982］2 All ER 67⑰、B & S Contracts & Design v Victor Green Publications ［1984］IGR 419⑱、Atlas Express v Kafco ［1989］1 All ER 641⑲）。不正な手段には違法行為や不法行為による方法が含まれるが、これに至らない不適正な方法でもよい。ただし、契約に違反することを仄めかすだけでは通常は不十分と解される。また、economic duress が契約締結の主たる原因であることの立証を要する。

(2) Undue Influence（不当威圧）

Undue influence は、当事者の一方が相手方からの不当な圧力により、契約締結や gift について自由な判断をすることができなかった場合、equity に基づいて、その契約や gift の解消を認める法原理である。これには、次の3つの種類がある。

（ⅰ） Undue influence presumed at law（法律上の推定による不当威圧）

契約を締結した当事者間に契約以前から特別な信認関係（confidential or fiduciary relationship）が存在する場合は、反証のない限り、当該信認関係上の弱い立場の者が、強い立場の者の undue influence をよって当該契約を締結したと推定される。親子関係（parent and child relationship）、弁護士と依頼者の関係（solicitor and client relationship）、受託者と受益者の信託関係（trustee and beneficiary relationship）、医者と患者（doctor and patient）、宗教家と信者（religious adviser and believer）、後見人と被後見人（guardian and ward）等が特別な信認関係の典型例である。ただし、労使関係（Mathew v Bobbins (1980) 256 EG 603）や夫婦関係（Royal Bank of Scotland v Etridge (No.2) ［2001］4 All ER 449）はこれに当らない。

(ii) Undue influence presumed at fact（事実上の推定による不当威圧）

当該契約や gift の重大性に鑑み、通常の関係でそのような契約や gift をするのは不自然と思われる場合は、当事者間において一方が他方に不当な影響を与え得るような関係が形成されていることを立証すれば、原則として、弱い立場の者は強い立場の者の undue influence により契約を締結したと推定される（Hodgson v Marks［1970］3 All ER 513）。

(iii) Actual undue influence

以上の2つに当らない場合は、実際に不当な圧力を受けたことによって契約を締結した事実の立証が必要である。

(3) Unconscionable bargains（非良心的取引）

取引上優越的な立場にある者が相手方の無知や窮状を利用して相手方に不利な条件の契約を締結させた場合に当該契約の解消を認めるため、Lord Denning が考え出した equity 上の法理である（Lloyds Bank v Bundy［1974］3 All ER 757[20]）。Common law に基づく duress により解決できない不公平を救済するための制度である点で undue influence と共通するが、undue influence は、一方当事者が相手方に対する優越した地位に基づいて相手方を圧迫して有利な契約や gift に同意させる意思（will）があることを要件としているのに対し、unconscionable bargain の法理はそのような場合に限らずに適用できると解されている。ただし、その要件はあまり明確ではない。

【CASES】

① *Coutrier v Hastie* (1856) 5 HLC 673

Coutrier sold Hastie a cargo of Indian corn which both parties believed to be in transit from Salonica to UK. Unknown to either party the corn had begun to ferment on the ship and the captain had sold it at Tunis before the contract was made. It was held that the contract contemplated that the goods actually existed. Since they did not, neither party was liable to the other.

② *Cooper v Phibbs* (1867) LR 2 HL 149 (HL)

Phibbs let a fishery to Copper. Unknown to the parties the fisheries already belonged to Copper. Thus the contract was void as it was impossible to perform.

③ *Bell v Lever Brothers Ltd.* [1932] AC 161 (HL)

Bell and Snelling, the chairman and vice-chairman of a company, which was a subsidiary of Lever Bros. ("LB"), were paid £50,000 for early termination of their service contracts. It then transpired that the two men had been in breach of their service contracts and LB would have been justified in dismissing them without compensation. LB attempted to have the severance contracts rescinded since it had contracted on the basis of a fundamental mistake. The jury found that the two men had forgotten about their breaches of duty when they had agreed to the compensation, and accordingly it was a common mistake. The House of Lords rejected LB's claim since the mistake was only as to the quality of the service contracts and was not fundamental enough to justify rescission.

"It would be wrong to decide that an agreement to terminate a definite specified contact is void if it turns out that the contract had already been broken and could be terminated otherwise ... Mistake as to quality ... will not affect assent unless it is the mistake of both parties, and is as to the existence of some quality which makes the thing without the quality essentially different from the thing it was believed to be.' ... for example ... 'A buys B's horse; he thinks the horse is sound and he pays the price of a sound horse; he would certainly not have bought the horse if he had known as the fact is that the horse is unsound. If B has made no representation as to soundness and has not contracted that the horse is sound, A is bound and cannot recover back the price. A buys a picture from B; both A and B believe it to be the work of an old master, and a high price is paid. It turns out to be a modern copy. A has no remedy in the absence of representation or warranty ..." (per Lord Atkin)

④ *Leaf v International Galleries* [1950] 1 All ER 693 (CA)

A painting called "Salisbury Cathedral" was sold in the mistaken belief that it was by John Constable. The Court of Appeal accepted that there was a mistake about the quality of the subject-matter and held that this was not enough to render the contract void.

"... that mistake was in one sense essential or fundamental. But such a mistake does not avoid the contract: there was no mistake at all about the subject-matter of the sale. It was a specific picture, "Salisbury Cathedral." The parties were agreed in the same terms on the same subject-matter, and that is sufficient to make a contract." (per Lord Denning)

⑤ *Solle v Butcher* [1950] 1 KB 671 (CA)

Charles Butcher let a flat to Godfrey Solle for £250 in the mistaken belief that the rent was not restricted by the Rent Restriction Acts. Solle later discovered that the Act did apply and that the maximum rent he could charge was £140. He sued for a refund and Butcher counter-claimed that the contract was void for mistake. It was held that the contract was not void in law, but was voidable in equity. It means that the tenant could chose to either rescind the contract or stay on, but in the latter case he would have to pay the full rent.

⑥　*Great Pearce Shipping Ltd. v Tsavliris Salvage (International) Ltd.* [2003] QB 679 (CA)

A contract was entered into for one ship to assist another ship, which was damaged at sea, on the common belief between the parties that the rescue ship was only 12 miles away from the damaged ship, but in fact she was 39 hours away. The owner of the damaged ship sought to cancel the contract and refuse payment on the ground that both parties had made a fundamental mistake as to the distance such as to render the contract void at law or, alternatively, voidable in equity. It was held that the ships were not that far apart that the contract could not have been performed. Further, it was not essentially different from that which the parties had intended. The contract was therefore, not void at law nor was it possible for equity to set aside a contract on such terms.

"... The following elements must be present if common mistake is to avoid a contract; (i) there must be a common assumption as to the existence of a state of affair; (ii) there must be no warranty by either party that the state of affairs exists; (iii) the non-existence of the state of affairs must not be attributable to the fault of either party; (iv) the non-existence of the state of affairs must render the performance of the contract impossible; (v) the state of affairs may be the existence, or a vital attribute, of the consideration to be provided or the circumstances which must subsist, if performance of the contractual adventure is to be possible." (per Lord Phillips M.R.)

⑦　*Smith v Hughes* (1871) LR 6 QB 597 (CA)

Smith offered to sell oats to Hughes and showed him a sample. The sample oats were 'green' (i.e. new), however, Hughes carelessly thought they were old, and ordered the whole quantity. It was held that the test for a mutual mistake is an objective one; where one party is simply careless, the doctrine of caveat emptor applies. Thus, where the buyer (Smith), due to his own carelessness, bought 'green' oats believing them to be 'old', he was bound to the contract.

⑧　*Raffles v Wichelhaus* (1864) 2 HC 906

第8章　Mistake、Duress、etc.

Wichelhaus agreed to buy '125 bales of Surat cotton to arrive ex Peerless from Bombay.' There were two ships called Peerless, both sailing from Bombay. One was leaving in October, the other in December. The buyer was referring to the former, the seller to the latter. It was held that as there was no consensus ad idem, there was no contract.

⑨　*Hartog v Colin and Shields* [1939] 3 All ER 566

The seller mistakenly offered to sell Argentine hare skins to Hartog for at a price per pound instead of per piece, a piece being about one third of a pound. It was obvious from the pre-contractual negotiations and normal trade practice that the intention was to sell the hare skins per piece. It was held that contract was void for mistake since the buyer could not reasonably have supposed that the offer contained the offeror's real intention.

⑩　*Cundy v Lindsay* (1878) 3 App Cas 459 (HL)

A rogue called Blenkarn sent a written order for handkerchiefs to Lindsay, a linen manufacturer in Belfast. He represented himself to be from the reputable firm of Blenkiron & Co. Lindsay had heard of Blenkiron & Co.'s reputation, although he did not know the exact address. Believing that letter, Lindsay sent the handkerchiefs at the rogue's address. The rogue sold the handkerchiefs to Cundy, who bought them in good faith. Payment was not made for the handkerchiefs, and Lindsay sued Cundy for unlawful conversion, claiming that title had not passed to the rogue as the contract with him was void for mistake. It was held that the contract was void as Lindsay never intended to deal with Blenkarn.

"Their minds never, even for an instant of time rested upon him, and as between him and them there was no consensus of mind which could lead to any agreement or any contract whatever." (per Lord Cairns LC)

⑪　*King's Norton Metal v Edridge, Merrett & Co.* (1897) 14 TLR 98 (CA)

The seller (King's Norton Metal) received an order for wire supposedly from Hallam & Co in Sheffield. The letter-head had a picture of a factory with several chimneys and a statement about various company depots. All this led the seller to believe that it was dealing with a creditworthy company, when, in fact, the letters were written by a fraudulent rogue called Wallis. Wallis sold the metal to Edridge, Merett & Co without paying for it, and the seller sued in conversion. It was held that this was not a case of an operative mistake. The seller was not mistaking one person for another. It was simply mistaken as to the creditworthiness of the client.

⑫　*Phillips v Brooks Ltd.* [1919] 2 KB 243

A rogue called North went into Phipplips' jewellery shop and selected pearls and a ring to the value of £3,000. He wrote out a cheque, claiming to be Sir George Bullough, a well-known wealthy person. The jeweler checked his address in the directory, and accepted the cheque. The rogue took away the ring and pawned it with Brooks Ltd. When the cheque was dishonoured, the jeweler claimed against Brooks Ltd. for return of the ring on the basis that the contract with North was void for mistake. It was held that the jeweller's mistake was only to the creditworthiness of his customer, not to his identity.

"He had contracted to sell and deliver the ring to the person who came into his shop...his intention was to sell to the person present, and identified by sight and hearing." (per Horridge J)

⑬　*Ingram v Little* [1961] 1 QB 31 (CA)

Three elderly sisters advertised their car for sale. A rogue, claiming to be P.G.M. Hutchinson of Stanstead House, offered to buy the car. They refused to accept his cheque until Hilda Ingram had gone to the post office to check his name and address in the phone directory. When she discovered it there, the sisters accepted the cheque. In fact, the real P.G.M. Hutchinson had died some time earlier. It was held that the contract was void, and the sisters could recover their car from Little, to whom the rogue had sold it. The court said that once the sisters had refused the cheque, the identity of the buyer (i.e. offer to the real P.G.M. Hutchinson) became fundamental to the contract.

'The parties were no longer concerned with a cash sale of goods where the identity of the purchaser was prima facie unimportant. They were concerned with a credit sale in which both parties knew that the identity of the purchaser was of the utmost importance." (per Pearce LJ)

⑭　*Lewis v Averay* [1971] 3 All ER 907

Lewis advertised his car for sale. A rogue, claiming to be the actor Richard Greene, offered to buy it and to pay by cheque. Lewis asked for proof of his identity and was shown a forged pass to Pinewood Studios in the name of Richard Greene. It was held, following Phillips v Brooks, that this contract was not void for mistake. Lord Denning said that the distinction between mistake as to identity and mistake as to attributes was 'a distinction without a difference' and 'do no good to the law'. According to him Ingram v Little was incorrectly decided..

"When two parties have come to a contract ... the fact that one party is mistaken as to the identity of the other does not mean that there is no contract, or that the contract is a nullity and void from the beginning. It only means that the contract is voidable, that is, liable to be set aside at the instance of the mistaken person, so long as he does so before third parties have in good faith acquired rights under it." (per Lord Denning M.R.)

⑮ *Shogun Finance Ltd. v Hudson* [2003] 3 WLR 1371 (HL)

A rogue, pretending to be Durlabh Patel, bought a Mitsubishi Shogun car from a motor dealer. He produced Mr. Patel's stolen driving licence, and asked to buy the car on hire purchase. The dealer phoned Shogun Finance, the hire purchaser, and faxed the draft hire-purchase agreement signed by the rogue as Patel, with a copy of Patel's driving licence. Shogun Finance verified Mr Patel's credit rating and approved finance. The rogue took the car and sold it to Hudson who bought it in good faith. Shogun Finance brought an action against Hudson for damages in tort of conversion, and argued that the rogue was not a hire-purchase debtor as there had been no contract with him on the ground of the mistake as to identity. It was held that the written agreement was made between Shogun Finance and the real Patel, which was nullity since it was made without Patel's authority. The claim was admitted since there was no valid contract between the rogue and Shogun Finance. It was not held to be a 'face to face' transaction, however, obiter indicated judges' disagreement with Ingram v Little.

⑯ *Frederick E Rose (London) Ltd. v William Pim & Co., Ltd.* [1953] 2 QB 450 (CA)

Frederick E Rose was asked to supply from the seller with 'Moroccan horsebeans described as feveroles'. Rose did not know what feveroles were, but he was told by the seller that feveroles were just another name for horsebeans. On this basis Rose entered a contract to buy 'horsebeans' from the seller. In fact, feveroles is a superior form of horsebeans, and when Rose claimed damages from the seller for supplying inferior horsebeans, he asked the court to rectify the contract to read 'feveroles' instead of 'horsebeans', so he could sue the buyer for supplying the wrong thing. The court refused to do so since Rose had agreed on a sale of horsebeans, and that is what the contract said.

"Rectification is concerned with contract and documents, not with intentions. In order to get rectification, it is necessary to show that the parties were in complete agreement on the terms of their contract, but by an error wrote them down wrongly; and in this regard, in order to ascertain the terms of their contract, you do not look into the inner minds of the parties ... into their intentions ... any more than you do in the formation of any other contract. You look at their outward acts, that is, at what they said or wrote to one another in coming to their agreement, and then compare it with the document which they have signed. If you can predicate with certainty what their contract was, and that it is, by common mistake, wrongly expressed in the document, then you rectify the document; but nothing less will suffice." (per Lord Denning MR)

⑰ *Universe Tankships Inc. of Monrovia v International Transport Workers' Federation* [1982] 2 All ER 67

A trade union (International Transport Workers' Federation) blacked a ship. To get it released the owner of the ship paid $6,480 into the union's welfare fund. It was held that the payment was recoverable as it had been extracted by duress.

"It is, I think, already established law that economic pressure can in law amount to duress; and that duress, if proved, not only renders voidable a transaction into which a person has entered under its compulsion but is actionable as a tort, if it causes damage or loss." (per Lord Scarman)

⑱ *B & S Contracts & Design v Victor Green Publications* [1984] IGR 419

Victor Green Publications hired the contractor to erect some exhibition stands at Olympia. The contractor's workers refused to complete the contract until a £9,000 demand for severance pay had been met. The contractor paid £4,500 and informed Victor Green that unless it paid the other £4,500 the job would not be carried out. Victor Green paid to avoid being sued by the exhibitors to whom it had let the stands, but then deducted the money from its final contract payment on the basis that it had been subjected to economic duress. It was held that in these circumstances there was duress and Victor Green was not liable for the £4,500.

"A threat to break a contract unless money is paid by the other party can, but by no means always will, constitute duress. It appears from the authorities that it will only constitute duress if the consequences of a refusal would be serious and immediate so that there is no reasonable alternative open, such as by legal redress, obtaining an injunction etc...." (per Kerr LJ)

⑲ *Atlas Express v Kafco* [1989] 1 All ER 641

A firm of carriers demanded extra charges from a small manufacturing company to deliver their goods. The company risked losing a valuable contract with Woolworths if its goods were not delivered and so paid the extra under protest. It was held that this amounted to economic duress.

⑳ *Lloyds Bank v Bundy* [1974] 3 All ER 757

Bundy was a farmer who had been a customer of the Lloyds Bank for many years. He gave a guarantee and a charge for £7,500 over his farmhouse to secure the overdraft of his son's company. He was advised by his solicitor not to increase the security, but was convinced by the assistant manager of the bank to increase the guarantee and charge to £11,000, even though, as the assistant manager knew, the farmhouse was his only asset. The Court of Appeal held that the charge should be set aside for undue influence since the bank was in breach of fiduciary duty. Lord Denning said that Bundy could have set aside the charge on the basis of 'inequity of bargaining power'.

"English law gives relief to one who, without independent advice, enters into a contract upon terms which are very unfair or transfers property for a consideration which is grossly inadequate, when his bargaining power is grievously impaired by reason of his own needs or desires, or his own ignorance or infirmity, coupled with undue influences or pressures brought to bear on him by or for the benefit of the other." (per Lord Denning M.R.)

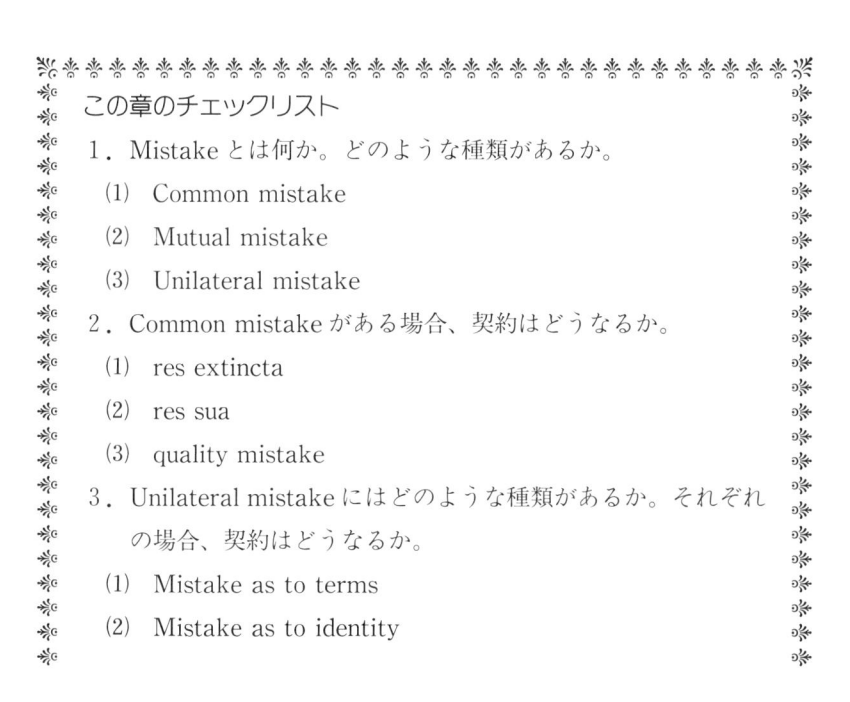

この章のチェックリスト

1. Mistake とは何か。どのような種類があるか。
   (1) Common mistake
   (2) Mutual mistake
   (3) Unilateral mistake
2. Common mistake がある場合、契約はどうなるか。
   (1) res extincta
   (2) res sua
   (3) quality mistake
3. Unilateral mistake にはどのような種類があるか。それぞれの場合、契約はどうなるか。
   (1) Mistake as to terms
   (2) Mistake as to identity

4．Rectification とは何か。

5．Duress にはどのような種類があるか。この場合、契約はどうなるか。

(1) Duress to the person

(2) Duress to goods

(3) Economic duress

6．Undue influence、unconscionable bargains とはそれぞれ何か。

(1) Undue influence presumed at law

(2) Undue influence presumed at fact

(3) Actual undue influence

(4) Unconscionable bargains

第9章

Discharge of Contract（契約の終了）

　Contractは、(ⅰ)当事者間の合意（termination agreement）、(ⅱ)契約違反（breach）、(ⅲ)不当表示（misrepresentation）、強迫（duress）等による解消（rescission）、(ⅳ)錯誤（mistake）による無効（void）及び(ⅴ)契約目的不到達（frustration）による失効（void）によって終了し、両当事者はそれ以降契約上の義務を免れる（discharge）。この内、misrepresentation、mistake、duress等は、前2章で扱ったので、以下、termination agreement、breach及びfrustrationによるdischarge of contractについて説明する。

1. Discharge by Agreement（合意による契約終了）

　契約を締結した当事者は、原則として、両当事者の合意によって、いつでも契約上の義務の変更や終了をすることができる。ただし、当事者間における契約の変更や終了の合意はそれ自体がcontract（契約）なので、法的拘束力を生じさせるためには、契約成立のための条件（agreement、consideration、intention to create legal relations等）を全て充足しなければならない。

　たとえば、契約の一方当事者の義務が履行済みであり、他方の義務のみが未履行の場合、当事者間の合意によって未履行当事者を義務から解放するためには、未履行当事者が新たなconsideration（約因）を提供するか、又は捺印証書（deed）によって合意をすることが必要である。これに対して、双方の義務が未履行の状態で契約終了の合意をする場合は、互いに相手方の義務を免除することが自己の義務から解放されることに対するconsiderationとなっているので、改めてconsiderationを提供する必要はない。

2．Discharge by Breach（契約違反による終了）

(1) Breach of condition、warranty、innominate term

　相手方当事者の契約違反を根拠に契約を解消（recession）して自己の義務を免れようとする場合は、まず違反された term（契約条項）が warranty、condition、innominate term のいずれであるのかを確認する必要がある。既述のとおり（本編第4章）、当事者は、breach of condition があった場合には、契約を解消（rescind）して損害賠償を請求するか、あるいは追認（affirm）して損害賠償のみを請求するかを選択することができる（Poussard v Speirs and Pond（1876）1 QBD 410）のに対し、breach of warranty の場合の救済手段は損害賠償請求のみであり、契約を解消することができない（Bettini v Gye（1876）1 QBD 183）。また、breach of innominate term の場合は、fundamental breach、すなわち、義務の性質及び違反の態様や程度に鑑みてもはや契約を継続する余地がないほど重大な契約違反である場合のみ breach of condition と同じ扱いとなる（Cehave NV v Bremer Handelsgesellschft mbH（1975）3 All ER 739）。

(2) Anticipatory Breach（履行期前の契約違反）

　当事者の一方が、契約の履行期到来前に履行を拒絶すること（anticipatory repudiation）、履行を不可能にすること（impossibility before performace is due）等、予め契約違反をすることが明白となる行為をすることを anticipatory breach（履行期前の契約違反）という。

　Anticipatory breach があった場合、相手方は履行期前であっても直ちに契約を解消（rescind）して損害賠償を請求することができる（Hochster v De la Tour（1853）2 E & B 678①、Omnium D'Enterprises and Others v Sutherland［1919］1 KB 618）。ただし、相手方は契約解消の義務を負うわけではないので、そのまま契約を存続させて履行期における義務履行の請求をする方法を選択することもできる（White and Carter（Councils）Ltd. v McGregor［1961］3 All ER 1178②）。この場合は、履行期において相手方の不履行を確認の上、契約違反による損害の賠償を訴求することになる。

ただし、anticipatory breach を知った後に直ちに契約解消をしなかった場合において、履行期に他の理由により契約の履行が不可能となったり、又は自らも契約違反をしたときは、もはや相手方の anticipatory breach を根拠として契約解消や損害賠償請求をすることができなくなる（Avery v Bowden (1885) 5 E & B 714③）。

3. Discharge by Frustration（契約目的不達成による履行義務の終了）

(1) 定義

　Frustration とは、(ⅰ)契約締結後に(ⅱ)契約締結時の予期に反して(ⅲ)何れの契約当事者の責任にもよらない事態が発生し、(ⅳ)その結果して契約上の未履行の義務の内容や目的が当該契約締結時に両当事者が合理的に期待していた内容・目的とは根本的に異なるものとなり、(ⅴ)契約当事者に当初の義務の履行を強制するのは不公平であると認められる状態となることをいう。Frustration によって履行が不可能となった契約上の義務は自動的に消滅し、当該義務を負っていた当事者は、その後に到来する全ての義務の履行責任を免れる。これを the doctrine of frustration（フラストレーションの法理）という。

　イギリス契約法には、日本民法のような過失責任の法理が存在せず、当事者の責任によらない事態が生じて契約の目的を達成できなくなった場合であっても、約束したとおりの義務の履行責任を負わなければならないのが common law 上の原則である（Paradine v Jane (1647) Aleyn 26 (KB)）。The doctrine of frustration は、重大な事情変更の後までも契約の文言どおりの義務履行を強制することが不公平で正義に反すると認められる場合に common law の原則を修正して正義を実現するために生まれた法理である。このような性格上、この法理の適用場面を安易に拡張することは許されず、要件を厳格に解釈すべきものとされている（J. Lauritzen A.S. v Wijsmuller B.V.: The Super Servant Two [1990] 1 Lloyd's Rep 1 (CA)④）。たとえば、後述のとおり、当事者の予期に反する事態が生じたことにより不測の費用その他の経済的な負担が生じたというだけでは frustration とはいえない（Davis Contractors Ltd. v Fareham Urban District Council [1956] AC 696 (HL)⑤）。

(2) Frustration の類型的要件

Frustration により契約上の義務が消滅するのは、契約の履行を不可能とするような事態が生じたときに限られる。その具体例は以下のとおりである。

（ⅰ） **Destruction of the subject matter of contract**（目的物の滅失）

契約の目的物が滅失したとき、その結果履行が不可能となった契約上の義務（目的物の給付義務、加工義務等）は frustration により消滅する（Taylor v Caldwell（1863）3 B&S 826⑥、Asfar & Co. v Blundell［1986］1 QB 123 (CA)⑦）。ただし、目的物が不特定の場合は、frustration とはなりにくい（Blackburn Bobbin Co., Ltd. v T.W. Allen & Sons Ltd.［1918］2 KB 467 (CA)⑧）。

なお、特定物に関する物品売買契約に関しては、the Sales of Goods Act 1979により、目的物の滅失が危険（risk）の移転前か否かが契約上の双方の義務の終了の基準になる（the Sale of Goods Act 1979 s7）。

> Where there is an agreement to sell specific goods and subsequently the goods, without any fault on the part of the seller or buyer, perish before the risk passes to the buyer, the agreement is avoided.

（ⅱ） **Temporary unavailability of the subject matter**（目的物の一時的使用不能）

契約の履行不能が一時的な場合であっても、それによって当初の契約の目的が達成できない場合は frustration となる（Jackson v Union Marine Insurance Company Ltd.（1874）LR 10 CP 125 (Court of Exchequer Chamber)⑨）。

（ⅲ） **Frustration of purpose**（目的達成の不能）

両当事者が意図していた契約の中心的な目的を達成することが不可能となる事態が発生したこと、又はそのような目的達成に不可欠な事態が発生しないことは、当該目的達成のために負担していた義務に関する frustration となる（Krell v Henry［1903］2 KB 740 (CA)⑩）。ただし、何が中心的な目的であるかは契約の内容との関連性によるので、必ずしも一義的には定まらない（Herne Bay Steamboat Co. v Hutton［1903］2 KB 683 (CA)⑪）。

（ⅳ） **Supervening illegality**（法の変更による履行の違法）

契約締結後に法が変更され、その結果として契約上の義務の履行が違法となった場合、当該義務は frustration により自動的に消滅する（Denny, Mott & Dickson v James B. Fraser & Co., Ltd. [1944] AC 265 (HL Scotland)⑫）。

(ⅴ) **Method of performance impossible**（履行の実現不能）

契約上の義務の履行が実現不可能となることも、当該義務に関する frustration の事由である（Nickoll & Knight v Ashton Eridge & Co. [1901] 2 KB 126 (CA)⑬）。ただし、義務の履行が商業上実現困難となっただけでは frustration とはいえない（Davis Contractors Ltd. v Fareham Urban District Council [1956] AC 696 (HL)、Ocean Tramp Tankers Corporation v VO Sovfracht, The Eugenia [1964] 2 QB 226 (CA)⑭、Tsakiroglou & Co., Ltd. v Noblee Thorl GmbH [1962] AC 93 (HL)）。

(3) 消極的要件（limitations）

Frustration の法理は契約上の義務を自動的に消滅させるという重大な効果をもたらすので、以下のような事情があるときは、その適用を制限している。

(ⅰ) **Self-induced events**（自ら招いた frustration）

第1に、義務者の過失（negligence causing event）により履行不能となった場合は、frustration は生じない（F.C. Shepherd & Co., Ltd. v Jerrom [1987] QB 301 (CA)）。この場合の義務者の過失の立証責任は、過失を主張する側が負担する（Joseph Constantine SS Line Ltd. v Imperial Smelting Corp. Ltd. [1942] AC 154 (HL)⑮）。

第2に、義務者の選択の結果、契約上の義務の履行が不可能となった場合（choosing not to perform）、たとえば、義務者が第三者との間で締結した別の契約上の義務を履行するために本件契約上の義務の履行ができない場合には frustration を主張できない（Maritime National Fisch Ltd. v Ocean Trawlers Ltd. [1935] AC 524 (PC on Appeal from the Supreme Court of Nova Scotia)⑯、J. Lauritzen A.S. v Wijsmuller B.V.: The Super Servant Two [1990] 1 Lloyd's Rep 1 (CA)）。

(ⅱ) **Events foreseen and provided for**（予期されていた事態）

契約の目的達成を不可能とする事態が生じたとしても、契約当事者がそのよ

うな事態の発生を予期して契約に規定していた場合は、これを原因とするfrustrationは生じない（Ocean Tramp Tankers Corporation v VO Sovfrcht, The Eugenia [1964] 2 QB 226 (CA)、Walton Harvey Ltd. v Walker & Homfrays Ltd. [1931] 1 Ch 274⑰、Amalgamated Investment & Property Co., Ltd. v John Walker & Sons Ltd. [1977] 1 WLR 164 (CA)⑱）。

ただし、戦争の勃発は、たとえ予期できたとしてもfrustrationの原因となることがある（Ertel Bieber & Co. v Rio Tinto Co., Ltd. [1918] AC 260 (HL)、W.J. Tatem Ltd. v Gamboa [1939] 1 KB 132⑲）。

(iii) Lease（リース契約）

リース契約は義務履行の期間が長いのでfrustrationが生じにくい（Criklewood Property Investment Trust v Leighton's Investment Trust Ltd. [1945] AC 22 (HL)⑳）が、the doctrine of frustrationが全く適用されないわけではない（National Carriers Ltd. v Panalpina (Northern) Ltd. [1981] AC 675 (HL)㉑）。

(iv) Contractual provision（契約条項）

契約当事者が契約の履行を妨げる一定の事態が生じたときの免責や契約終了に関する合意をしているときは、そのような事態が発生したときの効果は当事者間の合意に従うことになるので、その限度でfrustrationの法理の適用は制限される。実際上、重要な取引に関する契約書のほとんどは、いわゆるforce majeure clause（不可抗力条項）を設け、当事者の支配を越える特定の事態が生じた場合における契約履行義務の免責、及びその後の処置に関する事項（たとえば、frustrationによる契約の当然失効の排除、履行義務の中断等）を定めている。

継続的な取引に関する契約書には、hardship clauseと呼ばれる条項が含まれていることがある。これは、契約履行を主として経済的に困難とするhardship事由の特定及び当該事由が生じた場合における手続（条件変更、解約等）に関する合意であり、force majeure clauseとは目的が異なっている。

(4) Frustrationの効果

Common law上、契約上の義務は、frustrationの発生と同時に当然に終了

する。Breach（契約違反）、misrepresentation（不当表示）等による rescission や mistake による void の主張とは異なり、当事者による無効の主張や契約解消の通知によって終了するのではない。Frustration で終了した契約を追認することはできない（Hirji Mulji v Cheong Yue Steamship Co.［1936］AC 497 (HL)[22]）。

　問題は、frustration によって履行不能となった義務以外の義務、特に契約の相手方の義務がどうなるかである。これに関する common law の取扱いはあまり合理的といえないため、後記の制定法（the Law Reform (Frustrated Contracts) Act 1943）による修正を受けているが、先に common law の原則が適用される場合について説明する。

　まず、契約の一方当事者の義務が frustration によって消滅したとき、相手方当事者の前者に対する義務のうち、そのような事態が生ずるまでに発生していなかったもの（すなわち、履行期未到来の義務）は、同時に消滅する（Appleby v Myers（1867）LR 2 CP 651[23]）。これは、日本法上の危険負担に関する債務者主義と同じ結論である。

　これに対し、一方当事者の義務について frustration が生ずる前に既に発生していた相手方当事者の義務は、前者の義務が frustration で消滅しても原則として消滅しない（Chandler v Webster［1904］1 KB 493[24]）。たとえば、A と B との間で代金先払いの約定で製作物供給契約を締結していたとして、A の B に対する製作物引渡義務が frustration によって消滅したとき、B の A に対する代金が未払いの場合は約定の期日に支払わなければならないし、支払済みの場合は代金の返還を請求することができない。この結果は相手方にとってあまりに酷なので、判例法はこの原則を若干修正し、frustration によって一方当事者の義務が全て消滅した場合、相手方の義務は consideration の不存在を根拠として消滅することにしている（Fibrosa Spolka Akcyjna v Fairbairn, Lawson, Combe, Barbour Ltd.［1943］AC 32 (HL)[25]）。ただし、一方当事者の義務の一部だけが frustration となった場合の相手方の義務に関しては consideration の法理を使うことができない。

4．The Law Reform (Frustrated Contracts) Act 1943

　上記3(4)で説明したcommon law上の原則は、契約上の義務の一部についてfrustrationが生じた場合に既発生の相手方の義務が消滅しない点、及び契約履行着手前に準備のために要した費用の償還請求ができない点において、取引上の公平に反していた。そこで、この問題を解決するためにthe Law Reform (Frustrated Contracts) Act 1943が制定された。同法の適用範囲及び内容は以下のとおりである。

(1) 適用範囲（Scope）

　この法律には、以下の適用除外に当る場合を除く全ての契約に適用される。第1に、契約上の分離可能な義務の一部がfrustration発生時までに履行されていた場合、その部分については別個の契約があったものとして取り扱うものとし、この法律は適用されない（s2(4)）。第2に、charterparty（傭船契約）及びcarriage of goods by sea（海上物品運送）には適用がない（s2(5)(a)）。これらに関しては、先払いの約定の傭船料や運賃に関する義務は理由の如何にかかわらず消滅しない旨の商慣習が確立しているからである。ただし、time charter（定期傭船契約）にはこの法律の適用がある。第3に、contract for sale of specific goods（特定物売買契約）及びinsurance contract（保険契約）はこの法律の適用を受けない（s2(5)(b)、(c)）。特定物売買契約における物品の減失は、上記3(2)(ⅰ)のthe Sales of Goods Act 1979のs7によって処理される。第4に、frustrationとなり得る事態が生じた場合の処理に関し当事者間で法律の定めと異なる合意をしていた場合、裁判所はその限度で法律の適用を排除し、当事者間の合意の効力を認める（s2(3)）。すなわち、force majeure clauseによって法律の適用を排除することが可能である。

(2) Recovery（返還請求）

　相手方の義務がfrustrationにより消滅した場合、それ以前に支払済みの金銭については、その返還を受けることができる。ただし、相手方の義務が消滅する前にその履行準備や一部履行のための費用が相手方に発生していた場合、

裁判所が公平と認めるときは、その裁量により費用の全部又は一部が返還金額から控除されることがある（s1(2)、Gamerco S.A. v I.C.M./Fair Warning (Agency) Ltd. [1995] 1 WLR 1226）。

　相手方の義務がfrustrationによって消滅するより前に、これと対価関係にある金銭支払義務が発生していた場合、当該金銭支払義務はfrustrationの発生と同時に消滅するので、もはや支払いを要しない。ただし、相手方が契約の準備や一部履行に要した経費は、裁判所が諸事情を斟酌して公平と認める場合（if it considers it just to do so having regard to all the circumstances of the case）、相手方に補償しなければならない（s1(2)）。

(3) Where a valuable benefit has already been conferred（有価値な利益の供与がある場合）

　相手方の義務がfrustrationにより消滅するより前に相手方に対して有価値な物品を提供し、又は便益を供与していた場合は、以下の2つの条件を充たし、かつ裁判所が諸事情を斟酌して公平と認める場合（where the court considers just, having regard to all the circumstances of the case）、当該物品や便益の価額を上限とし、その返還を求めることができる（s1(3)）。

　（ⅰ）当該物品や便益が非金銭的な利益（benefit other than a payment of money）であること

　（ⅱ）契約上の義務から解放される前（before the time of discharge）に付与した利益であること

　この場合の物品や便益の価額は、frustrationが生じた後の残存価値について算定する（BP Exploration Co. (Libya) Ltd. v Hunt (No.2) [1982] 1 All ER 925 (HL)㉖）。したがって、たとえば、一方当事者が費用を投じて供与した物品の全てが火災によって消滅した場合、相手方に残っている利益の価値はゼロとなり、返還請求は認められない。

　The Law Reform (Frustrated Contracts) Act 1943によって、契約終了後の不公平が一応解消されたものの、the doctrine of frustrationは、（ⅰ）当事者の意思にかかわらず契約の上の義務の当然終了という効果をもたらす点、及び（ⅱ）事後処理は、裁判所の裁量に委ねられている点において法的安定性が不十

分であり、取引を行う上での障害となる可能性がある。よって、商取引に関してイギリス法に準拠する契約を締結する際は、契約当事者の意向を反映したforce majeure clauseを必ず設けるべきである。ただし、契約に影響する全ての事態を予想して規定することはできないので、そのような合意によってfrustrationを完全に排除するのは難しい。

【CASES】

① *Hochster v De la Tour* (1853) 2 E & B 678

De la Tour contracted to employ Hochster as a courier from June 1, 1852. On May 11 De la Tour informed Hochster that his services were no longer required. It was held that Hochster was given an immediate right of action for breach of the contract, and he did not have to wait until June 1.

② *White and Carter (Councils) Ltd. v McGregor* [1961] 3 All ER 1178

White and Carter, an advertising contractor, had contracted to advertise the garage business of McGregor on litter bins for a three year period. On the same day, McGregor requested that the agreement be cancelled, but the contractor refused cancellation, commenced and continued to display the advertisement on litter bins during the following three years, and then claimed the contract price. It was held that the contractor was not bound to accept the cancellation by McGregor, but was entitled to carry out the contract and claim for the full contract price.

③ *Avery v Bowden* (1885) 5 E & B 71

Bowden chartered a ship of Avery and agreed to load cargo on her at Odessa within 45 days. During the stay at the port Bowden told her captain that no cargo would be available for loading. However, the captain did not leave immediately, but stayed at Odessa hoping that Bowden would change his mind. Before the end of 45 day period the Crimean War broke out and the performance of the contract would have been illegal as trading with the enemy. It was held that Avery could not recover damages for the anticipatory breach since the captain affirmed by staying at Odessa, and the contract had been discharged by frustration.

④ *J. Lauritzen A.S. v Wijsmuller B.V., The Super Servant Two* [1990] 1 Lloyd's Rep 1 (CA)

第9章 Discharge of Contract

Wijsmuller contracted with Lauritzen to carry a drilling rig from Japan to Rotterdam, using either 'Super Servant One' or 'Super Servant Two'. Wijsmuller planned to use the Super Servant Two for this contract and the Super Servant One was used for other contracts with third parties. Prior to the performance, the Super Servant Two sank without fault on the part of Wijsmuller. It was held that the contract was not frustrated by the sinking of the Super Servant Two since it did not automatically bring the contract an end. The real cause was Wijsmuller's election not to use Super Servant One. The court summarised the doctrine of frustration as follows:

"Certain propositions, established by the highest authority, are not open to question:

1. The doctrine of frustration was evolved to mitigate the rigour of the common law's insistence on literal performance of absolute promises. The object of the doctrine was to give effect to the demands of justice, to achieve a just and reasonable result, to do what is reasonable and fair, as an expedient escape from injustice where such would result from enforcement of a contract in its literal terms after a significant change in circumstances.

2. Since the effect of frustration is to kill the contract and to discharge the parties from further liability under it, the doctrine is not to be lightly invoked, must be kept within very narrow limits and ought not to be extended.

3. Frustration brings the contract to an end forthwith, without more and automatically.

4. The essence of frustration is that it should not be due to the act or election of the party seeking to rely on it.

5. A frustrating event must take place without blame or fault on the side of the party seeking to rely on it." (per Bringham L.J.)

⑤ *Davis Contractors Ltd. v Fareham Urban District Council* [1956] AC 696 (HL)

Building contractors incurred massive expenses since a job, which had been expected to take eight months, took twenty two months due to labour shortages. The House of Lords rejected their claim that the contract was frustrated.

"It is not hardship or inconvenience or material loss itself which calls the principle of frustration into play. There must be as well such a change in the significance of the obligation that the thing undertaken would, if performed, be a different thing from that contracted for." (per Lord Radcliffe)

⑥ *Taylor v Caldwell* (1863) 3 B&S 826

Caldwell rented to Taylor the Surrey Gardens and Music Hall to give four grand concerts, etc. Before the first concert the Hall was destroyed by fire and Taylor sued for breach of contract in failing to supply the hall. It was held that the contract was subject to an implied condition that the parties would be excused if the subject matter was destroyed. As it was destroyed by no fault of the parties, the contract was frustrated and the parties were released from liability.

⑦ *Asfar & Co. v Blundell* [1986] 1 QB 123 (CA)

A cargo of dates worth £4,690 was sunk in the Thames and contaminated with sewage so that the dates were no longer fit for human consumption. The insurer claimed that the freight was not frustrated as there had not been total loss of the subject matter. It was held that there had been a total loss of subject matter and the cargo owner was discharged from his liability to pay freight, even though the cargo was still sellable for £2,400 if used for distillation into spirit.

⑧ *Blackburn Bobbin Co., Ltd. v T.W. Allen & Sons Ltd.* [1918] 2 KB 467 (CA)

Early in 1914, timber merchant agreed to sell a quantity of Finland birch timber. The seller did not keep stocks of the timber as the usual practice was to have it shipped directly from Finland, but this was not known to the buyer. Imports from Finland were stopped by the presence of German warship in the Baltic. The seller claimed that the contract had been frustrated, but the Court of Appeal held that it had not. German warship was an event, which rendered the mode of shipping contemplated by the seller practically impossible, however, such event was not provided for in the contract.

⑨ *Jackson v Union Marine Insurance Company Ltd.* (1874) LR 10 CP 125 (Court of Exchequer Chamber)

A ship sailed from Liverpool on January 2, 1872 with instructions to proceed 'with all possible dispatch (dangers and accidents of navigation excepted) from Liverpool to Newport, and there load a cargo for carriage to San Francisco.' The ship was stranded and delayed for over a month. It was held that the contract was frustrated. Even though the ship could have completed its voyage after repairs, this would have been a 'different adventure' to that originally embarked upon.

⑩ *Krell v Henry* [1903] 2 KB 740 (CA)

Henry agreed to hire a room in Pall Mall, from which to observe the coronation procession of Edward VII. When the procession was cancelled, the contract was held to be frustrated, even though technically he could still have occupied the room for the day. Vaughan Williams LJ, however, stated obiter that similar catastrophes would not have led to the frustration of a contract.

"... if a cabman was engaged to take someone to Epsom on Derby Day at a suitable enhanced price for such a journey, say 10l., both parties of the contract would be discharged in the contingency of the race at Epsom for some reason becoming impossible; but I do not think this follows, for I do not think the cab case the happening of the race would be the foundation of the contract. No doubt the purpose of the engager would be to go to see the Derby, and the price would be proportionately high, but the cab had no special qualifications for the purpose which led to the selection of the cab for this particular occasion. Any other cab would have done as well ... Whereas in the present case, where the rooms were offered and taken, by reason of their peculiar suitability from the position of the rooms for a view of the coronation procession, surely the view of the coronation procession was the foundation of the contract." (per Vaughan Williams LJ)

⑪ *Herne Bay Steamboat Co. v Hutton* [1903] 2KB 683 (CA)

Hutton hired a steamship which he planned to use to take passengers from Herne Bay to see the naval review conducted by the King at Spithead and to cruise round the fleet. When the review was cancelled due to the King's illness, he claimed that the contract had been frustrated. It was held that the contract was not frustrated since the naval review was not the sole basis of the contract. Hutton could still have conducted the cruise around the fleet, which was still anchored at Spithead.

⑫ *Denny, Mott & Dickson v James B. Fraser & Co., Ltd.* [1944] AC 265 (HL Scotland)

The parties entered into an agreement for the sale of timber, under which the buyer agreed to lease a timber yard to the seller, and to give the seller an option to purchase. Then, under war-time regulations it became illegal to trade in timber. It was held that the whole agreement, including the lease and the option to purchase, had become frustrated.

⑬ *Nickoll & Knight v Ashton Eridge & Co.* [1901] 2 KB 126 (CA)

A contract for the sale of cottonseed provided that the seeds were 'to be shipped per steamship Orlando from Alexandria during January.' The Orlando could not get to Alexandria in January as she ran aground in the Baltic. It was held that the contract was frustrated since it provided for performance only in the stipulated manner.

⑭　*Ocean Tramp Tankers Corporation v VO Sovfracht, The Eugenia* [1964] 2 QB 226 (CA)

The Eugenia was let to the charterer for a 'trip out to India via Black Sea' with the express provision that the ship should not be taken into a 'dangerous' zone where there were any hostilities or threatened hostilities. When the charter-party was negotiated the parties realized that the Suez Canal might be closed, but no express terms were inserted in the charter to meet that eventuality. When the ship arrived at Port Said, Egyptian anti-aircraft guns were in action. Nevertheless, the ship entered the Suez Canal. It was blocked by the Egyptian government and the vessel was trapped. The charterer claimed that the contract was frustrated by the closure of the canal. It was held that the charterer was in breach of contract to have taken the ship into a dangerous zone. The contract was not frustrated by the closure of the canal since it did not bring about a fundamentally different situation.

⑮　*Joseph Constantine SS Line Ltd. v Imperial Smelting Corp. Ltd.* [1942] AC 154 (HL)

The charterer of a ship, claimed the shipowner for damages for failure to deliver a cargo. The shipowner pleaded that an explosion on the ship had frustrated the chartered voyage. The cause of such explosion was unascertained. The court held that the explosion had frustrated the commercial object of the adventure and that the shipowner was not bound to prove that the explosion was not due to their neglect or default.

⑯　*Maritime National Fisch Ltd. v Ocean Trawlers Ltd.* [1935] AC 524 (PC on Appeal from the Supreme Court of Nova Scotia)

Maritime National Fisch was a fishing company, and hired five trawlers, including the St. Cuthbert, which was owned by Ocean Trawlers, to use for fishing. For fishing it needed to use 'otter trawlers' for which it required a licence, but the Minister would only grant it three licences, and asked the hirer to elect the three trawlers to which these licences would be granted. The hirer chose three but excluded St. Cuthbert, and then, claimed frustration of the contract of hire for St. Cuthbert because it was impossible to perform. It was held that the hirer could not claim frustration and was liable to pay for all the ships hired since it had selected itself which trawlers would remain unlicensed.

⑰ *Walton Harvey Ltd. v Walker & Homfrays Ltd.* [1931] 1 Ch 274
Walton hired advertising space in Walker's hotel for seven years, during which the hotel building was compulsorily acquired by the local authority and demolished. It was held that the contract was not frustrated since Walker was aware of such risk.

⑱ *Amalgamated Investment & Property Co., Ltd. v John Walker & Sons Ltd.* [1977] 1 WLR 164 (CA)
A building was entered in the statutory list of buildings of special historical interest a few days after the date of a contract for its sale. The listing had the effect of dramatically reducing its market value. It was held that the risk of a building listed was one that every owner and purchaser must recognize that he is subject to, and therefore that the contract was not frustrated.

⑲ *W.J. Tatem Ltd. v Gamboa* [1939] 1 KB 132
During the Spanish civil war, W.J. Tatem chartered to Gamboa, acting on behalf of the Republican Government of Spain, a steamship, for 30 days from July 1, 1937. The ship was to be used for the evacuation of refugees from Northern Spain to French ports. The ship was seized by the nationalists and detained in the port of Bilbao until September 11. It was foreseeable that the ship would be so detained, however, the court held that the contract was frustrated since the detention was unforeseeably long.

⑳ *Criklewood Property Investment Trust v Leighton's Investment Trust Ltd.* [1945] AC 22 (HL)
A 99 year building lease contract was granted in 1936 of certain land at Potters Bar on which lessees were to build a number of shops for the benefit of the lessors. Wartime restrictions meant it became impossible to build the shops, and the lessees claimed that the contract was frustrated. It was held that the doctrine of frustration did not apply because the interruption from 1939 to 1945 was not sufficient in duration to frustrate the lease.

㉑ *National Carriers Ltd. v Panalpina (Northern) Ltd.* [1981] AC 675 (HL)
The City Council closed the sole access road to a warehouse, which was leased to the lessee for 10 years, because a listed building nearby was in a dangerous condition. The access road was closed for 20 months. The lessee refused to pay

rent for this period. The House of Lords was of the opinion that a lease may be frustrated in rare circumstances, however, held that there was no frustration in this case.

㉒ *Hirji Mulji v Cheong Yue Steamship Co.* [1936] AC 497 (HL)

By a charter-party made in November 1916, the shipowner (Hirji Mulji) agreed that his ship should be placed at disposal of the charterer (Cheong Yue Steamship) on March 1, 1917, but the ship was requisitioned by the government before such date. The shipowner asked the charterer if it would be willing to take up the charter when the ship was released, and the charterer said yes. The ship was not released until February 1919, and when she was released the charterer refused to accept her. The shipowner contended that the charterer affirmed the contract after the frustration, however, it was held that frustration brought the contract to an end automatically, and the effect of frustration could not be waived in such manner.

㉓ *Appleby v Myers* (1867) LR 2 CP 651

Appleby took to erect certain machinery upon Myers' premises under the agreement, providing that the work was to be paid for on completion. Before the work was completed, the premises and the machinery already erected were wholly destroyed by fire. It was held that by frustration Appleby could recover nothing for the work already done since it had been agreed that the payment was to be made only on completion.

㉔ *Chandler v Webster* [1904] 1 KB 493

In a contract for the hire of a room to see Edward VII's coronation, it was provided that the rent was payable in advance. When the contract was frustrated by the cancellation of the coronation, it was held that the rent had to be paid since it was due before the frustration event.

㉕ *Fibrosa Spolka Akcyjna v Fairbuirn, Lawson, Combe, Barbour Ltd.* [1943] AC 32 (HL)

Fairburn contracted with Fibrosa, a Polish company, to manufacture certain machinery and deliver it to Gdynia. Part of the price was to be paid in advance, and Fibrosa paid £1,000 to the Polish manufacturer. Then, the contract was frustrated by the occupation of Gdynia by German forces in September, 1939, and the Fairburn requested the return of the advance payment. It was held that where the frustrating event caused the consideration wholly to fail, then no payment was due and payments already made could be recovered. The above Chandler v Webster [1904] was overruled to such extent.

㉖ *BP Exploration Co (Libya) Ltd v Hunt (No.2)* [1982] 1 All ER 925

Hunt had assigned to the oil company ("BP") a half share in the oil concession granted from Libyan government. BP spent considerable sum of money in exploration and found oil, however, the concession was expropriated following a revolution in Libya. BP brought an action against Hunt, claiming recovery of a 'just sum' under s 1(3) of the Act in respect of 'valuable benefit' obtained by Hunt prior to the frustration. The question was whether the benefit is to be assessed as it was before the frustrating event or after it. It was held that the benefit must be assessed as it is after the event. If the subject matter of the contract is destroyed by the frustrating event the value of the benefit will be nil.

【STATUTE】
Law Reform (Frustrated Contracts) Act 1943
1.-(2) All sums paid or payable to any party in pursuance of the contract before the time when the parties were so discharged (in this Act referred to as 'the time of discharge') shall, in the case of sums so paid, be recoverable from him as money received by him for the use of the party by whom the sums were paid, and, in the case of sums so payable, cease to be so payable:

Provided that, if the party to whom the sums were so paid or payable incurred expenses before the time of discharge in, or for the purpose of, the performance of the contract, the court may, if it considers it just to do so having regard to all the circumstances of the case, allow him to retain or, as the case may be, recover the whole or any part of the sums so paid or payable, not being an amount in excess of the expenses so incurred.

(3) Where any party to the contract has, by reason of anything done by any other party thereto in, or for the purpose of, the performance of the contract, obtained a valuable benefit (other than a payment of money to which the last foregoing subsection applies) before the time of discharge there shall be recoverable from him by the said other party such sum (if any), not exceeding the value of the said benefit to the party obtaining it, as the court considers just, having regard to all the circumstances of the case and, in particular,-

(a) the amount of any expenses incurred before the time of discharge by the benefited party in, or for the purpose of, the performance of the contract, including any sums paid or payable by him to any other party in pursuance of the contract and retained or recoverable by that party under the last foregoing subsection, and

 (b) the effect, in relation to the said benefit, of the circumstances giving rise to the frustration of the contract

---

この章のチェックリスト

1．契約が終了し、当事者が義務履行を免れるのはどのような場合か。
　(1)　Discharge by agreement
　(2)　Discharge by breach
　(3)　Discharge by frustration
2．Anticipatory breach とは何か。
3．Frustration はどのような場合に発生するか。
4．Frustration に該当する事態が発生しているのに frustration にならないのはどのような場合か。
5．Frustration の法律効果は。これにはどのような問題があるか。
6．Law Reform (Frustrated Contracts) Act 1943は、コモンローをどのように変更しているか。
7．Force majeure 条項とは何か。イギリス法に準拠した契約の場合、なぜ必要か。

第10章

Remedies for Breach of Contract
（契約違反の救済措置）

1．Damages（損害賠償）の基本的性質

　Damages は、breach of contract（契約違反）により被害を受けた契約当事者に対し法が認めている中心的な（コモンロー上はほぼ唯一の）救済方法（remedy）である。損害賠償を初めとするイギリス法上の救済措置（remedies）は、原則として、契約違反した者が得た利得よりも被害を受けた者が蒙った損害に着目し、被害を受けた契約当事者に対し、仮に契約違反が存在せず契約上の義務が適正に履行されていたとしたらその者が受けていたはずの経済的・財政的状態と同一の状態を与えることを目的としている。

　損害賠償の対象となる損害には、あらゆる種類の人的、物的損害（経済状態の悪化による損害を含む。）が含まれている。その金額は、全事情を総合的に評価、判断して算定する。また、損害賠償請求が認められるのは、契約違反の結果マイナスの影響がでた場合に限られる。たとえば、売買契約における物品引渡義務を遅滞している間に商品の市場価格が下落した場合は damage が生じているが、この間に上昇した場合は契約違反による damage はなかったことになる。

2．損害の範囲

　損害賠償請求が認められる損害は、契約違反を原因として発生した損害のうち、契約違反から疎遠過ぎる（too remote）ものを除いた損害である。すなわち、損害の範囲は、契約違反と損害との間の causation（因果関係）と remoteness（疎遠性）という2つの要件によって限定される。

(1) Causation（因果関係）

Breach of contract（契約違反）による damage（損害）の賠償を請求するためには、breach と damage の間に、当該 breach が damage の有効な原因（effective cause）であったといえる程度の適切な関連性（proper causal link）が必要である（Chaplin v Hicks ［1911］2 KB 786 (CA)）。

損害と契約違反との間に十分な関連性があれば、契約違反以外にも損害発生の原因（たとえば、戦争の勃発や第三者の行為等）があっても構わない（Monarch Steamship Co v Karlshamens Oljefabriker (A/B) ［1949］AC 196 ①、Heskell v Continental Express Ltd. ［1956］1 All ER 1033）。

損害の発生に第三者の犯罪行為が介在している場合であっても、当該行為の介在が契約違反者にとって予見可能（foreseeable）であれば、損害賠償義務を負担する（De la Bere v Pearson Ltd. ［1908］1 KB 280②、Stansbie v Troman ［1948］2 KB 48 (CA)③）。

(2) Remoteness（疎遠性）

契約違反と有効な因果関係（effective causation）のある損害のうち、損害賠償の対象となるのは、（ⅰ）契約違反の通常の結果（normal consequences）として自然に発生すると正当かつ合理的に考えられる損害（damages as may be fairly and reasonably be considered arising naturally）及び（ⅱ）契約締結時において、両当事者が契約違反の結果発生するであろうことを合理的に予期できたはずの損害（damages as may reasonably be supposed to have been in the contemplation of both parties, at the time they made the contract, as probable result of the breach of it）に限定され、それ以外の損害は契約違反から疎遠に過ぎる（too remote）ことを根拠として損害賠償請求の対象から除外される（Hadley v Baxendale (1854) 9 Exch 341④、Victoria Laundry (Windsor) Ltd. v Newman Industries Ltd. ［1949］2 KB 528 (CA)⑤）。これは、causation のある全損害を賠償させては契約違反者の責任範囲があまりに広がり過ぎるので、損害の範囲を限定するために裁判所が作り出した、remoteness（疎遠性）という要件である。合理的に予期すること（reasonable contemplation）が可能であった損害か否かは、いわゆる客観基準

(objective test) を用い、契約違反があったとしたら当該損害が発生することを、契約締結時に reasonable person（合理的な一般人）が予期できたか否かを基準に判断する（Koufos v C. Czarnikow Ltd. (The Heron II) [1969] 1 AC 350 (HL)⑥）。

なお、過失による不法行為（tort of negligence）における損害賠償の範囲を限定する際にも remoteness という要件が用いられるが、その意味内容は契約違反の場合と異なっている。すなわち、breach of contract では、損害発生の現実的な危険性（real danger）や高度の蓋然性（serious possibility）があり、そのような結果が発生するであろうこと（not unlikely to happen）を予期（contemplation）できた場合に限って賠償請求が認められるのに対し、tort に関しては、合理的に予見できた（reasonably foreseeable）損害、すなわち、発生する可能性（probability）が合理的に認められる損害は全て too remote ではないと判断されている。後者は reasonable foreseeability test（合理的予見可能性の基準）と呼ばれ、契約違反の損害に関する reasonable contemplation test（合理的予期基準）と区別されている（Koufos v C. Czarnikow Ltd. (The Heron II) [1969] 1 AC 350 (HL)⑥、H. Parsons (Livestock) Ltd. v Uttley Ingham & Co., Ltd. [1974] QB 791 (CA)⑦、Chiemgauer Membran Und Zeltbau GmbH v New Millenium Experience Co., Ltd. [2002] BPLR 42）。

3．損害の種類と損害額の算定

契約違反をした相手方に対して損害賠償を請求しようとする当事者は、まず当該契約違反によってどのような損害を被ったのかを確定する必要がある。契約違反による損害には、expectation loss（履行利益の損失）、reliance loss（信頼利益の損失）、speculative damages（推測的損害）、non-financial loss（非金銭的損害）等の種類があり、それぞれ損害額の算定方法が異なっている。1つの契約違反から複数の種類の損害が競合して発生している場合、被害を受けた当事者は、自己の選択により、その全部又は一部を請求することができる。ただし、expectation loss と reliance loss とは、以下に説明するとおりその内

容が両立しないので、同時に両方を請求することができない。

上記のどの種類の損害の賠償額算定にも共通する一般原則として、契約当事者は、契約違反がなかった場合における地位や利益以上のものを受けることはできない。すなわち、契約違反により被害を受けた契約当事者に対して裁判所が認める賠償額は、その者が実際に被った、又は被るべき損失額が上限である。

(1) Expectation loss（履行利益の損失）

Expectation loss とは、契約上の義務が約束どおりに履行されていたとしたらその約束を受けた当事者が得たであろう利益（expectation interest）を受けられなかったことにより被った損害のことである。これは、契約違反により被害を受けた契約当事者が、金銭的に可能な限り、契約上の義務履行があった場合と同じ状態にすることを求めて賠償を求める場合の損害を意味している。この典型例は、契約違反による目的物の減価額（difference in value）、契約違反を是正するための費用（cost of cure）等であり、これらは loss of bargain（取引利益の損失）と呼ばれる。いわゆる遺失利益（loss of profit）も expectation loss に含まれる。

（ⅰ）Difference in value（減価額）：土地建物や物品の売買、製造、加工、修繕等、目的物の引渡義務を含む契約における義務違反があった場合、原則として、被害を受けた当事者が受領することを期待していた目的物の価額と現実に受領した目的物の価額の差額に相当する金額が expectation loss となる。このような損害を loss of bargain（取引利益の損失）という。たとえば、欠陥品を引き渡した場合の loss of bargain は、欠陥がない物を引き渡した場合の価額と当該欠陥品の現実の価額との差額である。

また、目的物の引渡義務の遅滞の場合は、約束どおりの引渡があったときの価額と実際に引き渡された日における価額との差額である。他方、買主が約定の引渡日に目的物の受領を拒んだ場合、これによって売主が被る loss of bargain は、原則として、買主から受け取ることを期待していた目的物の代金とその現実の価額との差額である。これに関し、the Sale of Goods Act 1979には以下のとおり規定されている（the Sale of Goods Act 1979 s50（3）、s51（3））。

第10章　Remedies for Breach of Contract

50 Damages for non-acceptance

(3) Where there is an available market for the goods in question the measure of damages is prima facie to be ascertained by the difference between the contract price and the market or current price at the time or times when they ought to have been accepted or (if no time was fixed for acceptance) at the time of refusal to accept.

51 Damages for non-delivery

(3) Where there is an available market for the goods in question the measure of damages is prima facie to be ascertained by the difference between the contract price and the market or current price of the goods at the time or times when they ought to have been delivered or (if no time was fixed) at the time of refusal to deliver.

（ii）　Cost of cure（是正費用）：売主の契約違反により欠陥品を購入した買主がその物品の修繕のために要した費用が、当該欠陥を原因とするその物品自体の価値の減価額（deference in value）を超えている場合、原則として、買主が賠償を受けられる金額は価値の減価額分を限度とし、修繕費全額の請求は認められない（Phillips v Ward［1956］1 WLR 471 (CA)⑧、Ford v White［1964］1 WLR 885⑨、Lazenby Garages v Wright［1976］1 WLR 459 (CA)⑩、Watts v Morrow［1991］4 All ER 937 (CA)⑪）。たとえば、AがBから2,000ポンドでパソコンを購入したが、当該パソコンは欠陥品で1,500ポンドの価値しかなかったので、Aがこの製品を修繕した場合、修繕費用として1,000ポンドかかったとしても、AがBに請求できるのは、500ポンドが限度である。

　ただし、これには2つの例外がある。第1に、売買の対象が不特定の物品（chattel）ではなく特定物（たとえばreal property（土地建物））である場合は、他の物件との代替可能性がないことを考慮して、修繕費用の総額の賠償請求が認められることがある（Harbutt's Plasticine Ltd. v Wayne Tank & Pump Co., Ltd.［1970］1 QB 447 (CA)）。

　第2に、当事者間の契約において明示的に定められていた目的物の建造義務や修繕義務の違反があった場合、被害を被った当事者が自ら建造や修繕を行うために現実に要する費用（cost of cure）が義務違反による目的物の価値減額

分(difference in value)を超える場合であっても、建造費・修繕費相当額の賠償請求が認められることがある(Radford v De Froberville [1977] 1 WLR 1262⑫)。ただし、修繕費等としての請求金額が、これによって被害者が回復を受けられる利益との均衡上合理性を欠くほどに大きい場合は認められない(Ruxley Electronics and Construction Ltd. v Forsyth [1995] 3 WLR 118 (HL)⑬)。

(iii) Loss of profit(遺失利益):契約に基づいて目的物を受領することを期待していた者が、当該目的物を利用して事業を行う予定だった場合、事業ができなかったことによる損害も発生している。このような遺失利益(loss of profit)も、causation が認められかつ too remote でない場合は expectation loss に含まれる。Loss of profit を請求するためには、契約の履行があったときに得たであろう収益の金額を立証することが必要である。

(2) Reliance loss(信頼利益の損失)

Reliance loss とは、契約の一方当事者が契約の存在を信頼して行動したことにより生じた費用が、相手方の契約違反によって無駄になってしまったことによる損害である。契約違反により被害を受けた契約当事者が、契約を締結していなかった場合と同じ状態に戻すための費用の賠償を求める場合は、reliance loss の賠償請求をすることになる。相手方が売買契約上の代金支払義務を履行すると信じて、目的物の引渡準備のために費やした経費が典型例である。契約締結後のみならず締結前に費やした経費であっても reliance loss に含まれる(Anglia Television Ltd. v Reed [1972] 1 QB 60 (CA)⑭)。

Reliance loss は、契約が存在しなかった状態にするための費用の損失であり、契約が履行された場合の利益の損害である上記 expectation loss とは正反対の前提に基づいて算定される。したがって、reliance loss と expectation loss を両方とも請求することはできず、どちらか一方を選択する必要がある。

Reliance loss は、expectation loss とは異なり、契約違反者が義務を履行していたとしても何らの利益が生じなかった場合であっても、その賠償請求が認められる。しかし、契約違反がなかったとしても費やしたであろうことが明らかである経費は、reliance loss に含まれない。すなわち、契約当事者が元々不

第10章 Remedies for Breach of Contract

利益な合意（a bad bargain）をしていた場合における取引上の損失は、相手方の契約違反を理由に回復できない（C & P Haulage v Middleton [1983] 3 All ER 94 (CA)⑮）。なお、「契約違反がなくても費やしたであろう経費」であることの立証責任は、契約違反者の側が負担する（C.C.C Film (London) Ltd. v Impact Quadrant Film Ltd. [1985] 1 QB 16）。

(3) Speculative damages（推測的損害）

契約当事者が相手方の契約違反の結果利益を上げる機会を失ったとき（loss of opportunity to gain benefit）は、当該利益が確実に得られたであろうことの証明がなくても、因果関係が疎遠（too remote）でない限り損害賠償を請求できる。このような場合の損失を speculative damages（推測的又は偶発的損害）という（Simpson v The London and North Western Railway Co. (1876) 1 QBD 274⑯、Chaplin v Hicks [1911] 2 KB 786 (CA)⑰、Warner Bros. Pictures Incorporated v Nelson [1937] 1 KB 209、Dickson v Jones Alexander & Co [1993] 2 FLR 521）。

(4) Non-Financial or Non-pecuniary Losses（非金銭的損害）

イギリス法上、契約当事者が相手方の契約違反の結果、精神的な苦痛や失望（mental distress and disappointment）を受けたとしても、原則として、損害賠償請求をしてそのような苦痛や失望の回復を求めることはできない（Addis v Gramophone Co., Ltd. [1909] AC 488 (HL)、Cox v Phillips Industries Ltd. [1976] 1 WLR 638、Bliss v South East Thames Regional Health Authority [1987] ICR 700、Hayes v James and Charles Dodd [1990] 2 All ER 815 (CA)）。ただし、これには以下のような例外がある。

第1に、契約の目的が provision of pleasure and enjoyment（慰安、娯楽の提供）又は relief of discomfort（苦痛からの解放）である場合は、契約違反により被った精神的苦痛、不快感、失望等が損害賠償請求の対象となる（Jarvis v Swan's Tours Ltd. [1973] QB 233 (CA)⑱、Jackson v Horizon Holiday Ltd. [1975] 3 All ER 92 (CA)⑲、Ruxley Electronics and Construction Ltd. v Forsyth [1995] 3 WLR 118 (HL)⑬）。裁判所は、娯楽や慰安が契約の

唯一の目的でなくても、その重要な目的に含まれている場合であれば、契約違反によってこの目的が害されたときに損害賠償請求を認めている（Farley v Skinner (No.2) [2001] 4 All ER 801 (HL)⑳）。

第2に、精神的な苦痛の直接的な原因が契約違反による physical inconvenience（身体上の苦痛・不便）であるときは、当該身体的苦痛と関連する精神的損害も賠償請求の対象となりうる（Hobbs v London & South Western Railway Co., L.R. (1875) 10 QB 111、Watts v Morrow [1991] 1 WLR 1421 (CA)㉑）。

4．損害額の限定

(1) Mitigation（損害の拡大防止）

契約違反によって損害を被った当事者は、自らの損害をできる限り少なくするための合理的な処置を採るべきことが期待されており、これを行わなかったために損害が拡大した場合は、拡大部分については賠償を請求することができない（British Westinghouse Electric and Manufacturing Co., Ltd. v Underground Electric Railways Co. of London Ltd. [1912] AC 673 (HL)、Payzu Ltd. v Saunders [1919] 2 KB 581 (CA)㉒）。

ただし、損害の拡大防止措置を採らないことについて合理的な理由があるときはその義務を負わない（Banco de Portugal v Waterlow & Sons Ltd. [1932] AC 452 (HL)㉓）。

また、Mitigation の抗弁は、相手方による anticipatory breach（履行期前の契約違反）を accept せずに、契約履行期まで待ってから契約違反の責任を追及する場合には主張できない。すなわち、anticipatory breach があったときは、たとえその結果不要な費用が拡大することになるとしても、直ちに契約を解消する義務を負担することはない（White and Carter (Council) Ltd. v McGregor [1962] AC 413 (HL: Scotland)㉔）。

(2) Benefit Accruing

相手方の契約違反の結果として被害を被った当事者に benefit（利益）が発

第10章　Remedies for Breach of Contract

生したときは、当該利益の金額は、損害額から控除される（British Westinghouse Co., Ltd. v Underground Electric Railways Co. of London Ltd. [1912] AC 673 (HL)㉕）。

(3) Contributory Negligence（寄与過失）

Contributory negligence とは、自己の損害の発生に寄与した被害者自身の過失のことである。過失による不法行為を原因とする損害賠償請求（damages for negligence）の場合は、被害者の contributory negligence に応じて損害賠償額が減額される（the Law Reform (Contributory Negligence) Act 1945）。

イギリスの契約法は過失責任の原則を採っていないので、契約責任に基づく損害賠償請求に関しては、原則として寄与過失による損害額の減額はないが、契約責任と不法行為責任が競合する場合（concurrent liability in contract and in the tort of negligence）は、この法律の適用を受けて減額されることがある（Forsikringsaktieselskapet Vesta v Butcher [1989] AC 852 (CA)㉖）。ただし、製造物責任（product liability）のような厳格責任（contractual strict liability）に関しては、不法行為責任と競合する場合であっても contributory negligence の抗弁を主張することができない（Barclays Bank plc v Fairclough Building Ltd. [1995] QB 214 (CA)㉗）。

(4) Taxation

損害を受けた契約当事者が得られたはずである契約上の収益が、税務債務の対象となっていたはずである場合は、損害賠償金の算定上、当該税金分が控除される（B.T.C. v Gourley [1956] AC 185 (HL)）。これを Gourley Deduction という。

(5) Supervening events

契約違反により生じた結果がその後に被害当事者に生じた新しい事件や事故の結果によって中断（intervene）又は包含（subsume）されてしまった場合、新しい事件・事故の発生までに被った損害のみが契約違反による損害として算

定される（Beoco Ltd. v Alfa Laval Co., Ltd. [1994] 4 All ER 464 (CA)㉘）。そのような中断行為のことを、novus actus interveniens（a new act intervening、新しい介入行為）という。

(6) Limitation of Actions（消滅時効）

The Limitation Act 1980により、通常の契約に基づく債権の消滅時効期間は、契約違反の日から6年間である（s5）。ただし、deedによる契約の場合は契約違反の日から12年間である（s8）。なお、詐欺（fraud）その他損害を与える故意を伴う行為に対する訴訟の場合は、真実を知った日又は合理的に知り得た日を起算日として時効が進行する（Lynn v Bamber [1930] 2 KB 72）。時効は、書面による債務の承認又は一部弁済によって中断する（s29(5)）。

5．Liquidated Damages（損害賠償額の予定）

Liquidated damages（損害賠償額の予定）とは、契約違反があったときに賠償すべき損害額を予め合意しておくことをいい、その旨の条項をliquidated damages clauses（損害賠償額予定条項）という。契約の両当事者がliquidated damagesについて合意した場合、契約違反により被害を受けた当事者は、損害額の立証をせずに損害賠償請求をすることができる。損害発生の立証に関するremotenessの要件の適用もなくなるし、また、加害当事者からmitigationその他損害額を限定するための抗弁を主張することもできなくなる（White and Carter (Council) Ltd. v McGregor [1962] AC 413 (HL: Scotland)）。

このように、liquidated damagesの合意は、損害額に関する争いを避けて迅速な解決が期待できるので、契約当事者双方にとってメリットがある。ただし、契約違反があったときに一定の金額を支払うべき旨の合意の全てがliquidated damages clauseとなるわけではない。裁判所は、そのような条項をpenalty clause（違約罰条項）と解して法的拘束力を認めないことがある。Penalty clauseとは、契約違反の防止及び制裁を目的として、損害賠償とは無関係に、契約違反があったときに罰金として支払うべき金額を定めておく条項

である。イギリス法上、損害回復の限度を超えた punitive damages（懲罰的損害賠償）の請求は許されないので、penalty clause は違法かつ無効とされ、被害者は、現実に被った損害の限度でしか損害賠償を受けることができなくなる。実際上、liquidated damages clause に基づく損害賠償請求事件においては、当該条項が、liquidated damages clause、penalty clause のどちらであるかについて争われることが多い。この問題に関し、裁判所は、契約当事者が契約違反から生ずる可能性のある損害を誠実に予測（genuine pre-estimate of the loss）して損害額を見積もった上で賠償予定額を定めたのかどうかを客観基準により判定する方法を採っている。この判断にあたって、当該条項の表題（title）や文言（words）に penalty とか liquidated damages の語が用いられているか否かは一応の推定（prima facie supposed）の材料になるが、日常用語としての「penalty」は多義性があるので、これが決定的な要素となるわけではない（Dunlop Pneumatic Tyre Co., Ltd. v New Garage and Motor Co., Ltd．[1915] AC 79 (HL)㉙）。一般的な指針として、（ⅰ）合意した金額が契約違反によって生ずる可能性のある損害の最大額よりも極端に大きい場合、（ⅱ）金銭支払義務の不払による損害賠償予定額が当該義務を履行した場合の金額より大きい場合、（ⅲ）契約違反の程度、内容、結果にかかわらず同一金額の損害賠償額が定められている場合等は、penalty clause との推定が働きやすい（上記 Dunlop Pneumatic Tyre Co., Ltd. v New Garage and Motor Co., Ltd、Bridge v Campbell Discount Co., Ltd．[1962] 1 All ER 385 (HL)㉚）。

なお、liquidated damages clause は、損害賠償額を固定する合意であり、契約違反者のみならず被害を受けた当事者の側もこれに拘束され、the actual damage（実損害）が合意した金額を上回ったとしてもその請求をすることは許されない（Cellulose Acetate Silk Company Ltd. v Widnes Foundry (1925) Ltd．[1933] AC 20 (HL)㉛）。したがって、契約違反者だけの利益のために損害賠償額の上限を定める limitation clause（責任制限条項）とは異なり、the Unfair Contract Terms Act 1977の適用は受けない。ただし、消費者契約において、不当に高額の賠償金を定めた場合は、the Unfair Terms in Consumer Contracts Regulations 1999が適用されることになる（Sch.3(1)(e)）。

6．Restitution（原状回復）

　Restitution とは、契約違反や不法行為等の結果生じた不公平な状態を是正するために原状に復帰させること（restitutionary awards）を認める法理の総称である。コモンロー上、このような請求の根拠は、quasi contract（準契約）と呼ばれている。この法理の重要な適用場面は、契約が成立していないにかかわらず一方が他方から利得を受けているような場合である。たとえば、契約交渉中に一方当事者が他方のために契約成立を前提とする役務を提供したが、結局契約成立に至らなかった場合（本編第3章2参照）、又は成立したと信じていた契約が mistake（錯誤）その他の理由により無効（void）であった場合、便益を提供した当事者は、相手方が受けた利益（quantum meruit）の限度でその回復を求めることができる（Craven-Ellis v Canons Ltd［1936］2 All ER 1066）。

　Restitution（原状回復）は、契約違反に対する remedy としても請求できる場合がある。売買契約に基づいて買主が代金を支払ったのに、（ⅰ）売主が目的物の引渡義務を履行しない場合や（ⅱ）売主が引渡した目的物の所有者ではなかったため買主が所有者に返還しなければならなくなった場合における買主の売主に対する代金返還請求がその典型例である。これは、買主の代金支払義務の consideration（約因）となっている売主の義務が履行されなかった場合、代金支払義務に対する consideration が不履行によって消滅するので、quasi contract の法理に基づいてその返還を請求できるとする考え方である。このように、契約違反による restitution（原状回復）は consideration の法理を根拠としているので、この請求が可能なのは、原則として consideration となっている義務の全てが不履行の場合（total failure of consideration）に限られている（Rowland v Divall［1923］2 KB 500㉜）。

7．Specific Performance（特定履行）

　Specific performance は、裁判所が契約上の義務に違反した者に対し、その義務を約束したとおりの内容・方法で履行することを強制する救済手段のこ

とである。これは equity（衡平法）上の救済手段であり、裁判官が damages（金銭賠償）では契約違反による損害の回復手段として不十分であると判断したときだけにその裁量により認められる（Beswick v Beswick ［1967］2 All ER 1197）。通常、real property その他代替不能な特定物の給付や利用を内容とする契約でない限りは金銭賠償で十分と考えられるので、specific performance は容易には認められない。特に、以下のような契約上の義務の履行は、specific performance による救済は、原則として認められないと解されている。

第1に、長期間に亘って履行を強制することが必要な契約の場合は、裁判所が履行完了まで継続して監視・監督することが困難なので specific performance は認められない（Ryan v Mutual Tontine Westminster Chambers Association ［1893］1 Ch 116、Co-operative Insurance Society Ltd v Argyll Stores (Holdings) Ltd ［1997］2 WLR 898 (HL)）。

第2に、裁判所は、個人的な役務の提供を内容とする契約上の義務の履行を強制することは、原則として不適切と判断している（Rigby v Connol (1880) 14 Ch 482）。Employment contract（雇用契約）に関しては、この原則が制定法にも規定されている（the Trade Union and Labour Relations (Consolidation) Act 1992 s236）。

第3に、specific performance は equity 上の remedy なので、裁判所が当事者間の公平と正義に適うと判断できないような場合には認められない。たとえば、specific performance を命ずると義務者にとって苛酷な結果をもたらすこととなり、権利者の利益との均衡を著しく失する場合や specific performance を請求する権利者が契約に関して詐欺的な行為をしていたり相手方の錯誤に乗じていたり等 clean hands とはいえない場合である。

8．Injunction（差止命令）

(1) 定義

Injunction とは、被告に対し、一定の行為をなすことを禁じたり、契約違反状態解消のため一定の作為をなすことを命ずる裁判所の行為である。これには、mandatory injunction（作為命令的差止命令）、prohibitory injunction（禁止

的差止命令）及び freezing injunction（Mareva injunction、資産凍結命令）の種類がある。

Injunction は衡平法上の救済措置であり、裁判所の裁量に左右される。Prohibitory injunction は、個人的な役務提供義務の間接履行強制のために申し立てられる場合が多いが、裁判所がこのような目的での injunction を命ずるのは、契約にその根拠に関する明文規定がある場合等、例外的な場合に限られる（Warner Brothers Pictures Incorporated v Nelson［1937］1 KB 209㉝）。特に、義務者を契約上の義務を履行せざるを得ない状況に追い込むような injunction は、specific performance が認められるような場合でない限りは消極的である（Page One Records v Britton［1967］3 All ER 822㉞）。

(2) Freezing injunction（資産凍結命令）

Freezing injunction は、被告に対し、イギリス国内にある特定の財産、全財産又はその一部の処分や国外持ち出しを暫定的に禁止する裁判所による仮差止命令である（the Civil Procedure Rules 1998）。通常、イギリスの裁判所は債権回収を助けるために被告の財産処分を禁ずるのに消極的だが、この injunction は、資産の国外持ち出しを禁ずるため、その唯一の例外として認められる（Mareva Compania Naviera SA v International Bulk Carriers SA［1975］2 Lloyd's Rep 509、the Supreme Court Act 1981 s37）。

(3) Damages in lieu of specific performance or injunction（特定履行又は差止め命令に代わる損害賠償）

裁判所は、specific performance や injunction の請求があった場合であっても、損害額が比較的小さく、損害の金銭換算が可能であるとき、その他特定履行や差止命令が被告に酷な結果となる場合は、裁量により、損害賠償のみを認めることができる（the Supreme Court Act 1981、ss 49、50）。

【*CASES*】

① *Monarch Steamship Co v Karlshamns Oljefabriker (A/B)*［1949］AC 196
A British ship was chartered to carry soy beans to Karlshamns in Sweden.

Owing to a delay caused by the seaworthiness of the ship, she did not reach Karlshamns before the outbreak of World War II and the British Admiralty ordered the cargo to be discharged in Glasgow. The owner of the beans had to charter a neutral ship and claimed the shipowner to compensate expenses. The shipowner contested that the expenses for chartering another ship was not caused by the breach but by the war and the subsequent Admiralty order. It was held that the shipowner was liable since the effective cause of the Admiralty order was the delay caused by the unseaworthiness of the ship. The court stated obiter, that there must be a proper casual link between the breach and damage.

"It is well established that unseaworthiness, if it is to be a relevant factor of liability, must be "a cause" of damage or loss. That is necessary because unseaworthiness might take many different forms in the same vessel, so that before any one form can be relied upon, it must be a cause of damage; for instance, the failure to carry a proper medical chest, if it is a breach of the warranty, might have no relevance to the loss of a vessel by perils of the sea." (per Lord Wright)

② *De la Bere v Pearson Ltd.* [1908] 1 KB 280

The newspaper owner (Pearson) advertised that their city editor would give readers financial advice. Baghot de la Bere wrote to ask for the name of a good stockbroker, and the editor recommended an outside broker (a broker who is not a member of the Stock Exchange) without making reasonable enquiries about him. The broker was in fact an undischarged bankrupt, and de la Bere lost money invested in him, who misappropriated it. It was held that Pearson, in recommending the outside broker without making reasonable enquiries, had committed a breach of contract, and was liable for the loss, even though the misappropriation of the money by the broker amounted to a criminal offense.

③ *Stansbie v Troman* [1948] 2 KB 48 (CA)

A painter who in breach of contract leaves his client's house unlocked is liable for the value of goods stolen from it by thieves.

④ *Hadley v Baxendale* (1854) 9 Exch 341

Hadley owned a flour mill in Gloucester. He contracted with a carrier (Baxendale) to deliver his broken crankshaft to a maker in Greenwich for use as a pattern for making a new shaft. Due to the carrier's negligence the carriage was delayed and the new shaft was received late. As Hadley did not have a spare, the mill was stopped for a week and he lost a week's profits, which he claimed from

Baxendale. It was held that the loss of profits was not recoverable. The court said that damages were only payable for such losses as may fairly and reasonably be expected either to arise naturally from the breach, or to be in the contemplation of both parties at the time they made the contract, as a probable result. The stoppage of Hadley's mill was not anticipated by Baxendale.

"Where two parties have made a contract which one of them has broken, the damages which the other party ought to receive in respect of such breach of contract should be such as may fairly and reasonably be considered either arising naturally, i.e., according to the usual course of things, from such breach of contract itself, or such as may reasonably be supposed to have been in the contemplation of both parties, at the time they made the contract, as probable result of the breach of it. Now, if the special circumstances under which the contract was actually made were communicated by the plaintiffs to the defendants, and thus known to both parties, the damages resulting from the breach of such a contract, which they would reasonably contemplate, would be the amount of injury which would ordinary follow from a breach of contract under these special circumstances so known and communicated. But, on the other hand, if these special circumstances were wholly unknown to the party breaking the contract, he, at the most, could only be supposed to have had in his contemplation the amount of injury which would arise generally, and in the great multitude of cases not affected by any special circumstances, from such a breach of contract." (per Alderson B)

⑤ *Victoria Laundry (Windsor) Ltd. v Newman Industries Ltd.* [1949] 2 KB 528 (CA)

The engineering firm contracted to sell a boiler to Victoria Laundry, a launderer. The seller knew the nature of the business and was informed that the boiler was required for immediate use, but it delayed delivery for five months. The launderer clamed the £16 a week profit that they could have made from normal customers, and a £262 a week highly lucrative dyeing contract, which it could have accepted with the Ministry of Supply. It was held that, although the loss of normal business profit was a reasonably foreseeable consequence of the delayed delivery, the loss of profit from highly lucrative dyeing contract was too remote since the defendant had no knowledge of it.

⑥ *Koufos v C. Czarnikow Ltd. (The Heron II)* [1969] 1 AC 350 (HL)

The shipowner (Koufos) contracted to carry a cargo of sugar to Basrah for the charterer (Czarnikow). The shipowner knew that the charterer was a sugar merchant, and that there was a sugar market in Basrah, but did not know that the charterer intended to sell the sugar as soon as the ship arrived. The ship was 9 days late, and during the delay the price of sugar had fallen. The charterer claimed the loss of profit from the shipowner. It was held that the charterer was entitled to recover the difference in sugar price caused by the delay. Even though the shipowner did not know of the intention to sell the sugar immediately, 'if he had thought about the matter he must have realised at least that it was not unlikely that the sugar would be sold in the market at market price on arrival.' (per Lord Reid)

⑦ *H. Parsons (Livestock) Ltd. v Uttley Ingham & Co., Ltd.* [1978] 1 QB 791 (CA)

The parties entered into a contract for the supply and installation at a pig-farm of a large storage hopper to hold pig foods. Owing to the negligence of the supplier the ventilation cowl, sealed during transit to the farm, was opened, and the pig food went mouldy. Pigs suffered a rare disease from which they died. The pig farmer claimed damages for the value of the dead pigs and the loss of profits from selling the pigs when mated. It was held that since illness was to be expected, death (though not a normal consequence) was not too remote, and so the value of the dead pigs could be recovered. Lord Denning said that the Heron II test was applied only to loss of profits, and in respect of claim for physical damage (rather than economic loss) the rule in contract was the same as that in tort (i.e. reasonable foreseeability test). However, the other judges thought that the death of the pigs was a serious possibility, and satisfied the Heron II test anyway.

⑧ *Phillips v Ward* [1956] 1 WLR 471 (CA)

A surveyor did not draw his client's attention to the fact that the roof timbers of the house they were about to buy were rotten. The client bought the house at £25,000 although it was only worth £21,000. He claimed for recovery of £7,000 for new timbers, but it was held that he has entitled only to £4,000, i.e. the difference between the price he paid for the house and its value when he bought it.

⑨ *Ford v White* [1964] 1 WLR 885

Mr. and Mrs. Ford bought a house and adjoining plot for £6,350 after being advised by the solicitor that they could build on the plot. The solicitor was in breach of contract for not noticing a covenant against building on the plot. The property was in fact worth £6,350 but would have been worth £7,600 if there had been no covenant. It was held that the solicitor was not liable for the difference.

⑩　*Lazenby Garages v Wright* [1976] 1 WLR 459 (CA)
　Lazenby bought a secondhand car for £1,325 which Wright agreed to buy at a price of £1,670. Wright refused to accept or pay for it. Lazenby sold the car to another buyer for £1,770 and claimed £345 from Wright as the profit which they would have made on a sale to Wright (£1,670 minus £1,325). It was held that Lazenby's claim must fail since Lazenby had suffered no loss.

⑪　*Harbutt's Plasticine Ltd. v Wayne Tank & Pump Co., Ltd.* [1970] 1 QB 447 (CA)
　The defendant installed a heavy wax dispenser in the plaintiff's factory, but due to its breach of contract in installing a faulty dispenser, the factory was burn down. It was held that the plaintiff could recover the full amount for building a new factory even though it was more valuable than the original one.
　"The destruction of a building is different from the destruction of a chattel. If a secondhand car is destroyed, the owner only gets its value; because he can go into the market and get another secondhand car to replace it. He cannot charge the other party with the cost of replacing it with a new car. But when this mill was destroyed, the plasticine company had no choice. They were bound to replace it as soon as they could, not only to keep their business going, but also to mitigate the loss of profit (for which they would be able to charge the defendants). They replaced it in the only possible way, without adding any extras. I think they should be allowed the cost of replacement." (per Lord Denning M.R.)

⑫　*Radford v De Froberville* [1977] 1 WLR 1262
　De Froberville covenanted with Radford that she should build a brick wall on a plot of land to mark the boundary between their lands. When she failed to build it, Radford sued for the cost of carrying out the work himself. De Froberville claimed that the land had not diminished in value due to the lack of a wall, and a cheap pre-fabricated fence would be sufficient to mark the boundary. It was held that Radford was entitled to the price of a brick wall since that was what the contract stipulated.

⑬　*Ruxley Electronics and Construction Ltd. v Forsyth* [1995] 3 WLR 118 (HL)

第10章 Remedies for Breach of Contract

The constructor contracted to build a swimming pool for Forsyth in his garden. The contract specified that there should be a diving area of 7 feet 6 inches deep. When completed, the diving area was only 6 feet deep, which was still deep enough for diving off the edge, but precluded the addition of a diving board. The value of the pool was not diminished by the breach of contract, but the cost of remedying the defect would be £21,560. Forsyth argued that he needed the extra depth as he was a big man and did not feel safe diving in only 6 feet of water. The Court of Appeal decided for him and awarded the full cost of cure damages. On appeal, the House of Lords overturned such judgment, holding that the cost of cure damages could be recovered only if it was reasonable to do so, and that it would be reasonable only if the cost was out of proportion to the diminution in value. The court awarded nothing for swimming pool, but only allowed £2,500 for loss of amenity.

⑭ *Anglia Television Ltd. v Reed* [1972] 1 QB 60 (CA)

Reed, an American actor, contracted with Anglia Television ("ATV") to play the leading role in a television play called "The Man In The Wood". He was double-booked and repudiated the contract, and as a result, the project was abandoned. ATV sued Reed for their total wasted expenditures, including those incurred before hiring him. It was held that ATV could also recover pre-contractual expenditure since it was reasonably in the contemplation of the parties as likely to be wasted if the contract was broken.

⑮ *C & P Haulage v Middleton* [1983] 3 All ER 94 (CA)

Middleton (the "Licensee") was a car engineer, and was granted a 6 month contractual licence to occupy premises from C&P Haulage (the "Landlord"). The contract expressly provided that any fixtures put in by the Licensee would become the property of the Landlord. The Licensee spent money on fixtures, but he was evicted from the garage before the end of the term, which constituted a breach of contract by the Landlord. The Licensee claimed his wasted expenditure on installing the fixtures in the garage. It was held that he was not entitled to such expenditure since it would still have been lost even if the licence had been validly terminated at the end of the 6 month.

⑯ *Simpson v The London and North Western Railway Co.* (1876) 1 QBD 274

Simpson was a manufacturer of cattle-food. He entrusted samples of his products to the railway company for it to deliver them to Newcastle for agricultural exhibition. The goods were marked 'Must be at Newcastle on

Monday certain', but the goods arrived after the event. It was held that the railway company was liable for Simpson's prospective loss of profit for potential contract he might have made at Newcastle even with no evidence of his prospect of making a profit.

⑰　*Chaplin v Hicks* [1911] 2 KB 786 (CA)

Miss Chaplin, who had won the earlier stage of a beauty contest and selected as one of the fifty finalists, was not invited to the final by error of the organizer. She was awarded £100 in damages although it was not certain that she would have won the final.

⑱　*Jarvis v Swan's Tours Ltd.* [1973] QB 233 (CA)

Jarvis booked a holiday accommodation at a winter sports centre in Switzerland. Swan Tour's brochure stated: 'Why did we choose the Hotel Krone?... The Hotel Krone has its own Alphutte Bar which will be open several evenings a week ... No doubt you will be in for a great time, when you book this House-Party holiday ... Mr. Weibel, the charming owner, speaks English ... Welcome party on arrival. Afternoon tea and cake for 7days. Swiss dinner by candlelight. Fondue party. Yodeller evening. Farewell party in the "Alphutte Bar". Service of representative.' However, the services provided was much inferior to the description. When Jarvis arrived, there were only 13 people and all left by the second week, and he was having a party alone; the bar was only open one evening; the yodeller was a local man in his working clothes who sang a few songs very quickly; the representative left after a week; nobody in the hotel, except for Jarvis, spoke English, etc. Damages on the basis of financial loss were assessed at £32, but the Court of Appeal awarded him £125 to compensate for disappointment and distress.

⑲　*Jackson v Horizon Holiday Ltd.* [1975] 3 All ER 92 (CA)

The court additionally awarded £500 for the mental distress caused to the Jackson family during a disastrous holiday.

"It has often been said that on a breach of contract damages cannot be given for mental distress ... I think those limitations are out of date. In a proper case damages for mental distress can be recovered in contract ... One such case is a contract for a holiday, or any other contract to provide entertainment and enjoyment." (per Lord Denning)

⑳　*Farley v Skinner (No.2)* [2001] 4 All ER 801 (HL)

第10章 Remedies for Breach of Contract

Farley wanted to buy a weekend house, and hired Skinner to survey the property. Since the house was 15 miles from Gatwick airport, Farley particularly asked to check the possibility of aircraft noise. The surveyor reported that they thought "it unlikely that the property will suffer greatly from such noise, although some planes will inevitably cross the area." In fact, there was a navigation beacon near the house and accordingly there was substantial interference from aircraft noise. The Court of Appeal refused Farley's claim for damages because the contract was not for the supply of pleasurable amenity but for survey of a property. However, on appeal the House of Lords overruled and permitted the claim, holding that the contract needed not be exclusively for enjoyment or pleasure for an award of non-pecuniary damages to be made. If a major or important object of the contract was to ensure pleasure, relaxation or peace of mind, damages would be payable if these objectives were disregarded.

㉑ *Watts v Morrow* [1991] 1 WLR 1421 (CA)

The purchasers of the defective house claimed damages against the negligent surveyor. It was held that the purchasers were not entitled to damages for distress but they could be compensated for their physical discomfort caused by the defect.

㉒ *Payzu Ltd. v Saunders* [1919] 2 KB 581 (CA)

A contract for the supply of goods provided that delivery should be by instalments and payment within one month of delivery. The buyer failed to pay for the first instalment when due, and the seller declined to make further deliveries unless the buyer paid cash in advance. The buyer refused to accept delivery on those terms and sought damages for the seller's breach of contract. It was held that the seller was in breach of contract, but the buyer should have mitigated his loss by accepting the seller's offer of delivery against cash payment. Damages were limited to the amount of the buyer's assumed loss if he had paid in advance, which was interest over the period of prepayment.

㉓ *Banco de Portugal v Waterlow & Sons Ltd.* [1932] AC 452 (HL)

Waterlow & Sons contracted to print banknotes for the Bank of Portugal, and in breach of contract delivered a large number of notes to a criminal who circulated them in Portugal. On discovering this, the bank withdrew the issue and undertook to exchange all the notes in question for others. The printing company argued that it was only liable for the cost of printing the notes since any further loss were due to the bank's own act. It was held that it was liable for the full face value of the notes as the bank's conduct was reasonable having regard to its commercial obligations to the public.

㉔ *White and Carter (Council) Ltd. v McGregor* [1962] AC 413 (HL: Scotland)
McGregor was a garage proprietor in Clydebank, and made an agreement with the White and Carter ("W&C") whereby W&C agreed to advertise the McGregor's business on litter bins. Later, McGregor notified cancellation of the order, but W&C refused to accept it and proceeded to print advertisements and attached them to litter-bins. McGregor refused to pay the contract price, arguing that it was unreasonable of W&C to incur expenses after notified cancellation. It was held that W&C was entitled to recover contract price since it was not obliged to accept the repudiation.

㉕ *British Westinghouse Electric and Manufacturing Co., Ltd. v Underground Electric Railways Co. of London Ltd.* [1912] AC 673 (HL)
Electric manufacturer agreed to supply the railway company with turbines of a stated efficiency but supplied less efficient ones. The railway company accepted them, reserving the right to claim damages. After some years, the railway company replaced them with others. These were so much more efficient than the manufacturer's that the railway company actually used less coal than he would have done had the original contract been properly fulfilled. The House of Lords stated that the railway company was under no duty to mitigate by buying new turbines, but as he had bought them in consequence of the manufacturer's breach, the financial advantage he had gained by using them must be set off against the cost of buying them. As the railway company's savings in coal exceeded the cost of buying them, he recovered nothing in respect of it. However, he could recover for the loss suffered before replacing the turbines.

㉖ *Forsikringsaktieselskapet Vesta v Butcher* [1989] AC 852 (CA)
Norwegian insurance company ("Vesta") insured the owner of a Norwegian fish firm against loss of fish, and reinsured the risk with Lloyds underwriters through the broker. Conditions of the insurance were varied and Vest told the broker to make the same change to the reinsurance, but the broker failed to do so. When Vesta paid to the fish firm and attempted to claim under the reinsurance, Lloyds refused to pay, claiming that the reinsurance policy was void under its conditions, which had not altered. Vesta sued the broker for breach of contract, and the broker claimed that Vesta was contributory negligent for not following up the matter. It was held that where the defendant's liability in

第10章 Remedies for Breach of Contract

contract is the same as the liability in the tort of negligence, the 1945 Act applied to enable the court to apportion damages even though the claim was made in contract.

㉗ *Barclays Bank plc v Fairclough Building Ltd.* [1995] QB 214 (CA)

The contractor was in breach of a contract with Barclay to clean roof containing asbestos. It argued that the damages should be reduced for contributory negligence since Barclay had failed to supervise the work. It was held that contributory negligence was not a defence to a claim for damages based on a strict contractual obligation, even though the defendant might have also had a parallel liability in tort.

㉘ *Beoco Ltd. v Alfa Laval Co., Ltd.* [1994] 4 All ER 464 (CA)

Alfa Laval installed a heat exchanger at Beoco's premises. Later, a leak was discovered and Beoco employed a second engineer to fix it, but the repair work was done negligently and 2 months later the exchanger exploded, causing damage to property and economic loss of profit. It was held that the first engineer (Alfa Laval) was liable in damages for the cost of repairing the exchanger and for loss of profit up to the time of repair, but not subsequently since the cause of the explosion had been the plaintiff's own negligence in failing to carry out proper tests before using the repaired exchanger.

㉙ *Dunlop Pneumatic Tyre Co., Ltd. v New Garage and Motor Co., Ltd.* [1915] AC 79 (HL)

Dunlop supplied motor tyres, etc. to New Garage and Motor, a dealer, under covenants that the dealer should not resell the goods at less than Dunlop's list prices and should pay the sum of £5 by way of liquidated damages for every tyre, etc. sold in breach of the agreement. When the dealer was sued for damages, it pleaded that the clause was a penalty. It was held that the amount fixed by the parties was a genuine pre-estimate of damage.

"To assist this task of construction various tests have been suggested ... :

　(a) It will be held to be a penalty if the sum stipulated for is extravagant and unconscionable in amount in comparison with the greatest loss that could conceivably be proved to have followed from the breach.

　(b) It will be held to be a penalty if the breach consists only in not paying a sum of money, and the sum stipulated is a sum greater than the sum which ought to have been paid ...

　(c) There is a presumption (but no more) that it is a penalty when 'a single lump sum is made payable by way of compensation, on the occurrence of one or more or all of several events, some of which may occasion serious and others but trifling damage'.

On the other hand:

(d) It is no obstacle to the sum stipulated being a genuine pre-estimate of damage, that the consequences of the breach are such as to make precise pre-estimation almost an impossibility. On the contrary, that is just the situation when it is probable that pre-estimated damage was the true bargain between the parties ..." (per Lord Dunedin)

㉚ *Bridge v Campbell Discount Co., Ltd.* [1962] 1 All ER 385 (HL)

A car hire-purchase agreement between the parties contained a clause, providing that, in the event of termination of the agreement, the finance company shall be entitled to take possession of the car hired and to forfeit installments already paid, and further that the hirer shall pay a sum equal to two-thirds of the hire-purchase price as compensation of loss of profit. It was held that such additional sum to be a penalty and the finance company could recover only the actual loss.

㉛ *Cellulose Acetate Silk Company Ltd. v Widnes Foundry (1925) Ltd.* [1933] AC 20 (HL)

In a contract for the delivery and erection of plant it was provided that the contractors were to pay 'by way of penalty £20 for every week' after the date of delivery if delayed. The contractor was 30 weeks late, but the actual loss caused by the delay was £5,850. It was held that the sum was not a penalty, but was merely the amount agreed by way of compensation for delay, and that the damage must be limited to this agreed amount.

㉜ *Rowland v Divall* [1923] 2 KB 500

Rowland bought a motor-car from Divall for £334. He repainted the car and resold it on to a third party. Later, it was found that the car had been stolen, and police took possession of the car on behalf of the true owner. Rowland brought an action to recover £334 from Divall. It was held that the seller was in breach of s12 of the Sale of Goods Act (which implies conditions regarding the seller's right to sell), and there had been a total failure of consideration. Accordingly, Rowland was entitled to recover the whole purchase price, notwithstanding the car was used by him and his purchaser for 4 months.

㉝ *Warner Brothers Pictures Incorporated v Nelson* [1937] 1 KB 209

Bette Davis had agreed to give her exclusive services as a film actress to Warner Bros. for 52 weeks. In breach of contract, she entered into another contract with an English company. Warner sought an injunction, restraining her from carrying out the English contract. The injunction was granted with limitation that she just could not be a film actress in England since the contract did not completely prevent her from working at all.

"The case before me is, therefore, one on which it would be proper to grant an injunction unless to do so would in the circumstances be tantamount to ordering the defendant to perform her contract or remain idle or unless damages would be the more appropriate remedy ... The defendant is stated to be a person of intelligence, capacity and means, and no evidence was adduced to show that, if enjoined from doing the specified acts otherwise than for the plaintiff, she will not be able to employ herself both usefully and remuneratively in other spheres of activities, though not as remuneratively as in her special line. She will not be driven, although she may be tempted, to perform the contract, and the fact that she is so tempted is no objection to the grant of an injunction" (per Branson J)

㉞ *Page One Records v Britton* [1967] 3 All ER 822

Page One Records was a manager of a pop group, the Troggs. The management contract between them provided that the group could not employ anyone else as manager. An injunction to prevent the group employing the other firm as manager was refused, since this would have forced them to hire only Page One Records and thus amounted to specific performance of a service contract.

[STATUTES]
Law Reform (Contributory Negligence) Act 1945

1.--(1) Where any person suffers damage as the result partly of his own fault and partly of the fault of any other person or persons, a claim in respect of that damage shall not be defeated by reason of the fault of the person suffering the damage, but the damages recoverable in respect thereof shall be reduced to such extent as the court thinks just and equitable having regard to the claimant's share in the responsibility for the damage ...

4.-- [Fault is ...] negligence, breach of statutory duty or other act or omission which gives rise to a liability in tort or would, apart from this Act, give rise to a defence of contributory negligence;

Limitation Act 1980

5. An action founded on simple contract shall not be brought after the expiration

of six years from the date on which the cause of action accrued.

8.--(1) An action upon a specialty shall not be brought after the expiration of twelve years from the date on which the cause of action accrued.

(2) Subsection (1) above shall not affect any action for which a shorter period of limitation is prescribed by any other provision of this Act.

29.--(2) If the person in possession of the land .... in question acknowledges the title of the person to whom the right of action has accrued-

 (a) the right shall be treated as having accrued on and not before the date of the acknowledgement; ......

(5) Subject to subsection (6) below, where any right of action has accrued to recover

 (a) any debt or other liquidated pecuniary claim;

and the person liable or accountable for the claim acknowledges the claim or makes any payment in respect of it the right shall be treated as having accrued on and not before the date of acknowledgment or payment.

30.--(1) To be effective for the purposes of section 29 of this Act, an acknowledgement must be in writing and signed by the person making it.

(2) For the purposes of section 29, any acknowledgement ...-

 (a) may be made by the agent of the person by whom it is required to be made under that section ; and

 (b) shall be made to the person, or to an agent of the person whose title or claim is being acknowledged, or, as the case may be, in respect of whose claim the payment is being made.

32.--(1) .... where in the case of any action for which a period of limitation is prescribed by this Act, either-

 (a) the action is based upon the fraud of the defendant; or

 (b) any fact relevant to the plaintiff's right of action has been deliberately concealed from him by the defendant; or

 (c) the action is for relief from the consequences of a mistake;

the period of limitation shall not begin to run until the plaintiff has discovered the fraud, concealment or mistake (as the case may be) or could with reasonable diligence have discovered it .....

(2) For the purposes of subsection (1) above, deliberate commission of a breach of duty in circumstances in which it is unlikely to be discovered for some time amounts to deliberate concealment of the facts involved in that breach of duty ....

この章のチェックリスト

1. 契約違反があったときの救済手段として損害賠償請求が認められるための要件は。
2. 損害額の算定にはどのような根拠があるか。
3. Expectation loss, speculative loss, reliance loss にはそれぞれどのような損害、損失が含まれるか。
4. 非金銭的損害の賠償請求が認められるのはどのような場合か。
5. 損害額を限定するための抗弁にはどのようなものがあるか。
   (1) Mitigation
   (2) Benefits accruing
   (3) Contributory negligence
   (4) Taxation
   (5) Supervening event
   (6) Limitation
6. Liquidated damages clause は有効か。
7. Restitution とは何か。どのような請求ができるか。
8. Specific performance はどのような場合に認められるか。
9. Injunction とは何か。どのような場合に認められるか。

第11章

Privity of Contract（契約関係）

1．Doctrine of Privity（契約関係の法理）

　Privity of contract とは、契約を締結した直接の当事者間の関係のことである。Common law 上の原則として、contract は、その当事者（parties）以外の者に対して当該 contract に基づく権利を付与したり、義務を課したりすることができない。したがって、契約当事者が契約外の第三者に対して一定の義務を負担する旨を約束した場合、当該第三者が約束した者に対してこの約束に基づく請求をするために訴訟を提起しても、no privity の抗弁を主張されると敗訴することになる。この法原理を the doctrine of privity（契約関係の法理）という。The doctrine of privity は、本編第2章で紹介した the doctrine of consideration（約因の法理）と同様、裁判所が法的救済に値する合意を限定するために形成してきた伝統的法理の1つである。両者は全く異なる法原理ではあるが、適用場面が近似している。たとえば、原告からの契約に基づく請求に対する抗弁として、被告が、原告は契約当事者ではない（the doctrine of privity の抗弁）し、仮に当事者であるとしても consideration を提供していない（the doctrine of consideration の抗弁）と主張する等の方法で同時に主張されることが多い（Dunlop Pneumatic Tyre Co., Ltd. v Selfridge & Co. Ltd.［1915］AC 847 (HL)①）。実際上、ある者が consideration を提供したか否かは、その者が契約当事者であるか否かの重要な判断資料となる。

2．Avoiding the Doctrine of Privity（契約関係の法理の回避）

　Privity of contract の法理は、第三者に対して義務を負担することを約束した契約当事者の真意にかかわらずその法的拘束力を否定する要素となることか

ら、この約束を信頼した第三者に対して不当な不利益を与える結果となることが少なくなかった。たとえば、AB間の売買契約において、Aが契約外のCに売買代金を支払うことを約束していたので、Cはその期待の下にBに対して融資した場合、Cは、Bが破産すると、Bから貸金を回収することも、Aに代金を請求することもできないことになる。他方、他人間の契約の拘束を受けることが当初から予定されていた第三者が、privityを主張することによりその拘束から免れるのは不合理な場合もある。裁判所は、このような不公平な結果を回避するため、以下のような様々な方法を採ってprivity of contractの法理の適用範囲を限定してきた。

(1) Collateral Contract（付随的契約）

　契約の一方当事者と第三者との間で、付随的な契約（collateral contract）を別途締結することは自由である。このような契約の存在が認められる場合、第三者は、collateral contractの当事者としての立場で、契約上の義務の履行を求めることができる（Shanklin Pier Ltd. v Detel Products Ltd. [1951] 2 KB 854②）。Collateral contractが成立した時点において、主たる契約が存在していなくても構わない（Wells (Merstham) Ltd. v Buckland Sand & Silica Co., Ltd. [1965] 2 QB 170③）。ただし、collateral contractも契約である以上、明確かつ完全な意思の合致（clear and complete agreement）、consideration等の要件を全て充たしていなければならない。

(2) Action in tort（不法行為訴訟）

　The doctrine of privityは契約責任の追及に関する法理なので、契約の一方当事者が、第三者に対して契約外の注意義務（duty of care）を負っている場合、当該第三者は、liability in negligence（不法行為による過失責任）を追及することができる（Junior Books Ltd. v Veitchi Co., Ltd. [1983] 1 AC 520（HL Scotland）④）。ただし、第三者が被った損害が身体・財産等の物的損失ではなく経済的損失（economic loss）に留まる場合は、原則としてliability in negligenceを認めるべきではないとされている（D & F Estates Ltd. v Church Commissioners for England [1989] 1 AC 177 (HL)⑤）。

(3) Restrictive covenant in land lease（土地利用権の制限条項）

　衡平法（equity）上、土地（land）に関する権利（freehold（自由土地保有権）及びleasehold（不動産賃借権））の売主と買主との間で、当該土地の利用に関する制限条項（restrictive covenants）、たとえば、建物建築の禁止等を付した場合、買主から当該権利の譲渡を受けた転買人も、そのような制限条項の通知があることを条件として、その拘束を受ける旨の法原則がある（Tulk v Moxhay (1848) 2 Ph 774⑥）。一時期、この法原則が、動産（chattel）その他土地に関する権利以外の売買、たとえば、物品売買、船舶売買、株式売買等にも適用できるとする見解（Lord Strathcona Steamship Company Ltd v Dominion Coal Company Ltd [1926] AC 108 (PC)）とこれを否定する見解（Port Line Ltd v Ben Line Steamers Ltd [1958] 2 QB 146）との対立があったが、現在の裁判所は、買主が予め現実の通知（actual knowledge）を受けることを条件として、土地売買以外の契約にも拡張適用を認める考え方を採っている（Swiss Bank Corporation v Lloyds Bank Ltd [1979] Ch 548⑦）。

(4) Trusts in favour of the third party（第三者のための信託）

　Trust（信託）を用いれば、一定の財産に対する権利（property）を保有している者（holder）に対して、他人のために当該propertyを保有又は支配（hold）し、かつ管理する衡平法上の義務（equitable obligation）に従わせることができる。このような義務のことをfiduciary duty（信認義務）、この義務を負う者のことをtrustee（受託者）、これによって利益を受ける他人をbeneficiary（受益者）という。信託は、設定者（settlerといい、trusteeと同一人でもよい。）がその保有する財産に信託を設定する意思表示をすることにより発生する。契約当事者の一方が、当該契約に基づく相手方に対する権利に関して、第三者のために信託を設定する意思表示をしたことが認められれば、当該第三者は、受益者として衡平法（equity）上の権利を行使することが可能となるので、the doctrine of privityの適用を回避することができる。たとえば、AB間の契約において、Aが第三者であるCに対して一定の金銭の支払いをすることを約束し、BがCのためのtrusteeとして契約を締結したことが

立証された場合、Cはequityに基づいて、Aに対して直接に契約上の義務の履行を求めることができる（Re Flavell（1833）25 Ch D 89⑧）。ただし、この主張をするためには、Bにtrustを設定する旨の明白かつ明示的な意思があった旨の立証が必要なので、Bが自己の利益のために契約した場合は、たとえCの利益を同時に図る意図があってもtrustの成立は認められない（Vander-pitte v Preferred Accident Insurance Corporation of New York [1933] AC 70 (Privy Council, Canada)、Re: Schebsman [1944] Ch 83 (CA)⑨）。また、当事者間の契約において第三者に付与した権利の終了に関する合意があるときは、trustを設定する意思がないものと認定されている（Re: Sinclair's Life Policy [1938] 1 Ch 799⑩）。債権（choses in action）に対するtrustは一度設定すると撤回不能となり、beneficiaryの同意なしにその内容を変更することができないはずだからである（上記Re：Schebsman判決）。

(5) Specific performance to oblige promisor for the benefit of third parties（当事者による第三者のための債務の特定履行請求）

　当事者が契約外の第三者に対する義務を負担することを約束した場合、privity of contractは、第三者が当該義務の履行を請求することを制限するだけであり、第三者に対する履行の約束は、契約当事者間では法的拘束力を有する義務として成立している。したがって、そのような契約の相手方である当事者が約束者に対して、第三者の利益のために当該義務の特定履行（specific performance）を請求することは可能である（Lloyds v Harper (1880) 16 Ch.D. 290 (CA)、Beswick v Beswick [1968] AC 58 (HL)⑪、Jackson v Horizon Holidays [1975] 3 All ER 92 (CA)、Woodar Investment Development Ltd. v Wimpey Construction (UK) Ltd. [1980] 1 All ER 571 (HL)、Linden Gardens Trust Ltd. v Lenesta Sludge Disposals Ltd. [1994] 1 AC 85 (HL)、McAlpine (Alfred) Construction Ltd. v Panatown Ltd. [2001] AC 518 (HL))。ただし、特定履行の請求は、イギリス契約法上は、damages（損害賠償）による救済が不適当な場合の例外的なremedy（救済手段）に過ぎない。

(6) Promisee's action for damages（契約当事者による損害賠償請求）

　Common law 上、請求可能な損害賠償額は、liquidated damages（損害賠償予定額）の合意がある場合を除き、契約当事者が実際に被った損害の金額を限度とする。この原則によれば、契約当事者が、相手方が第三者に対して負担した義務違反を理由に損害賠償を請求しても、名目的な金額の賠償（nominal damage）しか認められないことになる。そのような義務違反によって損害を受けたのは第三者であって、約束を受けた契約当事者ではないからである。Lord Denning は、Jackson v Horizon Holidays Ltd.判決（[1975] 1 WLR 1468、3 All ER 92 (CA) ⑫）において、この損害賠償に関する一般原則を修正し、契約当事者は、第三者の利益のために締結した契約上の義務違反をした相手方に対して、契約に基づいて、第三者が被った損害についても賠償請求することができるとの判断を示した。しかし、the House of Lords はこの見解を完全には否定しなかったものの、基本的に反対した（Woodar Investment Development Ltd. v Wimpey Construction (UK) Ltd. [1980] 1 All ER 571 (HL)⑬）。ただし、その後の判例により、（ⅰ）契約当事者間において、第三者の損害分についても賠償請求できる旨の黙示の合意が認められ（Linden Gardens Trust Ltd. v Lenesta Sludge Disposals Ltd. [1994] 1 AC 85 (HL)⑭）、かつ（ⅱ）第三者が自ら賠償請求することができない場合（McAlpine (Alfred) Construction Ltd. v Panatown Ltd. [2001] AC 518 (HL)⑮）に限っては、契約当事者が違反者に対して第三者が被った損害の賠償請求することを認めている。

3．Exclusion clause and third party（責任排除条項と第三者）

　契約違反により損害を受けた当事者は、加害当事者に対して契約責任を追及すると同時に、当該契約の履行に関与した加害当事者の従業員、代理人（agent）、下請人（sub-contractor）等に対し、tort（不法行為）の一類型である negligence（過失）に基づく損害賠償責任を追及することがある。通常、取引契約の standard term は、責任排除条項（exclusion or exemption clause）や責任制限条項（limitation clause）を設けているので、そのような

不法行為責任の追及を受けた従業員等がこれらの条項の適用を受けることができるか否かがしばしば問題となる。後記の制定法（the Contracts (Rights of Third Parties) Act 1999）ができるまで、裁判所は、the privity of contract の法理に基づき、契約に責任排除条項があったとしても、被害を受けた相手方から negligence in tort の責任追求を受けた加害当事者の従業員や下請人が当該条項に依拠して責任制限を主張することは、原則として認めなかった（Consgrove v Horsfall（1945）62 TLR 140 (CA)）。ただし、当該条項が従業員、agent、sub-contractor に責任制限の効果が及ぶことを明記していた場合（"Himalaya" clause）はその例外としていた（Adler v Dickson: (The Himalaya)［1955］1 QB 158 (CA)⑯、Scrutton Ltd. v Midland Silicones Ltd.［1962］AC 446 (HL)⑰、Morris v C.W. Martin & Sons Ltd.［1966］1 QB 716 (CA)、New Zealand Shipping v A M Satterthwaite & Co.: (Eurymedon)［1975］AC 154 (Privy Council: New Zealand)⑱、KH Enterprise v Pioneer Container: (The Pioneer Container)［1994］2 All ER 250 (Privy Council: Hong Kong)、Starsin (Cargo Owners) v Starsin (Owners)［2003］UKHL 12）。

4．Contracts (Rights of Third Parties) Act 1999

　The doctrine of privity に対しては20世紀前半頃からその弊害を批判する声が上がっていたが、1991年、the Law Commission は、契約外の第三者が契約当事者に対して契約上の請求を行うことができるようにするための法律を制定する必要がある旨の Consultation Paper を提出し、1996年、これに基づく法案が公表された。1999年になって、ようやく the Contracts (Rights of Third Parties) Act 1999が採択された。

　同法により、契約において第三者に履行請求権があることを明記すること、又は当該条項が第三者に利益を付与することを目的としていること（契約が第三者による権利行使を制限していると解される場合を除く。）を条件とし、第三者による契約責任の追及、すなわち契約において相手方当事者以外の者が契約当事者に対して契約上の義務履行を請求し、執行することが可能となった。

　ただし、契約当事者が契約においてこの法律の適用除外を合意した場合、第

三者は当該契約に関する請求をすることができなくなる。実際上、2000年以降に締結された商取引上の契約の多くは、この法律の適用を除外する旨の条項を設けている。これは、この法律が適用された場合、契約当事者による自由な契約変更や権利放棄が制限されることになるためである。

【*CASES*】

① *Dunlop Pneumatic Tyre Co., Ltd. v Selfridge & Co. Ltd.* [1915] AC 847 (HL)

Dunlop supplied motor tyres to the dealer, under covenants that the dealer should not sell, and should not have its purchasers resell, the goods at less than Dunlop's list prices. Selfridge ordered Dunlop tyres from the dealer and agreed with the dealer that it would not resell the tyres at less that the list price. Selfridge did not observe the agreement with the dealer, and was sued by Dunlop for damages. It was held that there was no consideration moving from Dunlop to Selfridge. The court also mentioned the doctrine of privity as a distinct rule.

"My Lords, in the law of England certain principles are fundamental. One is that only a person who is a party to a contract can sue on it. Our law knows nothing of a jus quaesitum tertio arising by way of contract ……. A second principle is that is a person with whom a contract not under seal has been made is to be able to enforce it, consideration must have been given by him …'" (per Viscount Haldane LC)

② *Shanklin Pier Ltd. v Detel Products Ltd.* [1951] 2 KB 854

Detel Products Ltd., a paint manufacturer, promised Shanklin Pier that its paint would last for seven years if used to paint piers. Believing such promise, Shanklin instructed the contractor to buy and use Detel's paint for painting its pier, but it only lasted three months. When Shanklin sued Detel for breach of promise, Detel argued that there was no contract between them. It was held that Detel was bound by a collateral contract with Shanklin, whereby Detel's promised as to the durability of its paint in consideration of Sanklin's action in instructing the contractor to buy such paint.

③ *Wells (Merstham) Ltd. v Buckland Sand & Silica Co., Ltd.* [1965] 2 QB 170

A chrysanthemum grower made warrantee to the plaintiffs that its sand was suitable for growing chrysanthemum. The plaintiff bought the sand from a third party. It was held that the defendant was liable on the basis that there was a collateral contract, even though there was no specific main contract in contemplation at the time the warrantee was made.

④ *Junior Books Ltd. v Veitchi Co., Ltd.* [1983] 1 AC 520 (HL Scotland)
Veitchi subcontracted flooring in the factory of Junior Books and laid a defective floor. As there was no direct contractual relationship, Junior Brook sued Veitchi in tort. The House of Lords decided in favour of Junior Book on the basis that there was a duty of care.

"The appellants, though not in direct contractual relationship with the respondents, were as nominated sub-contractors in almost as close a commercial relationship with the respondents as it is possible to envisage short of privity of contract." (per Lord Roskill)

⑤ *D & F Estates Ltd. v Church Commissioners for England* [1989] 1 AC 177 (HL)
A block of flats was built on land owned by Church Commission. A subcontractor, who carried out the plaster-work, applied the plaster incorrectly and it began to fall off. D&F Estates, the lessee of the flat, sustained costs for remedial work, and sued the owner, the builder and the subcontractor. It was held that the loss was purely economical loss, which was not recoverable in tort.

⑥ *Tulk v Moxhay* (1948) 2 Ph 774
Tulk, who owned a house in Leicester Square, sold the garden in the centre of the square. The purchaser covenanted to maintain the garden and not to build on it. The land was sold several times with notice of the covenant. When Moxhay proposed to build on the land, an injunction was granted to restrain him on the ground that he was given notice of the covenant at the time of the purchase.

⑦ *Swiss Bank Corporation v Lloyds Bank Ltd* [1979] Ch 548
Swiss Bank made loan to the borrower to acquire securities, with the covenant that the proceeds of sale of the securities should be applied for repayment of the loan. The borrower granted charge over the securities to Lloyds Bank, who later acquired them by executing the charge. Swiss Bank claimed damages and repayment of loan out of the proceeds of sale. It was held that, if a person took a charge on property with actual knowledge of a contractual obligation, he could be restrained, however, in this case Lloyds Bank only had constructive knowledge, which was not sufficient.

⑧　*Re Flavell* (1833) 25 Ch D 89

　The partnership contracted with a retiring partner that it would pay him an annuity until his death, and, that after his death, it would pay such money to his personal representatives for the benefit of his wife and children. When he died, his creditors claimed the annuity to be part of his general assets. It was held that since the words of the contract established that the annuity had created a trust in Mrs Flavell's favour, she had a prior claim.

⑨　*Re: Schebsman* [1944] Ch 83 (CA)、[1943] 2 All ER 768

　Schebsman, upon his retirement from a company, agreed with the company that he was to be paid £5,500 in instalments over six years. It was also agreed that, if he died within the six years, payments were to be made to his wife. He adjudicated bankrupt and then died within such six years period and the trustee in bankruptcy claimed that as the money paid to Mrs Schebsman formed part of Schebsman's estate and should go to his creditors. The court held that the contract between Mr Schebsman and the company did not create a trust in favour of his wife, however, since the contract terminated upon his death, the money did not form a part of the estate. As the company was willing to continue payments to Mrs Schebsman, she was able to receive them.

　"It is true that, by the use possibly of unguarded language, a person may create a trust ... without knowing it, but unless an intention to create a trust is clearly to be collected from the language used and the circumstances of the case, I think that the court ought not to be astute to discover indications of such an intention." (per Du Parcq LJ)

⑩　*Re: Sinclair's Life Policy* [1938] 1 Ch 799

　Sinclair contracted a life insurance for the benefit of his godson. Under the term, the insurance policy would be valid as long as Sinclair continued to pay premium. When he died, the creditors claimed that the policy money belonged to his estate. It was held that, where a contract creates rights for a third party, a trust can only be found if those rights are irrevocable, and thus, the life insurance policy which contained a provision under which it could be surrendered did not create a trust.

⑪　*Beswick v Beswick* [1968] AC 58 (HL)

　A nephew had contracted in writing with his uncle to pay his aunt £5 a week after the uncle's death, but after his death the nephew refused to pay, and the aunt sued him. the Court of Appeal (Lord Denning) said that the doctrine of privity did not apply to a written contract according to s 56(1) of the Law of Property Act 1925, which states that 'a person may take an ... interest in property although he may not be named as a party to the conveyance or other instrument.' The House of Lords did not take such interpretation, but held that the aunt was entitled to an order for specific performance of the promise in her capacity as administratrix of her late husband's estate.

⑫ *Jackson v Horizon Holidays* [1975] 1 WLR 1468、3 All ER 92 (CA)

Julian Jackson booked a holiday for himself, his wife and his two small children. The hotel was disastrous in breach of the contractual terms, and he sued for the loss of holiday and distress. The Court of Appeal (Lord Denning) held that the victim of a disastrous holiday was entitled to claim damages not only for himself but also on behalf of the rest of his family who had also suffered, even though they were not privy to the contract.

⑬ *Woodar Investment Development Ltd. v Wimpey Construction (UK) Ltd.* [1980] 1 All ER 571 (HL)

Woodar agreed to sell the land for development to Wimpey. The contract provided for payment to both Wimpey and Transworld Trade Ltd., a third party. When Wimpey attempted to rescind the contract, Woodar sued for wrongful repudiation and damages both on its own behalf and on behalf of Transworld. The House of Lords held that the contract had not been wrongfully repudiated. The Lords stated obiter that they did not agree with the basis on which Lord Denning put his decision in Jackson v Horizon Holidays.

⑭ *Linden Gardens Trust Ltd. v Lenesta Sludge Disposals Ltd.* [1994] 1 AC 85 (HL)

The lessee of a building entered into a contract with the contractor to have asbestos removed from the building. The contract contained a non-assignability clause. Later, the lessee sold the property (the lease) and assigned the benefits under the contract. Then, defects in the contractor's work were found, and the assignor (the original lessee) and the assignee sued the contractor. It was held that the assignment was invalid since it was in breach of the non-assignability clause, and accordingly only the assignor could sue. However, the assignor no longer suffered financial loss since it transferred the property to the assignee. Nevertheless, the court held that the assignor could recover substantial damages since the building contract clearly contemplated that the property would be sold to a third party and the breach would cause damage to such third party, and therefore the contract was entered into on the basis that the assignor could recover damages suffered by the assignee for its benefit.

⑮　*McAlpine (Alfred) Construction Ltd. v Panatown Ltd.* [2001] AC 518 (HL)
　Panatown (the employer) contracted with McAlpine (the building contractor) for the design and construction of an office building in Cambridge. For taxation purpose, the owner of the building site, who was an associated company of Panatown, was not a party to the building contract, but it executed a separate 'duty of care' deed with the contractor. The deed was intended to create a right of action for the owner against the contractor. Later, the building was found to be so defective that it might have to be pulled down, and Panatown sought damages. The Court of Appeal applied the case law in Linden Gardens Trust Ltd. v Lenesta Sludge Disposals Ltd. [1994] 1 AC 85 (HL), and held that Panatown could recover substantial damages on behalf of the third party as it was contemplated by the contract. The House of Lords, however, held that where a contractor was in breach of a contract with the employer to construct a building for a third party, the employer could not recover substantial damages if it had been intended that the latter should have a direct cause of action against the contractor. Since the owner had a direct right to claim damages under the 'duty of care' deed, Panatown had no right to sue for damages suffered by the owner.

⑯　*Adler v Dickson: (The Himalaya)* [1955] 1 QB 158 (CA)
　The captain and boatswain of a P. & O. steamship were sued by a passenger for injury caused by their negligence. It was held that they are liable notwithstanding a clause in the ticket that the company should not be liable for injury. Denning LJ stated obiter that the servants would have defence if the clause had, in express terms, purported to cover them.
　"In the carriage of passengers as well as of goods, the law permits a carrier to stipulate for exemption from liability not only for himself but also for those whom he engages to carry out the contract, and this can be done by necessary implication as well as by express words. When such a stipulation is made, it is effective to protect those who render services under the contract, although they were not parties to it, subject however to this important qualification: The injured party must assent to the exemption of those persons. His assent may be given expressly or by necessary implication, but assent he must before he is bound for it is clear law that an injured party is not to be deprived of his rights at common law except by a contract freely and deliberately entered into him;

and all the more so when the wrongdoer was not a party to the contract, but only participated in the performance of it." (per Denning LJ)

⑰ *Scruttons Ltd. v Midland Silicones Ltd.* [1962] AC 446 (HL)

A drum of chemicals was shipped from New York to London. A bill of lading exempted the carrier from liability on excess of $500 per package. Scruttons, who was stevedore engaged by the carrier, damaged the drum whilst loading it onto a lorry, and caused £593 worth of damages. It was held that stevedore was not entitled to rely on the exemption clause contained in a contract to which it was not a party. However, it was suggested obiter that they might have relied on the exemption clause if the carrier had expressly contracted such clause as agent for the stevedores.

⑱ *New Zealand Shipping v A M Satterthwaite & Co.: (Eurymedon)* [1975] AC 154 (Privy Council: New Zealand)

A bill of lading exempted the carrier from liability unless action was brought within one year, and it also stipulated that the immunity was extended to the carrier's servants, agents or independent contractor. The stevedore, acted as the carrier's agent, damaged the cargo, and was sued by the owner more than a year later. The Privy Council applied obiter in Scrutton Ltd. v Midland Silicones Ltd. [1962] AC 446 (HL) and held that the stevedore was protected by the exemption clause.

[STATUTE]
Contracts (Rights of Third Parties) Act 1999

1.-(1) Subject to the provisions of this Act, a person who is not a party to a contract (a "third party") may in his own right enforce a term of the contract if-

(a) the contract expressly provides that he may, or

(b) subject to subsection (2), the term purports to confer a benefit on him.

(2) Subsection (1)(b) does not apply if on a proper construction of the contract it appears that the parties did not intend the term to be enforceable by the third party.

(3) The third party must be expressly identified in the contract by name, as a member of a class or as answering a particular description but need not be in existence when the contract is entered into.

(4) This section does not confer a right on a third party to enforce a term of a contract otherwise than subject to and in accordance with any other relevant terms of the contract.

(5) For the purpose of exercising his right to enforce a term of the contract, there shall be available to the third party any remedy that would have been available to him in an action for breach of contract if he had been a party to the contract (and the rules relating to damages, injunctions, specific performance and other relief shall apply accordingly).

(6) Where a term of a contract excludes or limits liability in relation to any matter references in this Act to the third party enforcing the term shall be construed as references to his availing himself of the exclusion or limitation.

(7) In this Act, in relation to a term of a contract which is enforceable by a third party-

"the promisor" means the party to the contract against whom the term is enforceable by the third party, and

"the promisee" means the party to the contract by whom the term is enforceable against the promisor.

2.-(1) Subject to the provisions of this section, where a third party has a right under section 1 to enforce a term of the contract, the parties to the contract may not, by agreement, rescind the contract, or vary it in such a way as to extinguish or alter his entitlement under that right, without his consent if-

(a) the third party has communicated his assent to the term to the promisor,

(b) the promisor is aware that the third party has relied on the term, or

(c) the promisor can reasonably be expected to have foreseen that the third party would rely on the term and the third party has in fact relied on it.

この章のチェックリスト

1. Privity of contract とは何か。Consideration とどこが違うか。

2. Privity of contract の主張が認めらないのはどのような場合か。

3. 会社と契約を締結した被害者から negligence の責任追及 (concurrent liability in negligence) を受けた会社の従業員や代理人は、会社と被害者との間の契約における責任排除条項 (exclusion clause) により免責されるか。

4．Common law 上、契約締結者以外の第三者が契約上の義務を負い、又は権利行使できるのはどのような場合か。
  (1) Collateral contract
  (2) Action in tort
  (3) Restrictive covenant in land lease
  (4) Trusts in favour of the third party
  (5) Specific performance for the benefit of third parties
  (6) Promisee's action for damages
5．Contracts (Rights of Third Parties) Act 1999とは何か。
  (1) 目的
  (2) 要件
  (3) 適用除外

第12章

Transfer of Contractual Rights and Obligation（契約上の権利義務の移転）

1．Contractual rights の法的性質

　これまでの章において、契約上の権利（contractual right）は、どのようにすれば適法かつ有効に成立し、かつ執行可能（enforceable）であるか、権利行使にはどのような制約があるか、また、enforceable であるとは誰がどのようなことをすることができるのか等を扱ってきた。最後に残された問題は、当該契約上の権利義務を第三者に移転することができるか否かである。この問題の前提として、契約上の権利の法的性質を確定しておく必要がある。Contractual right とは、intangible（無形）で、かつ personal（人的）な property（財産権）であり、かつ choses in action（債権）の１つである。Personal property（人的財産権）、intangible property（無体財産権）、chose in action（債権）の意味は、それぞれ以下のとおりである。

(1) Real and personal property（物的及び人的財産権）

　Property とは、物（choses）を使用・収益・処分等する権利としての財産権であり、これは real property と personal property の２つに大別される。

　Real property（物的財産権）とは土地及びその定着物（土地上の建物や樹木、農作物等）に対する権利としての財産権である。土地に関する権利として、freehold（自由土地保有権）と leasehold（不動産賃借権）の両方が real property に含まれる。これに対し、personal property（人的財産権）とは、chattel personal（動産）、intellectual property（工業所有権）等の intangible property（無体財産権）、株式（stock）、債券（debenture）、預金

(deposit)、売掛債権（account receivable）、現金（cash）、その他土地以外の一切の財産に対する権利である。

(2) Tangible and intangible property（有体及び無体財産権）

Property（財産権）は、土地建物、動産等の有体の財産権（tangible property）とそれ以外の無体財産権（intangible property）にも分類することができる。

(3) Chose in action and chose in rem（債権と物権）

Chose in action は、物理的な支配にはなじまず、原則として訴訟等の法的手続による金銭支払請求の形でのみ実現可能な財産権のことであり、日本法上の債権とほぼ同義である。これに対し、事実関係によって実現できる財産権（choses in possession（動産の占有）等）は、一般に choses in rem（対物権）と呼ばれる。

2．Assignment の一般原則（制定法によらない場合）

契約上の権利（contractual right）を有する者が、当該権利の assignor（譲渡人）として、第三者である assignee（譲受人）に対して、debtor（債務者）に直接契約上の義務履行を請求することができる地位を移転することを assignment（債権譲渡）という。

イギリス法において、assignment の方法には、コモンロー（common law）に基づく assignment（assignment at common law）と衡平法（equity）上の assignment（assignment in equity）の2種類が存在する。ただし、common law 上は、1925年に制定法ができるまで、原則として choses in action は non-assignable（譲渡不能）とされていた。

他方、equity 上の譲渡は可能であるが、choses in action には、legal chose（コモンロー上の債権）と equitable chose（衡平法上の債権）の2種類があり、譲渡対象がこのどちらであるかによって法的効果に違いがある。

(1) Legal choses とは、契約上の権利義務や保険証券上の保険金請求権等

の通常の債権のことである。Legal choses も equity（衡平法）上の assign（債権譲渡）をすることができるが、その債権譲受人（assignee）は、原則として、自己の名において債務者（debtor）に訴求することができない。Debtor に対して契約違反の remedy を求めたい場合は、assignor（債権譲渡人）の名で、かつ assignor と共同で裁判所に訴えなければならない。

(2) Equitable choses とは、信託財産に対する受益権（interest in trust fund）、遺言に基づく遺産請求権（reversionary interest under will）等、元々 equity に基づく権利として認められてきた特殊な choses in action のことである。原則として、assignee の単独名義で執行でき、assignor と共同で訴える必要はない。

3．Statutory Assignment（法令の規定による債権譲渡）

コモンロー上の債権譲渡に関して、the Law of Property Act 1925 は次のとおり規定している。

> Any absolute assignment by writing under the hand of the assignor (not purporting to be by way of charge only) ... of which express notice in writing shall have been given to the debtor ... is effectual in law (subject to equities having priority ...) to pass and transfer as from the date of such notice: (i) the legal right to such thing in action, (ii) all ... remedies for the same and (iii) the power to give a good discharge. (s136(1))

これにより、choses in action の assignment が common law 上も可能となったが、その要件は、以下のとおり極めて限定的である。ただし、これらの要件を備えた assignment は、consideration がなくても有効である。

(1) **Absolute assignment（完全な譲渡）であること**

The Law of Property Act に基づく assignment を行う場合、assignor は一切の interest を留保してはならない。したがって、条件付債権譲渡（conditional assignment）（Durham Bros v Robertson [1898] 1 QB 765①、The

Balder London［1980］2 Lloyd's Rep. 489）や担保のための債権譲渡（assignment by way of charge）をすることはできない（Jones v Humphreys［1902］1 KB 10②、Bank of Liverpool v Holland（1926）43 TLR 29）。また、債権の一部の譲渡（partial assignment）も認められない（Forster v Baker［1910］2 KB 636、The Mount I［2001］EWCA Civ 68）。

(2) By writing under the hand of the assignor（書面性）

Legal assignment は必ず assignor が作成した書面によるものでなければならない。また、取引上の売掛金その他の特定の債権の assignment は、登録しないかぎり破産手続の際に効力を生じない（the Insolvency Act 1986 s344（Book debts of a business））。

(3) Communication（譲渡の意思表示）

Assignor から assignee に譲渡の意思が伝達されていなければならない。

(4) Notice（譲渡通知）

Assignor 又は assignee のいずれかが debtor に対して書面により譲渡通知をしなければならない（Holt v Heatherfield Trust Ltd.［1942］2 KB 530）。この通知の時期は、譲渡債権の enforcement 前であればいつでもよい（Walker v Bradford Old Bank（1884）12 QBD 511）。なお、二重、三重の債権譲渡があった場合の優先順位は、通知の先後による（Dearle v Hall（1828）3 Russ. 1、Ellerman Lines Ltd. v Lancaster Maritime Co., Ltd.［1980］2 Lloyd's Rep. 497）。

4．Equitable Assignment（衡平法上の債権譲渡）

The Law of Property Act 1925に基づく法律上の assignment（legal assignment）には、上記3のとおり多くの制約があるので、この要件を全て充足することが不可能である場合、特に、security assignment（譲渡担保）、partial assignment（債権の一部譲渡）、conditional assignment（条件付債権

譲渡）が必要な場合には、equitable assignment の方法によることになる。上記3の要件の一部を欠いた債権譲渡であっても、equitable assignment としては完全に有効である。ただし、equitable assignment における assignee や assignor による権利行使には、以下のような制約がある。

(1) **権利行使上の制約**

契約上の一般債権等の legal choses（法律上の債権）の equitable assignment の場合、原則として assignee（債権譲受人）は自己の単独名義で debtor（債務者）に訴訟上の請求をすることができず、assignor（債権譲渡人）との共同名義で請求しなければならない（The Aiolos [1983] 2 Lloyd's Rep. 25、Three Rivers DC v Bank of England [1996] QB 292、Cator v Croydon Canal Co（1841）4 Y & C Ex. 405）。これは、権利者の不確定によるリスクから debtor（債務者、義務者）を保護し、かつ重複訴訟を防止するためである。

これに対し、assignor（債権譲渡人）は単独で debtor（債務者）に対して訴訟上の請求をすることができるが、assignee の trustee（受託者）としての地位に基づいてしか請求できない。

Assignor が債権の一部譲渡（partial assignment）をした上で、譲渡していない債権の一部を請求する場合、assignee と共同で訴訟を提起しなければならない。

後順位担保権（second mortgage）その他の equitable interests（衡平法上の財産権）は、equitable assignment の方法による譲渡しか認められない。また、必ず書面によらなければならない（the Law of Property Act 1925 s53 (1) (c)、Oughtred v IRC [1960] AC 206）。

(2) **手続（通知の要否）**

Debtor 又は obligor への通知は、equitable assignment の要件としては不要である（Holt v Heatherfield Trust Ltd. [1942] 2 KB 1、Gorringe v Irwell India Rubber, etc., Workers（1886）34 Ch. D. 128）。

ただし、通知がない場合、debtor や obligor は、assignor に対して債務履行をして、債務を免れることができる（Warner Bros Records Inc. v Rollgreen Ltd.［1976］QB 430、Herkules Piling v Tilbury Construction（1992）61 Build. L.R. 107）。また、書面による通知をしておけば、二重、三重の債権譲渡があった場合における優先権を確保できるので（Dearle v Hall（1828）3 Russ. 1、the Law of Property Act 1925 s 137）、一般的には通知した方が望ましい。

5．Exclusion of Assignment（譲渡制限）

　Statutory assignment、assignment in equity のいずれの場合であっても、personal contracts（一身専属的性質の契約）は譲渡できない（Nokes v Dominion Trust Ltd. v Parkway Motors［1955］1 WLR 719）。
　また、assign できるのは権利だけであり、契約上の債務、義務の assignment はできない（Linden Gardens Trust Ltd. v Lenesta Sludge Disposals Ltd.［1994］1 AC 85）。
　Creditor と debtor の間で assignment を禁ずる旨の明示の合意（non-assignability clause）をした場合、この合意は、イギリス法上拘束力を生じ、creditor がこれに違反して assignment をしても、debtor との間では assignment の効力を生じない（Helstan Securities Ltd. v Hertfordshire CC［1978］3 All ER 262、Linden Gardens Trust Ltd. v Lenesta Sludge Disposals Ltd.［1994］1 AC 85）。ただし、assignor と assignee との間では assignment は有効であり（Re Turcan（1888）40 Ch. D. 5、Re Westerton［1919］2 Ch. 104）、assignee は assignor に対して債権譲渡契約違反の責任を追及することができる（Bawejem Ltd. v M.C. Fabrications Ltd.［1999］1 All ER (Comm.) 377）。なお、non-assignability clause（債権譲渡禁止条項）は、creditor が第三者のために equity 上の権利を信託譲渡（declaration of trust）することまでは制限していないと解される場合がある（Don King Productions Inc. v Warren［2000］Ch. 291）。

6．債務者の抗弁権（Subject to equities）

Assignment at common law、equitable assignment のいずれの場合でも、debtor は、assignor に対抗、主張できた抗弁や契約の欠陥を assignee に対しても対抗、主張することができる。

(1) Defects of title（権利の瑕疵）

Assignor は自己が有する権利以上のものを譲渡できない（Tooth v Hallett (1869) L.R. 4 Ch. App. 242）。

(2) Claims arising out of contract assigned（譲渡債権に基づく抗弁）

Debtor は、assign された権利に係る契約に関する assignor に対するクレーム（たとえば、fraud を理由として契約を rescind（解消）する権利）を assignee に対しても主張できる（Graham v Johnson (1869) L.R. 8 Eq. 36）。ただし、debtor は、契約に基づいて相手方（債権者）に対して有することになった損害賠償請求権を契約上の債権譲受人に対して主張することはできない。たとえば、相手方の詐欺によって義務を負担した場合、債権の譲受人に対して当該義務の解消（rescission）を主張することは可能だが、詐欺による損害賠償請求権をもって債権譲受人に対して相殺を主張することはできない（Stoddart v Union Trust [1912] 1 KB 181③）。

(3) Claims arising out of other contracts（他の契約に基づく抗弁）

Debtor と assignor との間における他の契約に基づく債権との相殺は、債権譲渡通知前に発生したものに限り主張できる（Stephens v Venables (1862) 30 Beav. 625、Business Computers Ltd. v Anglo-African Leasing Ltd. [1977] 1 WLR 578）。

7．Novation（更改）

契約当事者の一方と第三者との間で、既存の契約の代わりに新契約を締結す

ることを novation という。たとえば、AとBとの間の契約において、Bは、当該契約上の債権債務を消滅させることに合意し、かつAとCとの間で、ABの間の契約と全く同一の権利義務を生じさせることを内容とする新契約を締結することについて合意すれば、AB間の契約におけるBの地位がBからCへ移転したのと同じ状態となる。このように、novationは、経済的にはassignment of liability と同一の結果を生じさせることができるので、債務（obligations）の移転に利用できる。

Novation の要件は次のとおりである。

（ⅰ） 全当事者（original creditor（A）、debtor（B）及び new debtor（C）の3者）の関与、合意があること（Tito v Waddell（No.2）［1977］Ch. 106）。

（ⅱ） Novation は3者間の contract なので、新たに契約に加わる第三者（C）から consideration が提供されなければならない。ただし、creditor（A）は、通常、original debtor（B）の債務を免除し、新たな契約に合意することにより consideration を提供している。また、original debtor（B）は、通常、new debtor（C）をAに対して提供することにより、consideration を提供している（Customs & Excise Commissioners v Diners Club Ltd.［1989］1 WLR 1196）。

【CASES】

① *Durham Bros v Robertson* ［1898］1 QB 765

A building contractor wrote to Durham Bros. in the following terms: 'Re Building Contract, South Lambert Road. In consideration of money advanced from time to time we hereby charge the sum of £1,080, being the price ... due to us from [Robertson] on the completion of the above buildings as security for advances, and we hereby assign our interest in the above-mentioned sum until the money with added interest be repaid to you'. It was held that the assignment was not within section 136(1) of the Act 1925 as it did not transfer the whole debt to Durham, the assignee, unconditionally, but only until the advances were repaid.

② *Jones v Humphreys* ［1902］1 KB 10

A schoolmaster borrowed £15 from Jones and in consideration of such loan, assigned to Jones such part of his income, salary from his employer as should be necessary and requisite for repayment of the sum borrowed with interest. It was held that this was not an absolute assignment, but was a mere security purporting to be by way of a charge.

③ *Stoddart v Union Trust* [1912] 1 KB 181

Union Trust was fraudulently induced to buy a newspaper at £1,000 and paid £200 immediately. The seller assigned the remaining purchase price of £800 to innocent third party, Stoddart. Union Trust insisted that it owed nothing to the assignee since it sustained damages of more than £800. It was held that Union Trust could not set off its claim for damages against the assignee since the claim of damages was a personal claim against the wrong-doer.

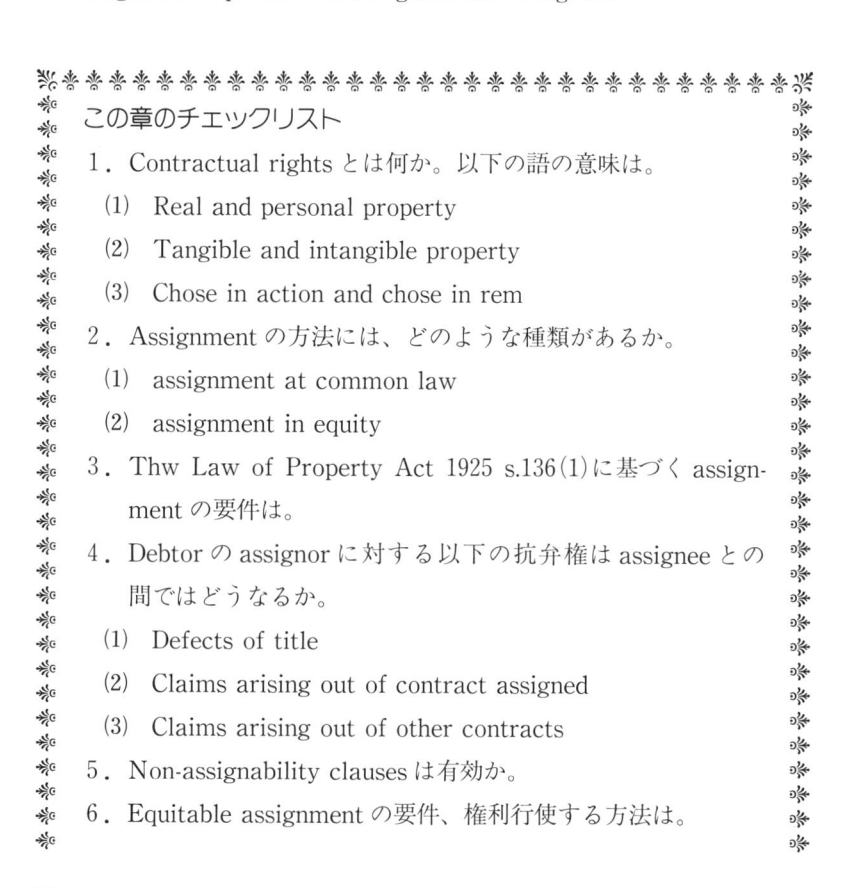

この章のチェックリスト

1. Contractual rights とは何か。以下の語の意味は。
    (1) Real and personal property
    (2) Tangible and intangible property
    (3) Chose in action and chose in rem
2. Assignment の方法には、どのような種類があるか。
    (1) assignment at common law
    (2) assignment in equity
3. Thw Law of Property Act 1925 s.136(1)に基づく assignment の要件は。
4. Debtor の assignor に対する以下の抗弁権は assignee との間ではどうなるか。
    (1) Defects of title
    (2) Claims arising out of contract assigned
    (3) Claims arising out of other contracts
5. Non-assignability clauses は有効か。
6. Equitable assignment の要件、権利行使する方法は。

7．Novation とは何か。要件は。

第Ⅲ編
国際取引法実務とイギリス法

第1章

国際契約交渉とイギリス法

1．契約交渉の目的

　契約交渉（contractual negotiation）とは、一定の（継続的であるか1回限りであるかを問わない）取引関係に入ろうとする複数の者又は企業の間で、当該取引の条件その他当該取引に関連する当事者間の関係を規律するための約束事を取り決めておくために行う、対面及び通信による当事者間の話し合いのことである。この定義から明らかなとおり、契約交渉の主要な目的は、取引の条件等に関する当事者間の合意を形成することである。しかし、この目的を達成するために行う交渉の方法や手段に関しては、国及び文化に応じて、とりわけ日本、韓国、中国などの東アジア人と欧米人（特に米英人）との間には大きな相違があるように思われる。一例として、契約交渉のために日本や中国の企業を訪問したイギリス企業の担当者から、交渉期間中における催しの多さ（たとえば、会議開始前の代表者の挨拶、歓迎パーティー、ゴルフコンペ、見学会、慰労会、送別会等）と面談する人物の多さ（たとえば、挨拶はいつも社長や重役（会議には出席しない）、会議ではそれ以外の10名前後（実際に話をするのは1、2名）、パーティー等ではその他の数名から数10名との名刺交換等）に驚かされた経験を聞かされることがある。また、日本側の交渉担当者が頻繁に入れ替わってその都度異なる説明や提案をしたため、真意が理解できず交渉が難航したという話も見聞する。他方、イギリス企業と取引交渉をした日本企業の担当者からは、イギリスの担当者と友好的かつ親密な関係が築けたと思ったのに、取引交渉の場では別人のように振る舞うので、その最後まで胸襟を開こうとしない融通性のなさに不信感を抱くに至ったという経験を聞かされることがある。私は、日本人と英米人とは契約交渉の手法に対する考え方が正反対であることが、このような誤解や不信感を生む原因ではないかと考えている。日

本人にとっての取引交渉の場は、実質的な契約条件の合意をするより前に、契約交渉を通じて相手との信頼関係を形成するための機会にもなっている。すなわち、日本社会では「契約は信頼できる相手と結ぶもの」との契約意識が今でも根強いので、多くの日本人は、意図的であるか否かはともかく、まず当該交渉相手が取引を始めても問題がない程度に信用できる人物又は企業か否かを確かめようとして交渉に臨むものである。そして、一度信頼関係が形成されると、具体的な取引条件等については互いに相手の立場と利益を慮り、譲り合いながら合意が形成できるはずであると考える傾向がある。よって、交渉期間中に企画される様々な催しは、担当者間の良好な人間関係の形成を通じて企業間の相互理解を深める上で重要な意味を有しているのである。しかし、英米人にとっての契約交渉とは自己に最大限に有利な条件を引き出すために互いの立場をぶつけ合うための一種の闘争の場であり、またそのような経過を通じてこそ双方が納得できる合意を導き出すことができると信じられている。これは、契約は信頼関係を前提として締結するものではなく、むしろ互いに信頼できない者同士を拘束するために締結するものであるという考え方を前提とすれば、当然の交渉方式である。よって、英米人にとっては、会議室での話し合い以外の行事は、交渉を円滑に進めるための潤滑油と息抜き以上のものではない。

　このような交渉相手との考え方の違いを意識せずに交渉に臨むと思わぬ落とし穴にはまる恐れがあるので注意を要する。たとえば、交渉相手を歓迎するためにわざわざ設けた催しの場等において取引条件にかかわる提案、発言、意見等を不用意に述べたりすると、英米人には会議室の延長の話と誤解され、かえってその後の話し合いに悪影響を及ぼすかもしれないのである。

　以上は、私が国際契約交渉において日本企業や欧米企業の代理や助言をした経験から受けた印象に過ぎず、これを裏付ける客観的な資料が存在するわけではない。しかし、様々な機会に諸外国の弁護士とこの問題について話し合った結果を総合すれば、欧米人（特に英米人）と日本人の間の契約交渉に臨む姿勢及び交渉の目的に対する考え方には大きな違いがあり、企業間の取引においても、この違いが互いの誤解や不信感の原因の１つとなっていることは間違いがないと思われる。私は、この交渉に対する意識の違いは、以下に述べるような、契約交渉中における当事者の権利義務を規律する法制度と密接不可分な関係を

2．イギリス法に基づく契約交渉中における当事者の義務

(1) 信義誠実（good faith）義務と契約締結上の過失責任

　イギリス企業との契約交渉に入る者は、イギリス法には契約交渉に関する一般要件としての信義誠実の原則が存在せず、原則として、契約交渉当事者は、信義則上の誠実義務を負うものではないということを認識しておく必要がある。

　日本法における契約締結上の過失責任の法理とは、契約準備交渉段階に入った当事者間の関係は、何らの特別な関係がない者の間の関係より緊密であることから、そのような関係にある当事者が負担すべき、相手方に損害を被らせないようにする信義則上の義務があるとする考え方である。この法原則は、大正年代にドイツのイェーリング（von Jhering）の学説が紹介されて以来、わが国の判例、学説上広く認められ、特に昭和40年代以降は、当事者の一方が契約交渉を理由なく打ち切り、それによって相手方の契約成立への期待を裏切り、相手方に無用の出費をさせた場合に、契約締結準備段階における信義則上の注意義務違反を理由とする損害賠償請求を認める判決が数多く存在する。

　しかし、イギリス法上、契約締結前において信義誠実義務が要求されるのは、消費者契約や保険契約等特定の取引分野だけに限られている。したがって、イギリスには、日本法上の契約締結上の過失責任に相当する法原則も存在せず、信義則に基づく契約締結協力義務（duty of co-operation to enter into an agreement）が発生することもない。もちろん、イギリス法上も契約交渉中に詐欺その他の不正な行為を行った場合は、misrepresentationの責任（第II編第7章参照）等が発生するが、これらあくまで不法行為法（tort）や特別の制定法（the Misrepresentation Act 1967）に基づく責任であり、その適用範囲は限定的である。この法意識の下で、イギリス人は、自己の利益のために交渉することこそ正しい交渉手法であり、契約交渉中の言動が交渉相手の利益に反していたとしても、原則として法的な問題が生ずることはないと理解しているのである。

(2) 情報開示義務

上記(1)のとおり、イギリス法上は契約締結上の責任の法理が存在しないので、原則として、信義則に基づく情報開示義務（duty to disclose information）が発生することはない。

ただし、契約交渉の一方当事者が、相手方が一定の事実について誤解をしていることを知りながらこれを黙っていた場合、既に告げた事実について変更が生じたのにそのことを告げなかった場合、真実の内の一部だけ告げて不利な部分を告げなかった場合等、特別な事情があるときは、情報開示義務違反としてmisrepresentationの責任追及を受けることがある（第Ⅱ編第7章参照）。

(3) 秘密保持（Confidentiality）義務

契約交渉中に相手方に情報を提供する場合は、その前に秘密保持契約書を締結しておくべきである。ただし、イギリスの裁判所は、書面による契約を交わさなかったとしても、以下の3つの要件が充たされた場合、黙示の秘密保持契約（implied confidentiality agreement）の成立を認めることがある。

第1に、情報を開示した相手方に秘密保持義務を負わせるには、当該情報が秘密性を有していなければならない（Woodward v Hutchins [1977] 2 All ER 751、Saltman Engineering Co Limited v Campbell Engineering Co Limited [1948] 65 RPC 203）。ある情報が秘密性を有するというためには、通常人が容易に知りえないような方法で管理されている情報でなければならず、情報を開示する際に秘密情報であると告げただけでは、秘密情報として保護されるわけではない。当該情報は、複雑であったり多量であったりする必要はなく、単純な方式や説明でも構わない。

第2に、秘密保持義務が発生するのは、秘密保持義務が当然に課されるような状況下において開示された場合に限られる（Coco v AN Clark (Engineers) Limited [1969] RPC 41①）。秘密保持義務を課すべき事情があるか否かを判断するに当って、イギリスの裁判所は合理的な一般人（reasonable person）を基準とする、いわゆるobjective test（*a reasonable man standing in the shoes of the recipient of the information would have realised that upon reasonable grounds the information was being given to him in confidence*）

を用いている。たとえば、情報を開示した当事者が当該情報を公知の情報と同じように取り扱っていた場合は、合理的な一般人を基準とした場合、受領者も開示当事者と同様に扱っても構わない、すなわち、秘密保持義務は負わないと判断される可能性が濃厚である（上記 Coco v AN Clark (Engineers) Ltd 判決、上記 Woodward v Hutchins 判決）。また、たとえ製品の製造に必要な設計図書等が秘密性を有していたとしても、市販されている製品自体を分析すれば誰でも知り得るような製品製造技術は秘密情報とはいえない。当該情報を暗号化していたとしても、容易に解析可能なものであれば同様である（Mars UK Ltd v Teknowledge Ltd［1999］All ER (D) 600②）。

第3に、情報を与えた当事者が相手方に対して、開示した情報の使用や第三者への開示に関する同意や承認（明示、黙示を問わない。）を与えていないと認められる場合であることを要する。秘密情報を受領した者が、そのような同意や承認を受けていない方法でこれを使用した場合や第三者に開示、漏洩した場合に、秘密保持義務違反（breach of confidence）の責任追及を受けることになる（上記 Coco v AN Clark (Engineers) Ltd）。

情報開示当事者は、当該情報を使用又は第三者に開示した者及び使用又は開示しようとした者に対して、損害賠償や差止請求の方法で、秘密保持義務違反の責任を追及することができる。ただし、差止請求が認められるのは、裁判官が損害賠償だけでは救済が困難であると判断した場合だけである（第Ⅱ編第10章8及び下記3(1)）。

秘密保持義務が発生した場合、情報開示当事者は、契約交渉の相手方から当該情報を受領した第三者に対しても、情報受領時に当該情報の秘密性を知っていたか否かにかかわらず、秘密保持義務の遵守を求めることができる。ただし、当該情報が秘密性を失ったときは、もはや保護の対象とならない。

契約交渉中には、当該契約の目的とは関連しない事項までも協議の対象となり、契約とは無関係な情報までも知られてしまうことがあるが、イギリスの裁判所がそのような情報に関してまで秘密保持義務を認めるか否かに関しては先例がない。このように、判例法によって発生する黙示の合意に基づく秘密保持義務には限界があるので、なるべく判例法には頼らず、きちんと秘密保持契約書を交わしておいた方が安全である。

3．契約交渉中に交わす書面

(1) 秘密保持契約書（Confidentiality agreement）

　ライセンス契約や企業買収契約の交渉に先立ち、ライセンサーや売主は、相手方に対し、秘密保持契約書（confidentiality agreement）や情報開示禁止契約書（non-disclosure agreement）への署名を求めるのが通例である。秘密保持契約書の締結が必要か否かは、ライセンス契約等が締結される前にどの程度の情報を開示するかにかかわっている。たとえばライセンス契約の交渉中に開示すべき情報の中に、契約締結後に実施許諾する秘密技術（特許出願中の技術情報や特許出願もしていない情報を含む。）の一部や売上予想その他経済的な価値がある営業上の情報が含まれている場合は、そのような情報を保護するために秘密保持契約を締結する必要がある。上記2(3)のとおり、秘密保持契約を締結せずに特定のノウハウや情報を開示した場合、イギリスのコモンロー上の原則だけでは、秘密情報が十分に保護されない可能性があるからである。

　秘密保持契約書においては、契約交渉中に相手方から情報の開示を受ける当事者に対して、当該情報及びこれに関する一切の資料に関する秘密を保持すべき義務、これらを自ら使用しない義務、及び許可なく第三者に開示・漏洩しない義務が定められる。更に、当該情報を無断で使用する第三者に対して、情報受領当事者の名で法的手続きを提起することを認める旨の規定を設けておくこともある。

　情報を受領した当事者が秘密保持契約に違反した場合、コモンロー上、違反者に対して契約違反による損害賠償を請求することができるが、これに合わせて、将来の当該情報の使用や開示を禁ずるために差止命令（injunction）を求める必要が生ずることが少なくない。そのような場合は、訴え提起と共に、暫定的な差止命令（interim injunction）を発してもらわなければ秘密保持の実効性が確保できない。イギリス法上、差止命令及び暫定的差止命令は衡平法上の救済手段であり、裁判所が損害賠償の方法では十分な救済ができないと考えたときにのみ裁判官の裁量によって認められるに過ぎない（第Ⅱ編第10章8参照）。ただし、秘密保持義務違反に関してはその義務の性質上、当該情報の秘密性の証明さえできれば、暫定的差止命令等の救済措置が認められる可能性が

かなり高いといえる。

　暫定的な差止命令（interim injunction）が認められた場合、被告は、本案の裁判確定まで秘密保持義務違反の行為を禁じられる。通常の場合、当該命令には、原告が、当該命令が間違っていた事実が後日（本案に関する裁判の際）判明したときに被告の損害を賠償することを約すること、及び一定の期間内にそのための保証金や担保を提供することが条件として付されている。

　暫定的な差止命令は、秘密保持義務違反の恐れを知ったときはできる限り速やかに申し立てる必要がある。秘密が開示された後に申し立てても、もはや損害の回復は不可能であることを根拠に申立てが認められない可能性があるからである。

(2) レター・オブ・インテント（Letter of intent）

　重要な取引に関する契約交渉中のある一定の段階において、交渉当事者間において正式契約とは異なる何らかの合意書が交わされることがある。これらの書面は、国際取引においては、letter of intent（レター・オブ・インテント）、memorandum of understanding（メモランダム）、heads of agreement（ヘッド・オブ・アグリーメント）、heads of terms（ヘッド・オブ・タームズ）等と呼ばれている（第Ⅱ編第3章2）。タイトルは様々であるが、その役割や表現、内容に関してはいずれも以下の記述が当てはまり大差がないので、以下、これらを総称して「契約締結前書面」と呼ぶことにする。

　契約締結前書面を交わす目的は、取引の種類、内容、契約交渉の経緯、特にどの段階で締結されるか等により様々である。ほとんどの場合に共通する最も一般的な目的は、当事者間で契約成立に向けて交渉を行う意思があることを確認し、かつ当事者間で了解している契約の目的や合意済みの事項を明示的に記録しておくことにより、今後の交渉を進めていくための前提を明確にしておくことである。

　契約締結前書面の内容もその目的に応じて様々であるが、両当事者が契約締結に向けて交渉を継続する意思を有していることを確認し、かつ当該書面締結までに合意に達している事項を記載している場合が多い。また、契約締結に影響を及ぼす可能性のある、当事者や契約目的物に関する事項の開示義務、契約

交渉中に知り得た相手方の情報に関する秘密保持義務、契約交渉に要した費用の分担（たとえば、契約準備費用は各自弁とする合意）等に関する条項を設けることもある。

　契約締結前書面がいかなる法的効力を有するかは、その目的、締結に至った経緯及び条項の内容により異なり一般化できないが、イギリスの取引実務上、契約締結前書面は法的拘束力を生じさせない書面とする意図の下に作成される場合が多い。よって、原則として、当該書面に契約を締結するために交渉する意思があることを記載したりその時点での了解事項を記載したりしても、それによって本契約を締結した場合と同一の義務を負ったり、あるいは当該書面記載どおりの法的義務を直ちに負ったりすることはない（第Ⅱ編第3章2参照）。ただし、裁判所によりこれと異なる認定をされる恐れもあるので、慎重にドラフトする必要がある。一般に、書面のタイトルはその内容の解釈に影響を与えるものとは解されないので、letter of intent というタイトルを付したという事実は、当事者の意図を推定する証拠の1つとなるだけである。当該書面の全部又は一部の法的拘束力を否定するためには、タイトルだけではなくその内容においても、当該書面が当事者間の意思を確認するためのものであることや法的拘束力がないことを明記しておく方が望ましい。

　契約締結前書面が法的拘束力のある書面として作成された場合、当該書面はそれ自体が contract となり、これに違反した者は契約違反による損害賠償責任を負うことになる。この場合の損害額は、交渉によって締結されたであろう本来の契約が締結されなかったことによる損害ではなく、契約交渉中に要した費用や経費に基づいて算定されることになる。契約締結前書面において損害賠償予定額を記載する場合は、罰則規定（penalty clause）として無効と解されないように、合理的な根拠のある損害額を予想して決定する必要がある（第Ⅱ編第10章5参照）。

　書面の文言が明らかに法的拘束力を生じない記載内容になってさえいれば、イギリス法上、作成者は信義則その他の一般原則を根拠とする法的義務を負担することはない。ただし、当該書面を作成した時点において記載内容が間違っていた場合は、作成者は misrepresentation を根拠として不法行為等の責任を負うことがある（第Ⅱ編第7章参照）。

また、仮に法的拘束力のない書面として合意した場合であっても、契約締結前書面を締結した場合は、当該書面において合意した事項を遵守すべきことが倫理的な義務となり、事実上、書面作成時に予測できなかった事態が生じた場合その他やむを得ない事情がない限り、この合意を覆すことが困難になる。したがって、たとえ法的拘束力を生じさせない意図を明らかにした上での合意であったとしても、その内容を慎重に吟味し、不用意な表明や約束を無条件で行わないように注意する必要がある。

(3) コンフォート・レター (Letter of Comfort, Comfort Letter)

コンフォート・レターは、ローンその他の融資取引の際に借主の信用を補完する目的で用いられる形式の契約締結前書面である。これは、契約交渉当事者間で締結する上記(2)の書面とは異なり、借主が銀行等の金融機関から借入をするに際し、借主以外の者が借主のために作成して銀行等宛に発行する書面である。一般的には、親会社が子会社の借入に関して銀行に発行する等、グループ会社のために発行されることが多い。当該書簡には、「子会社が銀行借入金を返済できる状態に保つことが親会社である当社の方針である。」との趣旨が記載される（Kleinwort Benson v Malaysia Mining Corp Sdn Bhd [1989] 1 All ER 785③、Re Atlantic Computers plc (in administration) National Australia Bank Ltd v Soden & Anor [1995] Bcc 696④）。親会社が子会社の債務について保証をしないでコンフォート・レターで済ませるのは様々な理由によるが、財務・会計書類の記載や親会社自身の信用評価 (credit rating) への影響を考慮している場合が最も多い。

子会社が借入金の返済を遅滞したとき、銀行はコンフォート・レターに基づいて親会社を訴えることができるか否かという問題に関して、イギリス法上の原則は未だ確立していない。一般的に、コンフォート・レターは、銀行が借主へ融資するか否かを決めるに当り、その決定を促進したり、助成したりするための書簡であるが、保証状 (letter of guarantee) とは異なり、その作成者が借主と同じ法的責任を負担するものではない（上記 Kleinwort Benson Limited v Malaysian Mining Corporation 判決）。ただし、当該書簡の記載内容が一定の法的拘束力を生じさせる合意であると解釈できる場合は、comfort letterというタイトルにかかわらず、発行者は名宛人である銀行に対して記載どおりの法的義務を負担したものと推定され、法的拘束力を生じさせる意思がなかったことについての立証責任は、発行者が負担する（Edwards v Skyways [1964] 1 All ER 494⑤）。その立証のためには、書面自体の内容に加え、書面発行について取締役会の承認を受けたか否か、当該書面の発行が銀行融資の条件（condition precedent）となっていたか否か等の要素が重要な意味を持つ。このようなリスクを避けるための最善の方法は、書面の中に一切の法的拘束力が生じない旨を明記することだが、それでは融資先の銀行が同意しない場合もある。

たとえ将来の行為に関する約束（guarantee等）を含まないコンフォート・レターであっても、少なくとも当該書面作成時における一定の事実（たとえば、その時において親会社が子会社を支払超過に陥らせない方針をとっていること）は必ず記載される。そのような記載内容に関して、当該書面を作成した時点において発行者が意図的に虚偽の事実を記載した場合や過失により虚偽に気づかなかった場合、これによって融資を決定した銀行から、被った全ての損害についてnegligent misstatementを根拠としてtortに基づく損害賠償請求を受ける恐れがある（第II編7章2(2)参照）。したがって、たとえ法的拘束力を生じさせないものとして発行する場合であっても、その内容の真実性について慎重に検討、確認するべきである。

(4) ロックアウト契約（Lock-out Agreement）

既述のとおり、イギリスには、いわゆる契約締結上の過失に相当する法原理は存在せず、原則として、信義則に基づく誠実交渉義務や排他的交渉権が発生することはないので、イギリス法に基づいて独占的交渉権が発生するには、明示的又は黙示的に、一定の交渉期間中、同一事項に関して第三者とは交渉しない旨の法的拘束力ある合意が成立していることが必要である。イギリスの企業買収における取引実務上、この目的のためにはロックアウト契約（lock-out agreement）という契約を締結する。ロックアウト契約の目的は、契約目的物の買主に対し、一定の期間中、売主と排他的に契約交渉をし、かつ目的物や売主に関する調査を独占的に実施する権利を与えることである。したがって、売

主は当該期間中、第三者と交渉に入ることが禁じられることになる。イギリス法上、企業買収のために交渉を行う旨の合意のような、いわゆる「合意のための合意」（agreement to agree）は、明確性を欠き、法的拘束力を有さないと解されている（Walford v Miles［1992］2 AC 128 HL（第Ⅱ編第3章⑨））。ただし、ロックアウト契約における第三者と交渉しない旨の合意（agreement not to negotiate with a third party）は、(1)交渉禁止期間が明定されていて、かつ(2)約因（consideration）があるか又は証書（deed）によって合意されていれば、法的拘束力を有している（上記 Walford v Miles 判決）。ロックアウト契約は、書面によることが通常だが、口頭の合意であってもその成立が立証されれば法的拘束力を有する（Pitt v PHH Asset Management Limited［1993］4 All ER 961）。Letter of intent、heads of terms その他の契約締結前書面においてロックアウト条項を規定しても構わないが、この場合は、法的拘束力を発生させる要件である約因（consideration）を落とさないように注意する必要がある。

　売主がロックアウト契約にかかわらず第三者と交渉に入った場合は契約違反となり、買主は、これによって被った損害の賠償を予見可能な範囲内で請求することができる。違反の結果として取引が成立するに至らなかった場合は、交渉期間中に支出した費用や経費の賠償請求ができるであろうが、取引が成立しなかったことによる遺失利益までも予見可能な損害として賠償請求するのは、通常は難しいと思われる。イギリス法上、第三者との交渉の差止・禁止命令（injunction）やそのための仮処分に相当する措置の命令（interim injunction）は衡平法上の制度であり、認められるか否かは裁判所の裁量にかかっている。裁判所は、事後的な損害賠償だけでは被害者に対して適正な救済を与えることができないと判断した場合にしか衡平法上の救済措置を与えないので、企業買収その他の取引に関する契約違反を是正し義務を履行させるための差止・禁止命令は、容易に認められない。

4．Subject to contract と Without prejudice

　Subject to contract という語句は、契約交渉中の両当事者がまだ完全な合

意には達していないことを表すために用いられる（第Ⅱ編第3章1）。両当事者がレター・オブ・インテント等の交換をせずに口頭及び書面による交信だけで契約交渉をしている場合は、交渉の途中におけるカウンターオファー（counter-offer）やこれに対する返信だけで契約が成立したと解されることがないように（第Ⅱ編第1章参照）、会議や交信文において、subject to contract の申入れであることを明記しておくべきである。

レター・オブ・インテント等の契約締結前書面を交わす場合は、当該書面に subject to contract の語句を記載しておけば、契約成立の法的拘束力を生じさせる意思がなかったものと一応推定されるが、当該書面を作成した時点までの交渉状況や合意内容、その後の事情等を総合し、契約が成立したものと認定される場合もあり得る（DMA Financial Solutions Ltd v (1) BaaN UK Ltd (2) BaaN International BV (3) BaaN CO NV [2000] CH.D (Park J) 28/03/2000（第Ⅱ編第3章⑩））し、付随的な契約（collateral contract）の成立が認められる場合もある（第Ⅱ編第3章2）。一切の法的拘束力ある合意をしない意図の場合は、subject to contract の文言に加え、その旨をも明記しておいた方が安全である。

Without prejudice は、厳密に言えば、紛争中又は和解交渉中の当事者間において、解決のために現に交渉している問題や事項に関する書面や会議における議論に対して用いられる表現である。紛争中又は和解交渉中に、意見や提案が without prejudice として提示された場合、当該書面、意見、提案等は、後の訴訟において without prejudice privilege を受けることができる。すなわち、和解交渉等を失敗し両当事者間で裁判上の争いとなった場合、いずれの当事者も当該書面や相手方の言動を、裁判手続において相手方の不利益に用いることが許されない。このように、without prejudice と subject to contract とは、その使用すべき場面と機能を異にしているが、実務上はよく混同して用いられている。

5．契約交渉の一方的な破棄と当事者の責任

契約交渉中には、交渉に関する法的費用、会計費用、契約準備費用その他

様々な費用が発生するので、契約が締結に至らなかった場合、一方当事者は、相手方に対して、そのような費用の全部又は一部の負担を求めようとすることがある。イギリス法上、契約交渉中の当事者は、いつでも自由に交渉を打ち切ることができるのが原則であり、特別な合意がない限り、交渉打ち切りによる責任を負うことはない。ただし、契約締結前書面において契約交渉中の協力義務、契約交渉を打ち切らない義務その他交渉継続に関する特別な義務の負担を合意したにかかわらず、一方当事者が契約交渉とは無関係な事情により、交渉継続を望む相手方の意向を無視して一方的に交渉を打ち切った場合には、相手方は当該義務違反を根拠として損害賠償を求めることができる（Radiant Shipping Co., Ltd. v Sea Containers Limited［1995］CLC 976 E&W）。この場合も、契約交渉を一方的に破棄（withdrawal）したのか、それとも双方に原因があって交渉が決裂したのかを判断するのはそれほど簡単ではない。また、当事者間で協力義務違反や交渉継続義務を定めた場合であっても、そのような義務違反の責任を負うべき場合は一方当事者が合理的な理由なく交渉を打ち切ったときに限る旨を合意するのが通常なので、「合理的な理由」の有無が必ず争点となる。更に、当該書面に記載された義務の内容自体が不明瞭であることを根拠として、その法的拘束力（enforceability）が認められない可能性もある。以上の理由により、実務上、lock-out agreement 以外の契約締結前書面（letter of intent, heads of terms など）においては交渉継続義務等を明確に合意しない方が一般的である。仮にそのような合意をする場合は、相手方から不測の負担を強いられることにならないよう、損害賠償の限度額を合意しておいた方が安全である。

6．契約交渉の準拠法

　契約や取引の準拠法について当事者間で合意がある場合はそれに従うのが原則であるが、契約交渉中や契約締結前書面においては、実務上、準拠法の合意までは行われていない。イギリス法は、当事者間で特別な合意がない限り、対象となっている取引と最も密接で現実的な関連性を有する法制度を準拠法とするので、契約交渉及び契約締結前書面の解釈やこれに関する紛争は、原則とし

て、当該契約を締結した国の法律に準拠することとなる。契約締結までに至らなかったとしても、主たる契約交渉地がイギリスである場合や契約の準拠法にイギリス法が選択されることが予定されていた場合は、契約交渉及びこれに伴う責任の有無や内容、範囲等は、イギリス法に基づいて判断されることになる可能性が高い。

【*CASES*】

① *Coco v AN Clark (Engineers) Ltd* ［1969］RPC 41

Coco and AN Clark began a joint venture relation to the production of a new engine. They decided not to continue and subsequently Coco alleged AN Clark had used formation imparted during the period of co-operation. There had been no contract between the parties, but it was held that the case was based on "the pure equitable doctrine of confidence unaffected by contract" (per Megarry J). The judge stated that there were three essential elements of an action for breach of confidence: firstly, the information must be of a confidential character, secondly, the imparting of the information must be in circumstances where the confidant ought reasonably to have known that the information was confidential, and thirdly the information must have been used or disclosed in a an unauthorised manner causing a detriment to the claimant.

② *Mars UK Ltd v Teknowledge Ltd* ［1999］All ER (D) 600

Mars UK Ltd designed and sold a new discriminator called the Cashflow. Teknowledge Ltd, who had bought it in the market, succeeded in reverse engineering it, and Mars UK commenced proceedings against it claiming, inter alia, breach of confidence in relation to the encryption system. It was held that in order to establish a breach of confidence the information itself had to have the necessary quality of confidence about it, and had to have been imparted in circumstances importing an obligation of confidence. In this case, the encrypted information in the Cashflow did not have the necessary quality of confidence since anyone could buy the Cashflow, and anyone with the skills to de-encrypt had access to the information. Further, the encrypted information had not been imparted in circumstances importing an obligation of confidence. The mere fact of encryption did not make the encrypted information confidential, nor should anyone who de-encrypted something which was in code necessarily be taken to be receiving information in confidence.

③ *Kleinwort Benson v Malaysia Mining Corp Sdn Bhd* [1989] 1 All ER 785

Malaysia Mining Corp ("MMC") issued to Kleinwort Benson ("KB") a letter of comfort, stating that it was a policy of MMC to ensure that its subsidiary company was 'at all times in a position to meet its liabilities' in regard to a loan made by KB to the subsidiary'. The High Court decided that such letter had contractual effect. On appeal by MMC, the Court of Appeal held that it was only a moral obligation as it stated the policy of MMC and accordingly it gave no contractual warranty as to MMS's future conduct.

④ *Re Atlantic Computers plc (in administration) National Australia Bank Ltd v Soden & Anor* (1995) Bcc 696

In 1988 British & Commonwealth Holdings P.L.C. ("B&C") purchased the whole of the share capital of Atlantic. The acquisition proved to be disastrous. Atlantic went into administration in 1990. A bank, which had financed B&C for purchase, claimed to be a creditor in a scheme of arrangement relating to Atlantic, arguing that it was entitled to recover damages from Atlantic under a letter of comfort given to it by Atlantic relating to a subsidiary's indebtedness. The court held that the letter of comfort did not constitute a contractual promise by Atlantic as to future conduct. Accordingly the bank's claim to be a creditor failed.

⑤ *Edwards v Skyways Ltd.* [1964] 1 All ER 494

Airline sought to rely on the use of the words "ex gratia" in a letter with regard to a pilot's redundancy payment. It was held that, such words were not sufficient to discharge that burden to make payment, so that the airline had to make payments and did not have discretion.

この章のチェックリスト

1．契約交渉の目的は何か。
2．契約交渉中の当事者は交渉相手に対してどのような法的義務を負うか。
3．明示的な合意なしに秘密保持義務が発生するのはどのような場合か。
4．秘密保持契約書の目的、内容及び法的効果は。

5．レター・オブ・インテントを結ぶ際、どのような点に注意を要するか。
6．コンフォート・レターとは何か。これを結ぶ際どのような注意が必要か。
7．ロックアウト契約とは何か。どのような場合に締結するべきか。
8．Subject to contract、without prejudice とは何か。
9．契約交渉を一方的に破棄した場合、どのような責任が生ずるか。
10．契約交渉の準拠法はどのように定まるのか。

第 2 章

英文契約書のドラフト

1．契約書作成の目的

　国際取引に関する契約は、契約の両当事者が契約書を作成の上これに署名する方法で締結するのが通例である。ただし、イギリス、日本を含む多くの国の法制度上、一部の特別な契約（不動産に関する契約、保証契約等）を除き、契約書の作成は契約締結に必要な要件、方式ではない（第Ⅱ編第 3 章 5 ）。そうであるにかかわらず契約締結のためにわざわざ契約書を作成する主たる目的は、以下の 2 つであると考えられる。

　（ⅰ）　様々な権利義務を含む複雑な取引関係に関する合意をした当事者間において、契約上いかなる義務を負担し、また権利を取得したかを記録しておくこと。

　（ⅱ）　後に争いが生じた場合に備えて、契約が成立していること及び契約当事者が法的拘束を受けている義務の内容に関する証拠を残しておくこと。

　契約当事者又はその代理人の立場で契約書をドラフトする際は、当該書面がこの 2 つの目的を充たすものでなければならないことを常に念頭に置き、この目的に適合するような内容及び表現の契約書として作成することを心がけなければならない。すなわち、契約書においては、両当事者が確かに合意している事項を漏れなく盛り込み、これを誰にも誤解されないような表現でわかりやすく正確に記載することが最も肝要である。

2．契約書作成の方法

　契約書、あるいはこれから相手方に提示するための契約書草案（ドラフト）を作成する方法には、（ⅰ）法律事務所の標準書式や市販の書式集に基づきこれ

を修正しながら作成する方法、(ⅱ)当事者が過去に締結した契約書に基づきこれを修正しながら作成する方法、(ⅲ)全く参考となる書式がない状態でスクラッチから作成する方法の3つが考えられる。多くの場合は(ⅰ)又は(ⅱ)の方法がとられるが、全く新しい取引や法分野に関する契約書を作成する際には(ⅲ)の方法によらざるを得ないことがある。

　いずれの方法による場合も、契約書又は契約書草案の作成者が最初になすべき作業は、これから作成しようとする契約書の骨子となる基本的な構成、各構成部分において一般的に定めておくべき事項及び各事項において通常規定しておくべき内容を予測し、これらをまとめたチェックリストを作成することである。この作業が済んだ後で、当該チェックリストに基づいて契約当事者に質問をして、各項目における当事者が求めている内容、あるいは両当事者間で既に合意した内容を確認することになる。上記1で述べたとおり、契約書（案）は、合意成立前の事項に関しては当該書面を作成する側の当事者の意向や要望を、合意成立後に関しては当事者間の合意内容を、それぞれ正確かつ明瞭に示すものでなければならない。この目的に照らし、契約書（案）作成中にチェックリストや当事者からの聴取内容が不完全であったことがわかった場合は、躊躇なく当事者に接触を取り、補充の質問をすべきである。

3．契約書の構成

　契約書の基本構成を策定する上でも、上記1の目的に照らして、当事者の意向や合意内容をわかりやすく表現する上で最も適した構成になるよう心がけるべきである。このための基本的な注意事項として、第1に、契約書の各条項は、記載漏れや重複や矛盾が生じることがないよう、論理的な順序に従って規定した方がよい。第2に、同種又は同一概念に基づく事項があるときは、それらはできるだけ分散させずに同じグループに分類して規定すべきである。第3に、異なる事項を定める規定や異なる概念に基づく規定はなるべく同一の条項に含めず、適宜に枝条項（sub-heading、sub-clause）を用いてわかりやすく整理すべきである。

　一般的な商取引に関する契約書の基本構成は、取引の種類や当事者や作成者

の個性によってある程度異なっているが、以下のような順序、内容になっていることが多い。

(1) Front cover（表紙）

契約書の表紙には、通常当該契約の表題（title）、契約当事者名、契約書を作成した法律事務所の名称、契約締結日及び（ドラフトの場合は）当該ドラフト作成日が記載される。

契約書の表題は、単に、DEEDとかAGREEMENTとのみ記載されることもあるが、原則として、そのような一般的なタイトルにするより、他の契約書と明確に区別できるように当該契約書が規律している取引の種類（sale、distribution、licensing等）に関する表示を含めた方が望ましい。

契約当事者名の表示については、一方当事者と他方当事者（たとえばsellerとbuyer）の間にANDを入れるべきである。いずれか一方の当事者（たとえばbuyers）が複数の場合は、契約におけるそれぞれの立場を明確にするため、その末尾に(1)、(2)などの番号を挿入して示す方法が用いられる。

当該書面が最終版ではないこと及び契約交渉中における最新のドラフトであることを明らかにするために、冒頭又は末尾にドラフト作成日を必ず記載すべきである。

(2) Contents（目次）

目次は契約書に不可欠とはいえないが、20ページを超える程度の契約書の場合は、設けておいた方が望ましい。なお、草案の段階ではドラフトが改訂されるごとにページも変更されることになるので、通常は最終版が確定するまで目次のページ番号を記入しない。

(3) Commencement（頭書）

契約書本文の冒頭に、契約書の表題、契約日、当事者名を記載する。当事者が会社の場合は、会社の登録番号も記載した方がよい。契約締結後に当事会社の一方の合併や企業買収により会社名が変更されることがあるので、契約当事者の特定上の混乱を避けるためである。なお、頭書において、当事者をその名

称の略語や取引上の役割（"Distributor"、"Licensor"等）により定義しておくことが多い。

(4) Recitals（前文）

契約の内容に入る前に前文を設けて両当事者が契約締結に至った背景事情を説明する形式の契約書もあるが、最近の契約書は、むしろ前文を省略し、ただちに各条項を規定する方法の方が一般的である。前文を設ける理由は、契約締結の目的を明確にしておくこと、契約締結の前提事実（たとえば、売主が売買目的物の所有者であること）について後日争われないようにすること、修正契約や補足契約等の場合は、原契約との関係を明らかにしておくこと等である。

イギリス法の解釈原理上、契約書の前文は契約条項の一部ではないが、主要な契約条項の意味内容が不明瞭である場合は、その解釈を補充するために用いられる可能性がある（第Ⅱ編第5章1参照）。そのような可能性を排除したい場合は、契約条項において、「前文は契約条項の解釈に影響を与えるものではない」旨を明記しておく必要がある。これとは逆に、前文の記載内容を契約条項の一部としておきたい場合は、たとえば、warranty clause（保証条項）において、前文記載の事実が真実であることを相手方当事者に保証させる方法をとる必要がある。

(5) Definitions（定義）

たとえば当事者名や他の契約書の名称、特定の出来事や商品等が契約書にたびたび現れる場合は、これらを1つか2つの単語だけで表示できるようにしておいた方がその都度繰り返すよりも便利である。また、契約書において用いられている特定の語句に関する一般的な意味内容が必ずしも明瞭とはいえない場合や当該契約書の中だけで通常の意味内容とは若干違った意味で用いたい場合にも、契約書における語句の意味を定義して明らかにしておく必要がある。このような語句が2つ以上の契約条項中に出てくる場合は、登場したときに定義するよりも、定義条項を設けて各用語の意味をまとめて規定しておいた方がわかりやすい。

一般に、定義には、'means' definitions と 'includes' definitions の2種類が

ある。'Means' definitions は、「AAA means……」とする定義であり、その語句の意味を当該定義条項に記載されたものだけに限定し、それ以外の解釈を排除したい場合に用いる。他方、「AAA includes……」との 'includes' definitions を用いた場合は、当該語句が定義条項に規定した意味を有することが明らかにはなるが、それ以外の意味が当該語句に含まれる可能性を排除するものではない。いずれを用いるかは、各語句を定義する目的に応じて使い分けるべきである。語句の意味を明確化するために、'means' definition をした場合でも、当該語句に必ず含まれるものを念のために明記しておきたいことがある。このような場合は、'means' definition の中で、'including but without prejudice to the generality of the foregoing …' の文言を加えて具体例を示す方法が用いられる。

　Definitions の規定は、語句の意味を明確化することに徹し、この条項の中で当事者の権利義務その他契約の履行に関連する定めをするのは、できる限り避けるべきである。たとえば、「"Price" means the price set out in the price list attached hereto, which may be changed by the Seller at any time by giving three months' prior written notice to the Purchaser.」と規定するよりも、「"Price" means the price set out in the price list attached hereto or its revisions, amendments or alterations made by the Seller in accordance with Clause 6.」と規定し、Clause 6において Seller の Price list を修正する権利及び修正手続について規定した方が望ましい。

(6) Operative clauses（主たる権利義務に関する条項）

　定義条項の後に、当該契約の中心的な権利義務を定める規定（たとえば、license agreement における実施許諾条項、sale agreement における目的物の引渡と代金の支払いに関する条項等）及び当該中心的な義務の実施に関連する付随的な権利義務を定める条項が設けられる。これらの規定は operative clauses と呼ばれている。Operative clauses の内容は、取引の種類、性質、内容、当事者間で合意した取引条件等に応じて大幅に異なる。たとえば、売買契約の場合は、特定された目的物の引渡義務、引渡の時期・方法その他の引渡条件、代金額、代金支払条件等、ライセンス契約の場合は、ライセンスを付与す

ること、付与されたライセンスの内容、範囲、制限、ラインセンス料、ロイヤルティの支払義務、計算方法、支払条件等がoperative clausesに含まれる。

(7) Conditions precedent（停止条件）

　契約の一方当事者は、ある一定の事態が発生しない限り、又は相手方当事者がある一定の行為をしない限り、契約上の主要な義務を負担したくないと望むことがある。そのような場合は、当該義務に関する停止条件（condition precedent）の合意をし、契約書にその旨の規定を設ける必要がある（第II編第3章4参照）。停止条件に関する条項は、契約の目的となる主要な義務にかかわる条件の場合は、上記(6)のoperative clausesの直前又は直後に規定するのが論理的でわかりやすいが、当該条件にあたる事態の発生が契約解除権の発生原因にもなっている場合は、権利義務条項（operative clause）や保証条項（warranty clauses）の後に定めることが多い。

(8) warranties（保証）

　保証条項（warranty clause）は、契約の一方当事者が相手方に対して、契約の対象となる取引、目的物、契約当事者に関する事実や約束その他、契約の締結及びその履行に影響を与える可能性のある事項について保証（warrant）する旨を規定している。保証条項は、契約締結前における事実や意見の表明や約束を契約条項として取り込んでおくことを目的とした規定なので、法律意見、税務上の意見その他、本来専門家にしか述べられない事項であってもこれに含まれていることが多い（第II編第4章2及び第5章1(2)参照）。保証の内容が多岐に及ぶ場合には、契約書に別表を添付して列記する方法をとることがある。

(9) Term and Termination（期間及び解除）

　Licensing、distributorship、joint ventureその他一定の期間継続することが予定されている取引に関する契約には、契約期間（term）及び期間満了後の更新手続き（renewal）に関する規定が設けられる。

　Termination clauseには、契約違反その他契約を終了できる事由が列記される。前述のとおり（第II編第4章）、契約条項（terms）にはconditions、 warranties 及び innominate terms の 3 種類があり、ある条項について裁判官に warranty と認定されると、当該条項違反を理由とする契約解消 (rescind) ができない。よって、そのような認定を避けるため、どのような規定に違反した場合に解除権が発生するかを契約書に明記しておくことが重要である（第Ⅱ編第 4 章 3 参照）。契約違反以外の解除事由として、破産その他支払不能事由の発生、解散・事業廃止、親会社や役員の交代等がよく規定される。また、一定の予告期間の経過を条件とし、当事者の一方又は双方の解約権を定める場合もある。

⑽ Boilerplaters（雑則）

Force majeure clause、confidentiality clause、notice clause、entire agreement clause、amendment clause、non-assignability clause 等は、あらゆる種類の契約書に共通に設けられるので、boilerplate clauses と呼ばれている。これらは、雑則条項（miscellaneous clauses）として総括され、取引に関する条項の後にまとめて規定される。雑則という呼び名にかかわらず、イギリス法の法原理との関係上いずれもきわめて重要な条項であり、十分な配慮をして作成しないと後日重大な問題を生ずる恐れがある。

（ⅰ） Force majeure clause（不可抗力条項）

当事者の支配の及ばない、予期せぬ事情による契約不履行について責任を負わないようにするための条項である。イギリス法に準拠する契約において、そのような事態が生じた場合は、the doctrine of frustration が適用される可能性があるので、これを排除するために不可欠な条項である（第Ⅱ編第 9 章 3 参照）。

（ⅱ） Confidentiality clause（秘密保持条項）

契約に基づき、又は契約に関連して相手方に開示、提供した秘密情報、契約締結の事実、契約内容等に関して第三者への開示や漏洩を禁ずる旨の条項である。ノウハウ・ライセンス契約等の場合は、契約の根幹をなす重要な規定である。秘密情報の範囲や開示が認められる第三者（従業員、子会社等）をどのように定義するかについて特に注意を要する。

（ⅲ） Notice clause（通知条項）

契約に基づいて一方から他方に通知や連絡をする場合の宛先、宛名人（担当者）名及び通知の方法（書留郵便、ファックス、e-mail 等）を定める。ただし、合意された宛先、方法によらない通知が常に無効と解されるわけではない。

（ⅳ） Entire agreement clause（完全合意条項）

当該契約書が当事者間の合意を定める唯一の契約であり、それ以前の合意や交信等は契約の内容とはならない旨を定める条項である（第Ⅱ編第 5 章 3 参照）。イギリス法上の口頭証拠排除の原則（parol evidence rule）を確認し、かつ規定内容によっては、契約書以外の証拠に基づく misrepresentation や implied terms に関する主張を排斥することを目的としている。ただし、mistake（錯誤）や rectification（誤記）を理由とする契約の無効や訂正の主張までも排除することはできない。

（ⅴ） Amendment clause（契約修正条項）

契約書の定めを変更、修正する場合は両当事者の書面による合意を要する旨を定める条項である。ただし、イギリス法上、契約の成立や変更には、原則として書面を要しないので、この規定を設けても、書面によらない明確な変更の合意を全て排除できるわけではない。Amendment clause は、entire agreement clause と同一の条項において規定されることが多い。

（ⅵ） Non-assignability clause（譲渡禁止条項）

契約上の権利義務の第三者への譲渡を禁ずる旨の条項であり、これに違反する assignment は、譲渡された契約の相手方当事者との関係上は無効とされる（第Ⅱ編第 12 章 5 参照）。契約上の権利に対する trust の設定、契約当事者の第三者との合併、契約当事者の支配株主の変更等による当事者の交替は、通常の non-assignability clause で禁ずることができないので、これらを制限したい場合は特別な定めが必要である。また、契約上譲渡を認めたとしても、assignment に関する法令上又は衡平法上の要件及び制約に従わなければ有効な譲渡はできない（第Ⅱ編第 12 章 3 及び 4 ）。

（ⅶ） Waiver clause（権利放棄条項）

相手方に対して契約違反の責任追及を直ちにしなかったとしても免責したことにはならず、また権利の不行使、一部放棄、猶予等があっても、当該権利のその後の行使やそれ以外の権利の行使までも放棄したことにはならない旨の条

項であり、権利行使の懈怠等について権利放棄やaffirmationとの認定を避けることを目的としている。ただし、この規定を設けたとしても、あらゆる懈怠がaffirmationにならないわけではない。

(ⅷ) **Exclusion of Contracts (Rights of Third Parties) Act 1999**（第三者の権利に関する契約修正法の排除）

2000年以降に作成されたイギリス法に準拠した契約は、the Contracts (Rights of Third Parties) Act 1999の適用を排除する旨の条項を標準書式として備えているものが多い。これは、同法の適用がある場合には、契約に基づいて便益を受ける第三者の同意がない限り、契約の修正や解約ができなくなるためである（第Ⅱ編第11章4参照）。

⑾ governing law、jurisdiction、arbitration（準拠法、裁判管轄、仲裁条項）

これらの条項は、通常、契約書本文の最後部、すなわち契約書末尾署名欄の直前あたりに設けられる。準拠法の規定がない場合は、訴訟を提起された裁判所が準拠法を決定することになるが、英文契約書がイギリスで締結された場合、イギリスの裁判所は、特にこれに反する主張がない限り、イギリス法に基づいて契約を解釈、適用する。

裁判管轄条項は、専属的管轄（exclusive jurisdiction）を定める場合と非専属的管轄（non-exclusive jurisdiction）を定める場合とがある。

最近の国際取引では、裁判管轄条項に代えて、あるいはこれに加えてarbitration clauseを設けることが多い（本編第3章1）。イギリス法上、arbitratorsの決定に不服のある当事者は、原則として、イギリスのthe High Court（高等法院）に不服申し立てすることが可能なので、裁判所による再審を避けるためには、契約書にarbitrationにおけるarbitratorの裁定を紛争解決の最終判断とする旨を明記しておいた方がよい。

⑿ Signatures（署名欄）

署名欄は契約書末尾に設けられ、会社の場合はdirectorが代表して署名（execute）する。Deedの場合を除き、common sealの押印やwitnessの立会いの必要はない。

4．契約書作成上の注意事項

(1) 語句の用い方

20世紀の末頃まで、英文契約書は、日常的な言語とはかけ離れた古式ゆかしい語句、文体、慣用句、ラテン語等を多用して法律専門家だけが理解できる書面として作成すべきものと考える人々が多かった。しかし、最近、多くの法律家及び法律事務所はこの古い慣行を改め、できる限り誰にでも理解できる簡易な語句や表現を用いて契約書を作成することが推奨され、また学生や若手弁護士に対してもそのような指導がなされるようになっている。以下は、最近のロースクールや大手法律事務所が法学生や新人弁護士に指導している、契約書作成上の注意事項の例である。

（ⅰ）　できるだけ短いセンテンスを用いること

（ⅱ）　できるだけ正確で慣れ親しんだ語句を用いること（たとえば、utiliseより use、forward より send、endeavour より try の方が望ましい。）

（ⅲ）　同じ意味の語句の繰り返しによる表現（assume and agree、change and alter、custom and usage、full and complete、furnish and supply、hold and possess 等）はなるべく用いないこと

（ⅳ）　修飾的な語句（たとえば、a little、very、relatively 等の修飾語、at this moment in time、in the first instance 等の付加的語句）や意味内容に解釈上の幅のある表現（たとえば、for the purpose of、from the point of view of 等による意味内容の限定）はできるだけ避けること

（ⅴ）　数箇所で同じ意味を表す必要があるときは、できる限り同じ語句や表現を繰り返して用いるようにし、特別な意図がない限り別の語句や表現に変更しないこと

（ⅵ）　ラテン語や古語や古文体（archaisms）は使わないこと（たとえば、in the event of より if、thereof より of the…、prior to より before、supra より above が望ましい。）

（ⅶ）　二重否定（not uninterested、not unnecessary 等）は用いないこと

（ⅷ）　動詞句（set forth、aware of 等の verb phrase）はなるべく用いないようにし、使用する場合は、できるだけ句と動詞を分離しないこと（たとえば、

the facts of which you are aware より the facts that you are aware of の方が望ましい。)

(2) 文法の用い方

契約書は、上記(1)と同様の理由により、できる限りわかりやすく誰でも理解できる表現となるよう、なるべく簡便な文法を用いるべきである。特に、現在形、過去形又は未来形を用いて表現すべき文章にそれ以外の時制を使ったり、権利義務の条件（conditions）を定める場合以外で仮定法を使ったりすると混乱の源となる。また、主語が不要又は無関係な場合や特別な理由（下記(6)の目的等）がある場合を除き、できるだけ受動態（the passive voice）は避けて能動態（the active voice）を用いるべきである。

最も重要なのは、shall、must、may の使い方である。契約により（通常は契約締結と同時に）一方が他方に財産や権利を与えたり、義務や債務を引き受けたりする場合は、現在形を用いるのが通常である。他方、契約において当事者が一定の行為や給付を約束する等、当事者の義務を定める場合は、原則として shall 又は must を用いるべきである。May は、当事者の一方が権限や権利を有する場合に用いられ、義務を課する規定とは解されない。

日本人が契約書を作成するときに迷うのは、契約書中に普通名詞を標記する場合に、単数複数のどちらを用いるべきか（たとえば、契約当事者の子会社を標記する場合、a subsidiary とするのか、それとも subsidiaries とするのか）という問題である。イギリス法上、原則として、契約において複数として表示された語句は単数を、単数として表示された語句は複数を含むものとされている（the Interpretation Act 1978 s6）が、国際取引に関する契約の場合は必ずしもイギリス法に準拠することになるとは限らないので、定義条項の後にその旨（すなわち、契約書中の単数は複数を、複数は単数を含む旨）を明記しておいた方が安全である。さらに、契約書の表現を明瞭にする上では、特別な理由（たとえば、下記(6)の目的等）がない限り、単語は単数にし、文法上も単数形で表現した方が望ましい。

And と or の使い方にも細心の注意が必要である。たとえば、契約解除事由として A or B と定めるべき場合に A and B と記載すると、A, B の双方が備

わっていない場合でないかぎり解除できないと解される。

(3) 期間、時間、数値の表現

契約において期間や期限を定める場合は、その初日や最終日を算入するか否かを明確に示しておく必要がある。By、from、until、to 等の語だけで始期や終期を示そうとすると不明確になるので、on or before…（…以前）、after…（…の翌日以降）、from and excluding…（…の翌日から）、to and including…（…日及びその翌日以降）、to but excluding…（…日の翌日以降）等を使い分けるべきである。また、between A and B や through A to B は、A と B が初日と終日を含むか否かを明記しないと、どちらの意味か不明確となる。

(4) 契約条項の区分けと分割

契約書の条項（clause）は、1つの条項において1つの事項だけを扱うように条文分けした方がよい。また、ある1つの事項の内容が複雑で、1つの条項だけでは長文になり、わかりにくいと思われるときは、sub-clause を設けて、その内容を更に分けて規定する方法が有効である。Sub-clauses を用いた場合、sub-clause の条番号は、枝番号（第1条の場合、1.1、1.2…）にしたり、括弧番号（(1)、(2)…）、ローマ字（A、B、a、b…）やローマ数字（ⅰ、ⅱ、ⅲ…）を用いたりして、紛れないようにする必要がある。また、その表記の仕方を契約書全体において統一すべきである。各 sub-clause の内容は、(ⅰ)当該条項（clause）の適用がある一般的な場合についての規定、(ⅱ)この一般的な場面に適用される基本的な義務又は要件の定め、(ⅲ)この基本的な義務又は要件に対する第1の例外規定、(ⅳ)これに対する第2の例外規定、(ⅴ)各例外規定の適用範囲を限定する規定、(ⅵ)本条項（clause）だけにおいて使用される語句の定義という順序で区分けするとわかりやすい。

(5) 条項間の矛盾を避けるための表現

たとえば、契約書のある条項において X が Y に対して一定の行為を行うべきことを規定し、他の条項がこれと同じ行為を行わなくてもよい旨を定めている場合、この2つの規定は、一方が他方の例外を定めているのか、あるいはい

ずれか一方が正しく他方は間違った規定であるかのどちらかということになるが、イギリスの裁判所は、文言上どちらとも判断できない場合は、不明確な条項として双方共に法的拘束力を認めない可能性がある。そのような事態を避けるためには、「subject to」や「notwithstanding」を用いて優先的に適用する規定がどちらであるか明確にする必要がある。「subject to」と「notwithstanding」は、ほぼ同じ目的で使用されるが、正反対の意味を有している。たとえば、ある条項（Clause X）に「Subject to Clause Y」と記した場合は、Clause Y は、必ず Clause X に優先することになるが、「Notwithstanding Clause Y」と記した場合は、その反対に Clause X が必ず Clause Y に優先することになる。Clause X に「Notwithstanding all the other provisions of this agreement」と記した場合、Clause X は、当該契約の全ての条項に優先することになる。Clause X に「Notwithstanding Clause Y」又は「Notwithstanding all the other provisions of this agreement」と記載したにかかわらず、Clause Y にも「Notwithstanding Clause X」又は「Notwithstanding all the other provisions of this agreement」と記した場合、少なくともどちらかの条項は間違っていることになる。

「Without prejudice」という表現も同じような目的で用いられることがあるが、その意味は「Subject to」とは異なっている。すなわち、Clause X に「without prejudice to Clause Y」と記した場合は、Clause X によって Clause Y の法的効果は何らの影響を受けないことになるだけである。これは、両条項の優劣というよりも、それぞれが無関係の事項を規律していることを表す場合の表現である。よって、両条項の内容が矛盾している場合は、少なくとも一方が間違っていると解される恐れがある。

(6) ジェンダー表現の回避

英文契約書に同じ人物（たとえば、a director 等）が2度以上登場する場合、he、she、his、her 等、その者の性別が特定される表現を使う必要が出てくることがある。この場合、he、his でよいのか、それとも都度に he or she とすべきか、あるいは she or he とすべきかという問題に悩まされることがある。イギリス法上は、契約において、特別な定めのない限り、男性として表示され

た語句は女性を、女性として表示された語句は男性を含むものと解する扱いになっている（the Interpretation Act 1978、s6）。しかし、契約書の作成に当っては、当該契約書に目を通す者が男女両方であることを考慮し、できるだけman、he、him等の男性だけを示す表現は避けるようにし、男女両性に共通する表現を用いた方が望ましい。すなわち、manの語はpersonにし、hisやherをtheに置き換え、またheやsheはtheyに代えて複数形にしたり、文全体を受動態に言い換えたりする等の工夫をして、性別を示す表現を用いない方がエレガントである。

5．契約解釈の基本原理とドラフト

イギリス法に準拠する契約書を作成する際には、イギリス法に基づいて当該契約書がどのように解釈されるかを考慮しておかなければならない。この観点から、第Ⅱ編において説明したイギリス契約法の解釈に関連する諸原則を再確認するため、以下に列挙しておくことにする。

(1) 文理準則（Literal rule）

裁判所が契約書を解釈する際、原則として、契約書に記載されている文言や文章の意味内容を、それを一般人が読んだときにおける通常の意味内容どおりに解釈し、契約を締結する前における当事者の言動、約束やそのような契約をした目的その他契約書に記載されていない事項や事情は考慮に入れない（the literal rule、第Ⅱ編第5章1）。また、不明瞭な条項や不完全な条項は法的拘束力を生ぜず、それが契約の成立に影響しない付随的な条項の場合は存在しないものとして解釈される（第Ⅱ編第3章3）。よって、契約書において用いる文言及び表現は、一般人が疑義を生じることがない程度に、簡易かつ明瞭にすべきである。

(2) 口頭証拠排除の原則（Parol evidence rule）

上記(1)と密接に関連するが、契約書の文言が曖昧で書面上だけでは解釈を確定できない場合を除き、契約書に記載されていない事項や事象を合意の内容を

証明するための証拠として使用することができない（the parol evidence rule、第II編第5章2）。

よって、契約書には当事者間で合意に達した全ての事項を漏れなく規定しておかなければならない。

(3) 契約解釈上の諸原則

契約条項を作成する際には、文理準則（the literal rule）を補完する様々な解釈原則にも注意を払う必要がある（第II編第5章）。たとえば、the ejusdem generis principle によれば、契約条項の適用範囲は契約書に例示列挙された事由と同種のものに限定される可能性があるし、また、the expressio unius est exclusio alterius principle によれば、契約書が言及していない事項は契約の適用が排除される可能性がある。よって、契約書に適用されるべき事項や事象を例示列挙する際には、あらゆる場合を想定して例示し、かつそれに限定されたくないときは、その旨（without limited to the foregoing 等）を明記しておく必要がある。

The noscitur a sociis principle は、契約書に記載された語句の意味は、当該記載された文脈に従って解釈されるべきこと、及び当該契約書の記載全体との整合性に基づいて解釈されるべきことを要求するので、契約書作成の際は、常に辞書を参照にして個々の語句や表現の正確な意味内容を確認すると共に、契約書全体と当該条項や語句との関係にも気を配らなければならない。

更に、the contra proferentem rule により、不明確な規定は、当該条項を作成した側、あるいは当該条項によって利益を受けようとする側の不利に解釈される可能性が高いことも常に考慮に入れておくべきである。

(4) 黙示の条項（Implied terms）

物品の売買に関する契約、サービスや労務の提供に関する契約その他一定の種類の契約は、契約書に明記されていなくても、法令により一定の黙示の条項（implied term）が契約の内容として組み込まれる（the Sale of Goods Act 1979、the Supply of Goods (Implied Terms) Act 1973、the Supply of Goods and Services Act 1982等）。また、特別な法令がない場合でも、商慣習

や取引慣行、契約当事者の過去における取引等や当事者間で明示的な合意をするまでもないと通常人が判断するような事項については、裁判所が一定の解釈基準（business efficacy test、officious bystander test 等）に基づいて黙示の合意による契約条項（implied term）を認定することがある（第Ⅱ編第4章2）。

予期していない黙示の条項を認定されないようにするためには、契約書において、合意しておくべき事項は全て明確に規定し、かつ完全合意条項（the entire agreement clause）等において、当該契約書に明記されているものを除き、明示又は黙示の合意による条項は一切存在しない旨を定めておくべきである（第Ⅱ編第5章3）。

(5) Conditions と Warranties

前述のとおり（第Ⅱ編第4章1）、イギリス法上、契約条項（terms）には、condition と warranty の区別があるが、innominate term の出現により、この分類はかなり曖昧になっている。特に、最近の判例法によれば、condition として規定した条項であっても innominate term と解されて契約解消（rescission）が制限されることがあるので、ある条項違反を根拠として rescission できるようにしておくためには、当該条項が重要であること、及び当該条項違反があれば契約解消できることを明記しておくべきである。また、重要ではない条項でも解除できるようにするためには、催告等の手続を定めておいた方が安全である。契約終了に関する条項が合理性を欠く場合は、the Unfair Contract Terms Act 1977により効力を否定されることがあることにも注意する必要がある（第Ⅱ編第6章3参照）。

(6) 責任排除条項（Exclusion clauses）

商取引に関するほとんどの契約は、何らかの責任制限に関する条項を含んでいる。責任排除条項の作成に当っては、the Unfair Contract Terms Act 1977 や the Unfair Terms in Consumer Contracts Regulations 1999を常に意識し、法令に抵触する無効な条項と解されないよう、合理的で公平な内容にしなければならない。また、the contra proferentem rule の適用があることを考慮し、

明確で疑義のない条項にし、かつ notice が不十分と解されないよう、当該条項の書式や表示上も十分な工夫と配慮をするべきである（第II編第6章参照）。

(7) **損害賠償額の予定及び罰則規定**（Liquidated damages and Penalty clause）

　損害賠償額の予定に関する合意条項（liquidated damages clause）は、特に損害額の算定が困難な取引において望ましい条項である。ただし、これを設ける場合は、当該予定額の算定方法について合理的に説明ができるように一応の根拠を予め準備し、罰則規定（penalty clause）として無効と認定されることがないようにしておくべきである（第II編第10章5参照）。

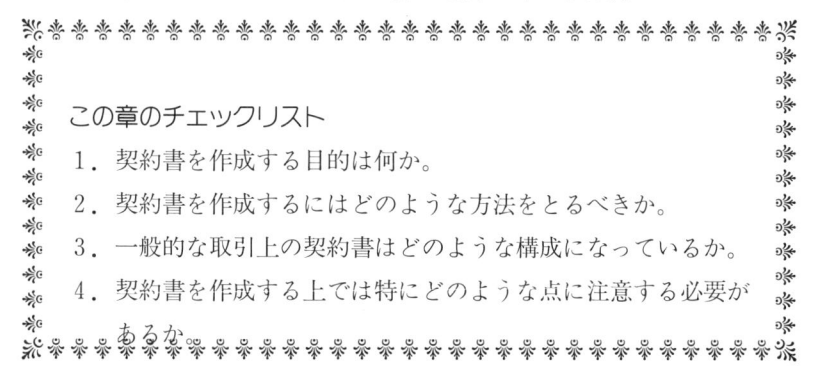

　この章のチェックリスト
　1．契約書を作成する目的は何か。
　2．契約書を作成するにはどのような方法をとるべきか。
　3．一般的な取引上の契約書はどのような構成になっているか。
　4．契約書を作成する上では特にどのような点に注意する必要があるか。

第3章

国際取引に関する紛争の解決方法

1．裁判と仲裁

　取引に関する紛争が生じ、話し合いによる解決が困難な事態に至った場合、紛争解決のために法的手続を採るべきか否かを決定しなければならない。この決定に当っては、第1に、当該紛争解決のためには、どのような手続をどこで採ることができるか、第2に、複数の可能性がある場合において、どこでどの手続を採るのが最も有利で、簡便で、迅速かつ経済的であるかの検討が不可欠である。

　第1の紛争解決のための主要な手続としては、裁判、仲裁、調停が考えられる。両当事者が契約において仲裁の合意をしていたときは、当該契約に関する紛争を解決するには原則として合意に従って仲裁の申立てをしなければならず、この合意を無視して裁判所に訴えを提起した場合、相手方の申立てにより訴訟手続は停止される（日本では仲裁法14条1項、イギリスは the Arbitration Act 1996 s9）。また、契約書に仲裁条項が定められていない場合であっても、紛争発生後に両当事者間で仲裁地及びその手続について新たな合意をして仲裁による解決の方法を採ることが可能である。

　裁判との比較における仲裁の利点として、（ⅰ）紛争の対象となっている取引や技術等を熟知した専門家を仲裁人に選任することが可能であること、（ⅱ）公開法廷でおこなう裁判と異なり、秘密性が保たれること、（ⅲ）裁判よりも柔軟な手続による迅速かつ妥当な解決が期待できること、（ⅳ）三審制の裁判よりも費用を節減できること等が挙げられている。ただし、裁判手続による場合であってもその管轄裁判所の所在する国によっては、専門性を必要とする特別な事件に関する専門裁判所を設けている場合もあるし、また、必要に応じて非公開の法廷を開くことが認められる場合もある。また、手続の柔軟性、妥当性、迅

速性、費用等の問題は、誰が仲裁人に選ばれるかにより大きく左右されるので、どちらが有利であるか一概には決められない。

実務上は、海事、物品売買、金融、造船、建設等に関する国際取引では、紛争当事者がイギリスとは無関係であっても、契約締結時又は紛争発生時において、イギリスにおける仲裁を紛争解決の方法とする旨を合意することが少なくない。これは、両当事者が互いに、紛争相手国の裁判所に解決を委ねるよりは第三国における仲裁の方が公平かつ合理的と考えるからである。そして、仲裁国としては、イギリスのように、対象取引に関連する法制度が発達し、かつ仲裁手続や仲裁人候補者が整っている国が選択されることになる。

最近、国際取引に関し、裁判、仲裁等の法的手続きに入る前に、調停、すなわち第三者を交えた話し合いによる解決を図る方法の有効性が注目されるようになり、このための手続を契約書において合意しておくことが増えてきている。調停前置の合意がある場合は、これを無視していきなり訴えを提起することができない。ただし、契約書において調停人の選任方法その他の調停のための手続や調停不成立の判定方法（たとえば、調停申立の後一定期間内に成立しない場合は不成立とみなす旨）を明記していない場合は不明瞭な規定として法的拘束力が認められないことがある（第Ⅱ編第3章4参照）。

2．裁判所の選択

仲裁や調停に関する合意がない場合の最終的な紛争解決手段は、裁判所に訴えを提起する方法である。契約において管轄裁判所に関する条項がない場合や非専属的な管轄裁判所の合意しかしていない場合、当事者は、どこの国の裁判所に訴えを提起することができるか、及びその内のどの裁判所に訴えを提起すべきかの選択をすることが必要となるが、国際取引に関する紛争において、この選択は非常に重要である。日本企業がイギリス企業に対し訴訟を提起しようとする場合、日本企業は、可能な限り地の利のある日本の裁判所で訴訟をしたいと望むのが通常である。しかし、日本、イギリスのいずれの国で裁判をした方が有利な紛争の解決を導くことができるかという問題は、様々な要素を総合的に考慮して検討すべき事項であり、実際上、日本での裁判の方が有利とは必

ずしもいえない場合が少なくない。以下は、日本とイギリスのどちらで訴えを提起するかを選択する上で、必ず考慮しておかなければならない事項である。

(1) 国際裁判管轄の有無

日本の裁判所で訴えを提起するには、（ⅰ）国際裁判管轄に関する日本の法原則に基づいて日本に管轄がある場合であることを確認しなければならないのは当然であるが、これに加え、（ⅱ）当該事件についてイギリスの裁判所が日本の裁判管轄を認めるか否かの点の確認も見落としてはならない。（ⅱ）を怠ったまま日本で訴えを提起した場合、相手方は同じ紛争に関する訴えをイギリスで提起した上で、イギリスの裁判所に、日本で継続中の訴訟を暫定的に停止する旨の差止命令（anti-suit injunction）を求めてくる恐れがあるからである（Andrew Frederick Beazley v Horizon Offshore Contractors Inc［2004］EWHC 2555、OT Africa Line Ltd. v Magic Sportswear Corporation and Others［2005］EWCA Civ. 710 (CA)①）。差止命令は日本の裁判所ではなく当事者である日本企業を名宛人として発せられる。この命令は、日本の裁判手続そのものに直接的な影響を与えないが、これに違反して訴訟追行した日本側当事者はイギリスにおける法廷侮辱罪の責任を問われ、会社の代表者がイギリスに入国した際に懲役刑を含む処罰が課せられる可能性がある。結局、先手を取ったつもりで始めた日本での裁判を継続することが困難となり、不利な立場でイギリスでの裁判に応ぜざるを得ないこととなる恐れがある。

どのような場合に日本の裁判所の裁判管轄が認められるかについて、イギリスの裁判所は、紛争の対象になっている契約の準拠法に従って決定する（Akai Pty Ltd v People's Insurance Co Ltd［1998］1 Lloyd's Rep 90）。通常の場合、当事者間においてイギリスの裁判所を専属管轄裁判所とする合意があるときは、特別な理由がない限りはイギリス以外の管轄は認められない（上記 OT Afirica Line Ltd. v Magic Sportswear Corporation and Others 判決）。特別な理由の有無は、証拠物や証人の所在地、契約の準拠法、当事者と管轄地との特別な関係の有無その他の事情を総合して裁判所の裁量により判断される（Donohue v Armco Inc［2001］UK HL 64②）。

(2) 執行可能性(財産の所在地での執行の可否)

　裁判により紛争を解決しようとする場合は、たとえ裁判で勝ったとしても、相手方がその判決に任意に従わないことがあるので、勝訴判決をどの国で執行する必要があるのかという問題を必ず考慮しておかなければならない。とりわけ、被告が日本に財産を有していない場合は、その財産所在地であるイギリスやその他の国において判決を執行しなければならないので、日本の裁判所の判決が財産所在地国において執行できるか否かが重要である。

　イギリスは民事訴訟手続に関する条約(1954年ヘーグ条約)に調印していないし、日英間には、外国判決の執行に関する2国間の取り決めがないので、日本の判決をイギリスで執行できるのは、コモンローの法原則に基づく要件を充足した場合に限られる。すなわち、イギリスで外国裁判所による人(法人を含む。)に対する判決(judgment in personam)の執行承認を得るためには、当該判決国の裁判所の国際裁判管轄がイギリスの裁判所により認められ(Pemberton v Hughes [1899] 1 Ch 781)、かつ原則として、被告が当該外国に所在するか、事業所を有するか、又は、当該外国の裁判管轄に合意し、もしくは任意に出頭して応訴していなければならない(Harris v Taylor [1915] 2 KB)。したがって、当事者間に裁判管轄の合意がない場合においてイギリス居住者に対して日本で訴えを提起した場合、相手方が出頭せず、何らの書面も提出しない状態のまま勝訴判決を受けたとしても、その判決はイギリスの裁判所による執行承認を受けられない可能性がある。

　以上により、執行の段階で争いが生じそうな事件の場合は、当初からイギリスで訴訟を起こした方が安全である。相手の資産がイギリスにある場合はもちろんだが、イギリス以外でもEU加盟国内や英連合(commonwealth)加盟国内にある場合も、それぞれの国が加盟している国際条約(the Brussels Convention 1968 Article 26、the Administration of Justice Act 1920、the Foreign Judgments (Reciprocal Enforcement) Act 1933)や2国間の取り決めに基づいて、イギリスの判決をとっておいた方が日本の裁判所の判決の場合よりも簡便に執行承認を得ることができる。

　執行可能財産の問題に関連して重要なのは、訴訟手続中に相手方が財産を処分したり消耗したりして判決を得たときには手遅れとならないよう、保全措置

を採るべきことへの配慮である。日本の裁判所は日本国外にある財産を差押さえることや日本国外に居るものに対して保全処分を命じることができないので、このような必要性があるときには、財産や相手方の所在地で訴えるしか方法がない。イギリス法上、暫定的な差止命令（interim injunction）や財産凍結命令（freezing injunction）は衡平法上の救済手段であり、裁判所が衡平の原則に照らして不可欠と判断したときにその裁量によって認められるに過ぎないが、これが認められた場合には、イギリス国外の財産の処分や行為を禁ずることもできる（第Ⅱ編第10章8参照）。

(3) 準拠法、実体法上の優位性

　取引に関する契約の準拠法をイギリス法とする旨を合意していた場合、日本で裁判を行うとしてもイギリス法に準拠して判断されることになるが、日本の裁判官は外国法に精通しているとはいえないので、当該紛争に適用されるイギリス法（制定法、判例法）は、その適用を主張している当事者が主張立証しなければならない。相手方がその法規の存在や適用を争った場合は、その分野の権威である弁護士や学者から法律意見書を取る必要があるが、相手方が意見書の内容を争った場合や有利な意見書が取れなかった場合、日本の裁判官が外国法を正しく適用して判断できるか否かのリスクがある。他方、準拠法として日本法が選択されている場合にイギリスで提訴したときも、その裁判手続上、日本法を適用した結果がイギリス法とは異なることを主張しようとする当事者が当該日本法の存在、内容、解釈、適用を主張立証しなければならないので（The King of Spain v Machado（1827）4 Russ 225、Ascherberg Hopwood and Crew v Casa Musicale Sonzogno［1971］1 WLR 173、Kutchera v Buckingham International Holdings Ltd［1988］IR 61）、日本の法律専門家による意見書を取らなければならないし、当該意見書の評価について同様のリスクを覚悟する必要がある。

　両当事者間で準拠法の合意がない場合は、訴えを提起した国の裁判所が自国の国際私法上の原則を適用して準拠法を決定する。日本の国際私法は、契約に最も密接な関係がある地の法を契約準拠法と定め、かつ契約において特徴的な給付（たとえば、売買の場合は、目的物の引渡し）を行う当事者の事業所所在

地の法は「最密接関係地」法と推定している(法の適用に関する通則法第8条1項、2項)。イギリスの国際私法も、当該契約と最も密接な関係を有する国の法律を適用する点では日本と同じである(the Contracts (Applicable Law) Act 1990, the Rome Convention 1980 Article 4(1))。しかし、イギリスの裁判所は、たとえば物品の移転や役務の提供を目的とする契約における売主や役務提供者の事業所の所在地と契約上の義務の履行地が異なる場合、「最も密接な関係を有する国(the country with which it is most closely connected)」は、義務履行地国であると判示している。このように、準拠法の決定に関する法原則は国によって異なるので、どの国で訴えを提起するかによって異なる法律が適用されることになる可能性がある。よって、契約の準拠法に関する合意がない場合は、日本法、イギリス法のどちらを適用した方が有利な結果を得られる可能性が高いかの予測が裁判地を決定する上での考慮要素となり得る。たとえば、契約に、契約違反の罰金を定める条項があったとした場合、イギリス法上は損害賠償額の予定に関する条項(liquidated damages clause)であることを立証しないかぎりpenalty clauseとして法的拘束力が認められないことになる(第Ⅱ編第10章5)が、日本法上は公序良俗に反する場合を除き有効な合意と解される。よって、この点に限っていえば、日本法を適用してくれる裁判所を選んだ方が有利ということになる。ただし、仮に日本で日本法を適用した判決を取得しても、イギリス法上違法と解される恐れがある内容の場合は、当該判決をイギリスで執行するときにそのイギリス法上の法的拘束力を争われる可能性が高いので、準拠法の選択が決定的な要素となるわけではない。

(4) 手続法上の優位性──証拠開示制度(Disclosure)

契約違反の事実の立証や損害額の立証のために相手方や第三者の手元にある資料が必要な場合、日本の裁判手続上は、これを調査したり、証拠として裁判所に提出したりするための手続が限定的である。文書提出命令の申立てをする際には、対象となる文書の特定を要し、相手方は専ら自己の利用に供するための文書であること等を主張してその提出を拒絶することができる(民事訴訟法220条)。証拠保全の申立ても、「あらかじめ証拠調べをしておかなければその証拠を使用することが困難となる事情がある」場合でなければ認められない

(同234条)。相手方当事者に対する照会の制度はある(同163条)が、違反者に対する制裁の定めがないこともあり、あまり有効に機能していない。これに対し、イギリスの裁判手続上は disclosure の制度によって、相手方の所持している立証に必要な資料の大半(privilege の対象となっているものは除く。)の開示を求めることができる。この開示義務に違反した当事者は法廷侮辱罪となる。したがって、手持ちの資料だけでは立証が困難な事件において相手方の資料を入手して有利な訴訟をしたいときは、日本で訴えを提起するよりも、イギリスの裁判制度を利用した方が有効である。

(5) 証人及びその能力

　事実に関する争いがある事件において勝訴判決を取ろうとする場合は、特にイギリスの裁判においては、証人尋問の役割が極めて重要であることに注意する必要がある。証人尋問は、証拠開示及び主張整理の手続が全て終わった後に設けられる審問期日(trial)においてまとめて実施され、その期間は、証人の人数に応じて1週間から2週間くらいであることが多い。当該事件に直接かかわった関係者は、バリスターとの事前準備と併せると、相当の長期間に亘ってイギリス国内でこの証人尋問とその準備に没頭しなければならない。バリスターは、証人尋問に特化したプロフェッショナルであるから、とりわけ勅撰法廷弁護士(Queen's Councel)のような一流弁護士による反対尋問の厳しさは、日本弁護士の比ではない。日本人の場合は、これに英語による質問に通訳を交えて回答しなければならないことによるハンディも加わるので、反対尋問で信用性を崩されることなく陳述書面等で述べたとおりの正しい主張を維持するのは、実際上容易なことではない。日本の企業人の中には、その知的レベルや実務能力とは関係なく、証人尋問、特に反対尋問における厳しい質問に耐え抜くことを不得意とする人物が少なからず存在する。誰が証人となる必要があるのかという要素は、一見見落としがちではあるが、実務的には裁判地を決定する上でかなり重要な決め手の1つである。

(6) 費用と期間

　企業が訴訟という解決手段を採るべきか否かを検討する際に最も重視するのは、裁判という解決手段が費用との兼ね合いにおいて見合っているのか否かという点である。日本の裁判とイギリスの裁判のどちらがより経済的かは、事件の性質・内容、当事者、担当裁判官の個性その他の要素に大きく左右されるので一概には決められないが、訴訟提起時に裁判所に支払うべき訴え提起の手数料に関して言えば、日本の印紙税額の方がイギリスの訴訟費用よりもはるかに高額である。しかし、訴訟に要する費用の大半は、裁判所に収める手続費用ではなく訴訟代理人となってもらう弁護士の費用である。この点を考慮に入れた場合、イギリスの裁判に要する費用は、日本よりかなり高額となることが多い。その理由は、（ⅰ）イギリスで裁判を行う場合には通常ソリシター、バリスター双方を雇う必要があること、（ⅱ）ソリシター、バリスター共に一般的には成功報酬方式ではなく、時間当たりの単価を基準にして報酬を支払う必要があるため（ただし、最近は成功報酬（contingency fee）方式の報酬契約も広く認められている。）、複雑な国際取引に関する訴訟の場合は請求額や勝敗に拘わらずに費用が拡大すること、（ⅲ）ソリシターの専門化が進んでいるため、複数の法律分野（契約法、不動産法、信託法、税法、金融法、会社法、労働法、特許法等）に亘る取引に関する事件の場合は多人数の専門弁護士の関与が必要となること、（ⅳ）需要の多い特定の分野（知的財産権訴訟等）を専門とするバリスターの報酬は特に高額であること、（ⅴ）勅撰弁護士（Queen's Counsel）を雇う場合は、そのアシスタントとなるバリスターも雇わねばならないこと等に加え、（ⅵ）日本企業の訴訟管理にも一因があると思われる。イギリスの弁護士は、サービス業の宿命として、当該事件を少しでも有利にするために必要又は有益な様々な付随的なサービス（たとえば、訴訟手続中における異議申し立て、反訴の提起、裁判所の決定や命令に対する抗告等）を提案してくる。当事者は自己のリスクで、このうちのどれとどれを行うかを決定しなければならないが、十分な判断能力のない企業は全ての提案を無条件で受け入れざるを得なくなり、結局弁護士費用が無制限に拡大していくわけである。以上のような様々な理由の複合により、イギリスで裁判をしているうちに弁護士費用が請求金額を越えてしまったという話は、冗談ではなく実際に頻発している。ただし、イギリス

における弁護士費用は敗訴者負担なので、裁判所は、一方を勝訴させる旨の判決、決定などを下した後で、勝訴者の申立てにより、その弁護士費用のうちの半分以上の金額については敗訴者に負担を命ずることが多い。日本の弁護士費用は、もちろん弁護士によって千差万別ではあるが、成功報酬の合意をしておきさえすれば請求額を超える心配はない。ただし、裁判で勝訴しても相手方から取り戻すことはできない。一般化はできないが、日本企業が、イギリスで取引紛争に関する訴えを提起して勝訴判決を勝ち取ろうとする場合、この全手続に要するイギリスの弁護士費用として、日本の弁護士費用の数倍から数十倍の金額を覚悟しておく必要がある。ただし、これは日本の裁判でも同様だが、イギリスの裁判の大半は、証人尋問手続（trial）に入る前に当事者間の和解によって解決している。訴えを提起した直後における暫定的差止命令（interim injunction）の申立てに関する攻防により和解に達する場合も少なくない。

　費用と密接に関連し、かつ場合によってはこれにも増して重要なのは、解決までの期間の長短である。裁判という解決手段を採る以上、ある程度の期間を要するが、イギリスで訴えを提起してから第一審の判決を得るまでの期間は概ね1年未満ではないかと思われる。日本の裁判は、近年集中審理方式が徹底し、相当に短縮してきているが、それでも、和解によらず判決を得ようとする場合には2年以上かかることが少なくない。また、日本国内で訴状の送達ができない場合は、訴訟開始のための送達手続だけで数ヶ月を要する場合がある。ただし、前述のとおり、事件の性質、内容その他の要素によっても期間が異なるし、日英を問わず、国際取引に関する企業間の紛争では、訴訟手続中における当事者間の和解により紛争が解決する場合の方が多いので、一般論としてはどちらが有利とはいえない。

　企業間の紛争が和解により終了するのは、予想される判決、敗訴のリスク、判決までの期間及び費用、勝訴後の執行の難易、今後の取引上の影響、企業の社会的評価等を総合して判断して、判決による解決が最善とはいえない場合である。そして、和解に応ずるべきか否か及びどの程度の条件ならば和解に応ずるべきかを各当事者が検討する際、当該訴訟における勝訴の見込みがどの程度かという点が最も重要な要素である。有利な条件による早期和解という経済的、効率的な解決を得るためには、目先の訴訟費用を気にかけるより、勝訴の見込

みの高い裁判所を選択して訴えを提起した方が結局は合理的である。この意味で、訴訟の経済性と迅速性は、当事者が必ず考慮する事項ではあるが、裁判所を選択する基準としては最優先事項ではない。

3．判決の執行

イギリスに所在する相手方に対して金銭の支払いを命ずる勝訴判決を得たにかかわらず相手方がこれを任意に支払おうとしない場合は、強制執行の方法によって回収する他ない。その場合には、まず相手方がどのような資産をどこに持っているのかを調査し、それぞれの資産に対して有効な方法で強制執行の手続をとる必要がある。

(1) 財産の調査

被告がイギリスに有している財産を調査する場合の通常の手順としては、先ず公開されている登記、登録情報を入手することである。イギリスには不動産登録制度（land registry）、株式登録制度（stock registers）、会社登録制度（Registrar of Companies）、判決登録制度（Register of County Court Judgments）等があり、不動産（freehold か leasehold）、公開株式等の資産、これに対する担保（charge、mortgage）、会社の財務状況や会社が負担している社債（debentures）、個人が差押えを受けている負債、破産宣告の有無等の一般的な情報を得ることができる。

(2) Freezing Order（財産凍結命令）

勝訴した原告が裁判所に被告の資産の凍結命令を申し立ててこれを得た場合、敗訴被告（個人、パートナーシップの構成員、会社の役員等）は、裁判所の命令に基づいて出頭し、宣誓の上、自己の財産に関する裁判所及び原告からの質問に答えなければならない。裁判所は更に、敗訴被告に対し、預金通帳等の銀行取引記録、過去2年間の会計書類、当期会計帳簿等の書類の提出を命ずることができる（the Civil Procedural Rules rule 25.1）。手元不如意を理由に支払を拒んでいた敗訴被告が、この命令を受けた途端に任意の支払いに応じてくる

こともある。

(3) 物品に対する強制執行 (Execution)

　高等法院 (the High Court) の勝訴判決を得た債権者は、the High Court に対して債務者が所持している物品に対する強制執行を申し立てることができる。この申立てを受けた裁判所は、当該物品所在地を管轄する行政区 (county) の the High Court Enforcement Officer (高等法院執行官、HCEO) に対して、債務者の財産を差し押えて競売するように命ずる (the Courts Act 2003、s 99)。County Court (県裁判所) の判決の場合も同種の手続が採られるが、5000ポンド以下の判決の場合は原則として、HCEO ではなく当該 County Court に配属されている court bailiff (執行官補佐人) が差押え及び競売を実施する (the County Courts Act 1984)。ただし、600ポンド以上の支払を命ずる判決の場合は HCEO が取り扱うこともできる。差し押えた財産は、全て一度に競売し、その代金から搬出、競売費用を差し引いた残金を債権者に交付する。HCEO や bailiff は、日本の執行官とは異なり、債務者の住居等の鍵をこじ開けて立ち入る権限までは認められていない。

(4) 不動産、株式に対する強制執行 (Charging order)

　勝訴判決を得た債権者は、裁判所に対し、債務者の不動産、株式、信託受益権 (債務者と第三者との共同名義の信託受益権等も含まれる。) 等に対する強制執行処分として、charging order (負担賦課命令) の申立てをすることができる (the Charging Orders Act 1979、the Civil Procedural Rules rule 73.3)。裁判所は、債権者が対象となる資産を特定して適式にこの申立てをしたとき、債務者には通知せずに暫定的な命令 (interim order) を発することができる (the Civil Procedural Rules rule 73.4)。債権者は、この interim order を登録することにより、その後に他の債権者が申し立てた charging order に対する優先権を確保することができる (the Civil Procedural Rules rules 73.6, 73.7)。ただし、charging order に基づく執行を行うためには、債務者も出頭した審問手続 (hearing) を経た上で final order を得なければならない。当該財産が離婚による財産分与の係争の対象であるとき、債務者が破産、清算手続

き中であるとき、当該財産が担保割れの状態（negative equity）であるとき等は、final charging order を得ることができない。この final charging order を得た債権者は、当該財産が売却されたときに、売却代金から優先的に債権回収を受けることができる。また、裁判所に対して、当該財産の売却命令を求めることもできる（the Civil Procedural Rules rule 73.10）。

(5) **債権に対する強制執行（Third party debt order）**

債権者は、債務者が第三者に対する売掛金、賃料債権、報酬債権、銀行預金その他の金銭債権を有していることを知ったとき、裁判所に対して、当該第三債務者が債務者に対して負担している債務を債権者に対して支払うように第三債務者に命ずることを求めることができる（the Civil Procedural Rules rule 72.2）。この第三債務者に対する裁判所の命令は、以前には garnishee order nisi（弁済禁止仮命令）と呼ばれていたが、現在は third party debt order（第三債務者弁済命令）という。この申立てを受けた裁判所は、まず審問手続をせずに暫定的な命令（an interim order）を発し、この送達を受けた銀行その他の第三債務者は、債務者に対する支払いをすることができなくなる（the Civil Procedural Rules, rule 72.4 rule 72.5）。第三債務者は、命令を受けた後7日以内に、裁判所に対して口座番号、債権額等の情報を提示しなければならない（the Civil Procedural Rules rule 72.6）。その後に開かれる審問手続には、債務者、第三債務者、他の債権者等、third party debt order に異議のある者が出頭することができる（the Civil Procedural Rules rule 72.7）。債権者は、final order を得た場合、第三債務者から直接取り立てて、自己の債権を回収することができる（the Civil Procedural Rules rule 72.9）。

(6) **賃金債権に対する強制執行（Attachment of earnings）**

敗訴判決を受けた債務者が労働者である場合、勝訴した債権者は、county court に対して attachment of earnings order（賃金差押命令）の申し立てをすることができる（the Attachment of Earnings Act 1971）。この命令が下された場合、債務者の雇い主は、債務者に支払う給料、賃金の内の裁判所が命じた一定の金額については、裁判所に支払わなければならない。裁判所は、受領

した金額から諸費用を控除し、残金を債権者に交付する。

(7) 将来債権等に対する強制執行（Equitable execution）
　上記(1)乃至(6)のような通常の手続では金銭判決の執行が困難な場合、債権者は、裁判所に対して、衡平法上の強制執行のための管財人（receiver by way of equitable execution）の選任を求めることができる（the Civil Procedural Rules, RSC Order 51）。管財人（receiver）は、債務者の資産を管理して賃料収入、生命保険の満期還付金等を回収し、経費を控除した上で債権者に支払う。この方法によれば、将来債権や共有名義の預金口座等に対する執行が可能であるが、管財人の報酬が大きな負担となるので、債務者の資産からの回収見込金額が相当に高額の場合でなければ利用できない。

(8) 破産申立による執行（Insolvency proceedings）
　債務者に対する破産申立ても債権回収のための選択肢の1つである。この申立ては、750ポンド以上の債権者は誰でも行うことができる。債権者が勝訴判決を得ておくことは破産申立ての要件ではないが、債務者が債権を争ってきた場合に立証しなければ申立てが棄却されるので、判決確定後に申し立てた方が安全である（Anderson v KAS Bank NV; [2004] EWHC 532 (Ch)）。破産手続は、債務者が破産申立ての通知を受けた後21日以内に債務を弁済しないときに開始される（the Insolvency Act 1986 s123）ので、債務者が破産を嫌って弁済してきた場合には迅速かつ経済的に債権回収を実現することができる。債務者が弁済をせずに破産手続きが開始した場合、債務者の全資産と負債が会計士等プロの公的破産管財人（official receiver）によって調査、管理され債権者に分配されるので、少なくとも債権者平等の下の公平な手続が保証される。ただし、債務者による相殺や反対請求申立てが認められて破産申立てが棄却された場合は、債権者にとっては大きな費用負担となるおそれがある（Popely v Popely [2004] EWCA Civ 463）。

【*CASES*】
　① OT Africa Line Ltd. v Magic Sportswear Corporation and Others [2005]

EWCA Civ 710 (CA)

Certain goods were shipped from New York to Monrovia in Liberia, in March 2002, but complaint was made of short delivery. The contract of carriage was evidenced by a bill of lading that included an exclusive English law and jurisdiction clause. In August 2003, the shippers (and the insurers, etc.) started proceedings in Toronto, relying on section 46(1) of the Canadian Marine Liability Act 2001 to give the Canadian court jurisdiction. In September 2003, the shipowners issued proceedings in England for an injunction restraining the Canadian action. The English court gave permission to serve the proceedings in Canada and granted an anti-suit injunction. The Court of Appeal held that the provision of the Canadian Act was an insufficiently strong ground for setting aside the jurisdiction agreement. "*the maintenance of the principle that parties should be free to choose the courts where their disputes are to be resolved must be of paramount importance and cannot be reduced to a mere legal aspiration.*" (Per Lord Justice Longmore)

② *Donohue v Armco Inc* [2001] UK HL 64

In 1998, the US conglomerate, Armco, brought proceedings in New York to recover damages from Donohue, a British man, who had been involved in the management buy-out (MBO) of a group of insurance companies which had formed part of the Armco Group. Armco alleged that, in connection with the negotiations for the MBO, Donohue had conspired with the American negotiators to defraud Armco of many millions of dollars. The contracts relating to these transactions included an exclusive English jurisdiction clause (EJC). In those circumstances Donohue had applied to the English court in 1999 for an injunction to restrain Armco from proceeding with the action in New York. The Court of Appeal granted Donohue the anti-suit injunction. In the meantime, Donohue's alleged co-conspirators had applied to the New York Court challenging its jurisdiction to deal with Armco's claims in view of the EJC, however, the New York Court had rejected this challenge to its jurisdiction. In view of such state, the House of Lords reversed the Court of Appeal's judgment and revoked the anti-suit injunction. It was held that, although he had a strong prima facie right not to be sued elsewhere than in England (derived from the EJC), it was apparent that the existence of an anti-suit injunction would not prevent the New York proceedings from continuing. It was in the interests of justice that the whole of the dispute should be referred to a single tribunal best fitted to make a comprehensive judgment on all the matters which arose. New York was the only place where this could be achieved.

この章のチェックリスト

1. 国際取引紛争解決のために仲裁申立てをするのはどのような場合か。
2. 仲裁による紛争解決は、裁判と比べてどのような利点があるのか。
3. 日英企業間の紛争解決のために、日本、イギリスのいずれの裁判所に訴えを提起するかを選択する上で、どのような事項を検討するべきか。
4. 金銭支払を命ずる判決を執行するために、被告のイギリス国内における財産を調査するにはどのような方法があるか。
5. 被告がイギリス国内に動産（物品）、不動産、銀行預金、売掛金債権、労働債権、将来債権を有していることがわかった場合、それぞれの財産に対して金銭の支払を求める判決を執行するにはどのような手続をとればよいか。

参考文献

第Ⅰ編

Catherine Elliot & Frances Quinn, English Legal System (Pearson Education, 6th edition, 2005) pp. 31-35（第4章）、62-92（第4章）、207-225（第2章）、455-490（第2章）

Gary Slapper & David Kelly, The English Legal System (Cavendish Publishing, 7th edition, 2004) pp. 63-75（第4章）、109-184（第2章）、621-643（第4章）

Martin Partington, Introduction to The English Legal System (Oxford Univ. Press, 2nd edition) pp. 30-66（第4章、第5章）、67-222（第2章）、223-251（第3章）

Phil Harris, An Introduction to Law (Cambridge University Press 6th edition) pp. 71-93（第1章）、114-154（第2章）、196-250（第4章、第5章）、251-437（第2章）

Granville Williams, Leaning the Law (Sweet & Maxwell, 12th edition, 2002) pp. 4-18（第2章）、21-27（第1章）、35-51（第5章）、51-68（第4章）、95-144（第4章、第5章）、225-264（第3章）

Ian McLeod, Legal Method (Palgrave Law Masters, 5th edition, 2005) pp.29-30（第2章）、41-56（第2章）、67-83（第4章）

Graig Osborne, Legal Practice Course Guide Civil Litigation 2005-2006 (Oxford University Press) pp. 265-278（第2章）

Denis Keenan, Smith & Keenan's English Law (Pearson Education, 14th edition, 2004) pp. 3-12（第1章）、12-17（第4章）、18-61（第2章）、173-209（第4章）

Gary Slapper & David Kelly, Sourcebook on the English Legal System (Cavendish Publishing, 7th edition, 2001) pp. 1-167（第4章）、169-

196（第2章）

Geoffrey Rivlin, Understanding the Law (Oxford University Press 3rd edition 2004) pp. 19-32（第1章）、85-113（第3章）、115-126（第2章、第5章）、149-168（第3章）

第II編

J. Beatson, Anson's Law of Contract 28th ed. (Oxford University Press, 2002) pp. 27-59（第1章）、60-88（第3章）、88-126（第2章）、134-159（第4章）、163-204（第6章）、236-275（第7章）、421-469（第8章）、470-495（第9章）

Jill Poole, Casebook on Contract Law 7th Ed. (Oxford University Press 2005)（全章）

Chitty on Contract vol. 1 (Sweet & Maxwell, 2004) pp. 121-169（第1章）、190-192（第3章）、198-213（第3章）、215-317（第2章）、329-370（第3章）、371-428（第8章）、429-508（第7章）、509-575（第8章）、707-729（第4章）、729-772（第5章）、773-790（第4章）、791-860（第6章）、1073-1162（第11章）、1163-1202（第12章）、1365-1403（第10章）、1423-1570（第10章）

Ewan McKendrick, Contract Law (Palgrave Macmillan, 2005)（全章）

Ewan McKendrick, Contract Law Text, Cases, and Materials 2nd ed. (Oxford University Press 2004)（全章）

G. H Treitel, The Law of Contract 11th Edition Vol. 1 (Sweet & Maxwell, 2003) pp. 8-45（第1章）、49-62（第3章）、67-161（第2章、第5章）、162-187（第3章）、191-214（第4章、第5章）、215-285（第6章）、286-329（第8章）、330-404（第7章）、405-428（第8章）、580-671（第11章）、672-704（第12章）、788-806（第4章、第5章）、832-865（第10章）、926-1064（第10章）

G. H Treitel, An Outline of the Law of Contract, 6th Edition (Oxford University Press, 2004)（全章）

第Ⅲ編

Cheshire & North's Private International Law 12th Ed. (1992) p. 458（第1章）

Chitty on Contract vol. 1 (Sweet & Maxwell, 2004) pp. 173-187、436-437、548-551（第1章）

Chitty on Contract vol. 2 (Sweet & Maxwell, 2004) pp. 662-663（第1章）

Dicey and Morris, The Conflict of Laws 13th Ed. (Sweet & Maxwell, 2000) pp385-425（第3章）、385-423（第2章）、467-564（第3章）、1216-1250（第1章）

Dicey and Morris, The Conflict of Laws 4th Supplement to the 13th Ed. (Sweet & Maxwell, 2004) pp. 172-202（第3章）

Graig Osborne, Legal Practice Course Guide Civil Litigation 2005-2006 (Oxford University Press) pp. 265-277（第1章）、421-460（第3章）

Bryan A Garner, Legal Writing in Plain English (The University of Chicago Press, 2001)（第2章）

Stuart Sime, A Pratctical Approach to Civil Procedure 8th Ed. (Oxford University Press, 2005) pp. 477-489（第3章）

Denis Keenan, Smith & Keenan's English Law (Pearson Education, 14PthP edition, 2004) pp. 152-172（第3章）

事項索引
（英文）

A
absolute assignment　244,250
acceptance　54,55,59,67,95
acceptance by silence　59
Acts of Parliament　8,34
actual knowledge　135,230,235
administrative law　8
advertisement　57
affirmation　111,159,164,278
agreement　54,55
agreement to agree　98,264
agreement to negotiate　98,105
ancillary contract　96
anticipatory breach　184,192,208
anti-suit injunction　289,300
Appellate Committee of the House of Lords　19
arbitration　15,278
attachment of earnings order　298
auction sale　58

B
bad bargain　207
Bar Vocational Course　29
bargaining power　140,141,147
barristers　26,27
battle of forms　61
beneficiary　10,230
bilateral contract　55
bilateral offer　55,59,64
bill　35
binding precedent　46,48
bona fide　170

breach of confidence　258
breach of contract　201
business efficacy test　114,285
business liability　138
bye-law　37

C
carriage of goods by sea　190
case law　4,44
case report　47
cases stated　23
causation　201,202
certainty　93,97
Chancery Division　47
change of circumstances　156,162
charging order　297
charterparty　113,190
chattels real　10
choses in action　242
choses in rem　243
condition subsequent　99
circuit judge　16,30,31
civil court　15
civil law　3,13
civil wrongs　13
claimant　14
classification of terms　110
clean hands　6,213
code of conduct　27
collateral contract　229,234,265
comfort letter　262
common law　2,4,44,46
common mistake　167,168,175,176

307

common seal   102,278
commonwealth   4,20,290
company law   11
compensate   14
completeness   93,97
condition   110,118,184,285
condition precedent   99,263,275
conditional agreement   99
conditional deed   102
conditional offers   64
confidentiality   257,276
confidentiality agreement   257,259
consideration   54,73,79,101,183, 189,198,234,244,249,212,264
constitutional law   7
constructive notice   135
constructive trust   10
consumer agreement   116
contemplation   202,216
contingent condition   99,111
contra proferentem rule   129,137, 284,285
contract   54
contract law   9
contractual rights   242
contributory negligence   209,223, 225
cost of cure   204,205,219
conciliation   15
counter-offer   60,68,69,265
County Court   15,16,26,50,297
course of dealing   136,144,145
court bailiff   297
Court of Appeal   6,14,19,23,49
Court of Chancellor   5
crime   13
Criminal Court   22
criminal law   8,13

Crown Court   15,23,50
Crown Prosecution Service   13
custom   45

D
damage   202
damages   5,111,113,153,157,170, 201,232
decisions   40
deed   100,101,183,278
definitions   273
delegated legislation   37
Denning J.   79,81,91
Department for Constitutional Affairs   14
descriptive ratio   48
deviation (4 corners) rule   137
devolution   35
dinning   29
directives   40
director   12,102
Director of Public Prosecution   13
discharge of contract   183
disclosure   292
distinguishing cases   47,50
distress   207,220,237
district judge   16,22,30,32
Divisional Court   18,50
Divisional Court of the Queen's Bench Division   18,23
doctrine of consideration   73,228
doctrine of frustration   185,191, 193,276
doctrine of precedence   3,46
doctrine of privity   9,228,234
duress   167,172,180
duty of care   229,235

E

economic duress 173,180
ejusdem generis principle 39,129, 284
enforceability 54,266
English Reports 47
entire agreement clause 131,133, 277,285
equitable assignment 245
equitable chose 243
equitable execution 299
equitable remedies 6
equity 4,9,79,168,172,176,213, 230,243
essential term 97,106
estoppel 79,89
European Commission 41,44,141
European Community 40,42
European Community law 40
European Council of Ministers 41
European Court of Human Rights 21
European Court of Justice 20,41
European Parliament 41
exclusion clause 129,134,232,285
executed consideration 74
execution 297
executory consideration 74
exemption clause 159,232,239
expectation interest 204
expectation loss 203,204
express term 109,135
expressio unius est exclusio alterius principle 39,128,284
extrinsic evidence 129

F

face to face transaction 170,179

Family Division 18,47
Family Proceedings Court 19,21
fast-track 16
fiduciary duty 230
fiduciary relationship 173
force majeure clause 188,190,192, 276
formality 93
fraud 143,163,164,170,210,226,248
fraudulent misrepresentation 155, 157
freehold 230,242
freezing injunction 214,291
freezing order 296
frustration 183,185
fundamental breach 137,146,147
fundamental mistake 169,170

G

General Council of the Bar 28
golden rule 39
good consideration 75,84,85
good faith 142,151,256
governing law 278
Graduate Diploma Course 27,29
Gourley deduction 209
guarantee 101,107,111,262
guilty 14

H

half-truths 155
Hansard 38
hardship clause 188
HCEO 297
heads of agreement 94,260
heads of terms 260
Her Majesty's Courts Service 14
High Court 6,8,15,17,30,50,297

309

House of Commons 7,35
House of Lords 4,7,14,19,24,35, 49

I
ICLR 47
illegal 13
implied condition 64,71
implied term 96,109,114,121,139, 284,285
in good faith 159
in honour only 93,103
in principle only 93
inadequate notice 136
incompleteness 97
indemnity 101,107
inequitable 79,80,89,90
inferior courts 14
injunction 5,213,225,259,264
innocent misrepresentation 158
innominate term 110,113,119,120, 184,285
Inns of Court 28,29
insolvency proceedings 299
instantaneous communications 63, 69
Institute of Legal Executives 33
insurance contract 112,190
intangible property 242
intention to create legal relations 54,93
interim injunction 259,264,291,295
intermediate terms 113
interpretation of contract 127
invitation to treat 57,65

J
judgment in personam 290

Judicial Appointments Commission 30
Judicial Committee of the Privy Council 4,20
judicial review 8,19
judiciary 29
jurisdiction 278

K
King in Parliament 7

L
land law 10
land registry 10,296
lapse of time 159
late notice 136
Law Commission Reports 38
law lords 19
law of landlord and tenant 10
law of trusts 9
Law Reports 47
Law Society 27
leasehold 230,242
legal assignment 245
legal chose 243
legal executives 33
Legal Practice Course 27
legal profession 26
letter of comfort 262,268
letter of commitment 94
letter of intent 94,103,104,260
Licensed Conveyancers 32
limitation clause 134,211,232
limitation of actions 210
liquidated damages 210,223,286, 292
literal approach 37
literal rule 38,128,283

Local Advisory Committee   32
lock-out agreement   98,105,263
Lord Chancellor   5,30
Lord Chief Justice   18,24,30,31
Lord Denning   6,20,38,62,138,141,
    168,232
Lords Justices of Appeal   24,30,31
Lords of Appeal in Ordinary   19,30,
    31
loss of profit   206

M
magistrates   22,32
Magistrates' Courts   15,21,22,26,
    50
Magna Carta   7
mandatory injunction   213
Master of the Rolls   6,19,30
memorandum of understanding   94,
    260
mere puff   154
mischief rule   38
misrepresentation   135,143,153,
    256,261
misrepresentation by conduct   155,
    162
mistake   167
mistake as to identity   170,178,179
mistake as to quality   168
mistake as to terms   170
mistake in documents   172
mistake res extincta   168
mistake res sua   168
mitigation   208
multi-track   16
mutual mistake   167,169,176

N
negligence   9,137,139,146,148,164,
    187,203,209,229,232,238
negligent misrepresentation   158
negligent misstatement   263
negotiable instruments   101
negotiation   94,103,104,105,106,
    128,254
non-assignability clause   247,277
Norman Conquest   2,10
noscitur a sociis principle   39,128,
    284
novation   248
novus actus interveniens   210

O
obiter   81,91
obiter dicta   48
objective approach   127
objective test   56,169,257
offender   14
offer   54,55,66,95,104
official receiver   299
officious bystander   114,121,285
order in council   37
out-of-court settlements   15

P
parliament   7
parliamentary sovereignty and
    supremacy   8,41
parol evidence rule   96,129,277,283
part-payment of debt   77,81
past consideration   75,83
penalty   210,224,261,286,292
personal contract   247
personal property   10,242
persuasive precedent   20,46,48,50

postal rule 62,69,70
pre-contractual document 94,96
preliminary contract 96
prescriptive ratio 48
President of the Family Division 18
principle of equity 5
private company 11
private law 8
privity of contract 228
Privy Council 50
prohibitory injunction 213
promise 54,73,79,101
promissory condition 99,111
promissory estoppel 73,79
property law 10
prosecutions 8
public company 11
public law 7
puisne judge 18,30,31
punitive damages 211
pupil 29
pupilage 29
purposive approach 37,39

Q
qualified acceptance 60
quantum meruit 212
quasi contract 212
Queen In Parliament 34
Queen's Bench Division 17,47
Queen's Counsel 28,293

R
ratio 50
ratio decidendi 48
real property 10,242
reasonable foreseeability 203,217

reasonable person 56,127,169,203, 257
reasonableness test 140,150,159
receiver 299
recorder 16,30,31
recovery 190,199
rectification 167,172,179
registrar 16
Registrar of Companies 12,296
regulations 40
reliance loss 203,206
remedies 14,157,201
remoteness 201,202
representation 109
repudiation 184,222
repugnancy rule 137
rescission 111,113,153,157,159, 170,285
restitution 96,212
revocation 63,70,71
Royal Assent 35,36
Royal Courts of Justice 17
royal writ 4
rules of interpretation 38,127

S
sanctions 14
sealing 102
seaworthiness clause 113
secretary 12,102
settler 10,230
shop display 57
small claims arbitration 16
Small Claims Courts 15
small claims procedure 16
solicitors 26
Solicitors' Disciplinary Tribunal 27
sources of English law 34

special notice 136
specific performance 5,212,225,
 231,237
speculative damages 203,207
standard terms of business 140,148
stare decisis 46
statement by conduct 156
statement of law 155
status quo ante 159
statute 4,34
statutory assignment 244
statutory instruments 37
subject to contract 93,264
suggestio falsi 155
superior courts 14
supervening events 209
suppresio veri 155
Supreme Court 20,30
Supreme Court of Judicature 15
system of assizes 2

T
tangible property 243
taxation 209
tender 58
term 109,275
term of years 109
termination agreement 183
terms and conditions 99,111
third party debt order 298
time charter 190
tort 138,158,203,229,232,256,263
tort of deceit 157,164
total failure of consideration 212,
 224
transfer of contractual rights 242
treaties 40
trust 5,9,230,236

trust property 10
trustee 10,230,236

U
uberrimae fidei 156
uncertainty 97
unconscionable bargain 174
undue influence 173,181
unfair term 142,151
unilateral contract 55,71,100
unilateral mistake 167,169
unilateral offer 55,59,64
unlawful 13
utmost good faith 156

V
victim 14
void 139,168,169,171,177,183,189,
 212
voidable 159,168,170,176,179,180

W
waiver 277
warranty 110,116,117,118,184,
 273,275,276,285
Weekly Law Reports 47
without prejudice 264
without reserve 58
writ system 4

Y
Youth Court 15,22

事項索引
（和文）

あ行

相対取引　170
遺失利益　206
一身専属的性質の契約　247
一方的契約　55
一方的錯誤　167,169
一方的申込　55
委任立法　37
違約罰　210
因果関係　201,202
インズ・オブ・コート（法曹院）　28, 29
英連合　4
エクイティ（衡平法）　4,168,243, 213,264
黄金律　39
欧州委員会　41
欧州議会　41
欧州共同体　42
欧州裁判所　20,41
欧州首脳協議会　41
欧州人権裁判所　21
欧州人権条約　21,35,39

か行

下位裁判所　14
解釈準則　127
会社印　102
会社登録所　12
会社法　11
海上物品運送　190
解除条件　99
過去の約因　75

家事訴訟裁判所　19,21
過失　9,137,139,232
過失による不実表示　158
家事部首席裁判官　18
慣習　45
完全合意条項　131,277,285
完全性　93
完全な譲渡　244
議会制定法　34
期間の経過　159
擬制信託　10
擬制通知　135
「起草者の不利に」の原則　129,137
貴族院　7,14,35
貴族院上訴裁判所　19
規定外排除原則　39,128
客観基準　56,169
客観的手法　127
救済措置　201
強制執行　297
行政法　8
共通錯誤　167
強迫　167,172
寄与過失　209
既履行約因　74
記録長官　19,30
禁止的差止命令　213
禁反言　79
近辺用語類推原則　39,128
偶発的条件　99,111
クリーンハンド　6
経済的強迫　173
刑事裁判所　22

索　引

刑事法　8
刑事法院　15, 23
競売　58
契約違反　201
契約解消　111, 153, 157, 159, 170
契約関係　228
契約関係の法理　9, 228
契約期間　275
契約交渉　94, 128, 254
契約条件条項　110
契約条件の錯誤　170
契約条項　109
契約上の権利　242
契約締結上の過失責任　256
契約の終了　183
契約法　9
契約目的不到達　183
県裁判所　15, 16, 297
原状の復元　159
憲法　7
憲務省　14
権利放棄　277
合意事実記載書　23
更改　248
公開会社　11
広告　57
控訴院　14, 23
控訴院裁判官　30
公訴局　13
公訴局長官　13
口頭証拠排除の原則　96, 129, 277, 283
高等法院　6, 15, 17, 297
高等法院執行官　297
衡平の原則　168
衡平法（エクイティ）　4, 168, 243, 213, 264
衡平法上の債権譲渡　245
公法　7

国王の議会　7
国際裁判管轄　289
コモン・ロー　2
根幹義務違反の法理　137
コンフォート・レター　262

さ行

債権　242
債権譲渡禁止条項　247
最高裁判所　20
最高法院　15
財産凍結命令　296
裁判外の和解　15
裁判管轄　278
詐欺　157, 170, 210
詐欺による不実表示　157
作為命令的差止命令　213
錯誤　167
差止命令　5, 213, 259
暫定的差止命令　259
資産凍結命令　214
事情の変更　156
執行官補佐人　297
私法　8
司法任命委員会　30
事務弁護士（ソリシター）　26, 294
修正命令　167, 172
自由土地保有権　230, 242
受益者　10, 230
受託者　10, 230
巡回裁判官　16, 30
巡回裁判所制度　2
準拠法　266, 278
準契約　212
上位裁判所　14
少額裁判所　15
少額請求仲裁　17
少額請求手続　16

315

条件付合意　99
条件付承諾　60
条件付捺印証書　102
条件付申込　64
証拠開示　292
承諾　55,59
譲渡禁止条項　277
常任上訴貴族　19,30
少年裁判所　15,22
消費者契約　9,116
情報開示義務　257
消滅時効　210
条例　37
女王座部首席裁判官　18
女王座部付属裁判所　23
女王の議会　34
女王の裁可　35
書式間の闘争　61
庶民院　7,35
信義誠実の原則　256
信義則　142
迅速手続　16
信託　5,230
信託財産　10
信託法　9
人的財産権　242
信認義務　230
信頼利益の損失　203,206
推測的損害　203,207
枢密院司法委員会　20
枢密院令　37
制定法　4
責任制限条項　211,232
責任排除条項　129,134,232
是正費用　205
設定者　10,230
説得的先例　46
善意　170

善意の不実表示　158
先例拘束の原理　3,46
相互的錯誤　167,169
双方的契約　55
双方的申込　55
疎遠性　201,202
ソリシター（事務弁護士）　26,294
ソリシター協会（ロー・ソサイェティ）　27
ソリシター懲戒審判委員会　27
損害　202
損害塡補契約（損害補償契約）　101
損害の拡大防止　208
損害賠償　153,170,201,232
損害賠償額の予定　210,286
損害賠償請求　157
損害補償契約（損害塡補契約）　101

た行

大憲章（マグナカルタ）　7,8
耐航性条項　113
第三債務者弁済命令　298
対物権　243
大法官　5,18,30
大法官部長官　18
大法官裁判所　5
多面的手続　16
治安判事　22,32
治安判事裁判所　15,21,22
地域諮問委員会　32
地区裁判官　16,22,30
中間条項　113
仲裁　15
仲裁条項　278
調停　15
懲罰的損害賠償　211
勅令状　4
賃金差押命令　298

索　引

追認　159
定義　273
定期土地利用権　109
定期傭船契約　190
停止条件　99,275
デニング卿　6
当事者の同一性の錯誤　170
同類解釈原則　39,129
特定履行　5,212,231
取消可能　168

な行

捺印証書　100,101,183
入札　58

は行

罰則　286
バリスター（法廷弁護士）　26,27,294
バリスター団体総評議会　26,28
判例法　4,44,46
非金銭的損害　203,207
非公開会社　11
秘密保持　276
秘密保持義務　257
秘密保持契約　257,259
ピューニ・ジャッジ（普通裁判官）　18
標準取引条項　140
不可抗力条項　188,276
不公正条項　142
不実表示　153
付随的契約　96,229
付随的条項　110
付属裁判所　18
負担賦課命令　297
普通裁判官（ピューニ・ジャッジ）　18
普通法　4
物的財産権　242
不当威圧　173

不動産譲渡士　32
不動産賃借権　230,242
不当利得　96
不法行為　157,158,229,232
不法行為法　9
フラストレーションの法理　185
文理解釈手法　37
文理準則　38,128,283
弊害準則　38
返還請求　190
法源　34
法曹院（インズ・オブ・コート）　28,29
法廷弁護士（バリスター）　26,27,294
法的拘束力　54,261,263,266
法的拘束力発生の意思　93
法律貴族　19
法律専務職員　33
法律の表示　155
保険契約　112
保証　101,111,262,273,275
補助裁判官　16
本質的な錯誤　169

ま行

マグナカルタ（大憲章）　7,8
未履行約因　74
民事裁判所　15
民事法　13
無効　139,168,169,171,212
矛盾原則　137
無体財産権　242
無名条項　110,113
明確性　93
明示条項　109,134
申込　55
申込の撤回　63
申込の誘引　57

317

黙示条項　　109
黙示的条件　　64
目的論的解釈手法　　37

や行

約因　　54,73,101,183,264
約因の法理　　73,228
約束　　79
約束的禁反言　　73,79
約束的条件　　99,111
有価証券　　101
郵便ルール　　62
要式性　　100
傭船契約　　113,190
予備的契約　　96

ら行

履行期前の契約違反　　184,208
履行利益の損失　　203,204
離路原則　　137
レコーダー　　30
レター・オブ・インテント　　94,260
ロー・ソサイエティ（ソリシター協会）
　　27
ロックアウト契約　　98,263

ABC

EU規則　　43
EU法　　40

法令・条文索引

A

Access to Justice Act 1999　23
Administration of Justice Act 1920　290
Administration of Justice Act 1970　17
Administration of Justice Act 1985　32
Amendment Order 1999　16
Arbitration Act 1996 s9　287
Attachment of Earnings Act 1971　298

B

Bills of Exchange Act 1882
—s3(1)　101
—s17(2)　101
Bills of Sale Act (1878) Amendment Act 1882　101
Brussels Convention 1968 Article 26　290

C

Charging Orders Act 1979　297
Civil Procedural Rules 1998　214
　—rule 25.1　296
　—rule 73.2　298
　—rule 73.3　297
　—rule 73.4　297,298
　—rule 73.5　298
　—rule 73.6　297,298
　—rule 73.7　297,298
　—rule 73.9　298
　—rule 73.10　298
　—RSC Order 51　299
Companies Act 2006　11
Constitutional Reform Act 2005　20,30
Consumer Credit Act 1974 s61　101
Contracts (Applicable Law) Act 1990　292
Contracts (Rights of Third Parties) Act 1999　9,233,239,278
County Courts Act 1984　297
County Courts Act 1959　15
Courts and Legal Services Act 1990　16,18,30
Criminal Justice Act 2003　24

E

EC Directive on Unfair Terms in Consumer Contracts 1993　142
European Atomic Energy Community Treaty (Euratom) 1957　42
European Coal and Steel Community Treaty (ECSC) 1951　42
European Communities Act 1972　34
　—s2(1)　40
European Community Treaty 1975 (the EC Treaty, the Treaty of Rome)　42
European Convention of Human Rights and Fundamental Freedoms　21,35,39

F
Foreign Judgements (Reciprocal Enforcement) Act 1933   290

H
High Court and Country Court Jurisdiction Order 1991   16
House of Lords Act 1999   35
Housing Act 1985   11
Housing Act 1996   11
Human Rights Act 1998   8,21,35,39

I
Insolvency Act 1986   11
   —s123   299
   —s344   245
Interpretation Act 1978 s6   280,283

J
Judicature Acts 1873-1875   5,15

L
Land Registry Act 2002   11
Landlord and Tenant Act 1954   11
Law of Property (Miscellaneous Provisions) Act 1989
   —s1(2)   102
   —s1(3)   102
   —s2(1)   101
Law of Property Act 1925   10,244
   —s53(1)(c)   246
   —s52   100
   —s54   100
   —1925 s136(1)   244
   —s137   247
Law Reform (Contributory Negligence) Act 1945   209,225
   —s1(1)   225

   —s4   225
Law Reform (Frustrated Contracts) Act 1943   189,190,199
   —s1(2)   191,199
   —s1(3)   191,199
   —s2(3)   190
   —s2(4)   190
   —s2(5)   190
Leasehold Reform Act 1967   11
Limitation Act 1980   210,225
   —s5   210,225
   —s8   210,226
   —s29   226
   —s29(5)   210
   —s30   226
   —s32   226

M
Marine Insurance Act 1906 s22   101
Misrepresentation Act 1967   165,256
   —s2(1)   159,165
   —s2(2)   159,165
   —s2(3)   159,165
   —s3   159,165

R
Rome Convention 1980
   —Article 4(1)   292
   —Article 4(2)   292
   —Article 4(5)   292

S
Sale of Goods Act 1979   115,121,139,149,159,168,284
   —s6   168
   —s7   186,190
   —s11(1)   159

索　引

—s12　115,121
—s12(2)(a)　115
—s12(2)(b)　116
—s12(4)　115
—s12(5)　116
—s13　122
—s13(1)　115
—s14　123
—s14(2)　115
—s14(3)　115
—s15A　125
—s15A(1)　116
—s23　159
—s48A(1)　116
—s50(3)　204
—s51(3)　204
—s57(2)　58
Single European Act 1986　42
Statute of Frauds 1677 s4　101
Supply of Goods (Implied Terms) Act 1973　139,149,284
Supply of Goods and Services Act 1982　284
Supreme Court Act 1981
—s37　214
—s49　214
—s50　214

T
Trade Union and Labour Relations (Consolidation) Act 1992 s236　213
Treaty of Amsterdam 1997　42
Treaty of European Union 1992 (the Maastricht Treaty)　42

U
Unfair Contract Terms Act 1977　134,138,147,148,159,211,285
—s2　148
—s2(1)　139
—s2(2)　139
—s3(1)　140
—s3(2)　140
—s5　139,148
—s6　115,149
—s6(2)　139
—s6(3)　139
—s7(2)　139
—s11　150
—s11(1)　166
—s11(2)　140
—s11(3)　140
—Schedule 2　140,150
Unfair Terms in Consumer Contracts Regulations 1999　44,134,141,151,211,285
—reg.4　151
—reg.4(1)　142
—reg.5　151
—reg.5(1)　142
—reg.5(3)　142
—reg.5(5)　142
—reg.8　142,151
—Schedule 2　142
Unsolicited Goods and Services Act 1971 s1(2)　59

判例索引

A

Actionstrength Ltd. v International Glass Engineering [2002] 1 WLR 566　　101,107
Adams v Lindsell (1818) 106 ER 250　62
Addis v Gramophone Co., Ltd. [1909] AC 488 (HL)　　207
Adler v Dickson: (The Himalaya) [1955] 1 QB 158 (CA)　　233,238
Aerial Advertising Co. v Batchelor's Peas Ltd. (Manchester) [1938] 2 All ER 788　　112,118
Akai Pty Ltd v People's Insurance Co Ltd [1998] 1 Lloyd's Rep 90　289
Alan Estates Ltd v W.G. Stores Ltd [1982] Ch 511　　103
Amalgamated Investment & Property Co., Ltd. v John Walker & Sons Ltd. [1977] 1 WLR 164 (CA)　188,197
Anderson v KAS Bank NV [2004] EWHC 532 (Ch)　　299
Andrew Frederic Beazley v Horizon Offshore Contractors Inc [2004] EWHC 2555　　289
Andrews Bros. (Bournemouth) Ltd. v Singer & Co. Ltd. [1934] 1 KB 17 (CA)　　137,145
Anglia Television Ltd. v Reed [1972] 1 QB 60 (CA)　　206,219
Appleby v Myers (1867) LR 2 CP 651

189,198
Ascherberg Hopwood and Crew v Casa Musicale Sonzogno [1971] 1 WLR 173　　291
Asfar & Co. v Blundell [1986] 1 QB 123 (CA)　　186,194
Atlas Express v Kafco [1989] 1 All ER 641　　173,180
Attwood v Small (1838) 6 Cl & F 232 (HL)　　156,162
Avery v Bowden (1885) 5 E & B 714　185,192

B

B & S Contracts & Design v Victor Green Publications [1984] IGR 419　　173,180
B.T.C. v Gourley [1965] AC 185 (HL)　209
Baird Textile Holdings Ltd v Marks & Spencer plc [2001] EWCA Civ 274, [2002] 1 All ER (Comm) 737　82
Banco de Portugal v Waterlow & Sons Ltd. [1932] AC 452 (HL)　　208,221
Bank of Liverpool v Holland (1926) 43 TLR 29　　245
Bannerman v White (1861) 10 CB NS 844　　110,116
Bannister v Bannister (1948) 2 All ER 133　　10
Banque Keyser Ullman S.A. v Skandia

(U.K.) Insurance Co., Ltd. [1991] 2 AC 249 (HL) 156

Barclays Bank plc v Fairclough Building Ltd. [1995] QB 214 (CA) 209,223

Barry v Davies [2000] 1 WLR 1962 (CA) 58,66

Bawejem Ltd. v M.C. Fabrications Ltd. [1999] 1 All ER (Comm.) 377 247

Behn v Burness (1863) 3 B&S 751 112,117

Bell v Lever Brothers Ltd. [1932] AC 161 (HL) 168,175

Beoco Ltd. v Alfa Laval Co., Ltd. [1994] 4 All ER 464 (CA) 210, 223

Beswick v Beswick [1967] 2 All ER 1197; [1968] AC 58 (HL) 213, 231,236

Bettini v Gye (1876) 1 QBD 183 112,118,184

Binions v Evans (1972) Ch 359 10

Bisset v Wilkinson [1927] AC 177 (Privy Council: New Zealand) 154,160

Blackburn Bobbin Co., Ltd. v T.W. Allen & Sons Ltd. [1918] 2 KB 467 (CA) 186,194

Blackpool and Fylde Aero Club v Blackpool BC [1990] 3 All ER 25 (CA) 58

Blake & Co v Sohn [1969] 1 WLR 1412 100

Bliss v South East Thames Regional Health Authority [1987] ICR 700 207

BP Exploration Co. (Libya) Ltd. v

Hunt (No.2) [1982] 1 All ER 925 (HL) 191,199

Bridge v Campbell Discount Co., Ltd. [1962] 1 All ER 385 (HL) 211, 224

Brikom Investments Ltd. v Carr [1979] QB 467 80

Brinkibon Ltd. v Stahag Stahl [1983] 2 AC 34 (HL) 63,69

British Crane Hire Corp. Ltd. v Ipswich Plant Hire Ltd. [1975] Qb 303 (CA) 136,144

British Movietonews, Ltd. v London and District Cinemas, Ltd. [1952] AC 166 (HL) 128,132

British Steel Corp. v Cleveland Bridge [1984] 1 All ER 504 95,97,103

British Westinghouse Electric and Manufacturing Co., Ltd. v Underground Electric Railway Co. of London Ltd. [1912] AC 673 (HL) 208,209,222

Brogden v Metropolitan Railway (1877) 2 App Cas 666 (HL) 59, 67

Business Computers Ltd. v Anglo-African Leasing Ltd. [1977] 1 WLR 578 248

Butler Machine Tool Co., Ltd. v Excell-o Corporation (England) Ltd. [1979] 1 All ER 965 61,68

Byrne & Co v Van Tienhoven & Co. (1880) 5 CPD 344 63,64,70

C

C & P Haulage v Middleton [1983] 3 All ER 94 (CA) 207,219

C.C.C Film (London) Ltd. v Impact

Quadrant Film Ltd. [1985] 1 QB 16   207
Carlill v Carbolic Smoke Ball Co [1893] 1 QB 256 (CA)   58,65, 154
Cator v Crydon Canal Co (1841) 4 Y & C Ex. 405   246
Cehave NV v Bremer Handelsgesellschaft mbH, The Hansa Nord [1975] 3 All ER 739; [1976] QB 44 (CA)   113,114,119,184
Cellulose Acetate Silk Company Ltd. v Widnes Foundry (1925) Ltd. [1933] AC 20 (HL)   211,224
Central London Property Trust Ltd. v High Trees House Ltd. [1947] KB 130   79,81,91
Chandler v Webster [1904] 1 KB 493   189,198,199
Chapelton v Barry UDC [1940] 1 KB 532 (CA)   136,144
Chaplin v Hicks [1911] 2 KB 786 (CA)   207,220
Chappell & Co., Ltd. v Nestle Co., Ltd. (1959) 2 All ER 701   75,84
Chiemgauer Membran Und Zeltbau GmbH v New Millenium Experience Co., Ltd. [2002] BPLR 42   203
City and Westminster Properties (1934) Ltd v Mudd [1959] Ch 129   131,132
Clarke v Dickson (1858) EB & E 148   159,164
Coco v AN Clark (Engineers) Limited [1969] RPC 41   257,267
Collins v Godefroy (1831) 1 B & Ad 950   76,85

Combe v Combe [1951] 2 KB 215 (CA)   82,92
Consgrove v Horsfall (1945) 62 TLR 140 (CA)   233
Cooper v Phibbs (1867) LR 2HL 149 (HL)   168,174
Co-operative Insurance Society Ltd v Argyll Stores (Holdings) Ltd [1997] 2 WLR 898 (HL)   213
Couchman v Hill [1947] KB 554 (CA)   110,112,116
Courtney & Fairbairn Ltd v Tolaini Brothers (Hotels) Ltd [1975] 1 WLR 297 (CA)   98
Coutrier v Hastie (1856) 5 HLC 673   168,174
Cox v Phillips Industries Ltd. [1976] 1 WLR 638   207
Craven-Ellis v Canons Ltd [1936] 2 All ER 1066   212
Criklewood Property Investment Trust v Leighton's Investment Trust Ltd. [1945] AC 22 (HL)   188,197
Cundy v Lindsay (1878) 3 App Cas 459 (HL)   171,177
Currie v Misa (1875) LR 10 Ex 153 (HL)   75
Curtis v Chemical Cleaning and Dyeing Co. [1951] 1 All ER 631   135, 143
Customs & Excise Commissioners v Diners Club Ltd. [1989] 1 WLR 1196   249

D

D & F Estates Ltd. v Church Commissioners for England [1989] 1 AC 177 (HL)   229,235

D&C Builders Ltd. v Rees [1965] 3 All ER 837; [1966] 2 QB 617 (CA) 78,80,90
Daulia Ltd. v Four Millbank Nominees [1978] 2 WLR 621 (CA) 64,70
Davis Contractors Ltd. v Fareham Urban District Council [1956] AC 696 (HL) 185,187,193
De la Bere v Pearson Ltd. [1908] 1 KB 280 202,215
Dearle v Hall (1828) 3 Russ.1 245,247
Denny, Mott & Dickson v James B. Fraser & Co., Ltd. [1944] AC 265 (HL Scotland) 187,195
Derry v Peek (1889) 14 App Cas 337 157,163
Dick Bentley Productions Ltd v Harold Smith (Motors) Ltd [1965] 2 All ER 65 (CA) 110,117
Dickinson v Dodds (1876) 2 ChD 463, 34 LT 607 (CA) 64,70
Dickson v Jones Alexander & Co [1993] 2 FLR 521 207
Dimmock v Hallett (1866) LR 2 Ch App 21 (CA) 154,155,161
Director General of Fair Trading v First National Bank plc [2001] 1 AC 481 (HL) 142,148
DMA Financial Solutions Ltd v (1) BaaN UK Ltd (2) BaaN International BV (3) BaaN CO NV [2000] CH.D (Park J) 28/03/2000; WL 1629568 98,106,265
Don King Productions Inc. v Warren [2000] Ch. 291 247
Donohue v Armco Inc [2001] UK HL 64 289,300

Drake v Thos. Agnew & Sons Ltd. [2002] EWHC 294 110,117, 157,163
Dunlop Pneumatic Tyre Co., Ltd. v New Garage and Motor Co., Ltd. [1915] AC 79 (HL) 211,223
Dunlop Pneumatic Tyre Co., Ltd. v Selfridge & Co. Ltd. [1915] AC 847 (HL) 73,74,228,234
Durham Bros v Robertson [1898] 1 QB 765 244,249

E

Edgington v Fitzmaurice (1885) 29 ChD 459 (CA) 155,161
Edmonds v Lawson [2000] QB 501 1091 (CA) 75,84
Edwards v Skywarys Ltd. [1964] 1 All ER 494 263,268
Ellerman Lines Ltd. v Lancaster Maritime Co., Ltd. [1980] 2 Lloyd's Rep. 497 245
Entores v Miles Far East Corporation [1955] 2 QB 327 (CA) 63,69
Errington v Errington and Woods [1952] 1 All ER 149 64
Ertel Bieber & Co. v Rio Tinto Co., Ltd. [1918] AC 260 (HL) 188
Esso Petroleum v Marden [1976] QB 801 (CA) 154,160

F

F.C. Shepherd & Co., Ltd. v Jerrom [1987] QB 301 (CA) 187
Farley v Skinner (No.2) [2001] 4 All ER 801 (HL) 208,220
Felthouse v Bindley (1862) 11 CB (NS) 869,142 ER 1037,31 LJCP

204   59,67
Ferguson v Davies (1997) 1 All ER (CA)   78,88
Fibrosa Spolka Akcyjna v Fairbuirn, Lawson, Combe, Barbour Ltd. [1943] AC 32 (HL)   189,198
Financial Ltd. v Stimson [1962] 3 All ER 386   64,71
Fisher v Bell [1961] 1 QB 394 (CA) 57,65
Foakes v Beer (1884) 9 App Cas 605 (HL)   77,81,87
Foley v Classique Coaches Ltd [1934] 2 KB 1   98,98,105
Ford v Beech (1848) 11 QB 852   128
Ford v White [1964] 1 WLR 885 205,217
Forsikringsaktieselskapet Vesta v Butcher [1989] AC 852 (CA) 209,222
Forster v Baker [1910] 2 KB 636 245
Frederick E Rose (London) Ltd. v William Pim & Co., Ltd. [1953] 2 QB 450 (CA)   172,179

G

Gamerco S.A. v I.C.M./Fair Warning (Agency) Ltd. [1995] 1 WLR 1226   191
George Mitchell (Chesterhall) Ltd. v Finney Lock Seeds Ltd. [1983] 2 All ER 803 (HL)   141,146
Gibson v Manchester C.C. [1979] 1 WLR 294 (HL)   60,68
Gillespie Bros. & Co v Cheney Eggar & Co [1896] 2 QB 59   130
Glasbrook Bros. Ltd. v Glamorgan C.C.

(1925) A.C. 270 (HL)   76,85
Good v Cheeseman (1831) 2 B&Ad 328 78
Gordon v Gordon (1816) 3 Swan 400 156
Gordon v Sellico [1986] EG 53 (CA); EGLR 71   156,161
Gorringe v Irwell India Rubber, etc., Workers (1886) 34 Ch. D. 128 246
Graham v Johnson (1869) L.R.8 Eq. 36 248
Great Northern Railway v Witham (1873) LR 9 CP 16   58,67
Great Pearce Shipping v Tsavliris Salvage (International) Ltd. [2003] QB 679 (CA)   169,176

H

H. Parsons (Livestock) Ltd. v Uttley Ingham & Co., Ltd. [1974] QB 791 (CA)   203,217
Hadley v Baxendale (1854) 9 Exch 341 202,215
Harbutt's Plasticine Ltd. v Wayne Tank & Pump Co., Ltd. [1970] q QB 447 (CA)   205,218
Hardwick Game Farm v Suffolk Agricultural etc., Association [1969] 2 AC 31   136,144
Hargreaves Transport Ltd. v Lynch [1969] 1 WLR 215   100,107
Harris v Nickerson (1973) LR 8 QB 286 (QB)   58
Harris v Sheffield United Football Club Ltd. (1987) 2 All ER 838 (CA)   76,85
Harris v Taylor [1915] 2 KB   290

Hartley v Ponsonby (1857) 7 E&B 872   76,85
Hartog v Colin and Shields [1939] 3 All ER 566   170,177
Harvela Investments Ltd. v Royal Trust Co. of Canada [1985] 2 All ER 966 (HL)   58
Harvey v Facey [1893] AC 552 (Privy Council: Jamaica)   56
Hayes v James and Charles Dodd [1990] 2 All ER 815 (CA)   207
Hedley Byre & Co Ltd. v Heller and Partners Ltd. [1964] AC 465 (HL)   158,164
Helstan Securities Ltd. v Hertfordshire CC [1978] 3 All ER 262   247
Herkules Piling Ltd. v Tilbury Construction (1992) 61 Build. L.R. 107   247
Herne Bay Steamboat Co. v Hutton [1903] 2 KB 683 (CA)   186,195
Heskell v Continental Express Ltd. [1956] 1 All ER 1033   202
Hirachand Punamchand v Temple (1911) 2 KB 330 (CA)   78,89
Hirji Mulji v Cheong Yue Steamship Co. [1936] AC 497 (HL)   189,198
Hobbs v London & South Western Railway Co., L.R. (1875) 10 QB 111   208
Hochster v De la Tour (1853) 2 E & B 678   184,192
Hodgson v Marks [1970] 3 All ER 513   174
Hollier v Rambler Motors (AMC) Ltd. [1972] 2 QB 71 (CA)   137,146
Holt v Heatherfield Trust Ltd. [1942] 2 KB 1   245,246
Holwell Securities v Hughes [1974] 1 All ER 161 (CA)   63
Hong Kong Fir Shipping Co., Ltd. v Kawasaki Kisen Kaisha Ltd. [1962] 2 QB 26 (CA)   113,118
Houghton v Trafalgar Insurance Co., Ltd. [1954] 1 QB 247 (CA)   137,145
Household Fire and Carriage Accident Insurance Co., Ltd. v Grant (1879) 4 Ex D 216 (CA)   62
Hughes v Metropolitan Railway (1877) 2 App Cas 439 (HL)   79,89
Hyde v Wrench (1840) 3 Beav 334   68

I

Ingram v Little [1961] 1 QB 31 (CA)   171,178
Inntrepreneur Estates Ltd. v Hollard [2000] WL 1084502 (CA)   155,161
Inntrepreneur Pub Co. v East Crown Ltd [2000] 2 Lloyd's Rep 611   131,133
Interfoto Picture Library v Stiletto Visual Programmes [1989] QB 433 (CA)   145

J

J. Evans & Son (Portsmouth) Ltd v Andrea Merzario Ltd [1976] 1 WLR 1078 (CA)   130,132
J. Lauritzen A.S. v Wijsmuller B.V.: The Super Servant Two [1990] 1 Lloyd's Rep 1 (CA)   185,187,

Jackson v Horizon Holiday Ltd.
[1975] 3 All ER 92; 1 WLR 1468,3
All ER 92 (CA) 207,220,231,
232,237 192
Jackson v Union Marine Insurance
Company Ltd. (1874) LR 10 CP
125 (Court of Exchequer Chamber) 186,194
Jacobs v Batavia and General Plantations (1924) 1 Ch 287 129
Jarvis v Swan's Tours Ltd. [1973] QB
233 (CA) 207,220
Jones v Humphreys [1902] 1 KB 10
245,249
Jones v Vernon's Pools [1938] 2 All
ER 626 (Livepool Assizes) 93,
103
Joseph Constrantine SS Line Ltd. v
Imperial Smelting Corp. Ltd.
[1942] AC 154 (HL) 187,196
Junior Books Ltd. v Veitchi Co., Ltd.
[1983] 1 AC 520 (HL Scotland)
229,235

K

KH Enterprise v Pioneer Container:
(The Pioneer Container) [1994] 2
All ER 250 (Privy Council: Hong
Kong) 233
King's Norton Metal v Edridge, Merrett & Co. (1897) 14 TLR 98 (CA)
171,177
Kleinwort Benson Ltd. v Malaysia
Mining Corporation, Berhad
[1989] 1 All ER 785 95,262,
268
Koufos v C. Czarnikow Ltd. (The

Heron II) [1969] 1 AC 350 (HL)
203,203,216
Krell v Henry [1903] 2 KB 740 (CA)
186,194
Kutchera v Buckingham International
Holdings Ltd [1988] IR 61 291

L

L. Schuler AG v Wickman Machine
Tool Sales [1974] AC 235 (HL)
114,119,128
Lambard North Central plc v Butterworth [1987] QB 527 (CA)
114,119
Lambert v HTV Cymru (Wales) Ltd
and Another [1998] FSR 874;
[1998] 15 LS Gaz R 30 99,106
Lampleigh v Brithwait (1615) Hob 105
75,83
Lazenby Garages v Wright [1976] 1
WLR 459 (CA) 205,218
Leaf v International Galleries [1950]
1 All ER 693; 2 KB 86 (CA)
159,165,168,175
Lefkowitz v Great Minneapolis Surplus Store (1957) 86 NW 2d 689
58,66
L'Etrange v F. Graucob Ltd. [1934] 2
KB 394 (CA) 135,143
Lewis v Averay [1971] 3 All ER 907
171,178
Library v Stiletto Visual Programmes
[1989] QB 433 136
Linden Gardens Trust Ltd. v Lenesta
Sludge Disposals Ltd. [1994] 1
AC 85 (HL) 231,232,237,247
Liverpool City Council v Irvin [1977]
AC 233 (HL) 115,121

Lloyds Bank v Bundy [1974] 3 All ER 757   174,181
Lloyds Bank v Rosset [1991] 1 AC 107   10
Lloyds v Harper (1880) 16 Ch.D. 290 (CA)   231
Long v Lloyd [1958] 1 WLR 753 (CA)   159,164
Lord Strathcona Steamship Company Ltd v Dominion Coal Company Ltd [1926] AC 108 (PC)   230
Lynn v Bamer [1930] 2 KB 72   210

M
Malik v BCCI [1997] 3 WLR 95 (HL)   115,121
Manchester Diocesan Council for Education v Commercial and General Investments [1969] 3 All ER 1593 (Ch D)   63,70
Mann v Nunn (1874) 30 L.T. 526   131
Mareva Compania Naviera SA v International Bulk Carries SA [1975] 2 Lloyd's Rep 509   214
Maritime National Fisch Ltd. v Ocean Trawlers Ltd. [1935] AC 524 (PC on Appeal from the Supreme Court of Nova Scotia)   187,196
Mars UK Ltd v Teknowledge Ltd [1999] All ER (D) 600   258,267
Martinez v Ellessee International SPA [1999] CLY 861 (CA)   98,105
Mathew v Bobbins (1980) 256 EG 603   173
McAlpine (Alfred) Construction Ltd. v Panatown Ltd. [2001] AC 518 (HL)   231,232,238

McInery v Llyods Bank Ltd [1974] 1 Lloyd's Rep 246 (CA)   154
Merrit v Merrit [1970] 2 All ER 760 (CA)   93
Monarch Steamship Co v Karlshamens Oljefabriker (A/B) [1949] AC 196   202,214
Morris v C.W. Martin & Sons Ltd. [1966] 1 QB 716 (CA)   233

N
National Carriers Ltd. v Panalpina (Northern) Ltd. [1981] AC 675 (HL)   188,197
New Zealand Shipping v A M Satterthwaite & Co.: (Eurymedon) [1975] AC 154 (Privy Council: New Zealand)   77,87,233,239
Nickoll & Knight v Ashton Eridge & Co. [1901] 2 KB 126 (CA)   187,195
Nicolene Ltd. v Simmonds [1953] 1 All ER 822 (CA)   99,106
Norfolk C.C. v Dencora Properties [1995] 9 Nov. 1995 (CA)   60

O
Ocean Tramp Tankers Corporation v VO Sovfracht, The Eugenia [1964] 2 QB 226 (CA)   187,188,196
Olley v Marborough Court Ltd. [1949] 1 KB 532   136,144
Omnium D'Enterprises and Others v Sutherland [1919] 1 KB 618   184
Oscar Chess v Williams [1975] 1 WLR 370   110,116

329

OT Africa Line Ltd. v Magic Sportswear Corporation and Others [2005] EWCA Civ. 710 (CA) 289,299

P

Page One Records v Britton [1967] 3 All ER 822   214,225
Pagnan S.p.A. v Feed Products Ltd. [1987] 2 Lloyd's LR 601   60
Pao On v Lau Yiu Long (1980) AC 614 (Privy Council: Hong Kong) 75,83
Paradine v Jane (1647) Aleyn 26 (KB) 185
Parker v South Eastern Railway Co. (1877) 2 CPD 416   135,143
Partridge v Crittenden [1968] 2 All ER 421   58,65
Payzu Ltd. v Saunders [1919] 2 KB 581 (CA)   208,221
Pemberton v Hughes [1899] 1 Ch 781 290
Pharmaceutical Society of Great Britain v Boots Cash Chemists [1953] 1 QB 401 (CA)   57,64
Phillips v Brooks Ltd. [1919] 2 KB 243   171,178
Phillips v Ward [1956] 1 WLR 471 (CA)   205,217
Photo Production Ltd. v Securicor Transport Ltd. [1980] AC 827 (HL)   138
Pinnel's case (1602) 5 Co. Rep 117 77,81
Pitt v PHH Asset Management Limited [1993] 4 All ER 961   264
Pollock v Marcrae [1922] SC (HL)

192   137,146
Popely v Popely [2004] EWCA Civ 463   299
Port Line Ltd v Ben Line Steamers Ltd [1958] 2 QB 146   230
Poussard v Speirs and Pond (1876) 1 QBD 410   112,117,184
Prenn v Simmonds [1971] 1 WLR 1381   128

R

R. v Clarke (1927) 40 CLR 227   59
Radford v De Froberville [1977] 1 WLR 1262   206,218
Radiant Shipping Co., Ltd. v Sea Containers Limited [1995] CLC 976 E&W   266
Raffles v Wichelhaus (1864) 2 HC 906 169,176
Ramsgate Victoria Hotel Co., Ltd. v Montefiore (1866) LR 1 Ex 109 64,71
Re Atlantic Computers plc (in administration) National Australia Bank Ltd v Soden & Anor [1995] Bcc 696   262,268
Re Flavell (1833) 25 Ch D 89   236
Re McArdle (1951) Ch 669 (CA) 75,83
Re Selectmove Ltd (1995) 2 All ER (CA), [1995] 1 WLR 474 (CA) 77,88
Re Turcan (1888) 40 Ch. D. 5   247
Re Westerton [1919] 2 Ch. 104   247
Re: Schebsman [1944] Ch 83 (CA), [1943] 2 All ER 768   231,236
Re: Sinclair's Life Policy [1938] 1 Ch 799   231,236

Re: Tachographs: EC Commission v The United Kingdom (1979) 43
Redgrave v Hurd (1881) 20 ChD 1 (CA) 156,162
Rice (T/A The Garden Guardian) v Great Yarmouth Borough Council [2003] TCR 1,(2001) 3 LGLR 4 (CA) 114,120
Rigby v Connol (1880) 14 Ch 482 213
Robertson v French (1803) 4 East 130 128
Roscorla v Thomas (1842) 3 QB 234 75,82
Rose and Frank Co v Crompton (JR) & Brothers Ltd [1925] AC 445 (HL) 93,103
Rowland v Divall [1923] 2 KB 500 212,224
Royal Bank of Scotland v Etridge (No. 2) [2001] 4 All ER 449 173
Royscott Trust Ltd. v Rogerson [1992] 2 All ER 294 (CA) 158, 163
Ruxley Electronics and Construction Ltd. v Forsyth [1995] 3 WLR 118 (HL) 206,207,218
Ryan v Mutual Tontine Westminster Chambers Association [1893] 1 Ch 116 213

S

Saltman Engineering Co Limited v Campbell Engineering Co Limited [1948] 65 RPC 203 257
Sauter Automation v Goodman (HC) (Manchester Services) [1987] CLY 61,69

Scammel & Nephew Ltd v Ouston [1941] AC 251 (HL) 97,104
Scotson v Pegg (1861) 6 H & N 295 77
Scrutton Ltd. v Midland Silicones Ltd. [1962] AC 446 (HL) 233,239
Shadwell v Shadwell (1860) 9 CB NS 159 (Court of Common Bench) 74,77,87
Shanklin Pier Ltd. v Detel Products Ltd. [1951] 2 KB 854 229,234
Shirlaw v Southern Foundries (1926) Ltd. [1939] 2 KB 206 (CA) 114,121
Shogun Finance Ltd. v Hudson [2003] 3 WLR 1371 (HL) 171,179
Shuey v United States (1875) 23 L ed 697,92 US 73 64,71
Sibree v Tripp (1846) 15 M. & W. 23 78,88
Simpson v The London and North Western Railway Co. (1876) 1 QBD 274 207,219
Smith v Butler [1900] 1 QB 694 100,107
Smith v Chadwick (1884) 9 App Cas 187 157
Smith v Eric S. Bush [1900] 1 AC 831 (HL) 156,157,163
Smith v Hughes (1871) LR 6 QB 597 (CA) 56,127,169,176
Smith v Land & House Property Corporation (1884) 28 ChD 7(CA) 154,160
Solle v Butcher [1950] 1 KB 671 (CA) 168,175
Spencer v Harding (1870) LR 5CP 561 (CP) 58

Spice Girls Ltd. v Aprilia World Service BV [2002] EWCA Civ 15; WL 45121 (CA) 155,156,162
Spurling (J.) Ltd. v Bradshaw [1956] 1 WLR 461 (CA) 136,145
Stansbie v Troman [1948] 2 KB 48 (CA) 202,215
Starsin (Cargo Owners) v Starsin (Owners) [2003] UKHL 12 233
Stephens v Venables (1862) 30 Beav. 625 248
Stevenson, Jacques & Co. v Mclean (1880) 5 QBD 346 60,68
Stewart Gill v Horatio Meyer & Co [1992] 1 QB 600 140
Stilk v Myrick (1809) 2 Camp 317 76,85
Stoddart v Union Trust [1912] 1 KB 181 248,250
Suisse Atlantique Societe d'Armement Maritime SA v NV Rotterdamsche Kolen Centrale [1967] 1 AC 361 (HL) 138
Swiss Bank Corporation v Lloyds Bank Ltd [1979] Ch 548 230, 235

T

Taylor v Caldwell (1863) 3 B & S 826 186,193
The Aiolos [1983] 2 Lloyd's Rep. 25 246
The Balder London [1980] 2 Lloyd's Rep. 489 245
The Good Luck (1991) 2 Lloyd's ep. 410 112
The King of Spain v Machado (1827) 4

Russ 225 291
The Moorcock (1889) 14 PD 64 114,120
The Mount I [2001] EWCA Civ 68 245
The Post Chaser [1982] 1 All ER 19 80
Thomas National Transport (Melborne) Pty Ltd. and Pay v May and Baker (Australia) Pty Ltd. [1966] 2 Lloyd's Rep 347 137,146
Thompson v ASDA-MFI Group plc [1988] Ch 241 100
Thompson v London, Midland & Scottish Railway [1930] 1 KB 41 136,143
Thornton v Shoe Lane Parking Ltd. [1971] 2 QB 163 (CA) 136,144
Three Rivers DC v Bank of England [1996] QB 292 246
Tillmanns v S.S. Knutsford [1908] 2 KB 385 129
Tinn v Hoffman & Co (1873) 29 LT 271 63,69
Tito v Waddell (No.2) [1977] Ch. 106 249
Tool Metal Manufacturing v Tungsten Electric [1955] 2 All ER (HL) 82,91
Tooth v Hallett (1869) L.R. 4 Ch. App. 242 248
Trollope & Colls Limited and Holland, Hannen & Cubitts Ltd. v The Atomic Power Construction Ltd. [1962] 3 All ER 1936 60
Tsakiroglou & Co., Ltd. v Noblee Thorl GmbH [1962] AC 93 (HL) 187

Tulk v Moxhay (1848) 2 Ph 774 230,235
Turiff Construction Ltd. and Turiff Ltd v Regalia Knitting Mills Ltd. [1971] (QBD) 9 BLR 20 96, 104

U
Universe Tankships Inc. of Monrovia v International Transport Workers' Federation [1982] 2 All ER 67 173,180

V
Vanderpitte v Preferred Accident Insurance Corporation of New York [1933] AC 70 (Privy Council, Canada) 231
Victoria Laundry (Windsor) Ltd. v Newman Industries Ltd. [1949] 2 KB 528 (CA) 202,216

W
W.J. Alan v El Nasr Export & Import Co [1972] 2 QB 189 (CA) 80, 82,89,91
W.J. Tatem Ltd. v Gamboa [1939] 1 KB 132 188,197
Walford v Miles [1992] 2 AC 128; WLR 174 HL 98,105,264
Walker v Bradford Old Bank (1884) 12 QBD 511 245
Walton Harvey Ltd. v Walker & Homfrays Ltd. [1931] 1 Ch 274 188,197
Ward v Byham (1956) 2 All ER 318 (CA) 76
Warlow v Harrison (1859) 1 E & E 309;

120 ER 925 (Exchequer Chamber) 58
Warner Bros Records Inc. v Rollgreen Ltd. [1976] QB 430 246
Warner Brothers Pictures Incorporated v Nelson [1937] 1 KB 209 207,214,225
Waltons Stores (Interstate) Ltd v Maher (1988) CLR 387 (High Court of Australia) 82
Watford Electronic Limited v Sanderson CFL Limited [2001] 1 All ER (Comm) 696 (CA) 141,147
Watts v Morrow [1991] 1 WLR 1421; 4 All ER 937 (CA) 205,208,221
Wells (Merstham) Ltd. v Buckland Sand & Silica Co., Ltd. [1965] 2 QB 170 229,234
West London Commercial Bank v Kitson (1884) 12 QBD 360 (CA) 155,161
White and Carter (Councils) Ltd. v McGregor [1962] AC 413; [1961] 3 All ER 1178 (HL: Scotland) 184,192,208,210,222
White v Bluett (1853) 23 LJ Ex 36 76
William v Stern (1879) 5 QBD 40 80,90
Williams v Cawardine (1833) 5 C&P 566 59,67
Williams v Roffey Bros and Nicholls (Contractors) Ltd. (1991) 1 QB 1 (CA) 76,86
Wilson Smithett v Bangladesh Sugar [1986] Lloyd's LR 1986 Vol.1 378 95,104
With v O'Flanagan [1936] 1 All ER

333

727 (CA) 156,161
Woodar Investment Development Ltd. v Wimpey Construction (UK) Ltd. [1980] 1 All ER 571 (HL) 231, 232,237
Woodhouse A.C. Israel Cocoa Ltd. S.A. v Nigerian Produce Marketing Co., Ltd. [1972] AC 741 (HL) 80,89
Woodward v Hutchins [1977] 2 All ER 751 257

X
Xenos v Wickham (1867) LR HL 296 102

Y
Yates Building Co. v R J Pulleyn & Sons (York) (1975) 119 SJ 370 63

島田真琴(しまだ・まこと)
慶應義塾大学大学院法務研究科教授、一橋綜合法律事務所パートナー(弁護士)
1956年生まれ。慶應義塾大学法学部卒業、ロンドン大学ユニバーシティカレッジ大学院法学研究科修士課程修了(LL.M)。1981年弁護士登録。長島・大野法律事務所勤務、ノートン・ローズ法律事務所(ロンドン)勤務、慶應義塾大学法学部講師(非常勤)などを経て、現在に至る。専攻はイギリス法、国際取引法。
主要著作に、Handbook on Cross-Border Industrial Sub-Contracting(共著、Kluwer Law Institutional)、International Libel Handbook: A Practical guide for Journalists(共著、Butterworth Heinemann)、「英国におけるマネジメント・バイアウトとわが国への導入の可能性」『NBL』377号、378号、380号、「ローン債権の売買—イギリス法と日本法」『慶應義塾大学法学部法律学科開設百年記念論文集』、「独占的契約交渉権の実効性と限界」『慶應法学』2号など。

国際取引のためのイギリス法

2006年10月16日　初版第1刷発行
2009年4月10日　初版第2刷発行

著者————島田真琴
発行者———坂上弘
発行所———慶應義塾大学出版会株式会社
　　　　　　〒108-8346 東京都港区三田2-19-30
　　　　　　TEL 〔編集部〕03-3451-0931
　　　　　　　　〔営業部〕03-3451-3584〈ご注文〉
　　　　　　　　　〃　　 03-3451-6926
　　　　　　FAX 〔営業部〕03-3451-3122
　　　　　　振替　00190-8-155497
　　　　　　URL http://www.keio-up.co.jp/
装幀————渡辺澪子
印刷・製本—株式会社丸井工文社
カバー印刷—株式会社太平印刷社

©2006 Makoto Shimada
Printed in Japan　ISBN4-7664-1312-1

慶應義塾大学出版会

新標準講義 民法債権総論
池田真朗編　民法主査として司法試験考査委員を務めた著者による本格的な債権総論の教科書。「紛争解決手段としての法」を説き、法科大学院時代に新たな「標準」を提示する。
●2500円

国際環境法
パトリシア・バーニー、アラン・ボイル著／池島大策・富岡仁・吉田脩訳　世界的に高い評価を得ている研究書、待望の翻訳。国際環境法のあらゆる局面における争点や定義、歴史および現状について詳述されている本書は、国際法および環境法の研究者、実務家にとって必携の大冊。
●10000円

破産法概説〔新訂第4版〕
宗田親彦著　第一線の弁護士かつ研究者の著者による、破産法の基本書。破産法の全面改正（平成16年）、新会社法の施行（平成18年）に対応した新訂第3版に、信託法の改正、信託財産の破産の制度の新設などの近年の法改正を反映。
●4600円

団体訴訟の新展開
宗田貴行著　近年、日本では法律違反行為により多数の消費者に拡散した被害が生じている。本書では、団体訴訟制度の母法国であるドイツの同制度の機能と理論を明らかにし、日本への消費者団体訴訟制度の導入を検討する。
●3800円

株式会社監査機構のあり方
倉澤康一郎著　一貫して株式会社における監査の必要性とわが国の特異な監査役制度の歴史的展開を説いた、倉澤監査機構論の集大成。新会社法以前における監査機構の法的変遷をたどる。
●8000円

表示価格は刊行時の定価（税別）です。